THE *PAST & PRESENT* BOOK SERIES

General Editor
ALICE RIO

Queen Boudica and Historical Culture in Britain

Martha Vandrei is Lecturer in Modern History at the University of Exeter.

Queen Boudica and Historical Culture in Britain

An Image of Truth

MARTHA VANDREI

OXFORD
UNIVERSITY PRESS

Great Clarendon Street, Oxford, OX2 6DP,
United Kingdom

Oxford University Press is a department of the University of Oxford.
It furthers the University's objective of excellence in research, scholarship,
and education by publishing worldwide. Oxford is a registered trade mark of
Oxford University Press in the UK and in certain other countries

© Martha Vandrei 2018

The moral rights of the author have been asserted

First Edition published in 2018
First published in paperback in 2026

All rights reserved. No part of this publication may be reproduced, stored in a retrieval system, transmitted, used for text and data mining, or used for training artificial intelligence, in any form or by any means, without the prior permission in writing of Oxford University Press, or as expressly permitted by law, by licence or under terms agreed with the appropriate reprographics rights organization. Enquiries concerning reproduction outside the scope of the above should be sent to the Rights Department, Oxford University Press, at the address above.

You must not circulate this work in any other form
and you must impose this same condition on any acquirer

Links to third party websites are provided by Oxford in good faith and
for information only. Oxford disclaims any responsibility for the materials
contained in any third party website referenced in this work.

Published in the United States of America by Oxford University Press
546 Fifth Avenue, New York, NY 10036, United States of America

British Library Cataloguing in Publication Data
Data available

Library of Congress Control Number: 2017958743

ISBN 9780198816720 (hbk)
ISBN 9780197904404 (pbk)

The manufacturer's authorized representative in the EU for product safety is
Oxford University Press España S.A. of Parque Empresarial San Fernando de Henares,
Avenida de Castilla, 2 – 28830 Madrid (www.oup.es/en or product.safety@oup.com).
OUP España S.A. also acts as importer into Spain of products made by the manufacturer.

For Paul Readman

What signify dates in a true story?
— Sir Walter Scott

Acknowledgements

This project began what seems a lifetime ago as a doctoral thesis in the history department at King's College London. The final typescript for this book was completed after I took up a post at the University of Exeter's idyllic campus in Cornwall. Throughout this period I have accrued many debts, large and small, professional, personal, and somewhere in between. Perhaps it is a hallmark of academic work, particularly in the humanities, that one's professional projects inevitably become a little personal; it is certainly true of this one.

First of all, I remain indebted to Ludmilla Jordanova for supervising my PhD from beginning to end, and for continuing to be a mentor and an inspiration to me in my career. I recall a conversation a year or two into my PhD during which I explained, with what I'm sure was inadequate clarity, my understanding of what I wanted the thesis to be. Ludmilla's response, delivered with something between exasperation and horror, was, 'But Martha—that's *everything*!' It's clear to me now what she meant, but I hope she can take some pleasure in the book that has finally emerged.

I am grateful also to my two brilliant examiners, Colin Kidd—I will never forget his warm welcome to me as a member of the 'craft'—and the inimitable Peter Mandler for conducting a rigorous but affirmative viva, and for providing countless references as well as sage advice and calm encouragement at pivotal moments thereafter. I have also benefited beyond measure from the support and example of David Cannadine, whose energetic dedication to the profession and the practice is without equal. I also wish to take this opportunity to thank the many other colleagues who have been generous with their time, advice, and expertise: Gareth Atkins, Richard Bourke, Matthew Cragoe, Rosemary Hill, Michael Ledger-Lomas, Ian McBride, Dave Monger, John Price, Karen O'Brien, Patricia Osmond, Ellie Reid, Miri Rubin, Richard Vinen, and Daniel Woolf. I am grateful to Miles Taylor for more than he might think.

I have had the good fortune to work in and with a variety of libraries and research institutions and to have benefited from a wealth of native expertise. I am grateful in particular to Abigail Kenvyn at the Brecknock Museum in Brecon, Wales, for sharing her gleanings about the statue of Boudica there, and to Gwyneth Gibbs for shedding light on the town of Stamford's interest in the ancient queen. The research and writing of this book, and the thesis on which it is based, was undertaken at the following: British Library, Institute of Historical Research (my thanks to Glen Jacques in particular), Senate House Library at the University of London, National Library of Wales, London Metropolitan Archives, Parliamentary Archive, Queen Mary University Archive, Hammersmith and Fulham Archive, Tower Hamlets Archive, Cardiff City Hall, British Museum, New College, Oxford, Essex Record Office, Suffolk Record Office (Bury St Edmunds Branch), Churchill Centre, Cambridge, Henry Moore Institute, and the British Film Institute, Reuben

Library. Much of the more recent research and writing was done at the London Library, scholarship's heavenly city. I am grateful to the staff and members for their refreshingly old-fashioned dedication to the cause.

Along similar though not identical lines, thought-provoking work-related conversation, as well as solace from such, has been had at the following establishments: the Seven Stars (three of them, in fact: in London, Penryn, and Falmouth), the Lord John Russell, the Edgar Wallace, the Harp, the upstairs cocktail bar at Rules, and the Hand in Falmouth. Staying with unconventional thanks, I have done more work than I wish to admit on Great Western Railway's 'Cornish Riviera' service from Paddington to Penzance. Thanks, GWR, for the Quiet Carriage: long may it last.

The University of Exeter has been a stimulating environment in which to begin my academic career and I am grateful to Kris Allerfeldt, Jo Esra, Nick Groom, Rob Magnuson-Smith, Richard Noakes, Catriona Pennell, and Natalie Pollard for being so helpful and welcoming, and to all my other colleagues—academic and administrative—and my lovely (really) students in the semi-autonomous republic of Penryn. I am grateful also to James Clark, Marion Gibson, and Andrew Thorpe for patiently supporting their junior colleague and for dealing with occasional bouts of fretting.

Matthew Hilton and Peter Coss at the *Past and Present* book series were supportive of the project from an early stage and, even more importantly, maintained incredible patience as it proceeded to take two years longer than I said it would. Stephanie Ireland and Cathryn Steele of Oxford University Press have been attentive and responsive editors. I am grateful to them, as well as to the four anonymous readers of the manuscript, to Gillian Northcott Liles for undertaking the copy-editing, and to Vijaya Manimaran for overseeing the production process. *The Historical Journal* and Cambridge University Press have kindly permitted me to reproduce sections of Chapter 5, which had previously been published.

The years I have spent thinking about historical culture have overlapped with the occasionally frustrating process of building a life in a United Kingdom that is increasingly hostile to newcomers. These years have therefore been simultaneously the most trying and yet still the happiest of my life. That I have been able to make a home here is due in large part to the friends I have made. In particular, I am thankful to (and for) Julie Hipperson, who combines a rare wisdom with the capacity for extreme silliness, and who shares my commitment to practical but rigorous feminism. Her friendship has been invaluable. I am also grateful for the support, camaraderie, and/or pot-valiance of the following: Marie and Steve Berry, Dan Browne, Michael Ciancia, Rona and Martin of the Cran/Spychal household (including their wonderful cheese-loving cats, Cousin and Lady), Stuart Drummings, Laura Forster, Mark Freeman, Tom Hulme, John Ingram, Gill Kennedy, Lindsay Meyer, William Mulligan, Niall O'Flaherty, Ann Poulson, and Tim Reinke-Williams. I am especially thankful for the support of the indomitable 'Auntie' Sue Drew, who welcomed me from the very start, and whose home in Sheffield has become a haven of stimulating conversation, gins and tonic, and countryside rambles.

Back in the US, I am grateful to my father, Charles, for igniting my interest in history and discouraging me from becoming an archaeologist. I am grateful also to my sister, Liz, for being an inspiration and for always keeping me laughing. My thanks go most especially to my mother, Eva, the most admirable woman I know; she has always asked the best questions and is too wise to claim she has all the answers.

In another lifetime, Paul Readman supervised this research in its very early stages. It was during the course of many memorable, often hilarious, conversations with Paul in his supervisory capacity that my ideas first took root, but it was only after he became my best friend that they could come to fruition. Although I continue to learn from him and to look up to his example he is much more than just a teacher to me now. Paul is my heart's protector, my brother-in-arms, and my constant companion in life's grand and occasionally serious adventure. This book is for him, with profound gratitude and infinite love.

Finally, all errors are of course my own, but I would ask the reader to bear in mind the humble words of William Camden, which summarize my own position: '...Neither have I affected to be thought knowing in any respect, unless it be that I am desirous to know. I frankly own my ignorance, and am sensible that I may oft-times have been mistaken; nor will I patronize my own mistakes. What Marksman that shoots a whole day, can constantly hit the mark?'

Martha Vandrei

Walworth, London and
Penryn, Cornwall
November 2017

Contents

List of Illustrations	xv
Introduction: Queen Boudica and the Idea of Historical Culture	1
1. 'Higher then to her no bookes doe reach': The Queen and the Antiquary	24
2. 'They that write to all, must strive to please all': Historians, Playwrights, and the Drama of History	51
3. 'Poetry and fiction intermixt with our history': Druids, Patriots, and Critics in the Eighteenth Century	81
4. 'Too strange to be popular': Negotiating Past and Present in Early Nineteenth-century Historical Culture	115
5. 'A great deal of historical claptrap': Heroine of Empire	146
6. 'That ubiquitous monarch': Boudica from Wales to Essex	170
Conclusion	203
Bibliography	209
Index	227

List of Illustrations

Cover image: Mrs Aylmer as 'Boadicea' at the Bury St Edmund's Pageant of 1907.

1. Woodcut of 'Voadica' in Raphael Holinshed's *Chronicles* (1577) — 17
2. Francis Delaram's frontispiece to Edmund Bolton's *Nero Caesar* (1627) — 39
3. 'Bonditia', by George Glover, in Thomas Heywood's *Exemplary Lives* (1640) — 52
4. Francis Hayman's frontispiece to Tobias Smollett's *Complete History of England* (1757) — 100
5. Illustration of Queen Boudica in John Baxter's *New and Impartial History* (1796) — 102
6. Queen Boudica in Emily Owen's *The Heroines of History* (1854) — 133
7. Thomas Stothard's illustration of Queen Boudica for G.F. Raymond's *New, Universal and Impartial History* (1790) — 142
8. Thomas Thornycroft's massive 'Boadicea group' on Westminster Bridge — 147
9. 'Buddug and her daughters' by John Havard Thomas in Cardiff City Hall — 187

Introduction
Queen Boudica and the Idea of Historical Culture

According to the extant sources, Boudica[1] was the queen of the Iceni who flourished during the opening stages of the Roman invasion of Britain.[2] The Romans had arrived in Britain, then populated by indigenous tribes, in 55–54 BC under the leadership of Julius Caesar. Caesar chose not to lead a full-scale invasion of the newly discovered island, and so initial contact between the Romans and the native Britons remained placid, with the former viewed as relatively benign by the latter. This remained the state of affairs throughout the reigns of Tiberius (AD 14–37) and Caligula (AD 37–41). It was Emperor Claudius (reigned 41–54) who finally resolved to conquer the land known as Britannia in 43. Claudius sent four legions to occupy the island and subdue the population. The sudden violent turn in the relationship between the Romans and the Britons did not fail to provoke an equally violent response from a people whom Tacitus described as 'broken in to obedience, not to slavery'.[3] But British resistance was shambolic and sporadic; the Romans benefited from the lack of cooperation between the disparate and historically quarrelsome tribes. The rebellion of Caractacus/Caradog, king of the Silures, was notable for its length and, at least initially, for its successes. However, it ended with Caractacus' betrayal by Queen Cartismandua of the Roman-allied Brigantes in AD 51, and his subsequent extradition to Rome.

Lacking any coherent strategy, each tribe reacted to the state of war in its own way. Like the Brigantes, Boudica's Iceni tribe of modern-day East Anglia were on relatively good terms with the Romans, although the relationship proceeded with some caution on the part of the Iceni. The tribe's king, Boudica's husband Prasutagus, died in AD 60 and, believing that by doing so he could protect his kingdom from wholesale annexation by Rome, he left half of his lands and riches to the emperor Nero. The other half he bequeathed to his two daughters, whose names and ages go unrecorded, under the guardianship of their mother, Boudica. The effect of Prasutagus' decision was the opposite of what he had intended: Roman

---

[1] 'Boudica', rather than the more familiar 'Boudicca' or 'Boadicea', has been shown to be the most likely to correspond to the Celtic original, according to K. Jackson, 'Queen Boudicca?', *Britannia*, 10 (1979), 255. I therefore use 'Boudica' throughout, and alternative spellings only when quoting or referring to a particular author's imagined version of the historical Boudica.
[2] Many archaeologists have attempted to piece together the story of Boudica's revolt, but see for instance G. Webster, *The British revolt against Rome AD 60* (London, 1999).
[3] Tacitus, *Agricola and Germania* (London, 2009), 10.

soldiers plundered the whole of the Iceni kingdom, the King's relatives were enslaved, his two children were raped, and his wife was publicly scourged. These outrages were but the latest and most horrifying to have been suffered by the Britons and, stirred to a renewed fervency, the Iceni and now the neighbouring Trinobantes rallied to Boudica. She became the leader of a full-scale rebellion against the most formidable human power then on earth. After sacking the settlements of Camulodunum (present-day Colchester) and Verulamium (now St Albans) Boudica's army brought its destructive force south to Londinium.[4] Tacitus records that 80,000 people were killed by Boudica's army, without regard for age, sex, or infirmity. The Britons were finally routed by the Roman governor Suetonius Paulinus, who had brought his army from the distant Isle of Mona (Anglesey) where they had been attempting to clear the Druids from their sacred forests, mostly by means of incineration. Her rebellion in ruins, Boudica took poison and died rather than allow herself to be captured alive.[5]

This, at least, is the Tacitean version of events. Cornelius Tacitus (AD 56/7–c.113) related Boudica's deeds first in the *Agricola* (AD 97), the eponymous biography of Tacitus' father-in-law, who also happened to be the military tribune in Britannia during the Boudican campaign. The treatment of Boudica's story in *Agricola* was very brief and suggests a lack of research on Tacitus' part. He made no specific mention of the wrongs Boudica and her family had suffered at the hands of the Romans, only summarizing a speech, which he attributed to Boudica, in which she exhorted her followers to rebel on the grounds that had been badly treated by the invaders. Later in *Agricola*, during a discussion of the rebellion by Galgacus some years after Boudica's death, Tacitus wrongly placed her at the head of the Brigantes tribe, having confused her with their queen, Cartismandua. The same mistake has been made on occasion elsewhere, almost certainly as a consequence of Tacitus' 2000-year-old slip of the pen.[6]

He corrected this in the *Annals* (c.113) and provided a fuller narrative of Boudica's rebellion during the reign of Emperor Nero. This account, written a few years after *Agricola*, told of Boudica's public humiliation, as well as of her daughters' torment and the enslavement of the royal family. Tacitus added further detail of omens seen in the town of Camulodunum, where the statue of the goddess Victory collapsed with no apparent cause. This portentous event occurred as the rebel armies rallied to Boudica, and to the greater goal of freeing the Britons from the insults of occupation. Again, before the final battle, Tacitus described Boudica as she delivered a moving speech to her troops, which he recorded in full in this instance.[7] Boudica was defeated and died by her own hand.

---

[4] The destruction of Verulamium follows that of Londinium in some accounts.

[5] This account is from Tacitus, *The Annals*, trans. A.J. Church and W.J. Brodribb (Mineola, NY, 2006 [first edition 1869]). References to the *Annals* are from this edition unless otherwise noted.

[6] The sixth-century Gildas referred to a 'deceitful lioness', who was occasionally identified with Boudica. Whatever her sins, Boudica is not recorded in the classical sources as having betrayed her allies, whether Roman or British; see J.A. Giles (ed. and trans.), *The works of Gildas and Nennius* (London, 1841), 9.

[7] For an illuminating discussion of Tacitus' language, see F.S. L'Hoir, *Tragedy, rhetoric, and the historiography of Tacitus's Annales* (Ann Arbor, MI, 2006) and for Boudica's speech, see E. Adler, *Valorizing the barbarians: enemy speeches in Roman historiography* (Austin, TX, 2011), 117–76.

In 1534, Polydore Vergil, an Italian in the court of Henry VII, published a new history of England, *Anglica Historia* in a Latin edition. This was the first history of any part of the British Isles to be based on Tacitus' account of the Roman invasion and the resistance it occasioned and, over time, this version would come to supplant earlier histories, particularly Geoffrey of Monmouth's mythic work composed around 1135, *Historia Regum Britanniae*, or the *History of the Kings of Britain*, known simply as the British History. Geoffrey of Monmouth, a Welsh monk resident in Oxford who later became the Bishop of St Asaph, wrote what had been the most influential account of early Britain using what he claimed were original British (that is, Celtic) manuscripts given to him by Walter, Archdeacon of Oxford. Geoffrey told of the foundation of Britain by Brutus of Troy, who had defeated the giants then dominant on the island and settled the three lands that would become England, Scotland, and Wales on his three sons.[8] This history unfolded over a period of about two thousand years, including the invasion of the Romans, and later the Saxons. It included heroically unverifiable tales of war on a global scale, in which the Arthurian army took on the entire strength of the Mediterranean world in the sixth century. But Tacitus' account put paid to this, telling instead how the Romans had descended on a land of near-naked savages who performed chthonian rituals under oak trees in the service of cruel, obscure gods. Over the course of the Renaissance and early modern period, Tacitus' histories reformed the entire landscape of early Britain and populated it with unfamiliar heroes and heroines, of whom Boudica would come to be one of the most enduring.[9]

In addition to Tacitus', there is one other written source which focused specifically on Boudica's actions and can be dated from a period in rough proximity to her own lifetime. This was the *Roman Histories* compiled by the Greek writer Dio Cassius in the second century AD. The books containing the history of Nero's reign did not survive in their original form, and thus the account we have from Dio of Boudica's rebellion comes instead from the epitome compiled by the eleventh-century monk John Xiphilinus; for simplicity's sake I will refer to the work as Dio's.[10] Dio's version of events differed in some respects from Tacitus'. These differences should be made clear at the outset because, although Dio's history did not have the popularity that the works of Tacitus did in later periods, subsequent writers sometimes combined Dio's account with Tacitus', without necessarily acknowledging which was which.

The first difference, and crucial to Edmund Bolton's seventeenth-century account in particular, is that Dio recorded the role played by Seneca, Nero's tutor

---

[8] This account is taken from T.D. Kendrick, *British antiquity* (London, 1950), Ch. 6. Kendrick pointed out that Polydore Vergil's was not even the most damning critique of the *British History*; that honour belongs to Scottish historian and tutor to James I and VI, George Buchanan, who published the *Rerum Scoticarum Historia* in 1582. But Vergil, an Italian, was a soft target, and many British antiquaries arrayed themselves against him over the next century.
[9] The importance of Tacitus to Boudica's reputation in Jacobean Britain forms the basis of Chapter 1.
[10] *Dio: the Julio-Claudians. Selections from books 58–63 of the Roman History*, ed. J. Edmondson (London, 1992), 31. The version of Dio's text which I have used throughout is 'Epitome of Book LXII', *Dio's Roman History*, ed. E. Cary (London, 1961), VIII, 83–105.

and later counsellor general, in the events that led up to Boudica's rebellion in Britain. It was Seneca, Dio wrote, who burdened the Britons with unwanted loans and demanded repayment on impossible terms.[11] Dio added this to the Britons' grievances, although he acknowledged Boudica's suffering as the primary reason the Britons finally chose to rebel. Secondly, unlike Tacitus, Dio recorded the conduct of the Britons during their rebellion at great length and with much more extensive, often lurid, detail. According to Dio, Boudica's troops butchered Roman mothers, murdered Roman infants, and engaged in all manner of looting, desecration, violence, and rapine in Roman-occupied towns.[12] Tacitus did not mention any of these particulars, although he did record that tens of thousands of Romans were killed. Third, Dio had Boudica deliver a much longer and more stirring speech to her troops. Tacitus' speech for her consisted of only a few sentences, albeit brimming with pathos; Dio's speech for Boudica carried on for some one thousand words and was followed by the recitation of a lengthy prayer to the goddess Andraste.[13] The Roman general Suetonius Paulinus' speech, which Tacitus had also recorded, was similarly lengthened by Dio, and split into three parts, delivered as the Roman general galloped between his divisions, exhorting his troops to victory. Lastly, Dio attributed Boudica's death to sickness, not suicide, as Tacitus had.[14]

* * *

These two scant source bases form the entirety of our original recorded knowledge of the story of Queen Boudica, her daughters, and the unfortunate Iceni rebellion: they are her beginning. But in this way, as in others, she is somewhat unusual. In general, it is difficult to locate beginnings in history; endings are even more elusive. Of course there are birth dates to mark the beginning of individual lives, and the death dates which bring them to an end. There are the beginnings of reigns, of wars, of institutions, and the death or cataclysm or slow decay that draws them to a close. But all of these are bounded by events which can be dated precisely, and, in the grand scheme of things, they are short-lived.

Beginnings and endings are common enough in this pointillist sense, but to locate the beginning of an *idea* is far more difficult—to find the end of an idea is perhaps even impossible.[15] This book is an attempt to piece together an idea and to tell its story through time to a by-no-means-definitive end point. It is the history of an idea, which this book tells through the posthumous life of my central figure, Queen Boudica, a figure with classical origins and a long posthumous life: she imposes a beginning of sorts, though the ending remains inconclusive. This book takes an unusually long chronological view, tracing Boudica's portrayals and uses through time, but also—and this is crucial to my overall argument—through multiple media, genres, and what we would today recognize as disciplines.

---

[11] Dio, *Roman History*, 83.
[12] Ibid., 95.   [13] Ibid., 85–95.   [14] Ibid., 105.
[15] Ideas reconstitute and reconfigure rather than disappear, and, for some, innovation is simply the recombination of existing ideas. See L.O. Mink, 'Change and causality in the history of ideas', *Eighteenth-century studies*, 2 (1968), 3–25, at 12. On ideas and 'originality', see D. Boucher, 'Ambiguity and originality in the context of discourse', in W.J. Van der Dussen and L. Rubinoff (eds), *Objectivity, method and point of view: essays in the philosophy of history* (Leiden, 1991), pp. 22–46.

Thus in telling the story of Boudica, this book seeks to map the idea of history itself across this long period of cultural, intellectual, and social change. In doing so, it seeks to challenge the conventional view of a rigid separation between 'popular' and 'academic' forms of history, as well as the accepted division between early modern and modern historical periods. It also questions the efficacy of recent approaches to studying the place of the past, such as cultural memory, public history, and the 'invention of tradition' paradigm. It argues that a different approach—a synthesis of all of these and more—is necessary to fully understand the emergence of history as a popular and academic preoccupation, as well as of figures like Boudica who are identified with a particular source base, and who have generated numerous depictions over many centuries. In order to fully understand ancient traditions, I argue here that we need to re-examine what it means to 'make history', and perhaps redraw the boundaries around what we conventionally recognize as fictional or factual genres. This book is a synthesis of ideas and practice; it draws on ideas perhaps more commonly discussed as abstractions, bringing them together with a practical historical case study in the figure of Queen Boudica in Britain.

At its core, what is presented here is a history of two ideas: the idea of history, and the idea of Boudica herself. It has been informed at various points by historical theory and the philosophy of history, as well as by the work of fellow historians, scholars of literature, drama, art, and political thought. This introductory chapter will examine the various currents of scholarship that have contributed to my understanding of historical culture as an emerging field of study in Britain.[16] I will begin by addressing heroic reputations and the notion of invented tradition, as usually understood, before explaining how a case study such as this of Queen Boudica can illuminate more complex questions, including what, precisely, history means and has meant over time. I will discuss other approaches to understanding the place of the past, in previous as well as present culture, particularly public and popular history and memory studies, all of which, I argue, address the present more than they do the past. I will go on to provide a more thorough explanation of the field of historical culture and what it means in the context of this book. This discussion will be followed by an exploration of previous scholarship about Boudica's posthumous life, focused particularly on the early modern period. This is a necessary preliminary to my own readings of lesser-known or misunderstood representations and their significance for a study of historical culture.

INVENTING TRADITIONS AND MAKING HISTORY

The study of the history of history is not usually organized around a single historical subject, whether a figure or an event. There are, of course, studies which focus on individual historical figures in Britain and their reputations over time, particularly

---

[16] The field in continental Europe is rather more advanced, exemplified by the Centre for the Study of Historical Culture in Rotterdam and the community of historical-cultural scholars active in Barcelona.

in the Victorian and Edwardian heyday of heroic commemoration. In the British context, individual reputations have been used to present cross-sectional analyses of British culture, reflecting preoccupations as diverse as gender, race, regional identity, nationalism, and imperial ambitions.[17] Yet these do not attempt to engage in any thorough way with what 'history' itself meant during these periods. Nor, given their restricted chronologies, is the question of earlier origins much discussed. This, coupled with the shared (and of course not unfounded) sense that history has been open to extremes of manipulation in the course of the modern period, which is instilled as the new orthodoxy following the cultural turn, has militated against a study of these past figures as possessing their own integrity.[18]

Indeed, that history is a tool, or even a weapon, to be deployed with purpose, has become the normative position for canny cultural historians to take. This follows a trajectory most forcefully articulated in British historiography by Eric Hobsbawm and Terence Ranger's argument that the nineteenth-century manipulation of present custom to appear ancient, especially by a body of elites, was intended to generate a sense of social cohesion and continuity. Although their approach has rarely been wholly endorsed by historians, its effects have been diverse and often implicit.[19] Yet in a sense, Hobsbawm and Ranger were merely repeating what had already become axiomatic. Writing in the late 1960s, the eminent Cambridge historian Sir J.H. Plumb stated bluntly, 'The past is always a created ideology with a purpose, designed to control individuals, or motivate societies, or inspire classes. Nothing has been so corruptly used as concepts of the past.'[20] The idea that history has been a malleable construct, a rewritable fable with its heroes and villains, whose authors search for contemporary relevance at the expense of other concerns, has sunk deep into the fabric of academic historical work, especially that which focuses on the Victorian period and later.[21]

There have been dissenting voices, at least when it comes to the invention of tradition. As J.G.A. Pocock has cogently put it:

> The invention of tradition is a phrase that encourages us to find an original set of inventors, specify their intentions or motives and the circumstances or context in

---

[17] Studies of historical figures of a comparable age or mythic quality to Boudica include S. Barczewski, *Myth and national identity in nineteenth-century Britain: the legends of King Arthur and Robin Hood* (Oxford, 2000); N. Vance, 'Roman heroism and the problems of nineteenth century empire: Aeneas and Caractacus', in G. Cubitt and A. Warren (eds), *Heroic reputations and exemplary lives* (Manchester, 2000), pp. 142–56; S. Heathorn, '"The highest type of Englishman": gender, war, and the Alfred the Great commemoration of 1901', *Canadian Journal of History*, 37 (2002), 459–84; I. Bryden, *Reinventing King Arthur: the Arthurian legends in Victorian culture* (Aldershot, 2005); J. Parker, *England's Darling: the Victorian cult of Alfred the Great* (Manchester, 2007).

[18] Boucher notes, for instance, Michel Foucault's dismissal of continuity and the search for originals as 'harmless enough amusement for historians who refuse to grow up'. Foucault quoted in Boucher, 'Ambiguity and originality', 33.

[19] E. Hobsbawm and T. Ranger, *The invention of tradition* (London, 1983), 9. Also, according to Hobsbawm and Ranger, invented traditions draw on a 'factitious' sense of continuity between past and present, 'Introduction: Inventing traditions', 2.

[20] J.H. Plumb, *The death of the past* (London, 1969), 17.

[21] For a brief but thorough discussion of this and other trends in the historiography, see B. Melman, *A culture of history: English uses of the past, 1800–1953* (Oxford, 2006), 5–10.

which they acted, and to suppose that we have thereby reduced the 'tradition' to historicity. So, it may turn out, we have: but we may need also to enquire what relations existed between the inventors and other members of their society who may have been involved in the action, and we need to enquire whether the invention was indeed instantaneous or took place over time. The longer it takes to 'invent' a 'tradition', the more will the words 'invention' and 'tradition' become interchangeable...[22]

As Pocock suggests, there is often a far more complex set of practices at play in the development of traditions—and indeed, historical knowledge generally—that invites sustained investigation over a long period of time.[23] Certainly, it is straightforward enough to find examples of history being 'used and abused', or presented, in Billie Melman's words 'as a key to "something else"'.[24] It is, however, far more difficult to tease out the less visible relationships between past and present to get to the heart of how human beings have engaged, reflectively, intimately, and humanely, with the past and the making of history.

One contention of this book is that approaches such as the 'invention of tradition' paradigm, as well as similar perspectives which view history as a mechanism of social control somehow epiphenomenal to successive presents, share a common disregard for historical and creative processes—that is, the processual and apperceptive nature of the development of historical ideas hinted at by Pocock. They focus instead on the product—that is, the representation—and its reductive significance to a contemporary setting. Boudica has been the subject of studies that take this approach, as we will see, but I hope to show that there was no single 'moment' of invention in Boudica's posthumous life, nor a single all-powerful body of knowing inventors. Instead, I propose that by enquiring into the processes by which aspects of the past—in this case Queen Boudica and ancient Britain—came into being through a discursive, even dialogic process, we can arrive at a fuller understanding not only of representations of this singular historical figure, but also of her authors; of how individuals in conversation with each other understood the act of making history. Ultimately, I hope to describe some part of the story of the development the idea of history itself within a cultural sphere.

In short, when it comes to the evolving (or revolving) idea of 'history', individual historical examples, be they of events or people like Queen Boudica, are uniquely suited to shedding light on a highly complex and potentially abstract cultural process. Boudica's example can illuminate how people interacted with the original source base, responded to the works of previous authors, and formulated their own notion of historical practice, sometimes in response to that of others. My argument here rests on the idea that to create an historical product—ranging from authoritative textbooks to imaginative history paintings, historical pageants, and films—is to engage, to varying degrees, in a series of actions: of knowledge-gathering, of synthesis, of interpretation, of negotiation, of narration, of assumption and

---

[22] J.G.A. Pocock, *Political thought and history: essays on theory and method* (Cambridge, 2009), 221.
[23] See also J. Rüsen, 'Tradition: a principle of historical sense generation and its logic and effect in historical culture', *History and Theory*, 51 (2012), 45–59.
[24] Melman, *A culture of history*, 9.

supposition. That is, to engage in a process of *making*, though not of making from nothing. The maker of historical products must begin with something unformed—the remains of the past—and end with something formed: the interpretation and recreation of that past, in whatever medium or genre the maker chooses. That process of forming is a self-conscious one, undertaken for various purposes, and, for all that it takes place within particular social circumstances and cultural contexts, it can also be considered as, to an extent, individualized, insofar as various environmental factors work on a single human mind.[25]

Therefore, to contend that the past is newly invented, newly constituted, or otherwise epiphenomenal to each successive present is to allow for only a partial and unsatisfactory understanding of continuity, or even, in extreme cases, to dispense with its possibility entirely. One foundational contention of this book, however, is that continuity is immanent in the act of reimagining the past—and not only in the obvious sense of the retention of content, or some resemblance of it. Nor by emphasizing continuity do I mean to argue that there is and was only one definitive way of interpreting the past, or of making it, or even of understanding the word 'history'. What I mean is that there is an extent to which the preoccupations of the makers of historical documents (or products, or representations—these could be used interchangeably) have remained much the same, or have at the very least maintained a discernible family resemblance to each other, throughout the four centuries examined in this book. And, even as writers and artists drew on the same historical content and moulded these to the conventions of disparate genres, there are underlying preoccupations that define all these products as 'historical', and their makers as historical authors, and attributes to their audience an awareness of their historical nature. My quarry, then, is the persistence, albeit in a variety of guises, of an idea of history.

As I have suggested briefly above, certain preoccupations constitute the act of making history, while also providing the tools with which to critique competing notions of the past. The necessity of assessing the 'truth' or 'falsehood' or simply 'relevance' of what remains of the past and might, in some circumstances, constitute reliable or merely plausible or useful evidence is just one prevailing concern. Another is the necessity of interpreting, interpolating, or imagining those details which the accessible record does not relay. Indeed, even more than the gathering of evidence and source material (important to the historical artist as much as to the writer of prose narrative), the act of interpretation, amorphous as it is and remains, forms the basis of all engagement with the past, whether for use in dramatic enactment, political argument, or academic writing. Indeed, every act of creation that can make any claim on the 'use' of the past embodies an act of (perceived) knowing, an act of interpreting, as well as an act of creating. It is thus a statement about

---

[25] R.G. Collingwood conceived of historical individuality as 'consist[ing] not of separateness from environment but of the power to absorb environment into itself'. Collingwood, *The idea of history* (Oxford, 1980), 162. Ernst Cassirer's understanding of culture as the cognitive aspects of individual minds given lasting communicable form is also illuminating, in Cassirer, *The logic of the humanities*, translated with foreword by C. Smith Howe (New Haven and London, 1961). See also my discussion in the conclusion to this book.

what history is and what it is not. It is, in the antiquary Edmund Bolton's words, 'an image of truth', but only one of many.[26]

'WHAT IS HISTORY?'

Scholars have long wrestled with that central question 'what is history?' Historians have largely done so from the perspective of professionals invested in a certain kind of historical writing and practice. E.H. Carr famously asked the question, but his answers were unapologetically—maybe unthinkingly—reliant on how professional practitioners have dealt with the methodological issues of fact-finding and interpretation.[27] As a consequence historians of history have placed great emphasis on the development of academic history, as recognizable by modern professionals.[28] In other words, the history of history can and has been treated as a sub-discipline of intellectual history, with its attendant focus on thinkers and texts deemed significant within the development of the discipline.[29] The approach to understanding what history is has been very different for philosophers, who readily acknowledge, and even revel in, the term's protean nature. Most famously, R.G. Collingwood's seminal text on 'the idea of history' ranged within the canon of historical writers and thinkers, while drawing equally on philosophers.[30]

---

[26] From Edmund Bolton's *Hypercritica, or a rule of judgement for writing or reading our history's*, published in *N. Triveti, Annalium Continuatio ut et…Edmundi Boltoni Hypercritica* (Oxford, 1722), 213–14.

[27] E.H. Carr, *What is History?* (London, 1961). See also K. Jenkins, '*What is history?': from Carr and Elton to Rorty and White* (London, 1995) and D. Cannadine (ed.), *What is history now?* (Basingstoke, 2002). See also S. Berger, 'Professional and popular historians, 1800–1900–2000', in B. Korte and S. Paletschek (eds), *Popular history now and then, international perspectives* (London, 2012), pp. 13–29. The most notable exception to the focus on the profession and the question of history is L. Jordanova, *History in Practice* (London, 2006) which is by far the most sensitive to matters of genre, media, and audience.

[28] For an overview of the debate about the origins of history in the early modern period, see D. Womersley, 'Against the teleology of technique', in P. Kewes (ed.), *The uses of history in early modern England* (San Marino, CA, 2006), pp. 91–104. The most influential works in this vein include F. Smith Fussner, *The historical revolution in English historical writing and thought, 1580–1640* (London, 1962); T.P. Peardon, *The transition in English historical writing, 1760–1830* (New York, 1966 [first edition 1933]); F.J. Levy, *Tudor historical thought* (San Marino, CA, 1967); H. Butterfield, *Man on his past: a history of historical scholarship* (London, 1969); J.M. Levine, *Humanism and history: origins of modern English historiography* (Ithaca, NY, 1987). For later periods, see the new edition by J. Robertson (ed.) of H. Trevor-Roper, *History and enlightenment* (New Haven, CT, 2010).

[29] LaCapra defines intellectual history as the study of 'situated language in significant texts', see D. LaCapra, *Rethinking intellectual history* (London, 1983), 19. See also J.M. Levine, *The autonomy of history: truth and method from Erasmus to Gibbon* (London, 1999). This story can also be told through milestones of professionalization, for which see R.A. Humphreys, *The Royal Historical Association, 1868–1968* (London, 1969); D.S. Goldstein, 'The organizational development of the British historical profession, 1884–1921', *Bulletin of the Institute of Historical Research*, 55 (1982), 180–93; D.S. Goldstein, 'The origins and early years of the *English Historical Review*', *English Historical Review*, 101(398) (1986), 6–19.

[30] R.G. Collingwood, *The idea of history* (Oxford, 1980). See also C. Parker, *The English idea of history from Coleridge to Collingwood* (London, 2000), which focuses in large part on the influence of idealist philosophy.

Indeed, theorists and philosophers have long considered questions that are at the heart of historical production.[31] One such question is: how do historical ideas come into being? A second, related question is: how is historical knowledge acquired? To imagine too clear a separation between these questions would be unhelpful. Ian Hacking's idea, derived from Foucault, of 'historical ontology' posits that our knowledge of the past can be best understood through studying how objects of that knowledge have been constituted over time.[32] But, perhaps tellingly, historical ontology and the inseparable area of historical epistemology[33]—the branch of philosophy that assesses knowledge claims—are more often encountered in the history and philosophy of science, where knowledge acquisition is a more straightforward concept because 'knowledge' is itself thought of as more concrete, rightly or wrongly.[34]

Meanwhile historians, as a rule, do not usually devote much attention to the philosophy of their discipline, nor to the fundamental questions that underpin it.[35] We do not tend to question the nature of historical knowledge or narrative, a shortcoming pointed out most famously by Hayden White.[36] White has thought very seriously—some might argue too seriously—about the overlaps between professionalized or 'scientific' forms of historical knowledge and the fictions, 'myths', and 'dreams' that denote other forms of historical imagining.[37] These forms could and should, White believes, come together to constitute the basis of a new kind of self-conscious 'metahistory', that would 'allow us to entertain seriously those creative distortions offered by minds capable of looking at the past with the same seriousness as ourselves but with different affective and intellectual orientations'.[38]

White's extensive oeuvre, especially what some have found to be its moral vacuity, remains controversial.[39] Yet his argument is in fact quite useful for historians

---

[31] For the links between the philosophy of history, the history of ideas, and the history of philosophy, see D.R. Kelley, 'What is happening to the history of ideas?', *Journal of the history of ideas*, 51(1) (1990), 3–25.

[32] I. Hacking, *Historical ontology* (Harvard, MA, 2002).

[33] Hacking refers to 'meta-epistemology', the study of 'epistemological concepts as objects that evolve and mutate', p. 9. See also M. Kusch, 'Hacking's historical epistemology: a critique of styles of reasoning', *Studies in History and Philosophy of Science*, 41 (2010), 158–73.

[34] For instance, U. Klein and W. Lefèvre, *Materials in eighteenth-century science: a historical ontology* (Cambridge, MA, 2007); H. Rheinberger, 'A plea for a historical epistemology of research', *Journal for the general philosophy of science*, 43 (2012), 105–11.

[35] C. Lorenz, 'Historical knowledge and historical reality: a plea for "internal realism"', *History and theory*, 33 (1994), 297–327. Lorenz points out that a gulf persists between some philosophy of history and actual historical practice, noting that philosophers must recognize the 'normative' elements of historical practice that some might dismiss as naïve realism.

[36] His critique is usefully summed up in H. White, *Tropics of discourse: essays in cultural criticism* (London, 1978), 27–50.

[37] A very useful digestion of White's work can be found in H. Paul, 'Hayden White and the crisis of historicism', in F. Ankersmit, E. Domańska, and H. Keller (eds), *Re-figuring Hayden White* (Stanford, 2009), pp. 54–73.

[38] White, *Tropics of discourse*, 47. See also H. White, *Metahistory: the historical imagination in nineteenth-century Europe* (Baltimore, 1973).

[39] White has responded to that criticism and many others most recently in H. White, *The practical past* (Evanston, IL, 2014).

looking to understand more deeply the power of history's boundaries, as much as its malleability, in the past. We rarely speak of knowledge as deriving from literature, drama, or imaginative forms of culture; yet, as may not have been the case when White began his career, these subjects form so much of the daily bread and butter of the practising historian in the twenty-first century. This, perhaps, means that we are now in a better position to consider these imaginative, 'non-professional' forms of history as fundamental to processes of making and disseminating historical ideas—yet without losing sight of their fundamental relation to the truth-bound activity of history-making itself. We, as cultural historians, must remember that truth is still fundamental to our enterprise.

Yet one could argue that asking straightforwardly epistemological or ontological questions has the potential to distance us from history-making as a self-conscious human act: as the accumulation of ideas, materials, and opinions, all tied to authors and in need of an audience to imbue them with meaning, and as a form of creation which is, at times, indistinct from reception.[40] In seeking to understand history—as generations of historians and philosophers of history have—in terms of 'what it is to reason and to gain knowledge', and thus to form a professionalized, 'modern' discipline around such principles, we necessarily privilege an idea of history that harmonizes with reason, logic, and scientific understanding, rather than with the fancy of poetry, the drama of the stage, or even the banal uncertainty of everyday human experience.

As I have argued above, to gain knowledge—or to convince oneself of having done so—is to engage in a process, one which takes place simultaneously with other mental activity, including reflection on the act of learning and of knowing itself, and the assessment, based on what is already 'known', of the validity or otherwise of new information. To gain knowledge is to seek stimuli, which in turn feeds perception; arguably, the seeking, perceiving individual—who need not be a historian—who is performing a conscious act of knowledge-gathering about the past, synthesizing her findings, and re-presenting them by her own chosen medium, is doing something quite different to an individual who happens upon the knowledge unintentionally, or with some intention other than to interpret and re-present it. From stimulus, to perception, to 'knowing', and onward to another process entirely, that is, to creating something original from the synthesis of what is known with what is believed, or imagined, or hoped: these constitute the complexity of historical work.

Perhaps, then, there are more productive questions for our purposes. One might be: how do conceptions of 'historical knowledge' manifest, across time, across genres, and in the works of individuals? Secondly, what vocabulary can historians use to trace this? I by no means wish to dispute the fundamental principle that historical 'objects of knowledge', or something approximating

---

[40] By far the most sensitive and well-conceptualized account of 'reception studies' is S. Goldhill, *Victorian culture and classical antiquity: art, opera, fiction, and the proclamation of modernity* (Princeton, NJ, 2011). Goldhill emphasizes the 'dynamic of classics' in the nineteenth century, and notes in particular the importance of individual artistic responses (especially within a self-conscious modernity) and the manner in which they can be mapped on to dominant themes and modes of reception, p. 9.

them, are indeed brought into being over time—that is a primary rationale for this book's chronology—but the processes by which that occurs, the individual actors involved, and the cultural and social contexts in which research, interpretation, creation, and reception have taken place have yet to be fully examined in relation to one another. Rather than offer a totalizing explanation for how objects of historical knowledge have come into being in all cases and at all times, this study uses a relatively unknowable, even 'mythic', figure, Queen Boudica, to demonstrate—insofar as it is possible to recover it—the ways in which acts of knowledge-gathering, perception, and interpretation have contributed to the bringing into being of a popular historical figure, without necessarily regarding her as a fully graspable 'object of knowledge'.

HISTORICAL CULTURE

Rather than approach the history of history as a history of the professionalized discipline or as an abstract, I follow Daniel Woolf and others in taking the view that history is a form of cultural production, discernibly 'subject to material, social and circumstantial forces...as much as the traditionally-studied intellectual influences'.[41] I further suggest that that the historical-cultural approach can help us to better understand how people in the past conceived of the very idea of 'history', by looking at the ways they critiqued themselves and each other on the basis of that idea. But, as this implies, conceiving of the history of history as a multi-generic, multidisciplinary field of culture does not allow us to escape that difficult, persistent question: what do we mean when we talk about 'history'? That is, how does an example of *historical* culture—a history play, for instance—differ from other cultural products, which are, after all, also socially created, circulated, affirmed, and interrogated over time?

The answer, as I have suggested, lies in the central preoccupation with one's distance from or proximity to something we can call 'historical truth'. To assert the importance of truth to the production of history is perhaps more contentious than it ought to be, especially among historians of culture; it remains the case in the early twenty-first century that the idea of 'truth' is more readily associated with authoritarian absolutes than free-ranging ideas. Yet the question of truth occupied the minds, and indeed consciences, of many makers of history—and for that matter fiction—in the past, long before the intervention of the profession. I use 'historical truth' then not as a single, attainable absolute, but simply as the ambiguous soul that animates the body of history.[42]

---

[41] D.R. Woolf, 'Little Crosby and the horizons of early modern historical culture', in D.R. Kelley and D.H. Sacks (eds), *The historical imagination in early modern Britain* (Cambridge, 1997), pp. 93–132, at 94. The title of Woolf's *The idea of history in early Stuart England: erudition, ideology, and the 'Light of Truth' from the accession of James I to the Civil War* (London, 1990), suggests the degree to which 'history' was a more malleable term in the past.

[42] There is a large and sometimes rebarbative theoretical literature here. See F. Ankersmit, *Meaning, truth and reference in historical representation* (Ithaca, NY, 2012). Also on 'representationcrisis' [*sic*], or

This approach brings to the fore questions around what defines historical knowledge, how evidence for the past is assessed by diverse human actors, and what role interpretation and imagination play in the narration, dramatization, and representation of the past. Thus it attempts to understand the origins and development of popular, or simply 'non-professional' notions of the documented past, or what Daniel Woolf calls the '1066 and all that' view of history, which has hitherto proved elusive.[43] There has been progress in the form of the developing fields of public history and cultural memory, but for the most part these approaches have primarily been focused on the place of the past in modern and contemporary society and are less illuminating when considering periods anterior to our own.

'Public history' is a term for which agreed definitions are scarce, though Ludmilla Jordanova's is perhaps the most useful: public history 'include[s] all the means, deliberate and otherwise, through which those who are not professional historians acquire their senses of the past'.[44] However, as David Glassberg notes, public history is inherently laden with questions about who defines and constitutes 'the public', and which version of the past ought to be presented to it.[45] Even more pertinent is that public history is of course contingent on modern notions of a public sphere, and of civic and national institutions for conserving and curating the past, especially in museums and archives.[46] Indeed, public history as a field of study today provides a lens on contemporary culture—that is, on the late twentieth and early twenty-first century—but offers little historical perspective.[47]

Perhaps surprisingly, a field defined as 'the history of popular history' does not exist in any thoroughly conceptualized or articulated way, although there is some work that defines itself as such.[48] However, cultural or historical memory studies is

---

the relationship between 'the representation' and 'the represented', see F. Ankersmit, 'The Three levels of Sinnbildung in historical writing: language and historical experience', in J. Rüsen (ed.), *Meaning and representation in history* (Oxford, 2006), pp. 108–22. Iit is worth noting that in both of these works, Ankersmit is concerned with historical writers, usually professional historians of the recent past.

[43] Daniel Woolf has opened up the field of historical culture more than any other historian of Britain. For a distillation, see D.R. Woolf, 'Disciplinary history and historical discourse; a critique of the history of history: the Case of Early Modern England', *Cromohs*, 2 (1997), 1–25. See the more fully developed D.R. Woolf, *The social circulation of the past: English historical culture, 1500–1730* (Oxford, 2003).

[44] L. Jordanova, 'Public history', *History today*, 50 (2000).

[45] D. Glassberg, 'Public history and the study of memory', *The Public Historian*, 18 (1996), 7–23, at 11.

[46] For a recent overview of the field and its practice, see F. Sayer, *Public history: a practical guide* (London, 2015).

[47] The field of 'new museology' attempts to unmask the ideological underpinnings of what might appear to be a passive or unthinking presentation of the past, especially in museums; see P. Vergo (ed.), *The new museology* (London, 2000 [first edn 1989]). David Carr argues for the differentiation between 'cognitive' forms of history, as practised by professional historians, and the 'practical' and 'future-oriented' form practised outside the academy; see D. Carr, 'The reality of history', in J. Rüsen (ed.), *Meaning and representation in history* (Oxford, 2006), pp. 123–36, at 132. This is not a wholly convincing distinction, given that the profession is by no means innocent of intellectual fashions.

[48] A field defining itself as the 'history of popular history' is only now emerging; see B. Korte and S. Paletschek (eds), 'Introduction', *Popular history now and then, international perspectives* (London, 2012), 10; see also S. Paletschek, 'Introduction: why analyse popular historiographies?', in S. Paletschek (ed.), *Popular historiographies in the 19th and 20th centuries: cultural meanings, social practices* (Oxford, 2010), pp. 1–18. And see important work on the English (and consciously urban) case in Melman,

perhaps its closest analogue, insofar as it takes seriously folk history, oral history, organized historical commemoration, and other forms of historical discourse that take place largely outside of an academic or institutional setting.[49] The study of 'memory' has generated an enormous amount of scholarship by professional historians and historical theorists, becoming a discipline in itself.[50] Under the auspices of memory studies, scholars have considered a range of historical consciousnesses outside the narrow limitations of academic opinion, blending the multimedia culture of history with the language of trauma and healing. However, the heuristic utility of 'memory' is limited by its imprecision, and, as with 'public' and 'popular' history, by its restrictive chronology. There is little scope for investigating the long legacies in popular culture of the classical, biblical, medieval, or early modern pasts.[51] Events which are chronologically distant and found only in slim documentary records do not possess the same power and immediacy as 'memories'; but they are nevertheless excavated by antiquarians, interpreted by historians, imagined by poets, and dramatized for audiences. Moreover, the division drawn between academic history and more 'popular' or 'public' versions of the past leaves little room for understanding the way in which artists and imaginative writers have engaged in the construction of historical ideas, especially in the *longue durée*.

Indeed, there is a growing sense among historical theorists active in the study of cultural or collective memory that we need new ways of understanding how people have engaged and continue to engage with the past; ways that do not rely so heavily on the normative experience of the professional historian resident in the Anglo-European world. For example, Jörn Rüsen's understanding of historical culture arises from an interest in multicultural histories, or the varieties of 'historical sense-formation' that are evident across diverse global cultures, and not merely in the European and American contexts.[52] Cross-cultural dialogue on the significance of the past demands a shared understanding of 'history' that is capacious enough to encompass the heterogeneous forms that 'sense-making' has taken in different parts of the world. This intercultural dialogue has the potential to destabilize

---

A culture of history. For contemporary popular history, see J. de Groot, *Consuming history: Historians and heritage in contemporary popular culture* (London, 2009); and W. Kansteiner and C. Classen (eds), *Historical representation and historical truth* (Middletown, CT, 2009), for a more theoretical perspective.

[49] K.L. Klein, 'On the emergence of memory in historical discourse', *Representations*, 69 (2000), 127–50, at 128.

[50] The most recent accessible introduction to the subject is A. Assmann, *Cultural memory and western civilization: functions, media, archives* (Cambridge, 2012). See also F. Ankersmit, 'Finding meaning in memory: a methodological critique of collective memory studies', *History and theory*, 41 (2002), 179–97.

[51] Scholars have of course studied 'memory' as it manifested during those periods, but the emphasis is on events of no great temporal distance; see D. Cressy, *Bonfires and bells: national memory and the Protestant calendar in Elizabethan and Stuart England* (London, 1989).

[52] 'Preface to the Series', in J. Rüsen (ed.), *Meaning and representation in history* (Oxford, 2006), x. This has also been the subject of D.R. Woolf, *A global history of history* (Cambridge, 2011), which confronts similar problems. For the most recent and informative treatment of historical culture, see P. Lambert and B. Weiler (eds), *How the past was used: historical cultures, c. 750–2000* (Oxford, 2017). I am grateful to Björn Weiler for sending me a copy of this work in proof, which I read after my own had been sent to reviewers.

accepted and conventional definitions of 'history'—especially those which rely on professional history as the normative form of 'sense-making'—and inaugurate 'a new opening of the academic discourse to its own historicity and cultural background, as well as a new acknowledgement that other cultural, non-academic, practices of "sense-formation" are equally important forms of human orientation and self-understanding'.[53] Although Rüsen's conception of historical culture is intended to facilitate academic discussions, it nevertheless suggests that disciplinary self-awareness amongst historians, and attentiveness to disciplines not one's own, as well as to things extra-disciplinary, is crucial for understanding the way that other cultures have created and consumed a sense of the past.

This foundation for cross-cultural dialogue is equally useful for conceiving of a cross-chronological historical culture: the human need to 'make sense' of the past and to 'make history' manifests itself in unfamiliar ways across different times, as well as places: the 'non-professional' might also be termed the 'pre-professional'. Thus 'historical culture' should be conceived of as an overarching and interconnected field of study that touches on, and, crucially, attempts to historicize the existing fields of memory, public history, popular history, and historiography. An idea of historical culture makes it possible to recognize the similarities and continuities between various forms of historical 'sense-making', and to describe and emphasize their deep, shared connection to an enduring human activity: the practices of knowing, interpreting, narrating, and creating that constitute our making, and making sense of, the past.

If historical culture has been an arena in which the past was 'constantly negotiated', my interest, then, is in the terms of that negotiation.[54] What were the limits imposed, whether by authors, critics, or audiences, on the interpretation or deliberate fictionalization of Boudica's story? In answering this question I hope to show that even when Boudica was reimagined or reframed for a new generation, the way of understanding her story maintained a degree of continuity across chronological and generic boundaries. Part of recognizing this continuity is to acknowledge that there are ways in which non-professionals, amateurs, writers, and artists have approached a similar source base with cognitive tools not unlike those of the historian. I hope to show that most individuals who came to Boudica's story did so with an idea of history in mind. That idea of history was not static, but it continued (and continues) to resemble itself even after the passage of centuries.

BOUDICA IN EARLY MODERNITY: ORIGINS AND SCHOLARSHIP

Thus far we have examined various frameworks for understanding the way historical ideas have emerged over time, and introduced key questions around the making of

---

[53] Rüsen, 'Preface', xiii–xiv.
[54] B. Forster, 'Popular history, gender and nationalism', in B. Korte and S. Paletschek (eds), *Popular history now and then, international perspectives* (London, 2012), pp. 149–68, at 150.

history and the idea of historical culture. But what of Boudica herself? I would like now to turn to a discussion of existing studies of Boudica. Scholarly studies of her posthumous life are relatively limited and have largely been conducted through the lens of literary criticism.[55] Much of this scholarship has focused on the early modern period, from the age of Elizabeth until the death of James I, and has used the gender politics of the era to dissect Boudica's contemporary reputation.[56] Jodi Mikalachki has identified a prevailing 'masculine anxiety' regarding Boudica in the work of early modern antiquaries and chroniclers.[57] It is worth examining this and similar claims in some detail, as doing so sheds light on the nature of historical culture at the close of the sixteenth century, and also foregrounds much of the discussion in the early chapters of this book.

One of the works Mikalachki points to is Raphael Holinshed's *Chronicles of England, Scotlande and Irelande* (1577). Holinshed's *Chronicles* was one of the first relatively accessible works—certainly compared to the Tacitean original, or even Vergil's Latin work—in which Boudica's story could be found.[58] Despite its large size, the *Chronicles* sold well and held remarkable appeal amongst religious scholars, antiquaries, and non-specialist audiences alike.[59] Holinshed's work—which was in fact more of an edited collection than a single-authored text—formed part of a tradition of chronicle-writing that extended back to the medieval period, when these were little more than lists of dates, events, or reigns of monarchs, with little attention given to narrative, to interpretation, or to general reflection.[60] However, Holinshed's *Chronicles* were somewhat different in that they drew on and interpreted the classical sources for early British history in innovative ways. More than any other Elizabethan work, Holinshed's *Chronicles* gave Boudica her beginning as a multifaceted character.

---

[55] C. Williams's *Boudica and her stories: narrative transformations of a warrior queen* (Newark, DE, 2009), which provides thematically organized discussions of works up to and including those produced in the late twentieth century. Works that consider Boudica in more sparse or schematic terms include M. Warner, *Monuments and maidens: the allegory of the female form* (London, 1985); S. MacDonald, 'Boadicea: Warrior, mother and myth', in S. MacDonald, P. Holden, and S. Ardener (eds), *Images of women in peace and war: Cross-cultural and historical perspectives* (Basingstoke, 1987), pp. 40–55. Richard Hingley and Christina Unwin's *Boudica, Iron Age queen* (London, 2000) is something of a catalogue of sources with limited contextualization and analysis. It is cited where relevant.

[56] J. Mikalachki, *The Legacy of Boadicea: Gender and nation in early modern England* (London, 1998); S. Frenée-Hutchins, *Boudica's odyssey in early modern England* (Farnham, 2014).

[57] Mikalachki misreads Camden's quotation of Tacitus as a deliberate appropriation of the voice of the conqueror, *Legacy of Boadicea*, 121.

[58] The recently published *Oxford Handbook of Holinshed's Chronicles* is by far the best resource for Holinshed's complex work; see P. Kewes, I.W. Archer, and F. Heal (eds), *Oxford Handbook to Holinshed's Chronicles* (Oxford, 2013). See also A. Patterson, *Reading Holinshed's Chronicles* (London, 1994), an earlier but still informative reading of Holinshed's work as a political statement. See also Frenée-Hutchins, *Boudica's odyssey*, 28–45.

[59] T.A. McElroy, 'Genres', *Handbook*, pp. 267–83; W. Herendeen, 'Later historians and Holinshed', *Handbook*, pp. 236–7. For the 'chronicle market', see A.T. Pratt and D.S. Kastan, 'Printers, publishers and the *Chronicles* as artefact', *Handbook*, pp. 21–42; see also F. Heal, 'Readership and reception', *Handbook*, pp. 356–72.

[60] See D.R. Woolf, *Reading history in early modern England* (Cambridge, 2000), Ch. 1; D.R. Woolf, 'From hystories to the historical: five transitions in thinking about the past, 1500–1700', in P. Kewes (ed.), *The uses of history in early modern England* (San Marino, CA, 2006), pp. 31–67.

Although the focus of the work was largely on political and military events, the *Chronicles* plotted a factual discussion of Boudica's rebellion within a narrative structure that allowed for interpretative latitude. The authors did not overly concern themselves with the interior lives or individual motivations of their human subjects, but nevertheless, the *Chronicles* found ways of appealing to an Elizabethan audience, whose sympathies were likely to be with the native Britons. The appearance of a woodcut illustration of Boudica in Elizabethan costume was only the most obvious of these means (see Figure 1).[61] Jodi Mikalachki has noted that Holinshed seemed to prefer the account of Boudica's rebellion found in the epitomes of Dio which, as we have seen, included stories of Boudica's atrocious vengeance. This, Mikalachki argues, suggests the antipathy of Holinshed towards his subject.[62] However, recent historians of the *Chronicles* have observed that the account of the Boudican rebellion was much more favourable toward the Britons than to their adversaries, the ostensibly more civilized Romans. Judith Mossman notes many instances in which Holinshed either deliberately mistranslated or misinterpreted Dio in order to make the Britons the bearers of superior numbers, technology, armour, defences, and discipline—attributes that had, in Dio's version, belonged

Figure 1. Woodcut of 'Voadica', courtesy of The Wardens and Scholars of New College, Oxford. Holinshed, R.: *The firste volume of the Chronicles of Englande, Scotlande, and Irelande*. (d7r, p. 61).

---

[61] R. Holinshed, *The firste volume of the Chronicles of England, Scotlande, and Irelande* (London, 1577), 60–5; the illustration appears p. 61.
[62] Mikalachki, *The legacy of Boadicea*, 14. Mikalachki's interpretation of Boudica has informed other accounts, such as W. Maley, ' "That Fatal Boadicea": depicting women in Milton's *History of Britain*, 1670', in D. Loewenstein and P. Stevens (eds), *Early modern nationalism and Milton's England* (London, 2008), pp. 305–30.

to the Romans. Holinshed also cast Boudica's suffering at the hands of the Romans as the primary cause of the Britons' anger.[63]

Why, then, if Holinshed was favourably disposed, did he choose to draw on the more scurrilous work? There was, in fact, a utility unique to Dio's version of events that might explain its appeal to Holinshed: the ancient account allowed the sixteenth-century chronicler to sensationalize without fictionalizing. Holinshed gave a detailed recital of the massacre of the Romans by the Britons as described by Dio, though he could easily have evaded the whole subject by simply leaving out Dio's own words. But the version of the destruction of London that was supported by Dio was undoubtedly the more arousing one for audiences inclined to prurience, and Holinshed, despite his own stance towards Boudica and the Britons, may not have been above such considerations.[64]

From the end of the sixteenth century, the intellectual currents of the time began to flow away from the chronicle's 'list' form of history; this, coupled with the banal machinations of audience demand for historical subject matter, brought about the genre's slow demise.[65] But, as the chronicle waned, the historical material, much of it based on the newly discovered classical sources, that they had done so much to document and disseminate, dispersed into other forms of historical culture that then eclipsed the chronicle in popularity and scope of content. The most notable beneficiary of the genre's subject matter was the history play, a form of historical production that was to maintain a growing popularity throughout the Elizabethan and Stuart eras; plays produced in the late seventeenth century will be discussed in Chapter 2, but I will focus here on the earliest.[66]

At the same time as the chronicles were fading, the death of Queen Elizabeth brought an end to any association Boudica might have had as 'Voada, England's happie queene', as Jonathan Aske had cast her following the defeat of the Spanish Armada.[67] Scholars have viewed the death of Queen Elizabeth as a milestone marking the retreat of the warrior queen from public view, or at least as a relatively

---

[63] J. Mossman, 'Holinshed and the classics', *Handbook*, 303–18, at 312. Annabel Patterson argues that Holinshed even attempted to weave Boudica into a 'discontinuous history of ancient constitutionalism'; this might push the argument too far, but it is certainly suggestive; see A. Patterson, *Reading Holinshed's Chronicles* (London, 1994), 105.

[64] R. Helgerson, 'Murder in Faversham: Holinshed's impertinent history', in D. Kelley and D.H. Sacks (eds), *The historical imagination in early modern Britain: history, rhetoric, and fiction, 1500–1800* (Cambridge, 1997), pp. 133–58.

[65] L.B. Wright, 'The Elizabethan middle-class taste for history', *The Journal of Modern History*, 3(2) (1931), 175–97, at 185; D.R. Woolf, 'Genre into artifact: the decline of the English chronicle in the sixteenth century', *Sixteenth Century Journal*, 19 (1988), 321–54, at 332.

[66] For the growth of 'chronicle plays', see F.E. Schelling, *The English chronicle play: a study in the popular historical literature environing Shakespeare* (London, 1902), especially 30–55. See also I. Ribner, *The English history play in the age of Shakespeare* (Princeton, NJ, 1957). For 'history play' as a genre in the age of Shakespeare, see B. Griffin, *Playing the past: approaches to English historical drama, 1385–1600* (Woodbridge, 2001); P. Kewes, 'The Elizabethan history play: a true genre?', in R. Dutton, and J.E. Howard (eds), *A companion to Shakespeare's Works, vol. 2, The Histories* (Oxford, 2003), pp. 170–93. It is notable that much of the scholarship about the relationship between drama and history rests heavily on Shakespeare, and little extends beyond the early modern period.

[67] J. Aske, *Elizabethan Triumphans* (London, 1588). Boudica also appeared in minor laudatory roles throughout Elizabeth's lifetime; see P.D. Green, 'Theme and structure in Fletcher's *Bonduca*', *Studies in English Literature 1500–1900*, 22 (1982), 305–16, at 307.

positive presence. As Frenée-Hutchins argues, following the arrival of James I, the hitherto heroic Boudica was transformed into 'a fierce, destructive and unnatural mother'; that is, she came to be seen as a stubborn obstacle to masculine civility of the Romans.[68] This was especially evident in the first history play about Boudica, John Fletcher's *Tragedie of Bonduca* (1612), in which Boudica and her daughters were portrayed as savages intent on bloody vengeance.[69] For all of its heavy fictionalization, Fletcher's play was likely to have been gleaned from the version of the Boudica story found in Holinshed's *Chronicles*.[70] In the play, the rape of Boudica's daughters is made light of, and the two young women are consistently portrayed unsympathetically. Boudica, meanwhile, is something of a harridan, whose tense alliance with her cousin, Caratach, collapses as he attempts to pursue an imagined ideal of masculine warfare against the Roman general, Suetonius—a dynamic that at least one scholar has read as having homosexual undertones.[71] Bonduca, meanwhile, tries unsuccessfully to take her personal vengeance against the Romans. After a final catastrophic failure in the battlefield, Bonduca and her two daughters take their own lives in the penultimate act of the play. In this moving scene, Fletcher imbued his three female protagonists with a degree of pathos absent from the rest of the play, in which the daughters tend to behave as at best uncouth and at worst barbaric. Yet her final act is not without an admixture of savagery. Bonduca taunts her youngest child, calling her a whore for her dalliance with Junius, a Roman soldier who has fallen in love with her.

Fletcher's play can easily be read in terms of simple binaries: femininity and masculinity, savagery and civilization, Briton and Roman.[72] Perhaps rightly, the

---

[68] Frenée-Hutchins, *Boudica's odyssey*, 5–6. This is also one of the arguments of Mikalachki, *Legacy of Boadicea*.

[69] See the biographical preface in F.E. Schelling (ed.), *Francis Beaumont and John Fletcher* (New York, 1912); P.J. Finkelpearl, 'Beaumont, Francis (1584/5–1616)', *Oxford Dictionary of National Biography* (Oxford, online edn, Oct 2006), http://www.oxforddnb.com/view/article/1871, accessed 20 Nov 2012. Hereafter *ODNB*. John Aubrey alludes to John Fletcher in his entry on Francis Beaumont as follows: 'They lived together on the Bankside, not far from the playhouse, both bachelors; lay together...the same clothes and cloak, etc, between them.' J. Aubrey, *Brief Lives*, ed. R. Barber (Woodbridge, 2004), 37.

[70] S. Doran, 'Tudor King's and Queens', *Handbook*, pp. 475–90, at 489. Fletcher had collaborated with William Shakespeare on *King Henry VIII (All is True)*, which drew on the 1587 edition of the *Chronicles*; see G. McMullan (ed.), 'Introduction' to William Shakespeare and John Fletcher, *King Henry VIII, all is true* (London, 2000), pp. 161–74. See also I. Ribner, *The English history play in the age of Shakespeare* (Princeton, NJ, 1957). Ribner identifies similarities between Fletcher's *Bonduca* and Shakespeare's *Antony and Cleopatra*.

[71] J. Crawford, '"The Tragedie of Bonduca" and the anxieties of the masculine government of James I', *Studies in English Literature, 1500–1900*, 39 (1999), 357–81, at 358. See also C. Jowitt, 'Colonialism, politics, and Romanization in John Fletcher's "Bonduca"', *Studies in English Literature 1500–1900*, 43 (2003), 475–94; G. McMullan, 'The colonisation of early Britain on the Jacobean stage', in G. McMullan and D. Matthews (eds), *Reading the medieval in early modern England* (Cambridge, 2007), pp. 119–42; C.D. Williams, '"This Frantic Woman": Boadicea and English Neo-Classical Embarrassment', in M. Biddiss and M. Wyke (eds), *The Uses and Abuses of Antiquity* (New York, 1999), pp. 19–35 discusses most of the major stage plays in brief, as does W.C. Nielsen, 'Boadicea on stage before 1800: a theatrical and colonial history', *Studies in English Literature 1500–1900*, 49 (2009), 595–614.

[72] The more recent discussion is S. Frenée-Hutchins, *Boudica's odyssey*, Ch. 4. Elsewhere, J.E. Curran has read the play as a subtle comment on contemporary religious controversy, arguing that Fletcher's

struggle between barbarism and civility as a preoccupation of masculine, colonizing nations underpins the majority of scholarly readings of the play. There may indeed have been a close connection between the disavowal of queenship and a sense amongst male writers—playwrights, historians, and poets alike—in Jacobean England that they must distance themselves from the barbarity of their national origins through testimonies of disownment such as Fletcher's play.

However, if John Fletcher had hoped to excise Boudica from the historical record, a more effective approach would have been not to write *Bonduca* in the first place.[73] As it happened, his negative view of her did not appear to have any long-lasting influence, possibly because Fletcher's play was 'not an exploration of the political implications of an historical period, but rather a skilful and effective use of history as a background for romantic themes'.[74] However, the diversity of readings of both the chronicle and the play show that early-modern historical culture was a complex generic mix. Authorial intentions—was Fletcher attempting to arrest the evolution of Boudica's myth, or was he simply exploring romantic themes?—can be very difficult to disaggregate in such a climate. Perhaps, then, the primary importance of these early-modern works is that they established Boudica as a free-standing presence outside of the classical accounts of Tacitus and Dio. Many characters from the classical histories passed unremarked, but Boudica—in spite of her womanhood, and in spite of her savagery—was lifted by Holinshed and Fletcher and projected onto a much larger canvas. In light of this contribution, the precise characteristics ascribed to her by either the chronicler or the playwright pale into lesser significance.

This early modern material is important in this study, not least for providing the background context of Boudica's emergence in the seventeenth century, the point at which we join the story. It is also important because, as I noted above, it is the period in Boudica's posthumous lifetime which has commanded the most attention from scholars. I have put it here in the introduction in order that the first full chapter can take up the story where so many other studies have left it hanging. The

---

Bonduca was the voice of a wave of 'Protestant anti-Romanism', the proponents of which equated the subjugation of native tradition by newly discovered Roman historical sources with the threat of Catholic oppression; see J.E. Curran, *Roman invasions: the British History, Protestant anti-Romanism, and the historical imagination in England, 1530–1660* (Newark, DE, 2002). Curran's view seems to equate the Rome of Tacitus with that of the papacy, but most contemporary commentator viewed the corruption of Rome as a gradual process, not as inherent to the place. See F. Heal, 'What can King Lucius do for you? The Reformation and the early British Church', *English Historical Review*, 120 (2004), 593–614; M. Vandrei, 'Claudia Rufina', in G. Atkins (ed.), *Making and remaking saints in nineteenth-century Britain* (Manchester, 2016), pp. 60–76.

[73] Like all plays, *Bonduca* was banned from performance after 1640, but the plays of John Fletcher, whether solo or collaborations, were among the most popular plays in print during the period 1642–60. See W. van Lennep (ed.), *The London stage, 1660–1800: a calendar of plays, entertainments & afterpieces, together with casts, box-receipts and contemporary comment compiled from the playbills, newspapers and theatrical diaries of the period*, Part I (1660–1700), (Carbondale, IL, 1962), cxxviii. Hereafter *TLS 1660–1800*. See also L.B. Wright, 'The reading of plays during the Puritan Revolution', *Huntington Library Bulletin*, 6 (1934), 72–108. *Bonduca* was in print and on sale in London in 1656, according to P. Massinger, T. Middleton, W. Rowley, *The Old Law, together with an exact and perfect catalogue of all the playes... more exactly printed then ever before* (London, 1656).

[74] Ribner, *English history play*, 58.

period after the death of Elizabeth, onward until the first British cinemas began to screen moving images of the ancient warrior queen, will be the focus of the rest of this work.

CHRONOLOGY, METHOD, AND STRUCTURE

This book aims to offer a sharper historical understanding of Boudica's place in historical culture, extending beyond the early modern focus offered by previous works. In turn, it provides a lens through which to view the development of history as a sphere of interest, whether popular, scholarly, or some less obvious category. The chronological boundaries of this study have been dictated by Boudica's posthumous existence, beginning, as we have seen, with the rediscovery of Tacitus, and extending into the twentieth century. Given the lengthy time period under consideration here, there will be extensive discussion of the relevant contemporaneous cultural, political, and social contexts in which individual representations of Boudica appeared, and in which individual producers worked.

But central to my method and overall argument is the sense that history is the product of many voices, not always in harmony. The role of individual authors, artists, scholars, and critics will also form part of the foundation for understanding representations. Many portrayals of Boudica can be embedded in personal as well as cultural, narratives: the life and opinions, motivations and intended meaning—when recoverable—of the author, artist, or scholar are, I believe, inextricable from the act of creation. Thus this book employs methods more often associated with literary scholars and cultural studies, particularly close readings of texts, thick description, and extensive contextualization. In using such an approach, I hope to excavate the multiple layers of meaning—cultural, political, even personal—that Boudica could and did embody, and what these can tell us about the making of history. This method, along with an attention to cross-chronological comparisons and to the essential questions discussed in detail above, presents an alternative way of understanding the place of the past: one which relies as much on contextualization within the cultural and social detail of successive presents as it does on the individual circumstances of production and reception, insofar as the two are distinguishable. It is worth noting that of course some authors led more well-documented lives than others, and I occasionally take the step of reading the works of less knowable figures as nevertheless articulating individual feeling.

The book is organized into six roughly chronological chapters. Chapter 1 is focused on the way in which Tacitus' histories became politicized through an association with the Roman philosopher Seneca's Stoicism in the seventeenth century, and the previously unacknowledged ways that Boudica fits into this story. In particular, this chapter will explore the work of Edmund Bolton, Catholic antiquary and staunch monarchist, whose *Nero Caesar; or monarchie deprav'd* (1624), cast Boudica's rebellion as a cautionary tale, sending a clear message to any who would threaten the king. Bolton's study of Boudica will be examined in light of his other writings and his own ambitions for his work in order to demonstrate how such an overtly prejudicial view was nevertheless upholstered with original antiquarian (which is to say philological and material) evidence, supposition, and what would appear to be a balanced view of the ancient historians. More perhaps than later chapters, Chapter 1 shows the individual against the backdrop of his period, and the way that this complex interaction could have interesting results for historical production.

Chapter 2 discusses the role of dramatic writers and 'hack' historians in establishing the spine of a popular narrative of national history—interchangeably, it seems, understood as English and British—during the mid- to late seventeenth century, with Boudica and her rebellion as one of its earliest fixed points. Once again, the work of less well-known writers, notably Thomas Heywood and Nathaniel Crouch, will illuminate the crossover between genres and discourses of historical truth that persisted into the latter half of the seventeenth century. This chapter will also suggest a relationship between 'popular' history and stage drama in the period from the late seventeenth and eighteenth centuries that has yet to be fully understood.

This concern also emerges in Chapter 3, which moves the story into the eighteenth century, focusing on the interaction between historical writers of opposing political opinions, and their differing interpretations of the ancient British past. These historical writings and the bases for their disagreement are discussed alongside the mid-eighteenth-century drama by Richard Glover, based on the life of Boudica. What emerges is a shared preoccupation with, and sensitivity to, the limits of interpretation, whether political or imaginative. Boudica's story was malleable, but the critical reaction to Glover's dramatic retelling reveals critics' uneasiness with his approach, akin to that felt by historians of differing political views.

Chapter 4 examines Boudica's portrayal in the first half of the nineteenth century, generally considered to be the point in time that saw the 'beginning' of popular history. This period is marked by a proliferation of historical material, but, although undoubtedly on a more widespread scale, much of the material reflects themes consistently present in discourses around Boudica. Thus one aim of this chapter is to understand how, in a rapidly growing popular culture of history, Boudica could play many roles, some of them new, but many of them with precedents in earlier periods. Yet changes are also evident, especially in the increasing significance ascribed to Boudica's identity as a woman, a mother, and a heathen. These concerns were reflected in older genres, such as drama, and new genres, particularly collective biographies aimed at young women. This, I argue, is reflective of history as a field of multifarious culture.

Picking up threads that begin to appear in Chapter 4, Chapter 5 examines the view that Boudica's image in the late nineteenth century was bound up with the expanding British Empire and imperialist sentiments. It looks in depth at the creation and placement of Thomas Thornycroft's 'Boadicea group', with detailed discussion of the thirty-year background of the statue's arrival in 1902. This iconic statue of Boudica belies the complexity of Boudica's meaning, to Thornycroft and to audiences. Through discussion of the near-contemporaneous historical novels in which Boudica appeared, and the incredulous public's response to what was at times a blatantly jingoistic interpretation of the ancient past, this chapter suggests that even past and present parallels that seem obvious are often far more complex than they appear; an incredulous public was not always so easy to convince. It also continues to follow discussions around what was allowable within the confines of fictionalization.

Chapter 6 extends this discussion further, focusing on the narratives of Boudica that persisted in different parts of Britain. It focuses in detail on Boudica's Welsh identity, traceable from the eighteenth century to the First World War. Welsh commentators, especially those with a cultural-nationalist agenda, drew on antiquarian research, tradition, and archaeological supposition to assert Boudica's Welsh identity, and reiterate the importance of the Welsh contribution to the palimpsest of the British past. The second half of the chapter shows how Boudica was important to other sub-national historical narratives in England through the medium of historical pageants and historical film. Overall this chapter argues for the multiplicity of local and regional historical narratives as a significant aspect of late nineteenth- and twentieth-century historical culture. A short concluding chapter reiterates my larger arguments, while also pointing to areas that invite further research by historians of historical culture.

1

'Higher then to her no bookes doe reach'
The Queen and the Antiquary

This steel Rule whoseoever honestly follows, may perhaps write incommidiously for some momentary Purposes, but shall thereby, both in present and to posterity, live with Honour, through the Justice of his Monuments.[1]

Historians of early modern culture have become increasingly attuned to the multi-generic and cross-disciplinary nature of the historical work produced in sixteenth- and seventeenth- century Britain, which ranged across antiquarianism, literature, drama, politics, satire, and law.[2] The slow and gradual process by which these various cultural spheres and 'shapes of knowledge' became disaggregated and were honed into the disciplinary structure familiar to today's scholars has been charted from a number of angles.[3] Recent studies of early historiography and historical fiction have also explored the complex, overlapping nature of scholarly and popular historical culture in this period.[4] Undoubtedly the late sixteenth and early seventeenth centuries—and for that matter the years following—was a time of flux, during which fact and fiction blended, sometimes seamlessly, together.

As discussed in the introduction to this volume, previous studies of Boudica's significance throughout the sixteenth and seventeenth centuries have contextualized her depiction within prevailing cultural discourses of femininity and early colonialism, with little acknowledgement of the significance to early modern

---

[1] Bolton, *Hypercritica*, 213–4.
[2] See Introduction n. 41 and D.R. Kelley and D.H. Sacks (eds), *The historical imagination in early modern Britain: history, rhetoric, and fiction, 1500–1800* (Cambridge, 1997); J.M. Levine, *The autonomy of history: truth and method from Erasmus to Gibbon* (Ithaca, NY, 1999). For history and legal matters, see J.G.A. Pocock, *The ancient constitution and the feudal law: a study of English historical thought* (Cambridge, 1957) and B. Shapiro, *A culture of fact: England, 1550–1720* (Ithaca, NY, 2000).
[3] For history and other disciplines, see D.R. Kelley (ed.), *History and the disciplines: the reclassification of knowledge in early modern Europe* (Rochester, NY, 1997); P. Hoffer, *Clio among the muses: essays on history and the humanities* (New York, NY, 2013). For the humanities, see A. Grafton and L. Jardine, *From humanism to the humanities: education and the liberal arts in fifteenth- and sixteenth-century Europe* (London, 1986); D.R. Kelley and R.H. Popkin (eds), *The shapes of knowledge from the Renaissance to the Enlightenment* (Dordrecht, Netherlands, 1991); J. Turner, *Philology: the forgotten origins of the modern humanities* (Princeton, NJ, 2014). See also the critique by S. Collini, 'Seeing a specialist: the humanities as academic disciplines', *Past & Present*, 229 (2015), 271–81.
[4] J.P. Hunter, 'Protesting fiction, constructing history', in Kelley and Sacks (eds), *Historical imagination*, pp. 298–317; A. Davis, *Renaissance historical fiction: Sidney, Deloney, Nashe* (Cambridge, 2011); N. Popper, *Walter Ralegh's 'History of the World' and the historical culture of the Renaissance* (London, 2012).

historical culture of rediscovered classical sources. Thus, for example, while Samantha Frenée-Hutchins distinguishes between the 'didactic nature' of early modern prose histories which, she argues, 'show the devastating effects of female leadership', and more 'literary' texts which 'advocated the need to tame the wild heart of women',[5] Boudica's identity as a Tacitean inheritance, and Tacitus' own growing importance in the period, goes unmentioned. This neglect in studies of Boudica in the early modern period is surprising given the extent to which the works of Tacitus infused Jacobean political and historical culture, but the overriding concern with issues emerging from Boudica's femininity has simply occluded other readings.

A further complication is presented by Tacitus' works themselves. Tacitus' importance in the period was multifaceted: his historical narrative, his rhetorical style, and especially his political-philosophical position—all held fascination for seventeenth-century historians, politicians, poets, and playwrights, making any single thread difficult to trace. However, Boudica's example allows us to focus in particular on Tacitus' influence on political thought and methods of historical discourse, and specifically on the manner in which Renaissance scholarship cemented Tacitus' association with Neostoicism in the Jacobean court. I will argue it was this association that led to the first (and for some time the only) truly original antiquarian-historical study of Boudica, published by the Roman Catholic antiquary Edmund Bolton (1574/5–c.1634). Bolton was a complex character, whose work furnishes a striking example of early modern historical culture as a landscape of fact, fiction, ideology, and intense antiquarian learning.

Blending opinion, material evidence, and historical narrative, Bolton's writing demands sensitive reading against the backdrop of his personal circumstances: he lived a precarious existence as a recusant, dependent on the goodwill of the sovereign, James I, and latterly Charles I, and on tenuous connections at court, especially with the Duke of Buckingham. However, Bolton also had a keen interest in Queen Boudica, ancient Britain, and the study of history itself. Excavating the various underpinnings and motivations of his work can reveal the contingency of historical interpretation, while also shedding light on the genuine fascination British antiquity held for this ambitious, but thwarted, antiquarian mind. Thus the aim of this chapter is to examine the case of Edmund Bolton and his writings, both on Boudica and on the nature of history, in order to understand the complex intersections between ideology and historical discourse in Jacobean England as they came together in the work of this unusual scholar.

There were undoubtedly tensions between Bolton's need to satisfy his benefactors and another duty of which he was deeply aware, namely that of the historian to relate a factually accurate version of events to his reader, while drawing out the lessons to be learned from the past—at least as he understood them. As we will see, this was an awareness he interrogated and honed throughout his career, especially in his reflections on the practice of reading and writing history. However, what is interesting here is that the balance between ideological necessity and historiographical

---

[5] Frenée-Hutchins, *Boudica's odyssey*, 10.

duty was easier to strike than we might suppose: Bolton's devotion to the monarchy and his antipathy do the influence of Neostoic ideas then current at court did not compromise his reasoning, even as his historical narrative was undeniably intended to show the dangers of pride, conspiracy, and sedition. That is, he presented a seamless, 'truthful' interpretation of Boudica's rebellion that both adhered to evidence and conveyed his cautionary message. We are left then with a contradictory personality: Bolton was probably one of the most critically self-aware historians in Jacobean England, even if he was also one of the most prejudiced.

As for Boudica herself, Bolton's work once again demonstrates that interest in her did not die with Queen Elizabeth, and neither did she suffer ignominy. Rather, her pedigree as a Tacitean historical figure and one of the first named personalities in British history made her an unignorable part of the national and, for Londoners, the local past. Bolton, however, did far more than not ignore her: he studied her rebellion in detail and made her a focal point of his work. This interest, I would argue, was no coincidence, nor was it mere antiquarian whim. Bolton's fascination can be explained by the fact that Boudica succinctly combined his interests in the classical past, the histories of Britain and of London, and his fascination with historical examples of anti-monarchical sentiment, sedition, and rebellion. Moreover, her story was easily interpretable within the confines of the antiquary's own decided opinions in favour of the monarch's absolute authority over his fractious subjects. Yet the Boudican rebellion also invited innovative thinking and erudite speculation on Bolton's part. His theories about the location of the final battle, the reasons for the queen's defeat, and her final resting place were all based on informed supposition, but he could rightly claim them as his own singular interpretations of a significant event in the country's earliest history. For Bolton, who believed that the history of England—he did not engage with the histories of Wales, Ireland, or Scotland—had yet to be satisfactorily written, Queen Boudica presented an opportunity to intervene in a past that was still in the process of solidifying.

TACITUS AND NEOSTOICISM IN EARLY MODERN BRITAIN

The first-century world had been dominated by Roman imperial power, and Tacitus' histories were among the most important documentary records of the period. Centuries after his death, Tacitus' histories introduced the scholars of Europe to what was in some cases, Britain's among them, a drastically new and challenging version of the distant past. But this was only part of the story. Most of Tacitus' works were concerned with his own Roman homeland, and especially with the political machinations of its emperors and senators. While Livy, for example, had witnessed the glory years of the Roman republic and recorded them for posterity, Tacitus' unfortunate task was to record the rise of tyrannical emperors, particularly in the *Annals* and the *Histories*.[6] In the *Annals*, he wrote of the long reign of

---

[6] A.T. Bradford, 'Stuart absolutism and the "utility" of Tacitus', *Huntington Library Quarterly*, 46 (1983), 127–55.

Tiberius and the relatively short but catastrophic years of Nero, whose cruel misgovernment bore responsibility for the Boudican rebellion and the ultimate destruction of Rome. The invasion of Britain, the arrival of Christians in Rome, their persecution under Nero, and the personal stories of famous Romans like Seneca, revered philosopher and dramatist, were all part of Tacitus' rich tapestry. In short, the history of the first century was a Tacitean one, seen through the eyes of a jaded Roman senator. And, in sixteenth- and seventeenth-century Europe and Britain, Tacitus' first-century Rome became a point of comparison and an analogy for the political and religious strife of the contemporary world.

Tacitus' emergence at the forefront of classical authors in the early modern world was gradual. Throughout the medieval period only a handful of scholars, clustered in southern and central Europe, encountered Tacitus' fragmentary record, and the majority of his works remained obscure into the sixteenth century. Of the *Annals*, only Books 1–6 and 11–21 have survived, and even these are only partially intact.[7] The earliest known example of the first six books is a single ninth-century manuscript in Carolingian miniscule, from which parts of the fifth book are missing; it is the sole ancestor of all later copies. By contrast, there are thirty-two known manuscript copies of Books 11–21, all of them complete up to Book 16, after which they vary slightly. There is evidence that scholars had consulted small parts of Tacitus' *Annals* in the sixth century, but it was not until ten centuries later that the work became more widely available when, under the auspices of Pope Leo X, Beroaldus published an edition of the rarest portion, the first five books of the *Annals*, in 1515. In 1533 Beatus Rhenanus compiled a new edition of the collected works of Tacitus, this time carefully distinguishing between the *Annals* and the *Histories*, and clearly marking the point in European history at which Tacitus became the object of philological and historical attention. Tacitus made his entry into Britain shortly after Rhenanus' Tacitus appeared.

Although the works of Livy and Cicero had dominated the intellectual landscape well into the Renaissance and continued to do so for some time, Tacitus surpassed all other classical authors as historian and rhetorician by the close of the sixteenth century.[8] By the beginning of the seventeenth century, 'Tacitism'—the widespread early modern interest in and enthusiasm for Tacitus as a prose stylist, moralist, historian, and political thinker all in one—had taken hold across Europe, including in Britain.[9] As Tacitus' influence grew, there emerged a sense among many contemporaries that their own political circumstances were analogous to first-century Rome, and that the world of Tacitus presented the denizens of a Europe in the midst of religious and political crises with examples and lessons for life. The *Annals* and the *Histories* documented the fraught period after Augustus' death in AD 14, when Tiberius succeeded his illustrious stepfather. Tiberius' leadership was marred by what Tacitus portrayed as flagrant abuses of power, in particular in the law

---

[7] The discussion in this paragraph is based on the account in C.W. Mendell, *Tacitus: the man and his work* (London, 1957).

[8] P. Burke, 'A survey of the popularity of ancient historians, 1450–1700', *History and Theory*, 5 (1966), 135–52, at 137. See also A. Momigliano, *The classical foundations of modern historiography* (Oxford, 1990).

[9] P. Burke, 'Tacitism', in T.A. Dorey (ed.), *Tacitus* (London, 1962), pp. 149–71.

courts. In the *Annals*, Tacitus described how laws against treason were deliberately employed to prey upon outspoken senators, whose wealth could be divided amongst their accusers following trial and execution.[10] Neither were the succeeding years of Claudius and Gaius (Caligula) glorious ones for Rome, though Claudius' saw the successful subjugation of much of southern Britain. Then, in AD 55, came Nero, inaugurating a new nadir even by Roman standards of megalomania. His life was recounted in the *Annals*, which broke off mid-sentence at the end of Book 16, meaning Tacitus' own record of the rebellion of the provincial governor Julius Vindex and the successful coup by Galba are missing. But the *Histories* picked up the story again in AD 69, the fatal Year of the Four Emperors: Galba, Otho, Vitellius, and Vespasian.

The political and historical innuendo in both the *Annals* and the *Histories* was obvious: these texts were freighted with examples for men and women who believed they themselves were living through an age of abuse of power, misgovernment by favourites, and civil war. But, of course, much was a matter of interpretation. Some read Tacitus as supporting republicanism among the rank and file (the 'red' Tacitus); others saw his works as being aimed at kings and princes, and promoting a veiled Machiavellianism (the 'black' Tacitus'); and still others, whom Peter Burke has called the 'pink Tacitists', read him as being in support of limited monarchy.[11] Tacitus, then, could teach tyrants how to oppress, and the oppressed how to resist. But there was more to this story than a simple *similitudo temporum*. Tacitus' work was considered increasingly dangerous because of its association with Stoicism, or, in its early modern guise, a set of principles that has come to be known as Neostoicism.[12]

Stoic philosophy, whether ancient or early modern, was and is difficult to codify, and thus its influence as a single body of ideas is equally difficult to trace. Stoicism had its beginnings in Greece as a philosophy of individual morality.[13] The Stoics esteemed the primacy of reason over emotion in decision-making and advocated for private retirement, solitary study, and 'constancy' in the face of harsh realities. However, beyond such generalities there is little to bind together the thought of the self-identified Stoics of Greece with those of Rome, or indeed, with those who came much later. What is clear is that, by the first century BC, Stoicism had undergone a metamorphosis. No longer confined to the plane of individuality, it had

---

[10] Tacitus, *Annals*, 48–50.   [11] Burke, 'Tacitism', 162–7.

[12] Momigliano, *Classical foundations*, 123–4; R. Tuck, *Philosophy and government, 1572–1621* (Cambridge, 1993), 39–45. Other accounts of the impact of ancient Stoicism in early modern Britain and Europe are M. Morford, *Stoics and neostoics: Rubens and the circle of Lipsius* (Princeton, NJ, 1991); A. Shifflett, *Stoicism, politics, and literature in the age of Milton: war and peace reconciled* (Cambridge, 1998); D. Allan, *Philosophy and politics in later Stuart Scotland: Neostoicism, culture, and ideology in the age of crisis, c. 1540–1690* (East Lothian, 2000); C. Brooke, *Philosophic pride: Stoicism and political thought from Lipsius to Rousseau* (Princeton, 2012). See also G. Oestreich, *Neostoicism and the early modern state* (Cambridge, 1982) and the brilliant dissection of that author's political motivations in P. Miller, 'Nazis and Neostoics: Otto Brunner and Gerhard Oestreich before and after the Second World War', *Past and Present*, 176 (2002), 144–86.

[13] The discussion in this paragraph is based on S. Braund (ed.), *Seneca: De Clementia* (Oxford, 2009), 64–70. See also S.K. Strange and J. Zupko, *Stoicism: traditions and transformations* (Cambridge, 2004).

become applicable to the practicalities of states and societies and was even linked to certain strands of political discourse, particularly Roman Republicanism. Ancient Roman Stoicism formed some part of Tacitus' historical writings, largely because Tacitus related the history of the celebrated dramatist and Stoic philosopher Lucius Annaeus Seneca, (c.4 BC–AD 65). Seneca's prominence in Roman society— he had been tutor to the young Emperor Nero—was to be his undoing: after his retirement from public life, Seneca was accused of conspiring against Nero and was forced by the emperor to commit suicide. For his part, Seneca accepted that rule by a single individual should and must exist in Rome. In AD 54 he addressed his *De Clementia* to the young Nero. *De Clementia*, the earliest example of what would become the Renaissance 'mirror for princes' genre, presented a Stoic's vision of the ideal king: a wise man, the embodiment of divine law, and a practitioner of the 'clemency' of the title. As for Stoicism's influence on ordinary citizens and politicians, it was most often interpreted as a philosophy of quiet acceptance of one's destiny—once that destiny was made clear by the course of events—on both a personal and political level.

Well into the sixteenth century, Stoicism maintained its association with the instinct to retreat from public life and cultivate one's proverbial garden rather than interfere in the messy, dangerous, and ultimately futile business of politics. Michel de Montaigne echoed the standard Senecan view in the late sixteenth century, and modern scholars of the Stoic movement of that period have associated it with political submission rather than resistance.[14] But this period also brought a change in the fortunes of both the Stoic philosophy and Tacitus' historical *oeuvre*, when the Flemish scholar Justus Lipsius (1547–1606) published new editions of Tacitus and Seneca, which became the basis for a more politically useful interpretation of the Stoic school of thought.[15] After editing Tacitus' *Annals* and *Histories* (1574), Lipsius read Seneca's philosophical works, which then informed his original tracts, *De Constantia* (1583) and *De Politica* (1589), and the handbooks, *Manductio* and *Physiologia* (both 1604). His efforts culminated in the publication of a new edition of Seneca's philosophical works.

Lipsius' understanding of the utility of Tacitus is attested to in the dedication, affixed to his edition of the ancient historian's writings, in which Lipsius quoted the penultimate, and last fully intact, sentence of the *Annals*. It was no coincidence that this happened to be the final phrase uttered by Thrasea Paetus at the moment of his enforced suicide—a common mode of death for Roman Stoics. A Senator, Thrasea had offended Nero by publicly refusing to share in the celebration of Agrippina's death, which was widely suspected to have been carried out on Nero's orders. Mark Morford has translated Paetus' last words as: 'Observe, young man, and may the gods avert the omen, but you live in such a time that it is good to strengthen your resolve by means of examples of constancy.'[16] The quote from Thrasea Paetus epitomized, so Lipsius believed, the utility of Tacitus for his own generation but, as Tacitus himself suggested, Thrasea's motivations in making such a

---

[14] Q. Skinner, *The foundations of modern political thought*, 2 vols (Cambridge, 1978), Vol. II, 279.
[15] Morford, *Stoics and neostoics*, 148–51.   [16] Ibid., 150–1.

public display of resistance in the face of what were certain to be dire consequences pointed to something like self-promotion, and even pride.[17]

Thus, while retirement and submission to tyranny characterized one side of Stoicism, as described by the doctrines of 'constancy' and 'prudence', there were other, less supine versions, namely the idea of the Stoic opposition, which grew out of the moralistic public resistance characterized by Thrasea Paetus.[18] As Christopher Brooke has so ably shown, even before Lipsius popularized Tacitus and Neostoic thought, critics of the doctrine acknowledged that the self-possession demanded by 'constancy' could easily slip into a more hard-minded and stubborn form self-control: resistance and obstinacy.[19] Even Tacitus found much that was objectionable in Stoic behaviour. In his opinion the Stoics were, at their worst, seekers after fame whose studied displays of virtue amounted to deliberate self-promotion. The three allegations of 'sedition, glory seeking, and hypocrisy' were levelled against the Stoics from Tacitus' day and well the seventeenth century.[20] These traits were thought to make the Stoic an unpredictable 'subtle casuistry of political activism' into the latter half of the seventeenth century.[21] This activism could range from public posturing to advocating tyrannicide.[22]

Self-possession and autonomy were inherent to the Stoic mindset, whether vocally oppositional or conceding, with silent reluctance, to authority. Thus the political message of Tacitus, especially as his works were translated in early modern Europe, was not received in any straightforward way by early modern commentators. In much of continental Europe, the Stoic opposition felt like a greater threat to the political order than it did in England, where, as Adriana McCrea's study has shown, Lipsian Neostoicism became an 'academic discussion' rather than a call to arms.[23] Nevertheless, the threat to the state from conspiracy and factionalism was alive in the minds of those who objected to the influence of Stoicism. The case of the Earl of Essex, executed after a failed rebellion against Elizabeth in 1601, illustrated the threat posed by those who adhered or claimed to adhere to some kind of continental Stoic philosophy. Essex had been a member of the circle around Sir Philip Sidney who, before his death in 1586, had been a popularizer of Lipsius' Stoicism, especially as it was connected with the anti-Spanish Protestant cause.[24] It is telling that Henry Savile, the first translator of Tacitus in Britain, was briefly imprisoned following the Essex rebellion. His earlier translations of the *Histories*

---

[17] Brooke, *Philosophic pride*, 64; Shifflett, *Stoicism, politics, and literature*, 24.
[18] For which, see Brooke, *Philosophic pride*, Ch. 3. Much of my discussion is based on Brooke's account.
[19] Ibid., 59–60.   [20] Ibid., 66.   [21] Shifflett, *Stoicism, politics, and literature*, 1.
[22] Brooke, *Philosophic pride*, 63. For Roman Stoicism and monarchy, see M. Griffin, *Nero: the end of a dynasty* (New York, 2001), 171–6.
[23] A. McCrea, *Constant minds: political virtue and the Lipsian paradigm in England, 1583–1650* (London, 1997), 4. See also P. Seaward, 'Clarendon, Tacitus, and the Civil Wars of Europe', in P. Kewes (ed.), *The uses of history in early modern England* (San Marino, CA, 2006), pp. 268–83.
[24] Brooke, *Philosophic pride*, 67. For a full discussion of the Sidney/Essex circle and Stoicism, see J.H.M. Salmon, 'Stoicism and Roman example: Seneca and Tacitus in Jacobean England', *Journal of the History of Ideas*, 50 (1989), 199–225 and J.H.M. Salmon, 'Seneca and Tacitus in Jacobean England', in L.L. Peck (ed.), *The mental world of the Jacobean court* (Cambridge, 1991), pp. 169–88.

and *Agricola* were read by some as directed at Essex, urging caution in the face of encroaching absolutism.[25]

For the reputation of Queen Boudica, none of this was inconsequential: the death of Elizabeth coincided with the increasing fame of Tacitus' account of ancient Europe, and thus with Boudica's own emergence in historical discourse. Thus, far from fading into insignificance at the arrival of James, Boudica's importance was, at this early stage, bound up with the growing influence of Tacitus' historical narrative and its relationship in the minds of many contemporaries to the political circumstances of seventeenth-century Britain and Europe. This connection brought her to the mind of Edmund Bolton.

THE STRUGGLES OF EDMUND BOLTON

Following Elizabeth's death, her successor, King James I and VI, was, at least at first, surprisingly sanguine about the potential conspirators in the ranks of his courtiers. Yet he had no love for Tacitus' dangerous lessons, nor for 'inconstant Lipsius'.[26] One of James's staunchest defenders and an enemy of Neostoic philosophy was the historian and antiquary Edmund Bolton. Bolton was no court politician; it is likely that his anti-Stoic stance had more to do with retaining the support of King James and his circle than any deeply held conviction on the subject. Indeed, Bolton had three overarching preoccupations: solving his financial problems, defending the monarch from subversive writers, and carving out a space for his original work in the contemporary landscape of historical and antiquarian studies. The ungenerous critic might say that he was not entirely successful at doing any of these things, but these were nevertheless the ever-present motivations behind much of his scholarly output.

Relatively little is known in detail about Bolton's life.[27] He was likely to have come to London from Leicestershire, a deduction supported by his connection with families in the area, notably the Beaumonts of Grace Dieu Manor, a seat of Roman Catholicism in the provinces. He married Margaret Porter, sister of the courtier Endymion Porter, and maintained good links with the Beaumonts. Sir John Beaumont, brother of Francis, John Fletcher's dramatic collaborator, was Bolton's supporter, and even penned the opening verses for the young antiquary's first published book, on the subject of heraldry, *The Elements of Armories* (1610).[28]

---

[25] P. Kewes, 'Henry Savile's Tacitus and the Politics of Roman History in Late Elizabethan England', *Huntington Library Quarterly*, 74(4) (2011), 515–51, at 526. For the Earl of Essex's place in contemporary and later political culture, see A. Gajda, 'Essex and politic history', in A. Connolly and L. Hopkins (eds), *Essex: the cultural impact of an Elizabethan courtier* (Manchester, 2013), pp. 237–59 and A. Gajda, *The Earl of Essex and late Elizabethan political culture* (Oxford, 2012).

[26] Quoted in Brooke, *Philosophic pride*, 67–8.

[27] See Woolf, *Idea of history*, 190–7 and D.R. Woolf, 'Bolton, Edmund Mary (1574/5–c.1634)', *ODNB* (2004), as well as T. Cooper, 'Bolton, Edmund Mary', *ODNB* (1885). Bolton's short autobiography can be found in his manuscript notes, BL Harl. MS 6521.

[28] E.M. Portal, 'The Academ Roial of King's James I', *Proceedings of the British Academy, 1915–1916* (1916), 189–208, at 191.

In 1619 Bolton published one of his most successful works, the epitomes of Lucius Florus, which became standard undergraduate reading by the 1630s.[29] But even so, as a recusant, Bolton was periodically subject to heavy fines and his life was marked by pecuniary woes—it is assumed he died at Marshalsea prison around 1634, having exhausted the goodwill of his friends and increasingly distant relatives.

Like many debtors, Bolton's quixotic ambitions exceeded his financial means and social position. The patronage of powerful Catholic sympathizers meant he was able to pursue a number of ambitious projects, including his acclaimed epitomes of Florus. It is likely that Bolton became familiar with James I's favourite, George Villiers, first Duke of Buckingham, through their mutual friends the Beaumonts. Having secured Buckingham's support, Bolton gained access to James I's inner circle; or, as Bolton himself put it, the obliging duke was 'the chrystall gate by which my labours first entered into the light of favour'.[30] Such oleaginous language was typical of his relations with social superiors and might in part explain why Bolton has not played a very significant role in the history of historiography. Among intellectual historians he has been dismissed, in Daniel Woolf's words, as an 'egregiously sycophantic, almost pathetic, suitor for office and favour'.[31] But even Woolf has also acknowledged, albeit in passing, that Bolton occupies a unique place in the historical culture of the period as one of the only English authors to blend minute details gleaned from antiquarian evidence such as coins, inscriptions, and other physical remains, as well as ancient documentary sources, with a form of reflective, humanistic historical narrative.[32] And yet Bolton, innovative in his practice, was emphatically conservative in his opinions, and his talent as an historical researcher became a tool for their justification.

However, Bolton never eschewed challenges: throughout his career, he was drawn to particularly unlovable Roman emperors, whose reputations he sought to recover from the prejudices of their primary historian, Tacitus. This point of view was the genesis of Bolton's history of the reign of Tiberius Caesar, written early in his career but which has not survived—or has not yet been found. However, some idea of its contents can be gleaned from another of the antiquary's works, *Ponderous and new considerations upon the first six books of the Annals of Cornelius Tacitus concerning Tiberius Caesar*, also known as *The Skowrers*, which has only recently been discovered in the Biblioteca Durazzo in Genoa.[33] Probably composed during the reign of King Charles I, possibly even near the end of Bolton's life, this was a detailed defence of Tiberius, whom Tacitus had accused of abusing his power in

---

[29] Woolf, *Idea of history*, 173.

[30] E. Bolton, *Nero Caesar, or monarchie deprav'd* (London, 1624), Dedicatory preface. The same preface appears in the 1627 edition, and all page numbers correspond.

[31] D.R. Woolf, 'Edmund Bolton, Francis Bacon, and the Making of the *Hypercritica*', *Bodleian Library Record*, 11 (1983), 162–8, at 166. For a similar opinion of Bolton's sycophancy, see Salmon, 'Stoicism and Roman example', 224.

[32] Woolf, *Idea of history*, 194–5.

[33] See P. Osmond, 'Edmund Bolton's Vindication of Tiberius Caesar: A "lost" manuscript comes to light', *International Journal of the Classical Tradition*, 11 (2005), 329–43. A large part of Bolton's manuscript notebook is devoted to 'Tiberiana', or material and passages for his history of Tiberius, as well as Neroniana, used for his later work. See BL Harl. MS 6521.

the legal courts. Some of Bolton's near-contemporaries, particularly the playwright Ben Jonson, had also homed in on Tiberius and his favourite, Sejanus, as homologues for the monarch and the dangers posed by favourites, and the taint had also, it seemed, infected James's successor.

But, for all its bias, even *The Skowrers* serves to build a picture of a talented scholar of history and the classics in deep dialogue with his source material. Patricia Osmond has assessed the work as Bolton's attempt to 'scour' away the taint left by Tacitus on Tiberius' reputation by enumerating the errors in the Roman historian's account and drawing on conflicting reports from other writers of the period.[34] In this manner, Bolton constructed a counter-claim, that Tiberius was in fact a relatively benign ruler with a sincere concern for the welfare of his subjects—not the insensate dictator described by Tacitus.[35] This typified Bolton's approach to Tacitus: he did not dismiss the Roman historian outright, but rather engaged with his arguments and presented contrary evidence, just as if the two were contemporaries. Bolton was, in short, a committed critical historian as much as he was James's servant. Indeed, it is possible to argue that throughout his life Bolton's primary concern was with defending and articulating the value of history and historical studies; this was a concern not wholly incompatible with his relationship to the king, especially as it allowed him to criticize others in their approach to similar subject matter.

From quite an early stage in his association with the court, Bolton advocated on behalf of historians and antiquaries. As early as 1617—the year he met King James for the first time—Bolton concocted a plan for a new 'Academ Roial', somewhat along the lines of the Elizabethan Society of Antiquaries but with a much more cosy relationship with the monarch. Bolton's scheme was ultimately unsuccessful, but it was testimony to his persistent belief in the importance of the past in the intellectual life of the court, even if this meant, at times, pandering to the needs of the sovereign.[36] Bolton undoubtedly had a personal desire to be at the forefront historical study, probably animated as much by his financial trouble as his admiration for the monarch.

Aside from such advocacy, Bolton made many private pronouncements on the paramount importance of the study of the past, in which he worked through his own ideas about the value of history in relation to other forms of writing. For example, among his unpublished manuscripts there is a rebuttal to Sir Philip Sidney's famous *Apology for Poetry; or A Defence of Poesie* (published posthumously in 1591). Sidney had painted a distressing portrait of the average historical writer:

> ... he, loaden with mouse-eaten records, authorizing himself (for the most part) upon other histories, whose greatest authorities are built upon the notable foundation of

---

[34] Osmond, '"Lost" manuscript', 332–3.
[35] There have been modern studies that have attempted the same exercise, for example, G.P. Baker, *Tiberius Caesar: Emperor of Rome* (New York, 1928).
[36] See Portal, 'The Academ Roial of King's James I'. The proposal exists in a number of versions in manuscript, with the last revision addressed to Charles I in 1625. See also J. Hunter, 'An account of the scheme for erecting a Royal Academy in England in the reign of King James I', *Archaeologia*, 32 (1847), 132–49. Bolton's notes for the proposal are in BL Add MS 24, 488, fol. 66-87/113-45.

hearsay; having much ado to according differing writers and to pick truth out of partiality; better acquainted with a thousand years ago than with the present age, and yet better knowing how this world goeth than how his own wit runneth...[37]

As Sidney saw it, even when the historian accomplished the highest aim, the recital of uncorrupted fact, his requisite fidelity to the record of the past left him with no moral compass. Without regard for either its nobility or venality, bad men could be rewarded and good men suffer. Only in the poet's unfailingly virtuous world could good men be celebrated as exemplars.

In his manuscript response, Bolton conceded that 'the windings and turnings which exercise readers in the labyrinths of a cunning plot, and the varieties of rare interwoven accidents (effects of memorie and witt) leade us up and downe with an ydle delight'.[38] But that was all they did, and that was not enough. Only 'sad and grave Histories' contained the truths conducive to 'heroick knowledge' and the spur to heroic, moral action that was the greatest benison conferred on the present by the example of the past. For Bolton, even the poet who portrayed the past in a fictionalized guise could not attain equal dignity with the historian. But there may have been more at stake here than merely defining the role of the historian against that of the poet. Sidney's own sympathy with Stoicism remained an abiding influence at court; this well-known position, and Sidney's anti-Catholicism, may have had as much to do with Bolton's ire against him as Sidney's views on the practice of history. The rebuttal from Bolton, directed at a man who had long been dead, demonstrates how closely the concerns of method and ideology could be bound up together, nearly to the point of inextricability—nearly.

The defensive spirit of Bolton's reply to Sidney ran throughout much the historical work he produced in the 1620s, but his most assertive statement on the subject came in the form of his *Hypercritica, or a rule of judgment on reading and writing our histories* (composed in or around 1621 but not published until 1722).[39] This was Bolton's original contribution to the Renaissance *ars historica*, all the more rare for being a British example of a genre more often associated with continental figures.[40] It is telling that Bolton drew on the work of Jean Bodin (1530–96), perhaps the most famous writer in the genre, whose essentially humanistic *Method for the easy comprehension of history* (*Methodus ad facilem historiarum cognitionem*) was published in 1566. Bodin blended a variety of classical currents in his treatise on

---

[37] P. Sidney, *An apology for poetry (or the defence of poesy)*, ed. R.W. Maslen (third edn, Manchester, 2002), 89.

[38] Quoted in T.H. Blackburn, 'Edmund Bolton's The Cabanet Royal: a belated reply to Sidney's Apology for Poetry', *Studies in the Renaissance*, 14 (1967), 159–71, at 170.

[39] N. Triveti, *Annalium Continuatio ut et ... Edmundi Boltoni Hypercritica* (Oxford, 1722). The 1722 edition was the first published version of the *Hypercritica*, so it could have had little impact during the author's lifetime. See T.H. Blackburn, 'The date and evolution of Edmund Bolton's *Hypercritica*', *Studies in Philology*, 63(2) (1966), 196–202; D.R. Woolf, 'Edmund Bolton, Francis Bacon, and the Making of the *Hypercritica*', *Bodleian Library Record*, 11 (1983), 162–8.

[40] Woolf, *Idea of history*, 173. For the *ars historia*, see A. Grafton, *What was history: the art of history in early modern Europe* (Cambridge, 2007). There were relatively few English examples, with Degory Wheare's *The Method and order of reading both civil and ecclesiastical histories* (1698) being the most well known; see J.H.M. Salmon, 'Precept, example, and truth: Degory Wheare and the ars historica', in Kelley and Sacks, *Historical imagination*, pp. 11–36.

history, but he harboured a suspicion of Tacitus' rhetoric and his politics. He had far greater esteem for the Greek historian Polybius, who championed impartiality and historical objectivity.[41]

In his *Hypercritica*, Bolton paraphrased and expanded on Bodin's treatise, defining and declaring the role of the historian in his own words:

> The reason of which speech Monsieur Bodin (whose also it is) giveth to be: for than an History ought to be nothing else but an Image of truth, and as it were a Table of Things done: permitting Judgment of all to the competent Reader, which Judgment we ought not forstall, howsoever in some rare Cases it may be lawful to lead the same.[42]

Bolton's interpolation—that it may be 'lawful' to lead the reader toward certain judgements—smacks of self-apology from a man who, as we have seen, was by no means free of bias in his own practice. But we might also read it as part of his ongoing response to Sidney's accusation that the historian—who by necessity of the facts must sometimes allow wickedness to go unpunished—was an uncertain moral guide for readers.

Aside from being well versed in the works of his contemporaries, Tacitus' influence is also evident in Bolton's treatise on method. Again, the picture is a nuanced one: Bolton the historian admired Tacitus the historian, even as he remained suspicious, not only of the Roman's politics, but also, perhaps, of his paganism. It has been suggested that the Catholic Bolton disapproved of the secularizing influence on Jacobean historiography that Tacitus exerted.[43] However, Bolton nimbly distinguished between the different forms that Tacitean thought could take, and he was thus simultaneously admiring and critical. He took an equally detached view towards Christian authors, discussing both in the same passage in the *Hypercritica*:

> ...as Cornelius Tacitus (let not plain dealing offend his other Admirers) either the most irreligious, or with the most and therefore the less worthy to be in Honour as a Cabinet Counselour with any man, to whom Piety towards powers divine is pretious...On the other side Christian Authors, while for their ease they shuffled up the reason of events, in briefly referring all causes immediately to the Will of God, have generally neglected to inform their readers in the ordinary means of Carriage in human Affairs, and thereby singularly maimed their Narrations.[44]

---

[41] See Salmon, 'Precept, example, and truth' and A. Momigliano, *Essays in ancient and modern historiography* (Oxford, 1977), esp. 67–77 and 79–98. Like Tacitus, Polybius' influence went beyond historical method and informed political ideas. Lesser points out that Bolton's book was published by Thomas Walkley (*fl.* 1618–58), who held 'Polybian' ideas about mixed government; Lesser also cites Bolton as an adherent. However, it was to Tacitus rather than Polybius that Bolton consistently referred, explicitly and implicitly, even if he may have been sympathetic to the idea of mixed government; see Z. Lesser, *Renaissance drama and the politics of publication* (Cambridge, 2004), Ch. 5 and p. 217. Bolton certainly admired Polybius, but his most spirited dialogues were always with the ghost of Tacitus.

[42] Bolton, *Hypercritica*, 213–14.

[43] Bradford, 'Stuart absolutism', 139. G. Burgess, *Absolute monarchy and the Stuart constitution* (London, 1996), 61, also views Bradford as overstating Bolton's absolutist and anti-Tacitean stance. However, Bolton is the voice of providentialist historiography in Ribner, *English history play*, 23.

[44] Bolton, *Hypercritica*, 202–3.

Thus Bolton cast a critical eye on Christian historians whose views blinded them to earthly matters, and bound them to implying that human beings are without agency in human affairs—a position that Bolton did not wholeheartedly endorse. As Ann Blair has argued, Jean Bodin himself had drawn a threefold division in historical writing: the histories of man and his society, of nature, and of God and divinity could all be subject to study in particular ways.[45] However, this distinction might also be applied to the method of reading other historians: Bolton probably was suspicious of Tacitus' opinions on the nature of divinity, but this did not make the Roman any less of an authority on man and society. Indeed, while Bolton criticized Tacitus' deficient religion and lack of piety towards 'powers divine' (monarchical, presumably), he was by no means an unquestioning providentialist himself. The peccadilloes of individual men and women were a constant source of fascination for him, and the amount of ink he devoted to sketching the character of his protagonists suggests that he too saw the conduct of mortal men and women as having a bearing on the course of history, more especially in making possible their own downfall. And although one objection to Neostoicism was that it ascribed too great a liberty to human will,[46] it would seem that Bolton's own objections to the modern version of the ancient philosophy were animated less by concerns of piety than by a historian's preoccupation with individual agency and causation.

From Bolton's point of view, by far the most objectionable aspect of Tacitus' histories was not the circumstances of their creation, but rather their misuse in the present, most especially in the imaginative parallel then being drawn between the historical events related by the Roman and the growing influence of Neostoicism in Bolton's own day. Bolton's anxieties on that score were long standing, as revealed in a letter he sent to Robert Cecil, first Earl of Salisbury in 1608. In the letter Bolton professes his esteem for philosophy generally, but cautions that by 'the error of students' 'divine Philosophie... chiefly Stoick', was being perverted into a much more dangerous form by its 'over-weening' followers.[47] Even at an early stage, before his first published work brought him any recognition, Bolton was aware of suspect innovations evident in Neostoicism. Yet his concern was evidently not an objection to the original pagan philosophy, nor to its impious recorder, Tacitus. After all, Lipsian Neostoicism was considered by most observers to be a Christianized form of the original philosophy, and it consequently developed a cross-confessional appeal.[48] And, as we have seen, Lipsius' Neostoicism did not disavow the influence of Providence—that is, it acknowledged a transcendental first cause. Thus it is probable that Bolton did not view atheism as immanent within Stoicism itself. With the Neostoics, Bolton could share a belief in God's ultimate supremacy in

---

[45] A. Blair, *The theatre of nature: Jean Bodin and Renaissance science* (Princeton, NJ, and Chichester, 1997), 69–70.
[46] Brooke, *Philosophic pride*, 101.
[47] Edmund Bolton to Lord Salisbury, 18 April 1608, BL Lansdowne MS Hicks Collection No 89.
[48] Salmon, 'Stoicism and Roman example', 222, and the introduction to *Two books Of Constancie written in Latine by Iustus Lipsius*, trans. J. Stradling (New Brunswick, NJ, 1939). The French Catholic Guillaume Du Vair's *La Philosophie Morale des Stoiques* had been translated into English as *The Moral Philosophy of the Stoicks* by the Calvinist Thomas James in 1598.

men's affairs, even if he also acknowledged the agency of men on earth and the significance of individual historical actors. But it was certainly the case that in Bolton's mind, God's authority must by right extend to the sovereign. That 'divine philosophie' could be perverted as a support to rebellion against the monarch was anathema to Bolton the historian. These corruptors of original philosophy suffered from the excess of overweening pride that had tempted Stoics in the past to commit acts of sedition. Bolton's distaste for the movement was to come to fruition in his longest extant work, in which Boudica was to loom up from the pages of Tacitus as a political lesson from the past.

Despite his scholarly investment in recovering the reputations of ancient Roman emperors, Bolton was also a keen student of the ancient British past, and, as occasioning the first classical reference to London, Bolton's adopted home, Queen Boudica played a role in his compositions on the subject of the city's antiquity.[49] But for the first time, in 1624, Boudica was to be the subject of Bolton's sustained attention; her life and rebellion would not be treated with the same scholarly thoroughness again until the early twentieth century. Without doubt, *Nero Caesar; or Monarchie Deprav'd* (1624; second edition 1627)[50] was Bolton's *magnum opus*. In *Nero Caesar*, he managed to combine all of his talents and preoccupations: minute antiquarian detail, classical learning, historical narration, ideological raillery, an avowed pride in the ancient past of Britain and London, and, above all, nimble argumentation.

BOUDICA, NERO, AND SEDITION

The Boudican rebellion broke out in the middle of Nero's reign, and Bolton's book more or less reflects that chronology by being divided roughly in half, with the first chapters being focused on the beginning of Nero's reign and a large section of the succeeding chapters devoted to events in Britain. Given this arrangement it proved difficult for later readers to accept Nero as the primary focus of the work. In a note on the title page of 1624 edition held in the British Library, a reader, probably in the eighteenth century, summarized the text as relating to '... the affairs of Britain from the time of Julius Caesar to the revolt under Nero. The author relates the history of Boadicea & endeavours to prove that Stonehenge was a monument erected to her memory.'[51] This mention of Stonehenge was an invention—or, more

---

[49] See, for instance, his *Vindiciae Britannicae, or, London righted by rescues or recoveries of antiquities of Britain in general and of London in particular, against unwarrantable preiudices, and historical antiquations among the learned* (c.1628) London Metropolitan Archives, CLC/270/MS03454. The 'vindication' in the work's title declares Bolton's intention to combat previous accounts of the foundation of London and to recover the native Britons' contribution to London's—and Britain's—glory. Boudica is mentioned in the very first sentence.

[50] The 1627 edition was printed with extra material, including an afterword in the form of a 'historical parallel' between the epitomes of Lucius Florus and the histories of Polybius, accompanied by discourse on the utility of epitomes and the superiority of histories.

[51] This annotation is in the 1624 edition of *Nero Caesar*, found in the British Library at shelfmark 196.e.15.

accurately, a deduction—which Bolton justified with the available evidence, and will be discussed below. But this lasting remnant of reader-criticism suggests that if Bolton ever intended Nero to be the star of this particular show, his choice of supporting cast rather stole the limelight in later years.

Indeed the 1627 edition of Bolton's work immediately introduced Queen Boudica as a central character, and one in opposition to Rome, by her appearance in an elaborate frontispiece (see Figure 2), which did not appear in the 1624 edition. This was the handiwork of Francis Delaram, a prominent artist in the London engraving trade from about 1615–24, who produced some forty-seven works which still survive, among them a large portrait of James I.[52] Delaram's frontispiece is dominated by two female figures on the left and right of the image, one representing 'Roma', the other 'Londinium'. Above Roma is a framed oval picture of the murder of Agrippina, the mother of Nero. On the right side of the frontispiece, opposite Roma, stands the female figure 'Londinium', whose own modest style of dress contrasts sharply with Roma's more opulent garb. Londinium also stands below a framed scene, this one of Queen Boudica addressing the Britons. Two female personalities thus occupy the periphery, while Emperor Nero's own portrait inhabits the centre.

This dynamic was not mirrored in the text, in which numerous personalities emerge as having a formative influence in Nero's early life; most of them did not long outlive the realization of the damage they caused. Bolton's initial focus in the text was on the first five years of Nero's reign, from AD 55 to 60, a period which concluded with the murder of Agrippina. As was befitting a period lurid with lust and violence, this was no dry narrative of events: Bolton gave his readers a detailed examination of the motivations, prejudices, weaknesses, and occasional strengths of the central figures, especially Nero, Seneca, and Agrippina. According to Bolton, Nero's depravity could ultimately be attributed to deficiencies in his education, which the antiquary judged to be the fault of Seneca and Agrippina, with the latter taking the larger part of the blame. Although the influence of Seneca on the impressionable Nero was dangerous from the outset, Bolton allowed that Nero may have had the potential to arrest his descent into depravity if only he had been given a well-rounded education—especially in the principles of 'philosophie'. It was, according to Bolton, Agrippina who had denied this to her son and thus condemned him to a lifetime of dissipation, dishonesty, and dissembling.

> For [Nero's] nature most undoubtedly affecting immortalitie of fame (which was truely princely, & truely ROMAN in him) by this abducement from the knowledge of honesty, and worth (the onely true grounds of glorie) he pursued showes, and seemings, and sought not... for that which makes men good or wise, but for that which might enable him to winn crownes of leaves, or garlands, for singing, fidling, piping, acting on stages, and the like ignobler trials, which neverthelesse through the error of his breeding, appeared to him such transcendently heavenly guifts, that in their perfection he constituted chiefe felicitie.[53]

---

[52] See A. Griffiths, *The print in Stuart Britain, 1603–1689* (London, 1998), 53 and A. Griffiths, 'Delaram, Francis (*fl.* 1615–1624)', *ODNB* (2004).

[53] Bolton, *Nero Caesar*, 4.

Figure 2. Francis Delaram's frontispiece to Edmund Bolton's *Nero Caesar* (1627). The Bodleian Libraries, The University of Oxford, Radcl. D. 8. Queen Boudica addresses her troops in the oval above the head of 'Londinium'.

As for Agrippina herself, she was equally bereft of an education in what Bolton termed 'true philosophie (for some philosophers are neither fit for kings nor subjects being falsely called wisdome)', the study of which 'would have taught her to consider, how much more glorious it is, to affect honest things rather than great, or to compasse great things honestly'.[54] Seneca, meanwhile, taught his charge

[54] Ibid., 5.

the skills to 'answear readely' when he might more profitably have learned to 'thinck deeply'.[55]

This has echoes of Bolton's earlier statement to Lord Salisbury on the subject of 'divine Philosophie' and is further testimony to his view that education in philosophical systems of the past was not immanently atheistic or subversive, but rather, if carefully handled, could have an improving effect on young minds—even those of women. Yet it was hardly a coincidence that all of the sinister features which Bolton saw as nascent in the young Nero—dissembling, self-serving tendencies, and a desire for fame above humility even as he affected the latter—were also identified by critics with the Stoic opposition. Bolton saw an analogy between Nero's early behaviour towards Emperor Claudius, his adopted father, with the attitude of a corrupted Stoicism and its corrosive effect on attitudes to regal authority—a clear reference to the Neostoic opposition of his own times. Unsurprisingly, Seneca was responsible for this 'weakening of pious respects in Nero' towards the Emperor Claudius. Seneca incited Nero to publicly, though obliquely, ridicule the emperor, and the two colluded in making thinly veiled jests at Claudius' expense. In so doing, Nero could boast of his own brilliance and suggest himself as a superior leader to the elderly Claudius, falling into that ever-present Stoic pitfall, pride. To Bolton, such behaviour was not only damaging to the individual character of the impressionable Nero, but it also amounted to treason; following Claudius' deification, it was little less than blasphemy. Bolton attributed responsibility for this entirely to Seneca, but his disapproval was once again leavened by a degree of admiration for that which remained uncorrupted: 'Therefore, howsoever I hartely love what Seneca's writings have good in them, and doe admire what is excellent either for wisdome, eloquence, or conceipt, yet I doe freely professe to hate that [Seneca's conduct], as all men certeinly doe, who esteeme the conscience of moral, and civil duties, above the flashes of ambitious wit.'[56]

Nero's behaviour only worsened: he poisoned his step-brother Britannicus, maltreated his wife Octavia, and ultimately committed the heinous crime of matricide. Weighing the available evidence from Tacitus, and presaging the treatment he would give to Boudica's story, Bolton provided an extensive description and analysis of Agrippina's violent death, and addressed in detail the evidence surrounding the rumour that she had been her own son's concubine. But all of this was, so to speak, by the by, for Bolton arrived at his overarching argument at the close of the First Book, encompassing Nero's first five years as emperor—the years when he was, in fact, at his least unreasonable. Bolton ends the first part of *Nero Caesar* by remarking:

> That sacred monarckie could preserve the people of Rome from finall ruine, notwithstanding all the prophanities, blasphemies & scandals of tyranous excesses, wherewith Nero defiled & defamed it, is the wonder which no other forme of government could performe, and is the principall both of his time, and of princedome it selfe.[57]

---

[55] Ibid.   [56] Ibid., 10.   [57] Ibid., 69.

This was in effect, the message of the whole study. Nero's singularly awful reign was so well documented that no historian could realistically hope to recover his reputation, and, sensibly, Bolton did not attempt to do this directly, instead allowing his argument to be buoyed by Nero's depravity. This made for an even starker contrast between the justness of the rebels' cause and the monarch's wickedness. Bolton's approach was to tell the story in the most evidence-laden manner possible, while drawing out what he took to be the inexorable lessons to be learned from it.

Beginning with a brief summary of the Romans' activities in Britain before the time of Nero, Bolton's account then moves on to the familiar events beginning with the death of Boudica's husband, Prasutagus, in the seventh year of Nero's reign. The Iceni king was considered to have been friendly with the Romans, but his death triggered a violent conflict over the lands he left behind. This Bolton primarily attributed to the widespread contempt for Nero which emboldened the Roman troops in Britain to abuse their power on the one hand, and which deprived the Britons of any 'orderlie redresse' of their wrongs on the other. In such a state of lawlessness, Boudica and her children were unable to escape the brutality of the Romans. 'For the princelie sisters (whether by force or fraud) were irreparablie dishonoured in their bodies, and Boadicia her selfe (their most unfortunate mother) full of most just griefe, and wrath, and full of all the tempestuous passions which nobilitie embased, or nature violated can suggest, did bleed & smart under whips, and cutting lashes. This the Cornelian Annals signifie; worthie of beliefe against the writers [*sic*] nation.'[58] Bolton was ever-attentive to the potential for bias in other historians' work, so he took Tacitus' admission of his countrymen's wrongdoing as supporting at least the possibility that Boudica and her daughters had personally suffered at the hands of the Romans and that this was the principal cause of the ructions. Yet he also questioned the veracity of Boudica's claim, which had not been repeated by Dio. This, however, was itself a comment on Tacitus rather than on Boudica.[59] Bolton was addressing the possibility that the accusations, which Boudica may or may not have made herself, could have been concocted by the incoming governor of Roman Britain, Julius Classicus, in an attempt to slander his predecessor, the cowardly Cerealis, and Suetonius Paulinus. In doing so, Bolton was suggesting that Tacitus might merely have been too gullible a historian.

Bolton had his own version of events that allowed him to fill in the blanks left by Tacitus and, in doing so, to make a broader point. Why, Bolton asked, might the Romans have treated Boudica so cruelly—if, in fact, they had done? He pointed out that Tacitus had similarly omitted any speculation for the rationale behind the (presumed) execution of Tigranes, an Armenian king, under Tiberius. Why should Tacitus leave out such crucial information? It was not, Bolton remarked sniffily, because Tacitus' 'conceipt of roiall majestie' was so reverent that he could conceive of no sufficient justification for the 'violation' of 'underling princes'.

---

[58] Ibid., 100.
[59] Daniel Woolf has argued that Bolton's scepticism 'deflated the myth of "Boadicea's quarrel"'. Woolf, *Idea of history*, 195.

> All that occurs to me as the most likely cause why centurions, and other the [sic] ravenous, and outragious officers of NERO, laid violent hands upon her, is meerely this, that it was the effect of their quicke, or captious sence of her words, upon expostulations in her palace, and kingdome, when they oppressed her.[60]

Bolton seems here to be apportioning blame to the cruel agents of Nero, who were intent upon taking Boudica's complaint as a direct threat to their authority and to the emperor.

> Among which words, if they were but the same, or the like, which she afterwards used in her armie (a matter not improbable) the admiration [mystery surrounding the Romans' conduct] is at an end. For they were so full of most just scorne, and open contempt of NERO's person, as could not but minister that advantage which their covetousnesse, and cruell iniquitie desired.[61]

The difficulty here is puzzling out whose cruel iniquity is being referred to in the final clause, but it seems likely, given that Bolton had just referred to the 'ravenous' and 'outragious' officers of Nero, that his meaning is as follows: Boudica's words were, perhaps justifiably, full of scorn and contempt for Nero, but her hasty remarks, 'full of all the tempestuous passions which nobilitie embased, or nature violated can suggest', were then interpreted by the Roman officers as sufficient justification for the cruel punishment meted out to Boudica and her daughters. Tacitus, by not revealing the precise circumstances of Boudica's punishment (or indeed Tigranes'), recused himself from having to consider whether such consequences were either true or warranted under the circumstances. In fact, so incendiary were Boudica's remarks likely to have been,[62] Bolton goes on to say that it seemed 'a favour, that they punisht her no more severely then so: *the blemishing of majestie, high treason among the ROMANS*'.[63] This final utterance shows that Bolton's long digression, as well informed and even-handed as it seemed, was no more than a circuitous way of arriving once again at the conclusion that the monarch had supremacy over 'underling princes'—Tigranes and Boudica—and that Nero's agents, not Nero himself, were responsible for administering what may well have been over-zealous punishments in his revered name.

But there were other causes which Tacitus did not mention, or certainly not in detail. These Bolton found in Dio Cassius' account of Boudica's story, which by the time Edmund Bolton was writing had fallen far behind Tacitus' as a legitimate record of ancient Rome. Dio mentioned two principal reasons for the British rebellion: 'the confiscation of goods' and, as Bolton put it, '... (I blush to write it) *Seneca's cruel usuries*'.[64] Dio Cassius maintained that Seneca, while he was Nero's trusted advisor, had forced unwanted loans on the Britons and then demanded repayment on extortionate terms. For his part, Bolton delighted in this example of Seneca's hypocrisy, providing as it did an opportunity for a subtle dig at the source of Stoic ideas. 'Yet this is he (o strange) who cryed out, when hee was at richest

---

[60] Bolton, *Nero Caesar*, 128. [61] Ibid.
[62] Presumably Bolton had in mind the insults recorded by Dio but unremarked by Tacitus.
[63] Ibid. Emphasis in original. [64] Ibid., 97.

How unknown a good is povertie!' That Bolton should appeal to Dio's history, a source held in inferior esteem to Tacitus', was potentially problematic, so he pre-empted his critics by allowing that: '... Dio is suspected by some of the most noble clarks of our age, as somewhat too unequall to the honour, and memorie of famous Seneca, the sharpest witt of Rome'.[65] Seneca, who, if Dio was to be credited, had given the Britons reason to band together 'under a most glorious title, the *recoverie of common libertie*' was, in Bolton's lifetime, considered a Stoic hero who stood in defiance of wanton authority.[66] For this reason, Bolton the antiquary may have taken some pleasure both in appealing to the lesser historian, Dio, over Tacitus, and in pointing out the revered Seneca's part in the abuse of the Britons. Indeed, Bolton had an idiosyncratic fondness for Dio's account, not least because the Greek writer seemed so taken by the story of Boudica. Bolton commented, '... there is not any thing of that bright author extant, upon which he can be thought to have dealt with greater care, or endeavour, then upon his Bunduca's storie...'[67] The same might be said of Edmund Bolton.

Although Bolton at least partially admitted the injustice of the Romans' conduct, he stopped short of blaming the system of Roman imperial government itself, instead citing the scandalous actions of a few powerful individuals whose judgement had failed them at a crucial diplomatic moment. However, as far as he was concerned the first truly sinful act on the part of the Britons came when, in response to the arbitrary brutality of the occupiers, they began to meet in secret, to conspire, and to bide their time. Having been uncertain about the exact causes of the revolt—he accepted that the Britons had genuine grievances, largely due to the fault of Seneca—it was this conspiratorial aspect to their conduct that offended the antiquary's sensibilities more than any remarks purportedly uttered by Boudica against Nero's person. Bolton's account emphasized the secretive nature of the Britons' conduct far more than the sources, either Dio's or Tacitus', justified doing. A single sentence in the *Annals*, '... the Trinobantes and others who, not yet cowed by slavery, had agreed in secret conspiracy to reclaim their freedom',[68] becomes in *Nero Caesar* an entire chapter entitled 'Boadicia, and the Britanns meet in great secrecie, and resolve to rise in arms'. As usual, Bolton was making a point with this diversion from the historical record, exploiting an opportunity to make more general remarks on the subject of civil unrest.

At the time of Boudica's rebellion, Suetonius Paulinus, then the Roman governor of Britain, was absent from the mainland, undertaking a campaign of destruction against the Druids on the island of Mona (modern-day Anglesey). At Bolton's estimation, Suetonius had taken with him 10,000 men, believing the remaining troops to be sufficient in force to put down any restiveness amongst the natives. However, it was not the strength of the men left in Britain that mattered in this account; Bolton pointed out that Suetonius' decision to leave had in itself been foolhardy because it was only the personal presence of the general which might have stopped what ensued. The want of this single powerful individual gave

---

[65] Ibid., 97–8. Emphasis in original.   [66] Ibid,. 151. Emphasis in original.
[67] Ibid., 116.   [68] Tacitus, *Annals*, 337.

the Britons licence to meet in secret, an occurrence which Bolton noted with disdain, was '... the first degree alwayes of a rebellion, next after the inward matter is inclinable'—the 'inward matter' referring to the individual mind, but perhaps also the very constellation of circumstances necessary for such meetings to take place.[69]

To compound the criminality of their secret machinations against Roman authority, Bolton then described how, with the intervention of the Druid priests, 'The head and members of this blacke agreement were fastened together in a most bloudie knot with speciall rites, and ceremonies.' However, no such rite was mentioned by Tacitus or Dio, so the antiquary fell back on testimony extraneous to Boudica's rebellion, which recounted the macabre rituals known to have been practised by the Druids in other times and places. From this general discussion Bolton deduced that, by a similar violent ritual, the conspirators had become bound to one another, severing the ties of peaceful intercourse that might hitherto of existing with the Romans. This, crucially, also deprived the Britons of the protection of Roman law:

> As for the sworne covenants betweene Romans, and the Britanns, ... by vertue whereof they had title to a lawfull redresse, they were all broken through as cobwebs. The sword their judge and umpire. Right, and common libertie the names of their quarrel: confusion, spoil, and thirst of bloud the sequel.... Most cunning and unavoidable, while the cold aër of fear (like a counter-circumstance of qualities) kept together the heat of counsel.[70]

Bolton had a clear aim in mind when taking this protracted detour into the realm of sedition. Secrecy and betrayal found fertile ground in the mind of the overweening opponent of rightful authority, whose skewed morality was wholly self-interested, and Bolton's extensive digression was thus a means of showcasing the danger posed by such rash undertakings. Subterfuge continued to be the order of the day as Boudica and her growing band of rebels approached Camulodunum[71] and made contact with sympathetic inhabitants there. As the Britons approached, those inside the town 'once covert enemies, and overt now' joined in with the Boudicans and laid waste to the community of veteran soldiers there. These veterans did not, however, get much sympathy from Bolton, who blamed their lack of foresight for allowing the Britons to so easily gain access to their stronghold. Having taken the battle to the Romans in Camulodunum and Verulamium, the rebels arrived, glutted with pillage, at Londinium, where Suetonius Paulinus had quickly made his way from Mona, only to find his forces insufficient to defend the inhabitants of the bustling city. He therefore abandoned it to the marauding Britons and, having done so, awaited the violent conclusion at a place outside of town, the exact location of which has confounded generations of antiquaries and archaeologists.[72] For his part, Edmund Bolton determined it to have been the area around the River Wylye, where there survived remnants of what he took to be ancient camps.

---

[69] Ibid., 109.   [70] Ibid., 110.
[71] Bolton erroneously believed Camulodunum to have been Maldon rather than Colchester.
[72] See Chapter 5.

Often it was the intervention of fate, or providence, which brought about the Stoic's submission to his circumstances, and it also became part of Bolton's depiction of Boudica's defeat. Here, the ultimate failure of the Britons to attain their aims was attributed to the *necessity* of defeat under the circumstances: the world, as ordered by Providence, could not allow for any other outcome. This was what Richard Tuck called the 'coercive character of destiny' at work in the Stoic mind.[73] As for the Romans and the Britons, from the start of the final battle the two sides were fixed in their positions, like actors in a scripted scene. 'Obstinacie on both sides fixed with trabal [beam-like] nailes of necessitie; the Britanns to maintaine what they had begunne; the Romans to maister their perill, or to die. No possibilitie to hang their quarell even upon the weighing beame of justice and peace... Boadicia at an instant strucke of all the locks of restraint on her side, by giving the word, and without God to friend, permits her cause to brute triall.'[74] Yet, in Bolton's mind, the ultimate result of the 'brute triall' was foretold from the beginning of the whole sorry saga. It was impossible for Bolton to unmoor Boudica's character flaws (what he termed her 'choler'), as well as her fatal feminine failures, from the conduct of her army and thus from the failure of her cause—all were linked in a trajectory mandated by the initial decision to secretly, then openly and violently, resist the divine authority personified in Nero. The Roman army was the better equipped and more disciplined force, but the 'barbarous sinnes of the Britanns' also told heavily, and retribution, in the form of defeat and death, was swift and comprehensive. This explanation combined the 'politic' historian's concern with individual decisions with the providentialist historian's insistence on divine will.

As for the aftermath of this violent episode, it was here that Bolton could make his unique mark on the nascent study of Britain's past and advocate for the significance of Boudica's case in the grand scheme of the history of the British Isles from its earliest moments. This he did by making Boudica's story integral to one aspect of the British past that had recently begun to invite widespread speculation: the origin of Stonehenge.[75] James I had sent his architect, Inigo Jones, to investigate the structure in 1620, which might explain Bolton's interest in the subject. While Jones and others had speculated that the stone circles were of Danish origin, Bolton was the first and possibly the only serious scholar to argue that Boudica's death occasioned such great sadness among her surviving countrymen that they erected the monument of Stonehenge in her memory. This was a supposition made more plausible by Bolton's locating the site of the final battle at the River Wylye, which runs near Salisbury Plain.

Bolton brought his antiquarian skills to bear and justified his assessment by reciting and refuting the accounts by previous antiquarian studies that attributed the megalith to the Danes. The very rudeness of the stones suggested it was of British workmanship. However, he dismissed one commonly held belief that Stonehenge marked the mass burial ground of Vortigern's Britons, who had been betrayed and slain by the Saxons, led by Hengist, who had been called in to assist

---

[73] Tuck, *Philosophy and government*, 54. [74] Bolton, *Nero Caesar*, 172, 174.
[75] For the place of Stonehenge in British historical culture, see R. Hill, *Stonehenge* (London, 2008).

after the Romans had abandoned Britain to the Danes. In Bolton's estimation, it was not a whole troop of Britons massacred in the fifth century, but rather a solitary warrior queen who lay under the dance of huge stones. Confronted with an opportunity to make an original and bold antiquarian claim, Bolton was full of praise for the 'magnanimous' Queen Boudica: 'Higher then to her no bookes doe reach, with any probabilitie of a person more capable of such a testimonie then she...'[76] The antiquary, hitherto somewhat equivocal, seemed to convince himself of her merit, at least amongst her countrymen, and his own Britishness swayed him to sympathy. If only the Britons had shown greater restraint, he lamented, but '...in the case of my dearest countrey, during this whole warre, there was nothing from first to last so unfortunately absent'.[77] The antiquary freely owned the barbarous past of his country, and his patriotism endeared the pagan Boudica to him. With a final note castigating Boudica for having permitted the Britons to engage in the dreadful acts of vengeance recorded by Dio, Bolton nevertheless declared her 'a great and noble ladie (the stay and anchor of her partie)', whose story was exceptional in the annals of Britain, and the world.

Bolton used the Boudica story to lampoon his enemies, by blaming Seneca for the Britons' grievances and taking the opportunity to vent his spleen at secret meetings, and to show the irony of constancy in the face of inevitable failure. He employed Boudica and her fellow Britons as representative of the less palatable characteristics of a particular political (mis)reading of Stoicism, which Bolton was seeking to discredit. Counterintuitive though this may seem—Boudica was anything but the ideal form of Stoic as calm, resigned, or submissive—there are echoes of the Stoic hero in the manner of her death. Her undiminished hatred of the Romans meant suicide was her only recourse, as it was for the many Roman heroes, among them Seneca and Thrasea Paetus, when faced with the threat of dishonour.[78] As for the disparity in the sources between the way in which Boudica met her death—either by poison in Tacitus or sickness in Dio—Bolton declares there to be no contradiction: she died by sickening from poison. He succeeded in ensuring she fulfilled the precepts of the Stoic suicide, while maintaining the dual authority of Dio– whose account was so crucial to his earlier remarks about Seneca—alongside Tacitus. This, however, is supposition; the antiquary was bound at some stage to narrate Boudica's death, and his reliance on Tacitus was by no means unusual.

Edmund Bolton has been cast by modern scholars as standing in judgement over Boudica, deriding her womanhood and glorying in her defeat.[79] However, as we have seen, Bolton was at least nominally committed to presenting balanced judgements of individual actors in history, especially as their deeds affected the course of events. True to form, Bolton minutely dissected Boudica's personality, and he undoubtedly did decry her intrigue and the passionate extremity of her vengeance. Indeed, he saw these actions as admixtures of the same toxic excess of

---

[76] Bolton, *Nero Caesar*, 183. [77] Ibid., 176.
[78] See T. Hill, *Mors ambitiosa: suicide and self in Roman thought and literature* (London, 2004).
[79] Frenée-Hutchins, *Boudica's odyssey*, 178. Frenée-Hutchins assumes that Bolton's Catholicism meant his sympathies were naturally with the Romans.

warm, dry choler, which made her prone to 'deceit' and 'adustion', or scorched dryness.[80] This height of temper was coupled, to dramatic effect, with a Stoic's overweening pride, or, as Bolton put it, 'Boadicia her selfe deepely tainted with that selfe-flattering pestilence' which contributed to her ultimate demise.[81] Thus Bolton's characterization of Boudica's rebellion drew on the worst sins of the Stoic movement—sedition and pride—while also inverting the virtue of constancy.

Just as his distaste for Seneca's teachings was tempered by admiration for the philosopher's learning, Bolton's opinion of Boudica cannot satisfactorily be categorized as either wholly laudatory or entirely condemnatory. He saw her as a subject worthy of scrutiny; he attempted to analyse her motives, the truth of her public statements, and the characteristics that led her to act as she had. He did the same in his discussions of Nero, Seneca, and Agrippina, and he was unusually even-handed in his assessment of the Roman general responsible for defeating the Britons, Suetonius Paulinus, whose individual character rarely attracted much attention:

> Arrogant nevertheless, and sowr, in his own case (as Tacitus notes him in his Agricola) when once he had gotten the upper hand. Which vices of minde, are familiar to armed might, and are as rarelie found several from deeplie musing and tardy natures. The servants of glorie doe not alwaies see the moral helpes they need. Nothing could prevent those blemishes but temperance.[82]

Indeed, *Nero Caesar* was as much a reflection on the lives, sins, virtues, and deaths of famous historical actors as it was an ideologically motivated study of an historical case study in sedition. Although he sometimes objected to Tacitus in matters of content, Bolton's method was, at least in this sense, indebted to the Roman historian.

But to paint Bolton as attempting to emulate Tacitus, or indeed any other single historian, whether ancient or contemporaneous, is to ignore what was original and interesting in his work. He had his own method, which he cobbled together from his wide reading, but also from his own experience. Buried in the 1627 edition of *Nero Caesar*, in an afterword addressed to his brother-in-law, Endymion Porter, Bolton summarized the position of the historian, beginning with the example of Tacitus and ending with a more general point:

> Orations such as were never spoken, and yet put into the mouths of actors by authors fitted to the matter, and sometimes used as artificiall places of recitall, or abridgement, the judgements also, with which Cornelius Tacitus, more than any other Roman aboundeth, uttered of men, and things, in the person of the historian himselfe (the first an office of prerogative, or rather of poëtrie, the second of censure and magistracie) fill bookes by leave, and not by the law of historie, and yet are not received but with honour: custome having prescribed therein against the rigour of fundamental axioms in the schoole of Clio.[83]

---

[80] Bolton, *Nero Caesar*, 101.   [81] Ibid., 173.   [82] Ibid., 103.
[83] 'An historical parallel' in *Nero Caesar* (1627), 16.

Here Bolton used Tacitus' example as a means of situating historical narrative between the imaginative privilege of poetry and the dignified authority of legal censure. In Bolton's estimation, historians of his own day continued to traverse a similar *via media* that allowed for a range of narrative techniques, including abridgement through speech and the explicit judgement delivered in the voice of the objective historian. The 'law of historie', Bolton argued, was rather more customary than rigorous, and so such interpolation and judgement by the historian was allowable within that law.

This idea of historical method as 'custom' suggests an organic development that reflects the elusiveness of the historian's quarry: recorded past action and its ambiguous relation to human thought, the latter of which must necessarily be subject to some degree of learned speculation. Only malleable custom, rather than unbendable rules, could hope to govern such unknowable quantities. Bolton's notion that the customs of history could be subject to growth and adjustment, and yet remain unchanged in their fundamental adherence to recorded evidence, captures the spirit of historical culture as simultaneously open to growth and to maintaining continuity.

Bolton's extended analysis of Boudica and her rebellion in *Nero Caesar* is notable for its nuance, sometimes bordering on contradiction; this was a consequence of the antiquary's purposes, which were, it must be said, in tension with one another. First, he was bound by his duty to James to show the rightness and necessity of monarchy in the face of the threat of sedition, rebellion, and even anarchy. *Nero Caesar* was written against a particular intellectual backdrop, in which the histories of Tacitus and the implications of Tacitism and Stoicism were at the forefront of many scholars' minds, most especially when it came to writing history. Bolton must have been intensely conscious of the histories and historical method of Tacitus at a time when the Roman historian's works were fomenting seditious ideas among his contemporaries and threatening the position of the King and all who depended on him. Bolton's history of Boudica was an antidote to Stoicism, a purpose for which her story was peculiarly suitable: it tarnished the reputation of Seneca, challenged the pre-eminence of Tacitus among readers and writers with malign intent, showed in violent detail the fated, even natural results of factionalism and rebellion against the divinely ordained monarch, and even perverted the notion of 'constancy' so dear to the hearts of the Stoics.

Bolton's second purpose in writing *Nero Caesar*, and arguably, the more significant was that he wished to showcase his own antiquarian and historical learning. This undeniably rendered his former purpose problematic. He was forced to embrace what at times bordered on bias, which he packaged as carefully weighed truth. Yet this he was able to do, whether because he sincerely believed he had arrived at conclusions based on a judicious reading of the evidence at hand, or because he had made his peace with the unfortunate lot of the paid expert. Nevertheless, aspects of his narrative, particularly his speculations on Stonehenge, would seem to have had no ideological objective behind them. While the claim regarding Boudica's burial at Stonehenge was not taken up by later scholars, it was a bold and original one, based on wide reading, possibly on observation of the site, and a smattering of antiquarian wishful thinking of the kind lovingly parodied by later generations.

Thus Boudica's reputation in early modern Britain and Edmund Bolton's place in historical culture were intertwined—and each was far more complex than they might at first appear. Alan Bradford has speculated that Edmund Bolton's *Nero Caesar* may have been completed as early as 1622, at which point he gave the manuscript to James I to personally correct, expand, or redact.[84] If this supposition is true,[85] far from conspiring to remove Boudica from British history, Edmund Bolton, backed by the king, was instrumental in cementing her story as a singular event in British history. While John Fletcher had made Boudica a semi-fiction, it was Edmund Bolton the antiquary who established her identity as an individual—a heroic figure who defined a pivotal moment in British history.

But the still larger point here is that, as the most highly regarded source for Boudica's story, Tacitus lurks in the background of her place in historical and political culture in this period. Previous analyses have focused too narrowly on Boudica's sex, significantly underplaying the extent to which Tacitus' reception in early modern Britain influenced Boudica's fate. Far from disappearing with the death of Elizabeth, or at the least being subjected to ignominy, Boudica thrived in the complex conceit of *Nero Caesar*. I have argued here that Edmund Bolton's *Nero Caesar* was shot through with Tacitist historical methodology and anti-Stoic ideas, and is thus a reflection of the layered nature of Jacobean historical culture. His work represented Boudica at a point when humanist history, in which the past was a mirror for the present, and the study of material and documentary remains, were only just beginning to operate as two aspects of the same method; a method pioneered in Bolton's study of Queen Boudica.

But Bolton purposes were best served by the fact that she was the leader of a rebellion against one of the most hateful rulers in the history of the Western world—and therein resided the coincidence that thrust Boudica into the limelight in *Nero Caesar*. Simultaneously political, antiquarian, and historical, *Nero Caesar* was a product of and for its time, but it was nevertheless a reflective exercise in historical scholarship. It was also the beginning of a new era for Boudica. Whatever the enduring merits or otherwise of Bolton's political and moral stance, *Nero Caesar* lifted her from the schematic backdrop of Holinshed's chronicle and (perhaps) salvaged her reputation from the over-dramatization of John Fletcher by making her, individually, a subject of serious historical interest that even the King found noteworthy. Moreover, in the context of debates around Stoicism, Boudica's rebellion showed the utility of the national past to historians and antiquaries, most of whom were at this stage more concerned with the glittering eminence of ancient Rome than with the crude insolence of ancient Britain.

---

[84] Bradford, 'Stuart absolutism', 139. A marginal note referring to an original manuscript given to James before the first edition appeared would seem to strengthen this theory; the note appeared in the 1627 edition, but not in the earlier one.

[85] Indeed, it seems certain that James had some role, even at the early stages of composition. Amongst his Neroniana, Bolton left a note next to a Latin passage relating to the murder of Agrippina: 'This particular the king would have inserted into my Nero'. Harl. MS 6521, 101.

Although there is a sense that Bolton was simply trying to create the vacuum he himself hoped to fill, he was wont to express concern that his country's history had yet to be satisfactorily written, despite his admiration for William Camden's *Britannia*. Yet even while lengthy national histories were becoming more commonplace, Bolton's sustained, minute treatment of a story of national importance set him apart. He even expressed a kind of pride in his parochialism, though it must have needled him. Close to the end of his career, he lamented, once again in self-apology, that he had never been nearer to Europe than the cliffs of Dover; yet his 'home-bred travails and home-bound studies' were no less truthful or reputable than those produced by his more cosmopolitan contemporaries. For all his poverty and hardship, Bolton declared himself 'fit, equallie, & solidly to deal or deliver truthes of this heroick nature'.[86]

Bolton's competing preoccupations should not detract from just how instrumental he was in historicizing Boudica during a period when many recent scholars have argued she was being written out of the historical record. Edmund Bolton's history served to show the significance and complexity of her rebellion, as well as to give a more balanced view of the first historically traceable female Briton. That his distaste for the views of some of his contemporaries drove him to this task is worthy of note, but it is by no means the whole story behind his intense interest in the ancient queen. Perhaps, then, it is a fitting tribute to Bolton's achievement that it would be nearly three centuries before another generation of scholars—this time in the guise of professional archaeologists—took up Boudica's case with anything approaching the dedication of this seventeenth-century antiquary. As the next chapter will show, following Bolton, interest in Boudica emerged in a different kind of historical narrative, one that was aimed at a wider audience than previous works, and which was infused with drama, imagination, and occasionally serious historical discourse.

---

[86] 'The Cabanet Royal, with the chief provisions which constitute and furnish it, for the service of civil wisdom & civil glorie', BL Royal MS 18 A. LXXI, 14–15.

2

'They that write to all, must strive to please all'

Historians, Playwrights, and the Drama of History

> *Sure, when our story in an After-Age*
> *Is represented on the Tragick Stage,*
> *No Savage Eyes in their struggling Tears shall keep;*
> *But for our Woes the whole sad Audience weep.*[1]

In the 1630s a new portrait of a woman called 'Bonditia' began to circulate in the London market (see Figure 3). 'Bonditia'—an unusual variant for Boudica—appeared along with an unattributed verse:

> Bonditia, the brave British Queene, in th'heade
> Of her owne Troopes, her hoast, in person ledd
> With warlike fight, Shee did soe well mayntayne,
> Full fowerscore thousand Romans there lay slayne.[2]

A serviceable potted history in four lines, it hit the highlights of Boudica's career, and in glowing terms. The portrait and verse were sold as part of a set of 'Nine Worthy Women'. The idea of a pantheon of 'worthy' men and women, often but not always nine of each, was an old one even in the seventeenth century, but the individual men and women celebrated in this way changed over time.[3] The nine women included in this example were famous queens from the Old Testament, as well as more recent women, notably Queen Elizabeth.

This particular portrait set was by the well-established London engraver George Glover (*fl.* 1634–52), who made a number of similar print series.[4] Like those of the

---

[1] C. Hopkins, *Boadicea, Queen of Britain, a tragedy, as acted by His Majesty's Servants at the Theatre in Lincolns-Inn-fields* (London, 1697), 33.

[2] The print with verse attached is reproduced in M. Jones, *The print in early modern England: an historical oversight* (London, 2010), p. 42, pl. 45.

[3] There is a reference to Nine Worthy Women taking part, along with their male counterparts, in the Chester Show of 1 August 1621. The relative proximity of this event to Glover's portrait set leads one to the tantalizing possibility that this was Boudica's first appearance in a civic pageant; see E. Baldwin, L.M. Clopper, and D. Mills, *Cheshire including Chester vol. I, Records of Early English Drama* (London, 2007), 461.

[4] M. Jones, *Print in early modern England*, 103, 108; A. Griffiths, *The print in Stuart Britain, 1603–1689* (London, 1998), 103; M. Corbett, M. Naughton, *Engraving in England in the sixteenth and seventeenth centuries. Part III, The Reign of Charles I, compiled from the notes of A.M. Hind* (Cambridge, 1964), 225–50.

Figure 3. 'Bonditia', by George Glover, in Thomas Heywood's *Exemplary Lives* (1640). The Bodleian Libraries, The University of Oxford, 4°A 47 Art (4), p. 69.

other worthy women, Boudica's portrait is a three-quarter length picture, designed as to show her manner of dress and accompanying ornaments. Boudica is one of three worthies shown with one breast exposed.[5] Her hair is portrayed as flowing loosely down her shoulders, and she wears a layered dress and sash, with a plume of feathers atop her head. Glover's picture bore little resemblance to the only other comparably detailed image of Boudica, found in Holinshed's *Chronicle*. Instead, Glover's image seems to follow, with some alteration, Edmund Bolton's description in *Nero Caesar*:

> Holinshed in her printed picture sets a crowne of gold upon her as a finall ornament; and it displeatheth not; though authoritie wants. An helme with a coronet, and a plume of feathers more proper…her shoulders sustained upon them a militarie cloake, or a thicke wrought mantle, buttond before, her goodlie tresses flowing in length downe her back…[6]

---

[5] Not, I would argue, a reference to the Amazons. Penthisilaea, who represented the mythical Amazons in the set, is shown with her chest covered, while the Old Testament Deborah and the Greek Artimesia, queen of Halicarnassus, also have one breast exposed. The significance, if any, is difficult to map.

[6] Bolton, Nero Caesar, 114.

It is likely that this was an original image of Glover's own creation, based loosely on Bolton's physical description. The inclusion of feathers seems particularly telling, as these were an interpolation on Bolton's part. That Bolton's sustained narrative and analysis of Boudica's rebellion appeared in English rather than Latin and in two editions lends further credence to the suggestion that his work provided the impetus for this later portrait. It is not possible to recover the precise mechanisms by which Bolton's description of Boudica came into the hands of the engraver, George Glover. It is, however, certain that by the 1630s, Boudica had become a recognizable individual for the maker and potential buyers of these portraits.

Glover's image is a bridge between Bolton's idiosyncratic, ideologically inflected retelling of the Boudica story and her emergence in the expanding market for history in the mid- to late seventeenth century. The work of Edmund Bolton presented an account of the people and events of Nero's reign which encompassed smatterings of politics, philosophy, history, antiquarian learning, and a Tacitean involvement in the minds and actions of complex characters. It was a compound of different elements, distilled through Bolton's singular apparatus; a similar dynamic is evident in the authors and works discussed in this chapter. But rather than layer ideology and history, the story here will be of the interactions between imaginative genres of history during a time when England's—and by extension Britain's—history was still forming in outline.

John Pocock pointed out some years ago that historical writing in the seventeenth century can be divided into two categories: history as a literary subject, and history as a serious area of study, particularly in faculties of law.[7] Yet the tendency amongst twentieth- and twenty-first-century scholars has been to identify historiographical debate and methodological discussion exclusively with the latter 'serious' history, rather than with the study and representation of the past by those outwith a recognizably scholarly sphere. This chapter will show how Boudica was very much a part of 'literary' history, much of it seemingly uncritical and unsophisticated to modern eyes. However, I will argue here that this work in fact offers a revealing commentary on contemporary perceptions of history's didactic possibility, its relationship with fiction and poetry, and its significance to ordinary readers; this extended even to a discussion of historical method, a subject of recondite interest even to the more 'serious' historical writers. Sustained attempts were being made to convey the gravity of history to decidedly unserious audiences, sometimes with reference to more recherché literature, particularly the *ars historica*.

As Daniel Woolf has argued, present-day historians of history have focused for the most part on the 'serious' histories produced during the seventeenth and eighteenth centuries, meaning that we have only a patchwork understanding of the way in which the English and British past came to be more widely disseminated during period.[8] What can be said for certain is that much of the process took place outside formal education structures. At the universities, for instance, Degory Wheare,

---

[7] J.G.A. Pocock, *The ancient constitution and the feudal law: a study of English historical thought in the seventeenth century* (Cambridge, 1987), 6–8.

[8] See especially the discussion in Woolf, 'Disciplinary history and historical culture'.

Camden Professor of History at Oxford from 1623 to 1647 insisted on the utility of the classical past for the youthful minds in his charge. This was not, it must be said, due to a snobbish disdain for 'modern' history harboured by classically educated elites, but rather because 'modern', and by extension national or even local history, was considered the preserve of only the most mature and promising minds.[9] Indeed, the most influential work on historical method, by Jean Bodin, formed the basis for this position.

Meanwhile, the state of antiquarianism in the latter half of the seventeenth century also worked against Queen Boudica and the British past as subjects of sustained attention. Antiquarian study was often narrow in its focus, limited to a particular locality or even one particular type of artefact, such as funeral monuments or heraldry.[10] Most antiquaries were interested primarily in physical remains, philology, numismatics, and linguistics; books and documents did not always draw the same keen attention, and, for a figure like Boudica, who existed in only a few written records, this was undoubtedly problematic. Moreover, although there were strong ties between the men who devoted their energies to antiquarian pursuits, the demise of William Camden's Society of Antiquaries, followed by the failure of Bolton's proposed 'Academ Roial', meant that prior to the Society's reformation in 1707, there was no single organized group whose task it was to study, interpret, or curate British history and antiquity, let alone to produce learned works for an interested public.[11] To be sure, there were forms of historical knowledge that penetrated across social divisions, especially oral culture[12] and the ubiquitous chapbooks and almanacs. However, the latter tended to present a patchwork version of history, usually in a muddled form, if at all.[13]

When it comes to Queen Boudica, we must turn to two media in particular to find her story packaged for audiences outside of learned circles: prose histories and historical stage dramas. Even as Boudica can tell us relatively little about formal historical education or even what would be recognized as antiquarianism during this period, she is unusually well placed to reveal the connections between history, classical learning, and drama, and the emergence of a 'popular' vision of the past. She can show how the broad arc of antiquity and history was constructed and shored up, not as an act of opposition to scholarly culture or appropriation of folk

---

[9] See M. Feingold, 'The Humanities', in N. Tyacke (ed.), *The History of the University of Oxford*, 8 vols (Oxford, 1997), Vol. IV, pp. 327–58.

[10] Woolf, 'Dawn of the artefact', 23–5.

[11] G. Parry, *The trophies of time: English antiquarians of the seventeenth century* (Oxford, 1995); D.R. Woolf, 'The dawn of the artefact: antiquarian impulse in England, 1500–1730', *Studies in Medievalism*, IV (1992), 5–35; M. Myrone and L. Peltz (eds), *Producing the past: aspects of antiquarian culture and practice 1700–1850* (Aldershot, 1999); R. Sweet, *Antiquaries: the discovery of the past in eighteenth-century Britain* (London, 2004). See also the catalogue of the Society of Antiquaries' anniversary exhibition held in 2007: *Making history: three hundred years of antiquaries in Britain, 1707–2007* (London, 2007).

[12] B. Worden, 'Historians and poets', in P. Kewes (ed.), *The uses of history in early modern England* (San Marino, CA, 2006), pp. 69–90, at 80. For oral histories, see A. Fox and D.R. Woolf (eds), *The spoken word: oral culture in Britain, 1500–1850* (Manchester, 2002).

[13] M. Spufford, *Small books and pleasant histories: popular fiction and its readers in seventeenth-century England* (London, 1981), Ch. 9.

beliefs, but as a commercially driven activity, subject to market forces and to a sense of history's potential to be both educative and entertaining.

Scholars have noted the growth of a 'history market' in Britain, particularly in light of the rise of the novel as both a complement to and a competitor for prose historical work in the first half of the eighteenth century. Karen O'Brien has argued that the period after 1700 marked a shift in the market for history books, when there occurred a 'generic evolution of history from political narrative to civil history, then [in the mid-eighteenth century] to a novelized kind of history incorporating biographical elements, anecdotes, and epistolary and other fiction formats... reflecting and instigating changes in the composition of the readership for historical works'.[14] Similarly, Mark Salber Phillips notes that the content of histories in the period shifted away from the military and political acts of great men, as authors began to place greater emphasis on the 'sentimental' aspects of history in the mid- to late eighteenth century.[15] The relationship between the fictions of novels and the realness of histories has been variously characterized as oppositional, critical, challenging, and occasionally complementary, but a relationship of some kind is taken as read: history would not be what it was without the intervention of the novel.[16]

But there is an older relationship that has yet to be fully understood: that between prose history and stage drama, particularly in the period from the Restoration to the middle of the eighteenth century.[17] Of course it is well known that historical source materials like the early chronicles provided inspiration for stage plays, which sometimes reciprocated by filling gaps in the historical record. As one scholar of

---

[14] K. O'Brien, 'The history market', in I. Rivers (ed.), *Books and their readers in eighteenth-century England: new essays* (London, 2003), pp. 105–33, at 110. This shift has also been noted in M.G.H. Pittock, 'Enlightenment historiography and its legacy: plurality, authority and power', in H. Brocklehurst and R. Phillips (eds), *History, nationhood and the question of Britain* (Basingstoke, 2004), pp. 33–44, at 36, and by J. Black, 'Ideology, history, xenophobia and the world of print in eighteenth-century England', in J. Black and J. Gregory (eds), *Culture, politics and society in Britain, 1660–1800* (Manchester, 1991), pp. 184–216, at 207.

[15] M.S. Phillips, *Society and sentiment: genres of historical writing in Britain 1740–1820*, (Princeton, NJ, 2000), 103. Affectations to literature were later derided by the more 'scientific' historians; see P. Craddock, 'Historical discovery and literary invention in Gibbon's "Decline and Fall"', *Modern Philology*, 85 (1988), 569–87. This discursive process, by which history and the novel variously separated and combined, is also linked to the feminization of reading audiences, characterized by the slow movement of history writing towards sentimentality, interiority, and personalization, which has been interpreted as an attempt to appeal to the growing number of female readers who might be seduced by the emotive appeal of novels; see D.R. Woolf, 'A feminine past? Gender, genre, and historical knowledge in England, 1500–1800', *American Historical Review*, 102 (1997), 645–79.

[16] There are a number of works one could point to here, but most relevant are E. Zimmerman, *The boundaries of fiction: history and the eighteenth-century British novel* (London, 1996); R. Mayer, *History and the early English novel: matters of fact from Bacon to Defoe* (Cambridge, 1997); K. O'Brien, 'History and the novel in eighteenth-century Britain', in P. Kewes (ed.), *The uses of history in early modern England* (San Marino, CA, 2006), pp. 389–405.

[17] This is an area that cries out for greater scholarly attention. There is of course a thriving literature about Shakespeare; see especially R. Knowles, *Shakespeare's arguments with history* (Basingstoke, 2002). Other works will be cited where appropriate. However, much remains to be understood about how history and performance intersected during the Restoration and beyond. For the novel's relationship to drama, see E.H. Anderson, *Eighteenth-century authorship and the play of fiction: novels and the theatre, Haywood to Austen* (New York, 2009) and A.F. Widmayer, *Theatre and the novel, from Behn to Fielding* (Oxford, 2015).

Stuart-era drama has noted, the instability of the relationship between the antiquarian raw material of the past and the historical narrative itself could be exploited by writers of history plays 'in order to intervene in the construction of the English [*sic*] past'.[18] For the writer of history plays, it was not simply a matter of staging imaginary events, yet neither was historical drama anything like an exercise in dry narration. Established historical narratives also acted as a 'check on the artificial virtuosity of the theatre' and tested its 'ability to stage reality'.[19]

However, I wish to make two related suggestions here. First, that writers of prose histories were aware of the particular qualities of historical drama that made it so appealing to audiences, not least its latitude for imagining personal relationships and portraying the emotional lives of historical figures. These elements of drama were likewise at the disposal of writers of historical prose, particularly new works aimed at a similar demographic to stage plays. Thus my second suggestion is that the relationship between drama and history was a reciprocal one. While history provided inspiration for and imposed limitations on the theatre, dramatic works presented historians with a template for retelling history in a more affective, and thus effective, guise.[20] Boudica's example demonstrates how from the middle of the seventeenth century we can begin to see a shift in history writing that reflects some of the tendencies of staged historical romance, especially, I argue, in appealing to the emotions of audience members and readers through a greater focus on Boudica's children, on the cruelties they suffered, and on the justness or otherwise of Boudica's revenge. Writers of history plays were attracted to the shadowy space between the documented past and the interpretable histories, and thus to the very human reactions of their central characters to momentous historical events.

This chapter will focus on writers whose works fall into the category either of engaging historical narrative or historical drama—indeed, authors often wrote both. The first two sections will focus on the works of Thomas Heywood (*c*.1573–1641) and Nathaniel Crouch (*c*.1640–1725) respectively. Both authors dabbled in the history of Britain and in the history of women—two areas of popular historiography in which Boudica often featured—and they both exemplify the overlap between different imaginative and factual genres. Heywood is a particularly significant figure for this purpose because, like Edmund Bolton, he reflected deeply—or convincingly affected to do so—on the nature of history and its benefit for his audience. But Heywood was first and foremost a dramatist and a translator of the classics, whose original historical compositions were written to complement an otherwise meagre income. Similarly, Nathaniel Crouch saw historical writing as a way of making ends meet, but he was no less invested in its didactic potential, both as a repository of facts about the national past and as a means of honing the audience's critical

---

[18] I. Kamps, *Historiography and ideology in Stuart drama* (Cambridge, 1996), 51.
[19] D. Goy-Blanquet, *Shakespeare's early history plays: from chronicle to stage* (Oxford, 2003), 291.
[20] In thinking about the commonalities between history and drama in their appeal to the emotions, I have found P.C. Hogan, *The mind and its stories: narrative universals and human emotion* (Cambridge, 2003) useful. Hogan does not give much attention to historiography specifically, but his ideas are nonetheless thought-provoking.

faculties. These first two sections establish Boudica as a part of a popularizing historical discourse in the latter half of the seventeenth century.

In the third section of this chapter, the discussion will shift to the two plays about Boudica written during the century's closing years. Like John Fletcher's *Tragedie of Bonduca*, the plays by George Powell (c.1668–1714) and Charles Hopkins (c.1671–1700) have been read as commentaries on war, masculinity, and colonization.[21] But for our purposes it is interesting to view these plays as responding to Fletcher's earlier work, and as competing with each other to attract playgoers. Rushed out within a year of one another, these two plays suggest that Boudica and ancient British history were able to draw in the crowds to London's theatres following the Restoration. Furthermore, their influence seems to have extended beyond the playhouse, a possibility explored in the final section of this chapter. A growing number of narrative histories of the nation's past—a genre of history I call 'panoramic history'—were written at the close of the seventeenth century and the beginning of the eighteenth. The details used to embellish the stage version of Boudica's story did, on a few occasions, find their way into the histories, but even more significant was their deployment of provocative, emotive language focused especially on the plight of Boudica's daughters. I argue that these histories show the longevity of emotionality as a marker of popular history, and link what might appear to be a new genre of marketable history to an older literary convention.

THOMAS HEYWOOD, THE 'POETICALL HISTORIAN'

Although rarely given much attention by scholars of Boudica, Thomas Heywood was a pivotal figure in her posthumous life, as the author of the only seventeenth-century prose account to be based on Edmund Bolton's earlier work. As classicist, dramatist, and historian, he was also an early popularizer of history, who sat easily between different forms of historical presentation.[22] Originally from Lincolnshire, Heywood came to London via Cambridge, where he gained the classical education that later allowed him to undertake serious translations of ancient works.[23] He is remembered mostly for his dramatic works, which took the form of upward of two hundred stage plays and seven Lord Mayor's Shows.[24] By far his most famous works were his 'domestic' tragedies, particularly *A Woman Kill'd With Kindness* (1603), in which a woman coerced into adultery is so ashamed of herself that she starves to death,

---

[21] Nielsen, 'Boadicea onstage', 600.

[22] L.B. Wright, 'Heywood and the popularizing of history', *Modern Language Notes*, 43 (1928), 287–93.

[23] A.M. Clark, *Thomas Heywood, playwright and miscellanist* (Oxford, 1931); B. Baines, *Thomas Heywood* (Boston, MA, 1984).

[24] For the latter, see D.M. Bergeron, *Thomas Heywood's pageants: a critical edition* (London, 1986) and J. C. Finlayson, 'Thomas Heywood's Panegyric to London's "University" in *Londini Artium & Scientiarum Scaturigo: or, Londons Fountaine of Arts and Sciences* (1632)', *The London Journal*, 39 (2014), 102–19. Heywood's writings have never been published in a satisfactorily complete edition, but a team at the University of Reading will publish a ten-volume edition from 2015 to 2022.

breathing her last as her husband grants her his forgiveness.[25] A domestic setting was typical of Heywood's drama, but ordinary people were not his only interest. Like Shakespeare, Heywood ranged from comedy and tragedy to history plays. He was among the first to dramatize the life of Queen Elizabeth in the two-part *If You Know Not Me, You Know Nobody* (1604–5), which recounted the early years of the queen's reign up to the defeat of the Spanish Armada. It is to these and other dramatic works that scholars have tended to pay the most attention.[26]

Both *A Woman Kill'd With Kindness* and *If You Know Not Me* exemplified Heywood's atypical—at least when compared to his contemporaries—focus on women and their travails, whether ordinary or extraordinary. Not only was he interested, he was also a staunch and eloquent defender of women at a time when the shortcomings of the female sex were the subject of serious polemic.[27] When Joseph Swetnam published his pamphlet *The Arraignment of Women* (1615), Heywood responded with a comedy, *Swetnam the Woman-Hater Arraigned by Women* (1620), in which the misogynist was tried and soundly browbeaten by a jury made up of members of the maligned sex. Lending weight to his unusually vocal defence of women, Heywood had become familiar with dozens—hundreds—of examples of female fortitude gleaned from his extensive studies in the classics.

Indeed, he was a prolific translator, producing English versions of Sallust's *Conspiracy of Catiline* and the *War of Jugurtha* in 1608, and he was the first to render Ovid's *Ars Ammoria* into English that same year.[28] Heywood's classical translations and prose works are discussed less often by modern scholars than are his plays, but these works in fact illuminate a point of connection between Heywood the dramatist, and Heywood the classicist and historian. A striking example can be found in his Sallust, to which was affixed a translation of the fourth chapter of Jean Bodin's *Methodus* in which Bodin had laid out the pedagogical schema a budding historian should follow.[29] This marked the first time that Bodin's *Methodus* appeared in English, and Heywood claimed to be influenced in his own historical works by the approach he was making available to those without his education. Thus Heywood combined a familiarity with the *ars historica* genre with a classical education and a declared intent to write for a wide audience, particularly an audience of women. Heywood understood the proscriptive nature of historical writing, but, as a man known for his stage plays, he was not bound to it, either by his own nature or his audience's expectations. His first history of women appeared in 1624.

Although he claimed to have written it very quickly, *Gynaikeion: or nine bookes of various history; concerning Women* was a magisterial survey which drew on the

---

[25] See L. Hopkins, 'The false domesticity of *A Woman Killed with Kindness*', *Connotations*, 4 (1994–5), 1–7.
[26] R. Rowland, *Thomas Heywood's theatre, 1599–1639, Locations, translations, conflict* (Farnham, 2010). For a study of Heywood's published plays, see D. Brook, *From playhouse to printing house* (Cambridge, 2000), Ch. 5, in which Heywood's prose works are briefly mentioned. These are treated somewhat more thoroughly in A.M. Clark, *Thomas Heywood: playwright and miscellanist*.
[27] K.U. Henderson and B.F. McManus, *Half humankind: contexts and texts of the controversy about Women in England, 1540–1640* (Chicago, 1985).
[28] L.F. Dean, 'Bodin's "Methodus" in England before 1625', *Studies in Philology*, 39 (1942), 160–6.
[29] Ibid., 163.

lives of women, named and unnamed, from the rustic to the divine, and from all periods. There were few references to figures from the British past—although Ethelfleda, the heroic Queen of the Mercians who defeated the Danes, figured prominently—and, curiously, no mention of Boudica. However, Heywood was more familiar with earlier periods of Roman history, Sallust's subject, and the myths of the ancients than he was with Tacitus.[30] Reading the *Gynaikeion* does give one a sense of what Heywood hoped to achieve with his prose histories and their particular emphasis on female accomplishments. Like Robert Burton, whose *Anatomy of Melancholy* (1621) became popular among learned men because it provided translations from ancient originals which were otherwise difficult to find, *Gynaikeion* could easily have functioned as a repository of anecdotal evidence, much of which would have been unknown outside of classical writings or ancient myths. For the young lady hoping to improve her conversation, especially if called upon to provide a sororal defence, *Gynaikeion* was a comprehensive guide, conveniently divided into sections devoted to women as mothers, daughters, wives, widows, leaders and queens, and even as prostitutes and killers.

For all its thoroughness, Heywood openly admitted to writing his *Gynaikeion* as if it were something not-quite-history, upon which the strictures of factual relation were consequently relaxed. He anticipated a backlash from learned critics, and provided a defence:

> ...I have therein imitated our Historicall and Comicall Poets, that write to the Stage; who least sic the Auditorie should be dulled with serious courses (which are meerely weightie and materiall) in everie Act present some Zanie with his Mimick action, to breed in the lesse capable, mirth and laughter: For they that write to all, must strive to please all. And as such fashion themselves to a multitude, consisting of spectators severally addicted; so I to an universalitie of Readers, diversely disposed.[31]

That this was, after all, a history of female accomplishments and deeds was by no means irrelevant to Heywood's self-defence. His condescension is evident, but his intention, to 'write to all', also suggests the unusual ambition of his project. Heywood combined the methods of the playwright with the content of historical works in what was, arguably, a new kind of prose literature aimed an audience of female readers, whose patience for 'weight' and 'material' was thought to be limited. He freely admitted than *Gynaikeion* contained purely fantastic elements, and in part, 'savour[ed] of lightnesse'. He made no apologies for confecting his history if it meant that it was read by the women and girls whose interests he hoped to pique.[32]

Although she was missing from *Gynaikeion*, Boudica played a central role in another of Heywood's later works on women, *Exemplary Lives and Memorable Acts*

---

[30] A passing reference on p. 344 to 'Lib. 17' of Tacitus would further suggest a degree of ignorance on Heywood's part. By the end of the sixteenth century, the *Annals* and the *Histories* had been confirmed as separate works, and Book 17 of the *Annals* had become Book I of the *Histories*.

[31] T. Heywood, *Gynaikeion: or, Nine bookes of various history. Concerninge women inscribed by ye names of ye nine Muses* (London, 1624), Preface to the Reader.

[32] *Gynaikeion* was digested and republished in 1683 under the title *Wonders of the Female World*.

of *Nine of the Most Worthy Women of the World* (1640), which was based on the existing portrait set by George Glover, discussed above. However, there were slight differences. Heywood's set of worthies was once again divided into three parts, based on the 'Three Jewes', 'Three Heathens', and 'Three Christians' who made up the nine, but Boudica appears in Heywood's account as a 'Heathen', while in Glover's original set she had been a Christian. This was possibly a mistake on the part of Glover, or it might have alluded once again to the account of Gildas, who believed that Christianity had arrived in Britain prior to Boudica's uprising. However, the fact that Heywood failed to mention Boudica in his comprehensive account of feminine history, and that there was a gap of nearly a decade between the appearance of Glover's 'Worthy Women' and Heywood's *Exemplary Lives*, suggests that Boudica's story was still only beginning to percolate through popular culture.

Heywood's *Exemplary Lives*, like the portrait set on which it was based, included laudatory verses on each of its nine subjects, accompanied by short biographical accounts in prose, not usually exceeding a few dozen pages. In the *Exemplary Lives*, Heywood distanced himself from his earlier unapologetic freedom with the facts of history. Instead, taking his cue from Bodin, Heywood made bold claims for the historicity of his potted biographies of women, and his audience, presumably unfamiliar with the *ars historia*, were treated to Heywood's own musings on the nature of historical writing. It seems remarkable given Heywood's popular subject matter and intended audience that he should profess on such a recherché subject, but his reasons for doing so were evident in the overall aim of his project, 'to dignifie the Sex'. By this he may have been alluding not only to the exemplary lives of his nine subjects, but also to the improving capacities of historical study.

In this miniature *ars historia*, Heywood explained to his readers that there were four kinds of History. Against the most noble form, the 'relatory', he opposed the 'nugatory', the 'adhoratory', and the 'fictionary'. The 'nugatory' was trifling and even comical, making it of least value, or of none at all to the serious reader; the latter two were 'exhortatory' in purpose and poetical in form, akin to Aesop's fables The most worthy, the 'relatory' were works which 'soly adheare to truth without deviation or digression; of which onely the ancient Grammarians admitted, as worthy the name' of history, and 'in which ranke I intrete thee to receive this following tractate'.[33] This last form compared to Bodin's remarks in the *Methodus*, translated into English by Heywood as 'Historie ought to be nothing but a representation of truth, and as it were a Map of mens action, sette forth in the publicke view of all commers to be examined.' On historical subjects, Heywood's Bodin had been equally clear:

> And therefore the predescanting opinion of the writer cannot but bring much discredite to the Action, in that hee presumeth to prepossesse the minds Artists with imaginarie assertions, seeming to teach those, who knew better then himselfe, what belongeth to such affaires.[34]

---

[33] T. Heywood, *Exemplary lives and memorable acts of nine of the most worthy women of the world* (London 1640), Preface to the Reader.

[34] T. Heywood, *The two most worthy and notable histories which remaine unmained to posterity; the Conspiracie of Cateline, undertaken against the government of the Senate of Rome, and The warre with Jugurth* (London, 1608).

These words, from Heywood's translation of Bodin's *Methodus*, acknowledged the conventional role of history as a tool for politicians and statesmen, who were able to learn from the examples of the past how best to govern and play at politics.[35] The historian himself could not and should not pretend to understand these arts, and thus was on more secure ground in relaying events without imposing 'predescanting opinion'. But this clearly was no matter for Heywood's *Exemplary Lives*, a work emphatically not aimed at statesmen. Nevertheless, Heywood claimed, his biographies should be read as nothing less than relatory accounts of the lives of these nine women.

He may have been emboldened by the fact that most of the *Exemplary Lives* was lifted, sometimes verbatim, from sources whose historical authority was perhaps less questionable than his own. In the case of Boudica, that source was Edmund Bolton's *Nero Caesar*. The verse that prefaced Heywood's version of Boudica's life was the only part of the account that was of his own composition. Given his nearly wholesale reliance on Bolton for the prose elements of the work, it is ironic that the verse should refer to the silence and ignorance of modern authors on the subject of the brave 'Bonduca':

> Witness this British Queene, whose masculine spirit
> Shall to all future, glorious fame inherit,
> Beyond all tongues or pens, who may be proud,
> Not thunders voice, can speake it self more loud,
> Of whom, although our moderne Authors wrote
> But sparingly, least they should seeme to dote
> Too much upon their Natives, forraigne inke
> Hath been so lavish, it would make man thinke
> Her valour inexpressible...[36]

Nowhere did Heywood acknowledge his debt to Bolton, referring only to 'a worthy and very learned Authour'.[37] Yet by making very slight omissions and additions, Heywood transformed Boudica's story from one that was overly detailed and at times objective to the point of ambivalence, as told by Bolton, to a more unquestioningly heroic story with a conscious appeal outside the learned world of court and politics. In this way Heywood's text acts as something of an editorial comment on Bolton's, revealing the words and phrases that the later author found objectionable. Instances of this are small, simple, and telling. Bolton had called Boudica's daughters 'poore, sillie ladies'; Heywood omitted the 'sillie' and left only the more sympathetic adjective.[38] Elsewhere, Heywood was able to reconcile Boudica's face as being at once 'excellently comely, yet with all incomparably terrible'.[39] Bolton had openly admitted to having been bamboozled by the double-meaning of the translation from Dio and had struggled with which to report. Heywood simply brought both

---

[35] For Bodin's historical thought, see J.H. Franklin, *Jean Bodin and the sixteenth-century revolution in the methodology of law and history* (New York, 1963).
[36] Heywood, *Exemplary Lives*, 68.   [37] Ibid., 75.
[38] Bolton, *Nero Caesar*, 99; Heywood, *Exemplary Lives*, 71.
[39] Heywood, *Exemplary Lives*, 72.

together as part of Boudica's charm. Also in his discussion of her physical attributes, Bolton conjectured that Boudica's 'choler' hinted at a tendency to deceit: 'And though be her colour her constitution might seem to bee cold, yet her doings declared, that choler had the maistrie in her, even unto deceit and adustion.'[40] In Heywood's hands, this became 'though by her complection, her constitution might seeme to be cold, yet her *noble actions* declared that choler had the predominance in her, even to adustion, her eyes were sparkling sharpe and piercing, her tongue shrill and harsh, as her person was tall and great...'[41]

As the translator of Bodin, Heywood gave the impression of being more than usually aware of the purposes that history could serve. However, even if he seriously aspired to Bodin's ideal of objectivity, Heywood left the hard work of historical criticism to be done by his source material, namely Edmund Bolton and *Nero Caesar*. Heywood turned to Bolton's existing account and moulded it to his own purpose, namely, to show Boudica as 'one of the bravest Shee Worthyes in the whole universe...'[42] and by doing so to market his books to a readership of women and girls. His protestation that *Exemplary Lives* was a 'relatory' work was likely little more than a self-conscious ploy to inflate its historical and hence its didactic value. In this he presents an interesting contrast to the popular historian, Nathaniel Crouch, whose work will form the basis of the next section. Crouch, who did not share Heywood's educational background, presented a far more intricate picture of the past to his audience, demanding their critical engagement.

NATHANIEL CROUCH, PUBLISHER AND POPULARIZER

It is highly likely that the narrative of British history, so often conveyed simply as the 'history of England' and told and retold for centuries, emerged first and foremost as a commercial proposition for writers looking to exploit a growing market.[43] The audience for these histories was largely composed, not of learned men, but of relatively ordinary people, male and female, neither poorly educated nor otherwise, with a degree of disposable income and some degree of literacy. Many authors believed that there was a gap in the public's knowledge, as well as a genuine demand for works of English history by 'native authors'. In his historical works, Heywood had not been concerned to convey to his readers a particular narrative of the nation's past from beginning to end, nor did he undertake his own original research—at least not in the case of *Exemplary Lives*. But his reference in the opening verse on Boudica to the silence of 'native authors' on the subject of her deeds harmonizes with the general sense among popular authors that their works were fulfilling a desire and a need. Indeed, Boudica's case is well suited to shedding light on the opportunities that antiquity, and for that matter the whole of the national

---

[40] Bolton, *Nero Caesar*, 101.
[41] Heywood, *Exemplary Lives*, 72. Emphasis is mine.   [42] Ibid., 91.
[43] For a general discussion of the marketing and selling of histories in this period, see Woolf, *Reading history in early modern England*.

narrative, presented to aspirant writers. Crucially, her identity was simultaneously English and British; English in the sense of modern geography, and more widely 'British' in her ethnic and linguistic affiliations. However, the history of England was often told as the history of Britain, and it is in this tacit sense that I employ the former.[44]

Nathaniel Crouch lacked Heywood's familiarity with the classics and made no attempt to induct his readers into the murky world of the *ars historia*. Nor did he embark on original, minute antiquarian research, or even return to the established works like Bolton's. Yet while he was no antiquary and no classicist, he was far more interested than the Cambridge-educated Heywood in conveying a full and clear picture of the period in which Boudica lived and her significance in British antiquity. Furthermore, he held a patriotic conviction that not only was learning about the nation's past important for improving the ordinary man or woman, this public consciously demanded access to its past. This may have been why Crouch had such an ambitious reach for his own books; he also had ready access to the means of achieving this reach as a publisher and bookseller in his own right. Through his second profession, he could more easily disseminate his own original works, many of which were historical, although he also dealt in travel and miscellany. Popularly known as 'Burton's Books', a reference to Crouch's tendency to publish under the initials 'R.B.' in homage to Robert Burton, author of the *Anatomy of Melancholy*, his histories were highly sought after, with new editions published throughout the eighteenth and nineteenth centuries. Although these were original compositions, Crouch's talent was for distillation: his works were valued as brief but accurate treatments of historical subjects. Samuel Johnson thought them 'very proper to allure backward readers', while fellow bookseller John Dunton noted that Crouch printed only 'what is very useful and very diverting'.[45]

This was high praise: to be useful and diverting was surely the ultimate aim of the humanistic historical writer, as opposed to the antiquarian. With his appeal to 'backward readers', Crouch was invested in disseminating a knowledge of history, particularly that of England, as well as Scotland and Wales.[46] In the preface to *England's Monarchs* (1685) he noted that foreign commentators accused the English reading public of preferring 'forreign' history to the 'remarkable Passages' of their own nation. He viewed this criticism as without foundation, finding instead that his books based on English history 'have received very great acceptation with the English Nation, So that many Thousands more of them have been vended, than of others which have concerned Forreign Matters'.[47] Like Heywood fifty years before,

---

[44] Crouch did write *A natural history of the principality of Wales* (1695) in which the story of 'Voadicia' and her husband Arviragus is recounted only briefly. He directed those readers with an interest in the story to consult his previous works in which Boudica featured more prominently (pp. 12–13).

[45] Quoted in W.E.A. Axon, 'Burton, Robert or Richard (1632?–1725?), miscellaneous author', *ODNB Archive* (1886), http://www.oxforddnb.com/view/olddnb/52645,accessed 1 Dec 2017.

[46] See n. 43 above. Crouch's *History of the Kingdom of Scotland* was published in 1696.

[47] R.B., *England's monarchs*, preface.

Crouch professed to be baffled by the sluggish response by authors and publishers to the demands of the reading public for histories of their own land.

But, unlike Heywood, Crouch made a career of seeking to improve the general audience's access to historical writing, which Boudica's example once again illustrates very well. As one might expect, Boudica had a brief cameo in *England's Monarchs*, but she played a more prominent part in *Female Excellency* (1688; there were two more editions before 1730). The latter was similar to Thomas Heywood's *Exemplary Lives* in that, drawing on an older tradition, it was organized around nine women as representative of female heroism.[48] Here he was free to enlarge on Boudica's rebellion to an extent not seen since Bolton's *Nero Caesar*. As Heywood had done in *Exemplary Lives*, Crouch began his account in *Female Excellency* with a celebratory verse:

> The Noble Voadicia whose hard fate
> Subjected her unto the Roman State
> O're which the bloudy Nero did command
> And cruel thraldom brought upon her Land
> Her countreymen doth gallantly incite
> That for their Ravisht freedoms they would fight
> And that her self will their Commander be
> And venture all, that their lost liberty
> They may redeem; And to fulfil her word
> Her utmostaid she doth to them afford
> Discomfiting their Roman enemies
> Then bravely in the bed of Honour dyes.

There could be no doubt in the reader's mind that this intended as a tribute to the ancient British heroine. To a greater extent than Heywood, Crouch made it clear that Boudica had commanded her fellow Britons as a military leader, and it was a matter of honour, not ignominy, that she should die by her own hand rather than submit to her enemies. But the prosopographical nature of the work belied his primary aim in writing *Female Excellency*. As Heywood had professed to be, Crouch was concerned with the ungallant nature of much contemporary writing about women, and he believed that, were they provided with an equivalent education to their male counterparts, women in the present age could easily match the attainments attested to in his history. Heywood had focused exclusively on the deeds of each of his female protagonists, omitting from Boudica's story the general narrative context of the Roman occupation, beyond, of course, noting the presence of Roman troops in Britain and their heinous treatment of Boudica's family. Crouch, on the other hand, prefaced Boudica's story by narrating the entirety of British antiquity; this went on for some forty pages before he finally commenced his narrative of Boudica's heroism. Such thoroughness was not a new departure for Crouch. He had taken a similar approach in the section devoted to Boudica in *England's Monarchs*, in which he had devoted much attention of the origins of the name 'Britain'. It might

---

[48] This time the nine women were: Deborah, Judith, Esther, Susanna, Lucretia, Voadica, Mariamne, Clotilda, and Andegona.

have come from the Greek word 'Prittania', referring to the rich metal deposits on the island; it may have come from the Danish, or it was an even older, mythical appellation deriving from the white cliffs. The author was in favour of the latter, but what is striking is the extent to which he was unwilling to lead his readers to absolute certainty, even as he presented all the competing alternatives.

The extensive detail in *England's Monarch's* notwithstanding, Crouch saw a biographical account of Boudica as 'so pertinent an opportunity to inlarge upon particulars as at this time' that he felt moved to provide yet another 'succinct account of the Original Inhabitants of these famous Islands with such truth and authority as things of so great Antiquity will allow'.[49] It is possible that he went over some of the same ground because *Female Excellency* was written with a female audience in mind, opening up the possibility that, as the first named female in the Britain's antiquity, Boudica's story might be a reader's first introduction to 'native' history. To that end, he neither omitted nor elided antiquarian and philological detail that, despite his pretences to Bodin's relatory history, Heywood would have considered superfluous to Boudica's exemplary deeds. Yet Crouch was very frank with his readers about the sketchiness of the evidence, giving implicit permission for each reader to form an individual judgement on the material at hand. For this reason he did not eschew the Galfridian legend whereby Britain was peopled by Brutus and the Trojans, but he was careful to explain that many disbelieved that story and instead favoured the possibility the Gauls were the first to settle in Britain. These ancient peoples would have left no written records, a point the author was also keen to make. Like John Milton—of whom more later—Crouch was openly suspicious of the Romans as foreign and therefore partial witnesses but even so, with a note of caution, he relayed the invaders' impressions of the customs, dress, and religion of the native Britons. He combined this keen attention to detail with respect for the interpretative autonomy of his audience, a strikingly different approach to that taken by Thomas Heywood and, later, John Milton, as we will see.

It was only after this lengthy prologue that Crouch eventually turned to a detailed narrative of Boudica's deeds. In its overall structure, it followed her story's familiar formula, but with a degree of thoroughness absent from Heywood's digest of Bolton. There is some original interpretation in his assertion that Boudica's death occurred in AD 73, more than a decade later than was usually claimed. But amidst all the detail, Crouch made clear that Boudica should be considered a 'Valiant Heroine' and, departing from his customary even-handedness, allowed her an unquestionably heroic death by suicide, without mention of the alternatives; she was, he said, 'another Lucretia'. Lest readers take this too much to heart, however, Crouch elsewhere noted that he was not undertaking 'to justifie self Homicide of which some of my Heroines were guilty, though the exigencies and extremities to which they were reduced, may be some kind of Justification, however I hope none will make that a President [*sic*], since so many worthy things may be observed in

---

[49] R.B., *Female Excellency, or the Ladies Glory, illustrated in the worthy lives and memorable actions of Nine Famous Women, who have been renowned either for Virtue or valour in several Ages of the world* (London, 1683), 128.

their Lives and Actions, both for information and delight'.[50] His concerns here were very different from Thomas Heywood's in *Exemplary Lives*, but they presage some of the moral difficulties encountered by later writers, particularly in the nineteenth century, when called upon to explain Boudica's suicide. This form of heroic demise was not entirely seemly for an audience of female readers, but Crouch was reluctant to deny Boudica her final act of bravery.

Crouch's claim to be bringing the history of the nation to 'the people' must be examined in the context of a long tradition of lamenting the lack of decent and accessible histories of England in particular. Heywood had been concerned about it, but the disparity between the price of a work like Heywood's *Exemplary Lives*, a much more expensive work, and Crouch's *Female Excellency* present an interesting contrast. Indeed, price rarely reflected the thoroughness of the historical narrative on offer. John Milton's *History of Britain*, which offered a broad-brush schematic of history, at least of the ancient past, yet sold at 5s; Crouch's extensive *England's Monarchs* sold at a mere sixpence.[51] Robert Mayer has stated that 'Crouch's histories argue powerfully for the productive, indeed the empowering, role of the oft-decried hack writer who puts elements of high culture into the hands of a new audience.'[52] There is no doubt that Crouch's histories, by virtue of their affordability, did enable a new audience to learn about their past, but Mayer's assertion that Crouch was a sort of Prometheus figure, stealing the flame of history from a body of elites intent on keeping it to themselves, requires some amending. If anything, Crouch improved on the less detailed historical picture presented by writers like Heywood. Indeed, there is no doubt that there was a greater degree of corner-cutting in *Exemplary Lives* than in *Female Excellency*. The former, for all its pretensions to mimicking Bodin, was little better than plagiary in which the original elements of Edmund Bolton's account, such as his conjectures on Stonehenge, were conveniently passed off as Heywood's but never subject to explanation or examination. By contrast, *Female Excellency* gave the reader a full disclosure of Britain's confused past, from Geoffrey of Monmouth's Brutus to the Roman invasion, all told in the author's own words and with minimal speculation, leaving the audience to assess the record with minimal intervention.

The question then is the rather vulgar one of value for money. Crouch's learned works reveal Heywood's prose writings as little better than vanity projects, intended to flatter the erudition of the author and impress literate women on moderate-to-high incomes. As works of history Heywood's *Exemplary Lives*, and even the *Gynaikeion*, although weighty with educative anecdotes, were largely fanciful; they can hardly be said to represent a 'high' culture of the past, impenetrable to the uneducated majority. We have seen that even men with a university education were denied access to 'modern' history, while antiquaries, occupied as they were the

---

[50] R.B., *Female Excellency*, Preface, n.p.
[51] See E. Arber (ed.), *The term Catalogues, 1668–1709* (London, 1903), Vol. I, 277.
[52] R. Mayer, 'Nathaniel Crouch, bookseller and historian: popular historiography and cultural power in late seventeenth-century England', *Eighteenth-Century Studies*, 27 (1994), 391–419. P. Hicks, *Neoclassical history and English culture: from Clarendon to Hume* (Basingstoke, 1996), 215 also refers to these 'hack' writers—perhaps ungenerously.

physical remains of particular locales and periods, were contributing to a learned but fragmented sense of the nation's past. Nathaniel Crouch's histories then were a necessary corrective or via media between patchwork antiquarianism and largely plagiarized histories of Heywood. In fact, by distilling the historical narrative of Britain for a wide audience, Crouch's works were forerunners to later narrative histories which were to draw on the substantive content of the sixteenth-century chronicles, repackaged in more pleasing language, with an admixture of authorial reflection and original argument. This suggests that the story of the nation's past was still in the process of being cemented in its general outline during the middle of the seventeenth century, and that genres of both imaginative and 'serious' history were contributing to that process.

BOUDICA RETURNS TO THE STAGE, 1696–7

As one of its first excursions into documented history, Boudica would come to represent the country's earliest antiquity in dozens of 'panoramic histories', a genre we will return to later in this chapter. Before turning to the most popular historical genre of the late seventeenth and eighteenth centuries, we will focus first on the two late seventeenth-century stage plays that were produced about Boudica in 1696 and 1697. In doing so, I wish to explore some of the overlooked links that existed between the early popular histories by Heywood and Crouch, the stage plays, and later the 'panoramic histories'. Although the porous nature of generic boundaries in this period has been acknowledged previously, there were clear and coherent connections between genres that were, by this relatively late stage, developing in divergent directions. Boudica's appearance in a drama, prose, and poetry speaks to the contrasts and commonalities between different forms of literary production, particularly historical drama and prose histories—both of which, for all they were distinct in their approach, method, and presentation, not to mention the differing expectations of their audiences, were nevertheless bound together by their shared historical subject matter and hence an investment in some understanding of 'history'.

I have sought to show how, in their respective and more or less subtle ways, Heywood and Crouch engaged readers in a degree of debate about what the activity of reading and writing history entailed. In Heywood's case, he gestured at educating his (in all probability female) readers in Jean Bodin's methods of history, perhaps as a means of legitimating what might, to some critics, appear to have been an exercise in valueless entertainment. In Crouch's case, the appeal of his histories was in exposing his readers to recherché philological and antiquarian debates, an approach that, advertently or not, encouraged them to make their own judgements on substantive matters of historical debate. However, in historical narratives written later in the century, we begin to see a shift away from this kind of educative aim, whether overt or covert, to a new form of emotive story-telling. This, I wish to suggest, is due to the influence of drama on historical writing—an influence that can be traced by looking first at the two new dramatic retellings of Boudica's deeds and then comparing some specific points raised in them to accounts in some later prose histories, extending into the early eighteenth century.

The first new play about Boudica was staged in 1696. It was a reworking of Fletcher's *Bonduca*, which had not been staged in its original form for decades. The second, performed in 1697, was a wholly original composition and by far the better of the two. But they shared a common and at this stage entirely novel focus on Boudica's daughters, portraying them as brutalized innocents caught up in the bloodshed of war-torn antiquity. By contrast, in John Fletcher's *Bonduca*, Boudica's two daughters acted as a single and at times absurd unit, nameless and devoid of pathos; they were unlikely to have provoked feelings of sympathy, at least, until the very end of the play when they take their own lives. However, in stage dramas produced after the Restoration, the historical Boudica played a much less central role than her children. The dramatic action of these plays largely centred on the relationships between her daughters and the men around them, while the queen herself was transformed into a presiding presence.

Arguably, this shift of focus away from Boudica's war to the young people whose lives went on in spite of it was a natural outgrowth of her heroization in the works of Heywood and Crouch. Although more restrictively bound to the historical record than Fletcher had been, Heywood and Crouch had nevertheless interpreted the material available to them in such a way as to valorize Boudica for her resistance, while downplaying the savagery of her vengeance. By raising Boudica to a pantheon of worthy women, popular historical treatments nourished an idea of her as a tragic figure whose cause was just, and who, rather than orchestrating a brutal campaign, was caught up in destructive events beyond her control. Equally, the portrayal of her daughters as articulate, proud, ultimately doomed young women was an extension of the sympathy elicited by their mother. Increasingly, they were cast as having been carried along by the same tide that would eventually overwhelm the unfortunate Britons.

The first Boudica stage play of the Restoration period was the work of George Powell (1668–1714), an actor and playwright as well known in his day for his drinking, womanizing, and pugnacity as he was for his thespian accomplishments.[53] Powell adapted John Fletcher's original work for the Theatre Royal Drury Lane's 1695–6 theatrical season, giving it the new title of *Bonduca, or the British Heroine*. In the published text, Powell claimed that 'the whole Play was revised quite through, and likewise studied up in one Fortnight', in order compete with the rival theatre company at Lincoln's Inn Fields.[54] This treatment did not reflect a lack of respect or enthusiasm for the subject matter of the current version, or for its spiritual co-author, John Fletcher. Like many of his literary contemporaries, and the theatre manager George Colman nearly one hundred years later, Powell voiced

---

[53] P.R. Backscheider, 'Powell, George (1668?–1714)', *ODNB* (2004), http://www.oxforddnb.com/view/article/22647, accessed 8 Aug 2017.

[54] G. Powell, *Bonduca, the British heroine, a tragedy, etc., Altered from the play generally attributed to Beaumont and Fletcher, but more probably by Fletcher alone* (London, 1696), preface. See also A.C. Sprague, *Beaumont and Fletcher on the Restoration Stage* (Cambridge, MA, 1926), 100–1.

disbelief that Fletcher's works had faded into relative obscurity, even after the publication of his and Beaumont's collected works in 1647:

> The Value of the Original [Bonduca] is not unknown to those who have read it in Fletcher: A Value that has often times been prized so high, that the whole Brotherhood of the Quill have for many Years been blamed for letting so Ingenious a Relick of the Last Age, as Bonduca, lie dormant, when so inconsiderable an Additional Touch of the Pen was wanting, to make it for an Honourable Reception in This.[55]

Powell's allusion to reading rather than viewing the play demonstrates how important this medium was for keeping alive dramatic works during the oppressive censorship of the previous decades, as well as the extent to which Boudica might have been encountered as an individual character through private reading rather than public performance. Given the age of the original, Powell also acknowledged the need to rework some of Fletcher's details in order to appeal to changed tastes. However, his published play shows tell-tale signs of haste: a character integral to the story, Comus, is misnamed in the *Personae Dramatis* as Macquaire, and variously spelled as 'Comes' and 'Comus' in the text. Occasionally a character's entrance is noted without that character uttering a line or taking part in the action. Such confusion was unlikely to have been evident in the performed play, but the published text has a distinctly slap-dash flavour.

As for the content, the broad constellation of characters and their relation to one another remained intact from Fletcher to Powell: Bonduca and her daughters are in favour of war, while Caratach, once again accompanied by Hengo, is more cautious, though willing to fight and die with honour. It is worth noting that Powell cast himself in the role of Caratach, which goes some way to explaining the focus on the male lead over the titular character. However, in Powell's reworking, the action centres not on a disagreement between Caratach and Bonduca on how to conduct the war, but instead on Bonduca's daughters, whom Powell portrayed as young noblewomen, granting them, for the first time, their own individual names: Claudia and Bonvica. Bonvica only rarely appears on stage and has relatively few lines. Claudia's role is much more complex, and provides the catalyst for much of the play's action: she has a lover in Venutius, a British prince, and has spurned the attentions of the traitorous Pictish interloper, Comus.

The most striking change from Fletcher is as a consequence of Powell's focus on the young Claudia, namely the very different tone with which her rape is treated. While all historical sources, and Fletcher's play, had implied that both daughters were victims of sexual violence, Powell portrayed the heroine, Claudia, as the sole victim sexual violence, not at the hand of a Roman, but the Pict, Comus. Although Comus openly threatens to carry out the act, the scene is interrupted by the arrival of Venutius, who rescues Claudia and kills Comus, before dying of his own wounds. In reorienting the action in this way, Powell, alighted on what was to become the most emotive aspect of Boudica's story in later depictions: the suffering of her children.

[55] Powell, *Bonduca*, preface.

However, this resulted in problems. In particular, Boudica's greatest dramatic moment, her suicide, was rendered inexplicable within the dramatic conceit constructed by the author. Although her suicide reflected the historical record, Powell's Bonduca was by no means a fully fleshed-out character in his play. She was no longer the shrill fury drawn by Fletcher, but a more aloof queen whose primary role was to attend at a Druidic ceremony and, eventually, to preside over the deaths of her daughters before killing herself. It was in many ways a more dignified role than Fletcher's had been, but it meant the Bonduca character was not a pivotal one, and Powell made no effort to explore the anger or despair that might have ultimately led to her suicide. As a consequence, her death, and the moving speech lifted from Fletcher, sits uncomfortably in Powell's play. This lack of attention to the titular queen could suggest that Powell was relying on the audience to be familiar with the historical narrative on which his drama was based. Arguably, John Fletcher had greater latitude to imagine a frantic female leader than Powell, who was writing after the publication of works by Bolton, Heywood, Crouch, and many other historical writers of varying accessibility. As her story was becoming more widely known, the plight of Boudica's daughters held greater interest, and freer dramatic licence, than the formulaic story told and retold by popular authors.

Interestingly, Powell's *Bonduca* was to remain in performance well into the eighteenth century, surpassing Fletcher's original in popularity. It was revived at Drury Lane in August 1715, and again in the summer of 1716, 'At the particular Desire of several Persons of Quality who are going out of England.'[56] It returned to the stage at Drury Lane in the summer of 1718, and to the Haymarket in 1723, as a benefit night performance for one of the theatre's actresses.[57] The final performance for Powell's play on record was in 1731.[58] In addition to its staged performances, Powell's work was printed and for sale in quarto editions across London. Advertisements for the play as a purchasable work appeared in a variety of newspapers, including the *Daily Courant*, a favoured organ for theatrical advertising, as well as the *Daily Advertiser*, the *Daily Journal*, and numerous other London dailies, advertised for between four and six pence. Even more enduring than the play was the music, written by Henry Purcell, which might account for the play's longevity.[59]

One year after Powell's play opened at Drury Lane, and in all likelihood as a reaction to its popularity, a second Boudica play in as many years made its way to the stage. It was for the rival theatre company at Lincoln's Inn Fields, which was by this time controlled by the actors Mrs Barry, Mrs Bracegirdle, and Mr Betterton, all of whom appeared in *Boadicea, Queen of Britain, a tragedy*, an entirely original play by Charles Hopkins (*c*.1671–1700). With Mrs Barry as the eponymous queen

---

[56] E.L. Avery (ed.), *TLS 1660–1800*, Part II (1700–29), 407.
[57] *Daily Courant*, 24 July 1718; Avery, *TLS 1660–1800*, Part II, Vol. II, 707.
[58] *Daily Post*, 8 June 1731.
[59] C.A. Price, *Henry Purcell and the London stage* (Cambridge, 1984), 117. The song's significance from the seventeenth century up to the First World War is the subject of M. Vandrei, '"Britons, strike home": politics, patriotism, and popular song in British culture, c. 1696–1900', *Historical Research* (2014), 679–702.

and the much-admired Mrs Bracegirdle as one of her daughters, called Camilla, the play was likely to have been well attended on opening, though recent scholars have speculated that the essentially pacifist message of its Irish-born author subsequently doomed it to oblivion.[60]

Firmly a writer of historical romance, Hopkins succeeded in transforming the war between the Romans and the Britons from a political affair to a purely personal one, while painting more vivid portraits of Boudica and her daughters than Powell had done. Hopkins focused his dramatic action on the relationship between Boudica's daughters, whom he called Camilla and Venutia, and two Roman soldiers, Decius and Paulinus; the latter was the only character of the younger generation to be based on a named historical figure, Suetonius Paulinus. Venutia harbours a secret love for Paulinus, while Camilla is betrothed to the British Prince, Cassibelan, who is the main male character on the British side.[61] He and Camilla are wholly unaware that the scheming Decius has been captivated by her beauty. The play revolves around this set of lovers rather than the actions of the rival commanders in battle. By depicting the personal side of the conflict, the author was able to examine the relationship between men and women, as well as conqueror and conquered. In Hopkins's version of events, the play begins as the Britons and the Romans are about to broker a peaceful settlement on the grounds of mutual respect and fairness. It is only when Decius, glimpsing Camilla, conspires with his evil aide, Caska, to prolong the war that matters begin to take a more familiar turn. Hopkins's empathetic portrayal of Camilla as at once a valiant, articulate woman and a pathetic victim of Roman aggression places his play alongside Thomas Heywood's dramatic oeuvre as an implicit defence of women against accusations of duplicity. Caska, the conniving attendant to the Roman generals, voices disgust for the female sex throughout the play, yet it is his false counsel that leads to much of the protagonists' misfortune. Caska hopes to prove woman's naturally fickle character, but he succeeds only in bringing ruin on Briton and Roman alike.

By far the most intense dialogue takes place between Decius and Camilla, revolving around the violent sexual intentions of the former. During the course of the war, Decius abducts Camilla and the ensuing exchange is overshadowed by the constant and explicit threat of rape. Decius makes clear that he would prefer if Camilla freely accepted his love, but that her failure to do so would not present an obstacle to his desire. For her part, Camilla's feelings for Decius are made very clear: 'I loath your Person, and your Love disdain'. Fed by the poisonous misogyny voiced by Caska, Camilla's protests serve only to convince Decius that she secretly desires him. Camilla is reduced to offering him her share of the British kingdom if only he will let her keep her honour. And, her fate almost sealed, she implores the gods to turn her into something foul, something Decius will despise. Finally, as she

---

[60] Nielsen, 'Boadicea onstage', 602.
[61] A prince by that name, who ruled over the Trinobantes, is thought to have lived some decades before Boudica's rebellion. Hopkins used the name without any of the biographical detail provided by e.g. John Speed, *The history of Great Britaine* (London, 1611), 186–7.

is being carried off the stage by soldiers, she falls into a swoon. Decius, in an aside to the by now presumably horrified audience:

> Away, she shall not long entrans'd remain,
> I'll quickly bring her back to Life again.
> My Soul is straining to the full delight,
> Gods! let me have this one, this charming Night,
> Put but my Pleasures out of Fortune's power,
> Then come whatever can, I've had my Hour.[62]

When we next meet Camilla, she is broken and disgusted with herself, her attacker, and a world in which so awful a crime can go unpunished by divine wrath. Decius, however, is unrepentant, and is instead convinced that he has won Camilla's affections by his use of force. Camilla resolves to starve herself, the only recourse left to a violated woman in a world of insensate men and cruel gods, and she leaves the scene. Immediately, Caska emerges to sneer that 'Women only wish and wait for Force.'[63]

Hopkins's play was not one of subtle morality: it is clear who is evil and who not. Paulinus is presented as Decius' opposite, refusing to accept Venutia as his bride if, in doing so, she must embrace the role of prisoner. Shortly before the end of the play, Boadicea confronts the noble general Paulinus with the truth about his favourite, Decius. Paulinus expresses shame and disgust on behalf of the Roman people and begs to be forgiven and to be allowed to prove his commitment to peaceful settlement, but Boadicea refuses his overtures and the war carries on. Cassibelan, loyal to his lover Camilla, kills Decius before succumbing to his own wounds. Decius' brutality has driven Camilla to madness and she takes her own life alongside her mother. Venutia, for her part, loves Paulinus willingly—the two are united at the end of the play, as all the rest have died or fled.

These new plays by Powell and Hopkins show a marked turn towards a novel perspective on Boudica's two children. While John Fletcher had made them nameless young savages who incited little sympathy, and whose plight was cast as almost comical, George Powell directly intervened in the original story by Fletcher, recasting the daughters as pathetic characters with strong moral views on their situation. Powell also intervened in the historical narrative, focusing on a single daughter as the victim of rape, or the threat of it. This was a dramatic interpolation that was repeated in Hopkins's play, and which allowed for a deeper exploration of the emotional and physical consequences of such torment. This new focus on the dire circumstances of Boudica's daughters meant that their mother was a somewhat less central figure in the drama, but it also heightened her psychological turmoil. Her vengeance was made to seem all the more justified, placing further pressure on competing duties to family and country.

Both plays were moving versions of Boudica's story, and in the next section, I wish to suggest that this emphasis on the emotional side of Boudica's rebellion was also becoming evident in the new narrative prose histories of the late seventeenth century.

---

[62] Hopkins, *Boadicea*, 23.   [63] Ibid., 26.

The last section of this chapter will examine more closely Boudica's part in the much longer narrative history of Britain's past, which to some degree mirrored the presentation of the stage dramas, and, occasionally, seemed even to draw on them as source material. This borrowing is significant in the long story of the interaction between historical fact and historical fiction—not only did dramas borrow from history, the histories found inspiration in drama, the most popular and enduring form of historical culture. Even as part of a much longer narrative of British history told over many hundreds of pages, Boudica's story retained its pathos, and, arguably, that pathos was intensified within the confines of the *longue-durée* of a historical genre I call 'panoramic histories'.

THE PANORAMA OF THE PAST

Continuing the trend exemplified by Nathaniel Crouch, a rapidly expanding number of histories of England and of Great Britain were being published in the period after 1650. Varyingly referred to as histories of England or Britain, there were also Scottish and Welsh examples of the panoramic history genre.[64] In some ways, panoramic histories were descendants of the chronicle, a genre of which even the most valued example, Holinshed's *Chronicles*, was 'much neglected, and almost laid aside' and thought of as 'very tedious and voluminous' by the first decade of the eighteenth century.[65] Panoramic histories filled the gap in the market left by the demise of the cumbersome volumes.

Like chronicles, panoramic histories took in the broad chronological sweep of the entirety of the past and were organized in a similarly linear fashion. The key difference between panoramic histories and chronicles was that the former placed greater emphasis on narrative inventiveness, authorial reflection, and emotional appeal. The emotionality of panoramic histories could take many forms, depending on the style of the author. But the emotive interpretation of history had significant implications for Boudica's individual story within the broad narrative of the British past. With only a few pages to fire the imaginations of their readers with the story of the tragic queen, authors of panoramic histories often reached for strong imagery, sentimentality or pathos, and even rancour. Yet the utility of panoramic histories for Boudica was that they demanded that her story be retold; if any author hoped to shy away from the warrior woman of Britain's antiquity, they were forced to explain themselves in ways that might not be entirely convincing.

This was John Milton's problem when he began to write his *History of Britain* in the 1640s; it remained unpublished until 1670. Milton was profoundly disgusted by the very notion of female rule, and yet there Boudica, inconveniently placed at

---

[64] Scottish historians such as Hector Boece and George Buchanan wrote antiquarian works about Scotland in the sixteenth and seventeenth centuries, and the trend continued, though some might argue that the great Scottish contribution to panoramic histories came later. The first Welsh-language history of Wales was T. Evans *Drych y prif oesoedd* (*The mirror of past ages*) (Shrewsbury, 1716); see Chapter 6.

[65] L. Echard, *History of England* (London, 1707), Preface.

the beginning of history by the venerated author Tacitus: she simply had to be dealt with. Thus in the early chapters of his history, Milton took the opportunity to traduce Boudica as the deranged leader of an uncivil band of thugs; he decried her conduct and even her words, derisively noting the frankness with which she publicly told of her own and her daughters' ordeal at the hands of the Roman invaders.[66] No writer before or since has told Boudica's story with such venom and, unsurprisingly, it is one of the few late seventeenth-century works about her to attract scholarly comment.[67] But Milton's misogyny, avowed though it was, should also be viewed in the context of the author's frustration with the records, or lack of them, for this early period of history. Milton admitted to including an account of British antiquity for the sole reason that his history would have been incomplete otherwise. He blamed the Roman writers for falsely portraying Britain's distant past, claiming that 'this they do out of vanity, hoping to embellish and set out thir Historie with the strangeness of our manners, not careing in the mean while to brand us with the rankest note of Barbarism, as if in Britain Woemen were Men, and Men Woemen'.[68] Thus, as an episode for which even the minimal extant source base was prejudiced, Boudica's story was rendered questionable, and therefore could be tactically shortened. Milton disbelieved Boudica's speech, especially Dio Cassius' version of it, thinking it too salacious and prurient, and so he left it out.[69] Indeed, Milton's entire account of Boudica has the quality of paralipsis.

John Milton could not hide his distaste and made no attempt to do so, and he could not feel for Boudica or her daughters the sympathy that was evident in the dramatic portrayals by Powell and Hopkins, or in earlier works by Bolton and Heywood. But Milton's overt anger is nevertheless interesting. In fact, his frustration with the source base and his disgust at Boudica amounted to no less than Milton's own original interpretation of British antiquity—one which, as we have seen, fell well short of that offered by Nathaniel Crouch. In a sense, his method was dictated by his emotions, not by any abstract sense of fidelity to the record or to a set of criteria for historical writing similar to that nominally upheld by Heywood.[70] Milton's distaste for the Boudica story added a layer of emotionality to the prose account found in his *History* that was more dramatic than it was rational and reflective. Similarly emotive, but more reverent in its view of Boudica, was Aylett Sammes's *Britannia Antiqua Illustrata* (1676). This was an expansively detailed illustrated history of British antiquity—I include it amongst the panoramic histories of the late seventeenth century because Sammes's work ran to a length comparable to the more chronologically wide-ranging histories and provided an unusually extensive survey of Britain's antiquity, real and imagined. In the relevant

---

[66] *Complete prose Works of John Milton*, 8 vols, ed. D.M. Wolfe et al. (London, 1953–82), Vol. 5.
[67] Maley, 'That Fatal Boadicea', 305–30.
[68] *Complete Prose Works of John Milton*, Vol. 5, 70.
[69] Patterson, *Reading Holinshed's Chronicles*, 220.
[70] For an interesting discussion of Milton's sense of history as 'the theatre of God's judgment', see D. Lowenstein, *Milton and the drama of history: historical vision, iconoclasm, and the literary imagination* (Cambridge, 1990), 25–8. Lowenstein also notes that the *History* reflects Milton's own contradictory views of historiography as both 'mythopoetic' and truthful, pp. 81–8.

section, Sammes included the usual prose narrative of Boudica's rebellion, but he coupled this with a laudatory verse and large, detailed, and original illustration. Boudica is depicted in a full-length portrait, showing her face, hair, dress, and demeanour; she is armed with a spear. There is little evidence that Sammes was influenced by the earlier descriptions by Heywood or of Bolton, or by Glover's illustration. Instead, in keeping with Sammes's avowed antiquarianism, he followed Dio's description to the letter.

The most interesting aspect of Sammes's Boudica story is to be found in the verse which accompanied the image:

> To war, this Queen doth with her Daughters move.
> She for her wisdom, followed They for Love,
> For what Roman force, Such joined powers could quell;
> Before so murdering Charmes whole Legions fell.
> Thrice happy Princesses had she rescued so,
> Her Daughters honour, and her Countrys too;
> But they being ravish't, made her understand
> This harder Beauty to secure, then Land.
> Yet her Example teaching them to dye.
> Virtue the roome of Honour did supply.

Here, Boudica's relationship with her daughters was the driving force behind her anger and her decision to pursue a war with the Romans. Far from dismissing this as poor governance on the part of the queen, Sammes's view of Boudica and her plight appears to have been that was she was drawn towards revenge by the cruel suffering endured by her children, who followed her unto death because of their own filial devotion. As in the imaginations of playwrights, Boudica's family becomes the centre of the conflict. Boudica's maternal need to protect her children is thwarted by the avarice of the Romans, who claim both their physical possessions and ancestral lands, but also their bodies. Wisdom, love, innocence, honour—all of these were the charms of Boudica's family. Sammes's ironic notion of these virtues as 'murdering' may be read as patronizing, but, more likely, as subverting the negative view of Boudica held by John Milton by suggesting that the victims were guilty of nothing beyond their own defenceless. Thus Sammes blended the emerging romantic view of Boudica as protective mother with a new sense that her daughters were abused innocents, identities which would become more common in the dramatic portrayals. Authors like Sammes, who was clearly moved by Boudica's plight, were inclined to labour at their works at least in part as creative endeavours, rather than settle for hastily stitching together existing accounts or drily narrating the facts.

Probably the most striking instance of Boudica's deeds being portrayed in a sentimental way in a panoramic history can be found in John Seller's *History of England* (first edition 1696). Seller was Hydrographer to the King, and later to Queen Anne, and his works are equally remarkable for their original maps. Moreover, Seller's history was published at around the same time that new stage plays about Boudica were being performed, and the language used to describe this most dramatic of episodes in early British history once again reflects a shift away from the 'dry as dust' chronicle and the simple repetition of Tacitus and Dio, and toward a more theatrical emotional vigour. As the playwrights Hopkins and Powell had done, Seller cast his narrative emphasis away from Boudica alone, placing much sharper focus on the suffering of her daughters following the death of their father, whose good intentions were thwarted by the rapine of the Romans:

> But the Young Ladies (being very Beautiful) contrary to the Trust reposed, were Ravished by a Roman Tribune, after he had labour'd in vain to tempt their Chastity with Gifts and Flatteries. The Queen (upon knowledge of this great Injury done to her Children) exceedingly Grieved; and perceiving she was like to have no Redress, though she had complain'd of the Injury and Violation of Trust: Mov'd by her Daughters Tears and her own Courage, she resolved to Revenge the Treachery. Whereupon, calling together the chief of her People, and some of the Neighbouring Princes, she presented the Young Ladies before them, with dishelved Hair, Raining a Shower of Tears from their Sorrow-clouded Eyes...[71]

The gifts and flatteries which Seller claimed had been showered upon the daughters by the lustful invaders were not recorded in any previous history, and the attribution of action on the part of the daughters, who moved their mother and her chiefs to revenge with their tears; they could not, it is implied, but be moved by such a pathetic sight. This is a far cry from John Milton's contention that to have made such a public declaration about sexual crimes was the mark of barbarism. For Seller, these were the actions of innocent women with no other recourse but to beg their kin for redress.

Similarly, the battle between the Britons and the Romans occasioned a breathless account by Seller:

> ...so secretly was the business [of gathering the Britons for battle] managed, that the Britains Assembling by small Troops in Woods, all on a suddain, at the time prefixed, joined their Forces and fell upon the Enemy, little suspecting it, with such fury, that before they could gather their scattered Forces, Forty Thousand were Slain, and Suetonius compelled to immure himself in Troynovant or London, and send speedily for succours; so that most of the Midland Countries were recovered, and the Roman Fortresses, built to bridle the Britains with Garrisons, Demolished: But the Carcasses lying un-bury'd corrupted the Air, and brought on a Plague which made great desolation. Yet the Queen pursuing this good success, in divers skirmishes destroyed 40000 more; however, at last being betrayed for a sum of Gold, she Poisoned her self to prefer her Captivity, or being carried to Rome to grace the Victors Triumph.[72]

Here Seller was reluctant to paint the Britons in anything less than a sympathetic light, judging perhaps that the audience's natural sympathies had been stirred by the portrayal of Boudica and her daughters as defenceless innocents. He relates the Britons' early successes, reminding the reader midway through the passage that the garrisons had been built by the Romans to 'bridle' the oppressed natives. Furthermore, Seller repeated the number of dead claimed by Tacitus—80,000—however, he

[71] J. Seller, *The History of England* (London, 1696), 18–19.   [72] Ibid.

misattributes this number of casualties to the Roman side alone, contrary to Tacitus, who had noted that the Britons lost 80,000 in the final battle, as opposed to the Romans' 400 in the final battle. Seller claimed these casualties for the Britons and further divided the numbers so that an equal number of Romans were killed at two distinct points: first as the Britons won back territory from Suetonius, who was forced to retreat into London, and then in pitched battles, which, Seller implied, ended as British successes.

Nowhere did Seller mention the claim by Dio that Boudica and her Britons had committed atrocities against Roman civilians, a point that had been stressed by Holinshed in his earlier account. Instead the overall impression given by Seller is that the Britons were fighting an organized military campaign and were within reach of victory. Although the reference to a plague—another inclusion of uncertain provenance—seems destined to doom Boudica to death by illness, it is by the intervention of a traitor, who sells Boudica's location to her pursuers that matters are finally brought to their customary conclusion, as derived from Tacitus. Boudica's defeat, having up to this point been consistently attributed to some failure on the part of the Britons—pride or disorganization or a combination—is here said to be due to a betrayal. The source for this remains obscure, though Edmund Bolton, writing much earlier and in a very different climate, had noted that some of his contemporaries believed there had been a conspirator in the ranks of the Britons. But it was not a belief often mentioned, and certainly never given much credence; it might perhaps have derived from the actions of the traitorous Cartismandua against Caractacus. However, Seller might also have included it for purely dramatic purposes, further implying that Boudica and the Britons had been denied the victory she deserved.

By the end of the seventeenth century, Queen Boudica had become a character whose life and qualities were recognized as sui generis and therefore of interest in their own right, and there is little doubt that Seller had been reading the Boudica story in contexts outside the classical sources of Tacitus and Dio. Seller could easily have drawn on the very different works of John Fletcher, Edmund Bolton, Thomas Heywood, or the popular works of Nathaniel Crouch, aside from numerous antiquarian works. His frontispiece, it should be noted, was taken from John Speed's chronicle of 1611, and Speed himself had given an extensive sympathetic account of Boudica's rebellion.[73]

A prime example of this reverential tone coupled with an emotive presentation can also be found in Bevill Higgins's *A Short View of English History* (1723). Higgins's *History* conformed more or less to the narrative formula for panoramic histories, and in most respects it was by no means a groundbreaking work. But Higgins's account of Boudica's rebellion may well have been partially influenced by fictional accounts he encountered elsewhere. Higgins related that:

> ...Boadicea, who by the repeated Victories, she snatch'd from the Conqueror, almost extinguish'd the Roman Name in this Island; till at last by a Reverse of Fortune, being

---

[73] Speed, *History of Great Britain*, 198–200.

> reduc'd to great Extremeity in a Seige, and one of her Daughters ravish'd, she could no longer bear the lost Honour of her House, and Slavery of Country, but by her manly Resolution with her own Hands put an End to her Glorious Life, not more like a Roman than a Briton.[74]

There are a number of discrepancies between Higgins's portrayal and the standard version of Boudica's story; indeed, his depiction takes on an interesting similitude with Charles Hopkins's play. First, the author intimates that Boudica was close to victory, as she had been at the beginning of Hopkins's *Boadicea*. And, as in the play, the denouement comes during a siege, when Boudica and her daughters end their lives. Also, the reference to only one daughter's having been raped—not both, as was the standard account—mirrors the fate of Camilla, who alone was brutalized by the Romans in Hopkins's drama. As we have seen, historical writers had tended to treat Boudica's offspring as a unit because there was no extant detail about them; not even their ages were known. But for dramatists the lives of Boudica's two daughters presented the greatest opportunity for dramatic embellishment, allowing them the latitude to invent two distinct personalities for them, as Charles Hopkins had done, and to thicken their respective plots by subjecting them to very different fates. Bevill Higgins, in a work of history, made invented detail a part of his fact-based account. He suggested that the daughters suffered their misfortunes after the rebellion had begun, and that their fate added to an emotional burden on the ancient queen which led to her suicide, other elements of the story borrowed not from historical or classical sources, but from drama.

Boudica's story continued to be a fruitful area for emotive, dramatic treatment well into the eighteenth century, a period more conventionally associated with these 'novelized' tendencies that I am here connecting to an older generic form, the history play. One such work was William Guthrie's (1708?–1770) *General History* (1744) which, the author hoped, would 'write as much to the heart as to the head'. According to Guthrie, a journalist by trade, one of the aims of all the best history should be 'to describe the great scenes of action, with the characters of its chief performers, in as warm and animating a manner as possible, without deviation from truth'.[75] Thus it is unsurprising that Guthrie gave a large amount of space to Boudica's story, drawing on a language similar to that used by historians at the end of the seventeenth century.

> As to Boadicea, she seems to have cherished life only that she might have the means of a sure and speedy vengeance...Meeting with dispositions in the Britons so answerable to her own, [Boudica] took care to keep their sentiments alive, be representing their injuries with all their aggravating circumstances, till the people were thoroughly convinced of the necessity, nay, the wisdom, of making one struggle for recovering their independency...Having assembled her army, she mounted upon a suggestum, or a throne of turf, with a lance in her hand, to give a more warlike majesty to her person,

---

[74] B. Higgins, *A short view of the English history* (London, 1723), 10.
[75] W. Guthrie, *A general history of England from the invasion of the Romans under Julius Caesar*...(London, 1744), iii.

which was of the largest size; her face beautiful, but the softness of her features, tempered by a sternness and fierceness in her look...[76]

Guthrie's footnote also suggests that Boudica may herself have been raped by the Roman soldiers, a claim not made elsewhere but which he may have extrapolated from Dio Cassius.

Another evocative example of Boudica's emotional appeal in panoramic history can be found in Charles Granville's *A synopsis of the troubles and miseries of England during the space of 1800 years* (1747). After an explanation of Boudica's speech to her assembled troops, Granville continued:

> The Vigour and Vivacity with which this Lady pronounced her Speech, and the warlike Majesty of her Person and Dress, inspired Fire and Fury into the Britons and drew a Shout of Applause from their whole Army. Boadicea then, lifting up her Hands to Heaven, recommended herself and her Army to its Protection; and concluded with reproaching the Romans as govern'd by an infamous Fidler, with all the Follies and Vices, but without any of the Virtues, or even the Spirit of a Woman.[77]

This account presents a curious mix of the words of Tacitus and Dio, but parts of it, such as the applause of the troops, were Granville's invention. The inclusion of the 'Fidler', a reference to Emperor Nero, was a repetition of Guthrie's account, which was itself an embellished version of Dio's.

Thus well into the eighteenth century, even as 'Enlightenment' historians were sharpening their quills, the history market was flooded with histories that appealed to the sentiments of the average reader. Long before novelists, imaginative writers whose livelihoods depended on their ability to appeal to a wide audience exploited Boudica's story, as well as that of British antiquity more generally, for commercial gain. But in doing so they contributed, knowingly or unknowingly, to the growing appeal of English and British history, and to the changing nature of historical culture. By combining dramatic embellishment with historical stories and heroic personalities, writers of prose history were able create entertaining, informative works that simultaneously flooded and fuelled the market for the past. There were writers, among them Thomas Heywood and Nathaniel Crouch, who were spurred on by the demand for history that had been growing since the era of the chronicle and would continue to expand into the eighteenth century. As the translator of Sallust and Bodin, Heywood's interest in and enthusiasm for the past was genuine and in some manner scholarly, but he combined this impulse with an appeal to a large and diverse audience by writing accessible historical works. Similarly, Crouch was a conscious popularizer, but one who improved on the historical works other authors had offered to their readers at a higher price. Thus Crouch and Heywood, writers who are not seen as integral to the development of 'serious' history, belong to a long tradition of historical writing that appealed to the emotions of its audience.

---

[76] Guthrie, *General history of England*, 32–3.

[77] C. Granville, *A synopsis of the troubles and miseries of England during the space of 1800 years* (London, 1747), 13.

The overlaps between history as it was performed on stage and prose historical narrative looms larger in the story of historical culture than has previously been acknowledged. Indeed, one might take the view that the mid-seventeenth-century presentation of Boudica, particularly in Heywood's work, was a substitute for the dramatic performance of historical episodes that had been banned from the stage. Small changes in the ways authors interacted with readers point to forms of engagement analogous to that which had, before their closure, been unique to the physical space of the theatre. For instance, authors, by directly addressing their reading audience in prefaces, a practice of which Thomas Heywood was an early adopter, reinforced the idea of the author as performer, the reader as audience.[78] This suggests there was a reciprocal relationship between dramatic performance and history writing during the seventeenth century that lasted into the Restoration and beyond. Histories written in the early decades of the eighteenth century infused Boudica's story pathetic appeal, further suggesting that the effect of the closure of the playhouses on wider historical culture was real and long lasting. However, Boudica's example alone can only be suggestive of this relationship, lengthy and complex as it is, and much remains to be done in the field.

What is certain is that there was an enduring and inherent drama to Boudica's life, meaning she was never to be far from the stage, whether in original productions or revivals of older ones. This was true even in the politically charged culture of the eighteenth century, when history became a lens through which to expose the follies of the present. In the next chapter, we will also see how present-day politics shaped the prose narratives of antiquity which Boudica inhabited. Yet even in the shadow of party politics, the dialogue between history and drama remained an important backdrop to discussions of what it meant to write 'true' history. The politicized present never entirely overshadowed the appeal to evidence and the binding ties of authenticity that defined historical culture as 'history'.

---

[78] C.S. Clegg, 'Renaissance play-readers, ordinary and extraordinary', in M. Straznicky (ed.), *The book of the play: playwrights, stationers, and readers in early modern England* (Boston, MA, 2006), pp. 23–38.

3

'Poetry and fiction intermixt with our history'
Druids, Patriots, and Critics in the Eighteenth Century

> *There were of old, and still are, Indolent Readers, who turn to an Author with the design rather of killing than improving their time;.... With such Readers, every step an Historian takes towards determining the weight of evidence, or the degrees of credibility, is an excursion into the regions of dulness; but while the Writer proceeds in his narrative, without reflection, they continue to read without reflecting: and his history enlightens them just as much as a romance would have done: for they are equally unconcerned about truth in either.*[1]

The eighteenth century was arguably the golden age of the prose historical narrative. The century of David Hume, Edward Gibbon, and William Robertson[2]—that is, of 'enlightened' history writing—must be and has been viewed as a time of huge significance in the evolution of modern historiographical practice, and thus we should not be surprised that this period has garnered such extensive attention from historians of history. This was the period in which 'rationalism, empiricism, scepticism and progress' were brought to bear on British historical writing.[3] But beyond the evolution of historiography, this was a period of unprecedented growth in the number of histories in print, a trend that began in the latter half of the seventeenth century and continued apace. Devoney Looser has estimated the number of books on British history published in the eighteenth century to have been about 10,000.[4] To this number must be added the topographical works that included long sections on historic events, the number of which is difficult to judge, and also to the growing prevalence of local and urban histories covering lengthy periods in smaller areas, such as William Maitland's *History of London* (1739) and Philip Morant's *History and Antiquities of the Town and Borough of Colchester* (1748), the number of which is equally difficult to estimate.[5]

---

[1] Anon. review of Tobias Smollett's *History of England*, *Monthly Review*, June 1757, XVI, 530–6, at 531.
[2] Hay called these three writers the 'triumvirate' of British historians; see D. Hay, *Annalists and historians: western historiography from the eighth to the eighteenth centuries* (London 1977), 175.
[3] E. Jenkins (ed.), 'Introduction: Eighteenth-century British historians', *Dictionary of Literary Biography*, vol. 336 (London, 2007).
[4] D. Looser, *British women writers and the writing of history, 1670–1820* (London, 2000), 10. Looser's method is not clear, but this probably includes any books that encompassed discussions of any period, no matter how long or short, of Britain's past.
[5] See R. Sweet, *The writing of urban histories in eighteenth-century England* (Oxford, 1997).

In part this explosion in the sheer volume of histories available for readers to peruse was due to the increased prominence of political debate as a facet of historical discourse—or indeed, of historical discourse as a facet of political debate. The struggle that followed the Glorious Revolution of 1688, between Hanover-supporting Whigs (who later split along anti-Walpolean and pro-Walpolean fissures) and nominally Roman Catholic, Stuart-supporting Tories and Jacobites, had the effect of politicizing history writing to a degree not seen in earlier periods.[6] J.G.A Pocock has argued that the history of England—if not of all of Britain—was written to reflect the politically charged literary culture of the eighteenth century.[7] However, this was not a straightforward binary opposition. The extent to which the labels 'Whig' and 'Tory' could be used is open to debate, and often shifted through the course of the century.[8] But it is certain that the origins of the constitution and the balance of its essential constituent parts were the subject of intense disagreement, and each side of the debate could find supporting evidence for their side's case in historical precedent. This led to a surge in the number of prose histories about the development of English—and by extension British—politics.[9] The consequence of this pressing of history into partisan service, particularly in the era of Walpole, as Christine Gerrard notes, was to bring about a new level of historical awareness in public culture.[10]

Yet even as contemporary tensions came to dominate discussions of the past, this by no means detracted from a sense among historical writers that there were interpretative limits to historical discourse. Thus I argue that one unexpected consequence of this heavily politicized, occasionally emotive history writing was an emphasis on and attentiveness to the importance of strictures on interpretation. As political opinions became the stuff of historical argument (and vice versa) and dramatized language became suspect, individual approaches to the style and method of history became open to challenge, and were used as a means of undermining both the political subtexts of a work and the historical rigour of the author. More often than not, an appeal to the ideal of historical practice was cynical at best; and yet there undoubtedly were ideals of historical practice, and they, like narratives of the past, were continually negotiated in the historical writing of the period. Although history remained an agreeably flexible medium, this flexibility was by no means without limits.

In particular the sense that the past was a repository of examples for the present, there to draw upon as analogies, which had been part of conventional historical discourse for centuries, sat less comfortably as historians increasingly expressed

---

[6] R.C. Richardson, *The debate on the English revolution* (Manchester, 1998 [first edition 1977]), Ch. 2.

[7] J.G.A. Pocock, *Barbarism and religion*, 6 vols (Cambridge, 1999–2015), Vol. II, 167. For a thorough discussion of the political persuasions of individual historians, see L. Okie, *Augustan historical writing: histories of England in the English Enlightenment* (Lanham, MD, 1991).

[8] R. Fabel, 'The patriotic Briton: Tobias Smollett and English politics, 1756–1771', *Eighteenth-century studies*, 8(1) (1974), 100–14 gives an overview.

[9] Fussner, *The historical revolution*, 106–10.

[10] C. Gerrard, *The patriot opposition to Walpole: politics, poetry, and national myth, 1725–1742* (Oxford, 1994), 101–2.

detachment from the present as a means of lending a sense of objectivity and thus legitimacy to their arguments. This amounted to a more rigorous policing of the perceived boundary between past and present. Mark Salber Phillips has described the emphasis eighteenth-century historians, both 'Enlightenment' and 'romantic', placed on a sense of 'distance' as strategy for understanding the past with greater clarity and for narrating it with greater (or lesser) affect.[11] Indeed, as Phillips also points out, that 'distance' from the past could afford greater objectivity is and has been taken as a historiographical axiom. However, the historian's detachment from his or her own present was equally significant for eighteenth-century historical writers as a sense of historical distance. As some saw it, the historian, rather than living in the present, must immerse himself in the world of the past, be deaf to the clamour of his contemporaries, and remain unswayed by the temptation to allow his understanding of the past to be infected by his or her assessment of society's present circumstances. The distance between past and present was thus mirrored by the historian's own idealized position as above and beyond time. However, this ideal was more often sought in the work of others than practised in one's own writing. Historians who claimed a sense of distance were, as we will see, often the least objective in their assessments of the past—and their contemporaries were quick to point this out. Yet these acknowledged historical standards meant that political disagreement could and did become a form of historical argument.

What, then of Boudica? In such a heady atmosphere of political tension and intense historical disagreement, Boudica's individuality was bound to be somewhat occluded, as more focused works about 'worthy' men and women were eclipsed by panoramic narratives, in which constitutional issues were embedded and negotiated. Moreover, there is a less robust historiography around uses of the past in eighteenth-century historical culture: less serious works of prose history or historical drama have been eclipsed in modern scholarship by the canon of Enlightenment historians. The eighteenth century is a similarly unchartered area for Boudica. Only three studies of the warrior queen go so far as to mention eighteenth-century depictions, and there has been little sustained interrogation of Boudica's significance in the political and cultural contexts of the period.[12] Sharon MacDonald contends that popular interest in Boudica was 'sporadic' because she was a more apt symbol at times of war; when her utility waned, she simply faded from view. But Boudica was by no means silent in the period. As one of the first named figures in British history, and with a good classical pedigree, she found her way into the opening chapter of dozens, more likely hundreds, of panoramic historical narratives.

---

[11] Mark Salber Phillips has written with great eloquence and subtlety on the subject; see Phillips, *Society and sentiment*, as well as M.S. Phillips, 'Rethinking historical distance: from doctrine to heuristic', *History and theory*, 50 (2011), 11–23, and M.S. Phillips, *On historical distance* (New Haven, CT, 2013).

[12] For the most recent detailed treatment, focused on Boudica's femininity, see C.D. Williams, '"On Boadicea think!": In search of a female army', in C.D. Williams, A. Escott, and L. Duckling (eds), *Woman to woman: female negotiations in the long eighteenth century* (Newark, DE, 2010), pp. 204–24.

Yet, in the context of panoramic histories, the ancient queen Boudica—indeed, any individual figure from the period—was liable to be overshadowed by discussions of constitutional concerns, especially the origins of power balances in the distant past, a matter of intense debate, especially after 1688.[13] Thus, in narratives of the ancient past, although Boudica was almost always mentioned by name, the degree of detail that accompanied her story varied. Her importance could also occasionally be asserted without the need for a lengthy textual treatment: she was the subject of a number of new illustrations in the period, for example. But, for the most part, rather than take top billing, she was often portrayed as part of a panorama of the ancient past, populated by Druids, Romans, and Britons. This chapter will begin by exploring the appearance of the ancient Britons and the Druids in panoramic histories. The focus here will be on specific authors and their works, particularly Paul Rapin, Thomas Carte, Thomas Salmon, and Tobias Smollett, as well as a handful of others who wrote histories in the middle decades of the eighteenth century from different partisan viewpoints.

My rationale in choosing these specific historical writers is threefold. First, they all wrote extensively about the ancient past, including Boudica's role in it, as part of their panoramic histories. Compared to some earlier works in which Boudica was a representative 'great woman', these works offered less biographical detail, but often gave extensive accounts of the society in which Boudica lived, particularly the role of the Druids. In addition, Carte, Rapin, Smollett, and Salmon represent a cross-section of views about the ancient past and its relationship to contemporary politics. Their views brought them into an occasionally tense dialogue with one another, as well as with other critics. This leads to the third reason I have alighted on these four writers: each of these authors specifically addressed the relationship between history, politics, and imaginative genres. Tobias Smollett, for instance, was known as a novelist, and his work did not escape criticism as a result. But similarly, Thomas Carte's and Thomas Salmon's political views were very different to those of Paul de Rapin de Thoyras and other historians whose views were more 'Whiggish' than otherwise, be that Tory or, in Carte's case, Jacobite. These disagreements gave rise to revealing critical and authorial commentary on the production of history for popular audiences in an age of party-political tension.

Boudica's supporting cast, the Druids and the ancient Britons, were highly malleable figures open to a variety of readings. This meant that Boudica herself could be and often was positioned within versions of the ancient past which reflected the partisan present. Yet while it is important to acknowledge all of the various biases that influenced the differing visions of British antiquity portrayed in the histories, the aim of this section is primarily to recover the dialogue between historical writers of

---

[13] For the tangled relations between the constitution, antiquity, and ethnicity, see C. Kidd, *British identities before nationalism: ethnicity and nationhood in the Atlantic world, 1600–1800* (Cambridge, 1999). More generally on the revolution, see the classic Q. Skinner, 'History and ideology in the English Revolution', *The Historical Journal*, 8 (1965), 151–78; and J.M. Levine, 'Fact and the English revolution', *Journal of the history of ideas*, 64 (2003), 317–35. However, Kidd's work deals specifically with the role of British antiquity in political thought.

the period, and to engage with the criticisms that were levied against them. Their evident political disagreement was conducted in the language of historical argument, with accusations of misrepresentation, misinterpretation, and presentism employed by the opposing sides. Disinterest and impartiality, a fixed gaze on the past to the exclusion of the present, and the consultation of newly available sources were all expected to play a part in the historian's undertaking. Even as these rules were wantonly flouted on all sides, writers were nevertheless keen to claim that the historical endeavour was subject to certain guidelines and strictures that were constantly violated by opponents.

However, to view these histories in isolation would be to lose sight of the degree to which eighteenth-century history writing was indebted to other genres. In the second part of this chapter, I turn again to the underexplored relationship between stage dramas and 'true' prose histories. In 1753 Boudica appeared in an original stage play by Richard Glover, *Boadicea, queen of Britain*. This was arguably her most important appearance in the eighteenth century, at least for our purposes. Like the histories, Glover's play was intended to speak to contemporary politics, but the critical commentary around the play is revealing of concerns remarkably consistent with those expressed by critics of historians. As a playwright writing about the past, critics expected Richard Glover to adhere to the facts of history in a manner similar to historians working in the traditional vein of prose narrative. However, there were additional and rather interesting pressures on Glover. As well as the requisite fidelity to the facts, Glover was bound by another, somewhat more ambiguous measurement: the possibilities and limitations inherent in human behaviour, dictated by some notion of human nature. In this sense, the dramatist was under greater pressure even than the historian, being expected to produce a convincing representation of the enduring reality of human experience, in the present and the past.

POLITICIZING ANTIQUITY, NEGOTIATING HISTORY

We have seen that, with works such as that of John Seller, the genre of panoramic history was coming into its own in the late seventeenth century, and there were many more examples soon to follow. After the upheavals of the Civil War, the Restoration, and the Glorious Revolution, the popularity of panoramic histories, which encompassed such long periods of time, and allowed for sustained reflection on the origins of political institutions, seems wholly understandable. Although any and all forms of narrative history were open to politicization, panoramic histories laid open the entirety of the British past as a contestable field; this in part explains their growing prominence. Stretching from the ancient Britons to the recent revolutions, the genre of panoramic history—hardly innovative even before 1688—became an even more vigorous form of historical writing during the eighteenth century. Of course for some writers, it was easier to ignore the ancient British past than to expend valuable energy searching for answers that could not be found in the slim evidentiary record. As the author of *A Compendious History of the Monarchs of England from King William I* (1712) wrote:

> If any object against this History, because it omits the Times of the Romans, Saxons and Danes, I answer, that many fabulous Accounts, that we have of those Times, and the little that is material in 'em, is sufficient Excuse besides that the Smallness of the Volume would not afford sufficient Room to say much; and it is better to say nothing at all than nothing to the Purpose.[14]

Many serious writers took a similar view: that the history of ancient Britain was simply too distant, too unknowable to be of more than speculative interest. As we have seen, John Milton, whose history of ancient Britain was to be republished in White Kennet's *General history* (1706) admitted to including the earlier part of British history purely out of a dutiful sense of necessity. Much later, David Hume, in volume one—the last to be published, even though it was the first in chronology—of his *History of England* (1754–62) expressed his own misgivings, noting wistfully that 'The curiosity entertained by all civilized nations, of enquiring into the exploits and adventures of their ancestors, commonly excites a regret that the history of remote ages should always be so much involved in obscurity, uncertainty, and contradiction.'[15] For his part, Hume's recitation of the Boudica story gave only the barest outline, noting that she had been Queen of the Iceni, that she had been treated in 'the most ignominious manner' by the Romans, and that she had taken poison rather than be captured alive by the conquering army.[16] Although Hume omitted the strong judgements evident in Milton's history written nearly a century earlier, what both Milton and Hume demonstrate is that Boudica's non-appearance, or the manner of her appearance, in histories was not solely determined by the political persuasion of the author. It was also a matter of fidelity to trustworthy evidence, of which vanishingly little existed for ancient Britain.

If the lack of firm evidence meant that the ancient Britons were less central to the debate around the ancient constitution than were the Anglo-Saxons, they were by no means wholly irrelevant to it.[17] Much discussion in the early part of such histories centred around the role of the Druids, the ancient religious order that was the subject of increasing interest in the early part of the eighteenth century.[18] The Druids were also alive in dramas dedicated to their time, exemplified in Ambrose Philips's *The Briton*, performed in 1723. Like Glover's *Boadicia*, discussed under the next section, the performance of *The Briton* occasioned the publication of a pamphlet containing the historical narrative on which the play was founded, available for

---

[14] G.L., *A compendious history of the monarchs of England from King William I* (London, 1712).

[15] D. Hume, *History of England, from the invasion of Julius Caesar to the revolution in 1688*, 6 vols (London: A. Millar, 1762), Vol. 6, 1.

[16] Hume, *History of England*, 6.

[17] Colin Kidd has pointed to the genuine need for historians to investigate more closely what is meant by the word 'Britons'; see C. Kidd, 'Wales, Enlightenment and the new British History', *Welsh History Review*, 25 (2010), 209–30, at 212, and Vandrei, 'Britons strike home'. For Druids and Welsh cultural nationalism, see Chapter 6.

[18] For a full treatment, see R. Hutton, *Blood and mistletoe: the history of the Druids in Britain* (London, 2009), esp. Ch. 2.

sixpence.[19] However, there are also histories that sought to explicate the unique history of the earliest form of British religion. In the same year as Philips's *The Briton* appeared on stage, Henry Rowlands published *Mona Antiqua Restaurata*, a discourse on the antiquities of the Isle of Anglesey, known in antiquity as Mona, reputedly the seat of the ancient Druid order which has been so cruelly cut to pieces by Suetonius Paulinus shortly before Boudica's rebellion. Three years after Rowlands, the republican John Toland's *A critical history of the Celtic religion* was published. Both Rowlands and Toland cast the Druids as oppressors and the Britons as gullible followers—Rowland from the point of view of a devout Anglican cleric and Toland from that of a free-thinker.[20] But Druids cropped up most often in the very place one might expect to find them: at the beginning of panoramic histories. They rarely passed without comment.

However, a greater focus on the Druids did not necessarily lead to a correspondingly intense interest in Boudica, the depth of whose association with the Druids was not perceived statically. The reason for this was that the scraps of documentary evidence for the customs and manner of the Druids were not gleaned from the same sources as Boudica's life and times. For instance, the account given by Julius Caesar in the *Gallic Wars* was an oft-cited source for the Druids and ancient British society, but it was produced long before Queen Boudica's lifetime.[21] Caesar had landed in Britain more than a century before Boudica's rebellion and had been among the first to record the strange barbarism of the ancient religious order then dominant in the lands occupied by the Celts and the Gauls. Caesar related how the Druids practised human sacrifices and divined the future by reading the spilled entrails of their victims. He observed similarly questionable customs amongst the general populace in ancient Britain, including their practice of polyamory.

Caesar was also an acute observer of their manner of making war: it is from Caesar that we learn that the Britons rode into battle on chariots, for example. Thus Caesar's version of ancient British society, though one hundred years out of date by the time of Boudica's rebellion, was one of the most authoritative sources available for the context in which she and the ancient Britons lived. Of course Caesar did not mention Boudica, so the connection between the ancient queen and the Druids was the subject of speculation and interpretation; thus the degree to which Boudica was personally associated with the Druids, or the Druids with her rebellion, was a fruitful area for historical writers, whose interpretative stance could feed into very different views of ancient Britain that were variously amenable to supporters of opposing political factions in the present.

Written over a century after Caesar's, Tacitus' account could be taken to suggest that Boudica's rebellion was, at least in part, caused by the desecration and destruction of the Druidic oak groves on Mona, and by Suetonius' brutal massacre of the priests and priestesses on the island. This link was sometimes exaggerated by

---

[19] *Memories of Venutius and Cartismandua, extracted from the most authentic accounts, and explaining the Historical parts of the Tragedy called The Briton* (London, 1723).
[20] Gerrard, *Patriot opposition*, 139–45.
[21] Caesar discussed Britain in Book V of *The Gallic Wars*, see also Hutton, *Blood and mistletoe*, 2–7.

eighteenth-century writers, particularly those with Tory leanings. In fact, the two events were related in tandem by Tacitus, but the historian did not make a direct causal link. Likewise, Dio, in his characteristically overblown fashion, had Boudica praying to the goddess Andraste and releasing a hare as an omen of victory, two allusions to her intimacy with Druidism. Similarly, the barbaric acts of vengeance recorded by Dio had the effect of suggesting Boudica had absorbed the flippant attitude toward human life endemic in a class of elect priests who practised human sacrifice. A given author's positioning of the Druids, then, could have an effect on Boudica's own portrayal as representative of either arbitrary despotism or enlightened governance. However, this gerrymandering of the evidence did not usually detract from her the generally accepted view of her as a heroic figure. Her status as a defender of British liberties—acknowledged as long ago as Holinshed's *Chronicles*—to an extent elevated her above the factional fray, though not without exception.

The politicization of the culture of the Druids by historians began very early in the development of panoramic history, with the Whiggish Paul de Rapin de Thoyras's *History of England* (1725), one of the most successful and well-read political histories of the first half of the eighteenth century. Rapin (1661–1725) was a Huguenot refugee and soldier who landed with William of Orange at Torbay.[22] Scholarly by nature, Rapin was taken by the history and politics of his adopted island and, by 1705, had begun to think seriously on the idea of writing a history of England for a European audience. His vision of history, like that of many other writers, was bound to his understanding of the current English party system and methods of government. Prior to writing his history, Rapin published the *Dissertation sur les whigs et les tories* (1717) as an explanation of the party-political system in England (Rapin did not account for other parts of the British Isles) for a continental audience. Tellingly, the tract began with the Anglo-Saxon parliaments, or Wittena-Gemot, and moved swiftly to the dispossession of the English under William the Conqueror, leaving out the ancient Britons completely. The *Dissertation* emphasized the mutual agreement that existed between the King and his people, an arrangement Rapin traced to the Anglo-Saxons.

An English version of the *Dissertation* prefaced the translation of Rapin's *History of England*, which was done by Nicholas Tindal in 1725, two years after it appeared in French in The Hague. The translator's introduction to the English text made much of the privations Rapin had to endure in order to write his great work. After a long battle with ill-health, made worse by his historical labours, Rapin died in the same year Tindal's translation was published, leaving a final volume unfinished. Given the author's state of health, Tindal dwelled on the numerous instances when Rapin was tempted to give up his *History*. The first of these instances was when he came to narrate the ancient past, up to and including the Anglo-Saxons, a period

---

[22] H. Trevor-Roper, 'A Huguenot historian: Paul Rapin', in I. Scouloudi (ed.), *Huguenots in Britain and their French background, 1550–1800* (London, 1987), pp. 3–19. M. G. Sullivan, 'Rapin de Thoyras, Paul de (1661–1725)', *ODNB* (2004), http://www.oxforddnb.com/view/article/23145, accessed 21 Nov 2012.

Tindal liked to 'a wild and untrodden desert', which was so difficult to research that it nearly drove the historian to put down his pen.[23]

Rapin attached great importance to the Anglo-Saxons, so his treatment of the period prior to their arrival in the *History of England* was not lengthy, nor did it traverse new ground. Yet his version was to stand as the interpretation of antiquity most in keeping with principles of parliamentary sovereignty and freedom from a cabal of religious elites. Rapin painted the Druids as an all-powerful class of despots who 'made Religion a handle to procure themselves the management of Private as well as Publick Affairs', a strategy that 'kept the People in great Awe and Dread of them'.[24] However, Rapin's Whiggish opinions of the Druids did not infect his depiction of Boudica's rebellion. His recitation of Boudica's story was fairly straightforward and there was no evident lack of respect in his views of her as an individual. He described her as 'a Woman of great spirit', whose desire for revenge was judged, rightly he thought, by historians to have been justified by the treatment she had endured. Rapin attributed the general unrest of the Britons in large part to the cruelty suffered by Boudica and her family, an important point, as this amounted to a diminishment of the role of the Druids in the events. To make that point, he included a paraphrased version of her speech: 'She came not there, as one descended from Royal Progenitors, to fight for Empire or Riches, but as one of the common People, to revenge the Loss of their Liberty...'[25] As Rapin had it, the Romans' behaviour toward the beleaguered Britons 'bred in the Minds of the People so utter an Aversion to a Foreign Yoke, that they were all at once inspir'd with a Resolution to shake it off' and so they 'join'd themselves to the rest of their Countrymen, for the Recovery of their Liberty'.[26] The image of the Britons presented here was one of a bravery and resistance, while the Druids were despotic, but also ultimately ineffectual.

As we saw in the last chapter, emotive language was becoming a regular feature of prose histories, and there is some flavour of this affective history in Rapin's version of events as translated by Tindal. Boudica is described as 'burning with a Desire of Revenge'.[27] Rapin included Dio's version of events, and he managed to make them even more striking by noting that the Roman virgins of Camulodunum had their breasts cut off and 'cramb'd into their Mouths, that they might seem in the Agonies of Death, to eat their own Flesh'.[28] That single word, 'cramb'd', makes Dio's word as usually translated, 'sewn', seem pedestrian. Rapin also added small editorial flourishes, such as his suggestion that, after her defeat, Boudica was 'touch'd with so deep a Sense of Shame and Loss' that she readily took her own life by poison.[29] Although such injections of style and reflection were few and may well have come from Tindal, even with minimal original research Rapin had managed to write a convincing enough version of the ancient British past, tinged with principles that his contemporaries derided as Whiggish. But in the main, Rapin's

---

[23] P. de Rapin de Thoyras, *The History of England from the invasion of the Romans to the end of the reign of William the Conqueror*, trans. N. Tindal (London, 1725), preface, n.p (9).
[24] Ibid., xix.   [25] Ibid., 53.   [26] Ibid., 51.
[27] Ibid., 54.   [28] Ibid., 51.   [29] Ibid., 55.

rendition of the ancient British past was quite conventional; even his objections to the Druids were hardly original, taken as they were from Rowlands and Toland.

Rapin's reluctance to politicize Boudica can be compared to a less well-known account, by Thornhagh Gurdon (1663–1733), a minor antiquary and historian. He took a more adventurous view than Rapin, managing to construct a truly Whiggish interpretation of Boudica's place in the history of parliament. 'The magnanimous Heroine Boadicea Queen or Princess of the Iceni, so successfully commanded the British Armies, as to beat and conquer the Roman Vice-Roy, or Lieutenant Suetonius Paulinus: And no doubt, that noble Lady was a deliberative Member of the Council where the Resolution was taken to fight the Romans, and that she should command the Force.'[30] Of course no such consultative process appeared in recorded history, so Gurdon was reliant on conjecture and his own opinions to make this statement, but his triumphalist tone, unusual in recitations of the Boudica story in any period, suggests that he wished to guide the reader toward the view that the cooperative proto-parliamentarian nature of ancient British government was the key to Boudica's early victories.

Yet despite the overtly Whiggish histories by minor historians like Gurdon, it was Rapin's work that was considered the most dangerous. Opponents lost little time in crafting a view of the British past that fit more comfortably with their own vision of the present. The first to undertake the task was the travel writer Thomas Salmon, who published his *Modern History, or the Present State of All Nations* in 1732, in which he attacked Rapin as a foreigner, a Presbyterian, a mountebank, and a menace. Rapin was an 'utter enemy of our Constitution', whose history had been an attempt to show that the government and church in the island had been originally republican and presbyterian. Hammering home his criticisms, Salmon claimed that Rapin's editors had colluded with this view and 'dress'd up the Story in such a pleasing Form, that young People read it as greedily as they would a Novel or a Play, not considering the Tendency of it', and that Rapin's work was 'Poetry and Fiction intermix'd with our History.'[31] Here Salmon conflated different forms of interpretation. Rapin's historical deduction, controversial though it may have been, was not an outright invention, yet it was treated as such in order to make the point that political positions could be masked by pleasing language and entertaining presentation. These three authorial strategies—fictionalization, sensationalism, and informed interpretation—could be deployed in histories, novels, and plays. However, Salmon's contention was that the strictures binding history were so tight that even interpretation amounted to invention.

Yet Salmon, for his part, attempted greater originality than Rapin, goaded by what he perceived as weaknesses in the latter's research. Rapin was reluctant to say much about ancient Britain, but what little he had said, and much that he had not, became ammunition for his political enemy. This was a tit-for-tat exercise as much as a serious attempt to write a new and useful history. Salmon alighted on a passing comment by Rapin, in which he wondered at the efficacy of the British war chariots,

---

[30] T. Gurdon, *History of the high court of parliament* (London, 1731).
[31] T. Salmon, *Modern History or the present state of all nations*, 32 vols (London, 1732), Vol. XVI, xii.

since it seemed strange to him that the Britons leapt from their chariots in order to engage the enemy's mounted troops; it seemed much more advantageous to remain in the chariot.[32] Thus Salmon's account of ancient history included a lengthy digression into all the possible ways a chariot could be used in battle, noting, unconvincingly, that the natural swiftness of the Britons on foot was more than a match for Roman horses.[33] On more substantive matters, such as the probable form of government in ancient Britain, both authors had recourse to the evidence of the Gauls, who were organized as independent petty states under heads or kings. Rapin noted that these kings met and chose by consent one of their number to lead the army and execute the laws.[34] Salmon did not mention this essential aspect of consent, though he did make the point that the formation of empires through the amalgamation of petty princes was 'the Original Government of the World, deduced from the Natural Force and Right of Paternal Dominion'.[35] The inviolate nature of hereditary succession among the ancients was also demonstrated, Salmon argued, by the passage of power to female heirs as well as to male. The same argument was made in a sermon during the reign of Queen Anne preached before the House of Commons to commemorate the anniversary of the restoration of the throne under Charles II.[36] Salmon was not the first to make this point, but by doing so in a work of history, he was making a more direct link between the distant and recent past.

Salmon's account of Boudica's rebellion stands out as one of the more sceptical in regards to the original material of Tacitus and Dio. Yet this scepticism was to little purpose except, perhaps, to call into question the implication that the ancient Britons were an ignorant rabble led by a distracted woman—a notion that did not trouble Rapin. Salmon did mention the atrocities Boudica is said to have committed, but with the grudging caveat, 'if we may credit the Roman authors'. By the time Salmon came to the final battle scene, he had lost patience completely with his sources, refusing to include Boudica's prayer or her speech, or to give any credit to Dio's version of events. Salmon huffed, 'But how impracticable Speeches are at such times, I need not suggest to any considering Man: They are usually drawn up by Historians to give us wrong Impressions.' The impression the ancient authors wished to give was of a great Roman victory over a 'Hairbrain'd Rabble', a version of events Salmon dismissed outright.[37] Salmon's incredulity can be attributed to the relatively uncritical stance taken by Rapin, whose conventional recitation of the ancient British past was in contrast to his more thorough treatment of later periods. Salmon undermined the source base as a backhanded attack on Rapin's approach, but he simply lacked the ingenuity to create an alternative narrative to challenge that of the sources, or of Rapin.

Salmon and Rapin represented two different approaches to the ancient Britons, loosely mapping on to rival interpretations based on their differing politics. But Salmon's scepticism notwithstanding, neither he nor Rapin delved into the ancient

---

[32] Rapin, *History*, xviii.
[33] Salmon, *Modern history*, 42–3.
[34] Rapin, *History*, xxii.
[35] Salmon, *Modern history*, 40.
[36] H. Todd, *A sermon preach'd before the honourable House of Commons* (London, 1711).
[37] Salmon, *Modern history*, 61–2.

past with any great zeal, reserving intense scrutiny for later, more revealing periods in history. Thomas Carte's *General History of England*, however, was in a rather different mould to either of the preceding works. It was written as a much more consciously engaging history than Thomas Salmon's, and very much a Tory view to Rapin's Whiggish one. But rather than simply assert his disagreement with Rapin and the ancient authors as Salmon had done, Carte offered what he hoped to be the most creditable alternative to the Rapin's view of antiquity, adorned with original research and ingenious, if idiosyncratic, arguments.

Carte was a well-known member of the Nonjuring community, having refused to take the oath of allegiance to the Hanoverian line following the removal of James II. Before turning his hand to history, he had been implicated in the Atterbury Plot of 1722 and had fled to France to avoid prosecution. He returned to England in 1728, where he turned his hand to writing histories of a distinctly Jacobite hue. In 1734 Carte published *A defence of English history against the misrepresentations of M. de Rapin Thoyras in his History of England*, a lengthy tract lampooning Rapin's 'knowledge of history and his integrity in writing it'. The criticisms contained in the tract, though derived from Carte's own extensive researched and translation of original materials, were written in a mood of evident frustration, which spilled over into the full response that was Carte's *General History of England*. He set about raising subscriptions shortly after the publication of his *Defence*, publishing *A proposal for removing the impediments of writing an History of England* in 1736, a shameless plea for funds, of which more were to follow. Carte reasoned that because the projected history would be 'for the publick good and the Honour of the country', it seemed only right that it should be paid for by public subscription.[38] Yet despite the support of a large number of subscribers, Carte struggled to complete the first volume in ten years; he did, however, manage to publish a 'Specimen' of his history, which proved as controversial as any full-length history, as we will see. The whole work finally appeared in 1747, but its contents—especially Carte's endorsement of a recent incident of touching for the 'king's evil' by the Old Pretender—and the response from derisive critics led many of his supporters to withdraw. The second and third volumes barely limped through the presses.

Carte made great claims for the first volume of his *History*, casting it as an original work of research, a monument to the public and the nation, and above all a contribution to great literature. It possessed:

> ...a clearness of narration, proper for instruction, as well as necessary for their being rightly understood; not with the pomp of sounding words, the flourishes of an orator, or the paintings of a poet, which history rejects as unworthy of her dignity, and which are certainly an improper language to come out of the mouth of truth; but still with a force, and elegance, and (as occasions require) a life of expression; in an easy flow of style; such as, without veiling any of the narrative charms of Truth, may yet give her ornaments agreeable to her modesty, and make her appear amiable in the eyes of

---

[38] Carte's various prefatory pamphlets were eventually published together as *A Collection of Several Papers published by Mr Thomas Carte in relation to his History of England* (London, 1744).

those, who might be shocked to see her in a dress either forbidding or negligent; is the proper business of an historian.[39]

This passage signals that Carte was very much aware of the accusations made by historians against one another that they had dressed up their histories in pleasing guises, the better to occlude the real truth of matters and covertly instil their own opinions in the unwary. Rather than own, as Thomas Heywood had a century earlier, that his history was written to entertain first and to inform second, Carte claimed to have carved out a mixed identity for history as amenable to the same elegance and liveliness as poetry, but without sacrificing the inherent primacy and dignity of its claim to truth.

Given the barrenness of the source base, Carte thought it particularly important when dealing with the ancient past to resist the inclination toward dry narration, or to swing to the other extreme of 'inserting amusing tales without any foundation in fact'.[40] Instead, he packed his account with new research and arresting, if tenuous, arguments. In particular, Carte drew on Abbé Paul Pezron's *Antiquité de la nation, et de langue des celtes* (1703), which neither Rapin nor Salmon had addressed, and he gave a lengthy account of Celtic origins and the settlement of Britain.[41] Beginning with the sons of Noah, carrying on to the Titans, and the Belgae, who settled amongst the 'Old Britains', Carte engaged in great depth with innovative, though largely fantastic, accounts of the period. The unusual attention Carte gave to the pedigree of the Britons served as a preface to his own novel conclusion, that the ancient Hyperboreans, a mythical people known (or imagined) by the Greeks and thought to be the origin of much of Greek religion and culture, were none other than the inhabitants of the Hebrides; thus all that was great in Greek culture had its origin in ancient Druidic learning. Indeed, Carte took an exceptionally positive view of the Druids and their role in ancient Britain. Though he did not deny that the Druids had practised human sacrifice, he insisted that this was entirely normal and therefore acceptable practice in ancient civilizations. As for their domination over both civil and criminal matters, Carte argued that the Druids' supremacy was legitimated by right, as well as by the consent of the governed.[42]

In Carte's history, the Druids' power and influence was richly evidenced by the case of Boudica's rebellion. He followed Tacitus in attributing the rebellion to widespread national anger at the destruction of the sacred groves and the defenceless Druid community of Mona.[43] Carte argued that although the wrongs done to Boudica and her family were a proximate cause, the threat posed by the Romans to the Britons' common religion provoked rival tribes to forge an unprecedented

---

[39] T. Carte, *A General history of England*, 2 vols (London, 1747), Vol. I, 2.
[40] Ibid., Vol. I, xii.
[41] Kidd makes a distinction between the myth-making of Abbé Paul Pezron and the sober antiquarianism of men like the philologist Edward Lhuyd. However, Carte's interest in the former seems to have been at least in part animated by a sense that Pezron's work was a corrective to existing scholarship. Carte was certainly a poor scholar, but I would stop short of saying he was an entirely insincere one. Kidd, 'Wales', 221–2.
[42] Carte, *General history*, Vol. I, 42–7.   [43] Ibid., Vol. I, 116.

common bond. However, just as Whig commentators had done, Carte cast Boudica as a figurehead in this newly united front, describing her as, 'a woman of venerable aspect, graceful person, high spirit, masculine courage, and warlike disposition', a description which combined Tacitus and Dio with Carte's authorial interpolation. His account deviated from the usual when he stated that the Britons, although they were beaten, were mustering for another attack 'when the sudden death of Bonduica, caused probably by grief, vexation, and despair, or hastened (as some say) by poison, disconcerted all their measures, and caused them to disperse into their several countries, an usual consequence of disappointments, in armies collected out of several nations'.[44] The attribution of Boudica's death to the strain caused by her defeat, rather than sickness or suicide, was Carte's own innovation. It seemed that Carte's protestations of Druidic civility made him reluctant to allow Boudica the violent death usually attributed to her. Interestingly, this cause of death was to enjoy a certain popularity among nineteenth-century moralists, as well.

Carte also undertook the unusual practice of employing modern or contemporary terms to explain ancient words and concepts to uninitiated readers. In his discussion of the suffering of Boudica's extended family, deprived of their land and riches by the Roman occupiers, Carte noted that this was done by 'escheat', an arrangement whereby land reverted to the Crown or the state upon the death of the holder without a qualified heir.[45] 'Escheat' was a legal term of post-Conquest origin, not one that would have been employed during Boudica's lifetime. Elsewhere, Carte wrote that '[t]he druids composed in those days, (if I may be allowed to borrow expressions from more modern times,) the principle part of what hath been since called, in France the Court of Peers, and in England the court or Great council of the Barons. See here, in a constitution founded by the Old Britains, the first draught of that which hath since obtained in this nation...'[46] Carte's borrowing of later or contemporary terms to make them easier to grasp was unusual, and judging by his interpolated plea that allowance be given, he was conscious that it would appear so, and might even attract criticism.

Assuaging his conscience, Carte claimed that he '...judged and wrote of ancient ages, as if I lived only in them, without any application to later times'.[47] This, however, was clearly erroneous. Even as Carte himself castigated others for the mixing the worlds of past and present, pointing out that by doing so they were weakening their historical judgement, he painted a portrait of ancient Britain in which a strong class of religious leaders played a vital and entirely positive role in society, human sacrifices notwithstanding. The ancient Britons, Carte claimed, ceded authority willingly to the Druidic order as a class of nobles suited to power; they esteemed their learned governors and celebrated them for their equitable administration of justice. While other historians had suggested that the power of the Druids was tempered by civil authority, held independently by cities or provinces, Carte intoned that these authors were judging 'of ancient times, by the usages of modern, the ordinary source of endless mistakes'.[48] The ancient Britons, Carte argued, were

---

[44] Ibid., Vol. I, 118.   [45] Ibid., Vol. I, 115.   [46] Ibid., Vol. I, 47.
[47] Ibid., Vol. I, xii.   [48] Ibid., Vol. I, 41–2.

governed in all matters by men who were effectively clergymen, with no check on their power from other quarters.

Carte's tendency to invoke without clear explanation terms alien to the ancient world and to so clearly mirror the present in his portrayal of the past jarred with his tendency to point out this failing in others. In such a febrile political atmosphere, his hypocrisy could not go unnoticed, and, with its unmistakable current of Jacobitism and crypto-Catholicism, it is hardly surprising that the *General History* was roundly condemned. The author incurred the biting derision of the novelist Henry Fielding, who was a vocal Patriot-Whig critic of Walpole as well as a bitter opponent of Jacobitism. As the editor of the satirical *Jacobite's Journal* under the *nom de plume* Mr John Trot-Plaid, in the issue of 20 February 1748, Fielding verbally hauled Carte before the *Journal's* textual 'Court of Criticism'. Referring to Carte, rather tellingly, as 'that learned and facetious novelist', the historian was accused of 'not having the Love of Truth before his Eyes, nor weighing the Duty of an Historian' and he was subsequently convicted of 'perverting the Intent of History and applying it to the sordid and paltry Use of a Party'.[49]

As incisive as Fielding's assault was, the earlier intervention of Samuel Squires, Bishop of St David, was more damning still. In the spring of 1746, Squires had written a response to the early publication of a 'Specimen' of Carte's history, which had appeared in print over a year before the first finished volume went to the presses. The 'Specimen' contained only one section of the final text: Carte's chapters on British antiquity. To this 'Specimen' Samuel Squires responded, not with satire, but with a level-headed and learned commentary; it was a response to Carte the historian, but which also landed a glancing blow against Carte the purported Jacobite and professed Nonjuror. Point by point, Squires addressed Carte's unconventional notions about ancient British society in solemn, strangulating detail. Squire accused Carte of having deliberately chosen the Druids as the subject of the 'Specimen' because they allowed him the greatest latitude to make the case for the authority of the priesthood in matters of state, civil society, and even in warfare. As a defender of the Hanoverian Church of England, Squires was moved to point out Carte's tendency to extend the authority of the the Druids to the point that these priests became. '... Dictators, Vergobrets, Kings, hereditary-right Kings, hereditary Legislators, hereditary Nobles, Augurs, Sacrificers, Generals of Armies, Commanders of Cavalry, Princes, Tribunes, Ephori, Philosophers, and Academicians'.[50] In short, Squires viewed Carte as being 'far more conversant with modern Notions and Ideas, than he is with genuine Antiquity', and of using history to fight the battles of the present.

Squires's attack on Carte's deliberate use of the past, along with accusations of fictionalization and misrepresentation of the kind Salmon had levied against Rapin are indicative of an emerging understanding amongst historical writers that their

---

[49] W.B. Coley (ed.), *The Jacobite's Journal and related writings* (Oxford, 1974), 168–72. Carte was also the subject of the satirical *A Letter to John Trot-Plaid, Esq. Author of the Jacobite Journal, concerning Mr Carte's General History of England., By Duncan Mac Carte, a Highlander* (London, 1748).

[50] S. Squire, *Remarks upon Mr. Carte's Specimen of his General History of England very proper to be read by all such as are Contributors to that great Work* (London, 1748), 21.

works should abide by certain strictures. Of course, there had long been a dialogue around history as being more or less supported by extant evidence, but this period saw a greater emphasis placed on identifying the various means by which an historian's objectivity—and by extension his commitment to telling the historical truth—might be compromised. The guiding assumption was that historical narratives would be read by unsuspecting audiences and consumed as 'true'; this assumption made exposing the deficiencies of authors all the more urgent. Although it remained important to point out one's opponent's use of 'novelized' language to expose these partial narratives of the past, it was equally important to uncover the subtle ways that the present was being reflected in a purportedly impartial genre.

In short, the strictures on how history could be used by historians and other authors were tightening. Carte's awareness of the variable proximity between past and present, which was determined by the author, differed from the *similitudo temporum* espoused by seventeenth-century authors. It was no longer seemly to judge of the present as though it were a reflection of the past, nor was it unquestioningly acceptable to use the past as a field on which to fight the political battles of the present. Rather, the ideal, which Carte acknowledged but failed to practice, was of the historian, appraising the past as an object entirely separate from the author's present.

Interestingly, dubious presentations of the past could be conveyed in histories by means other than the author's prose. This was the case in Tobias Smollett's *Complete History of England* (1757–8). A Scottish physician and novelist, Smollett's politics are difficult to characterize, and he seems to have 'understood the essential meaninglessness of party labels' in the period.[51] He was no supporter of Walpole, although he had Whiggish sympathies, and he dedicated his history to William Pitt the Elder, 'not to the minister, but to the patriot', who was then secretary of state.[52] Indeed, Smollett's views have proven difficult for historians to characterize. Lending some credence to his disavowal of prejudice, the author was not afraid to expose even his own side, declaring to his friend, Dr John Moore, that the final volume of his *History* was certain to ruffle the feathers of 'the west country Whigs of Scotland' because 'in the course of my inquiries some of the Whig ministers turned out such a set of sordid knaves, that I could not help stigmatising them for their want of integrity and sentiment'.[53]

However, Smollett sensibly restricted his political sermonizing, at least in the first three volumes of his history, preferring instead to respond to what he perceived as a gap in the market and 'present the Public with a succinct, candid, and complete History of our own country, which will be more easy in the purchase, more agreeable in the perusal, and less burthensome to the memory, than any work of the same nature, produced in these kingdoms'.[54] Smollett took the additional step of publishing a second edition of the *Complete History* in 110 serialized six-penny numbers. His work was succeeded in reaching reach a larger audience than previous

---

[51] Fabel, 'Patriotic Briton', 104.
[52] T. Smollett, *Complete history of England*, 5 vols (London, 1757), Vol. 1, Dedication.
[53] Smollett to Dr John Moore, 2 Jan 1758 in *Life and letters of Tobias Smollett (1721–1771)*, ed. L. Melville (London, 1926), 161.
[54] T. Smollett, *Plan of the Complete History of England* (London, 1757), 1.

histories, with weekly sales reaching 10,000 by 1758.[55] Significant to the work's success was that it lacked the scepticism evident in David Hume's history, finished only a few years later, making Smollett's a safe alternative.[56]

Smollett's view of Boudica and the ancient Britons was distinctive. As was by now common practice, the opening pages of the history dealt with the ancient Britons and the Druids, but, in keeping with his relatively judicious views on controversial events, Smollett did not paint a wholly unflattering picture of the Druids. He acknowledged that they had held 'dangerous power', but also allowed that this was a necessary corrective to the savagery of the people over whom they ruled. Indeed, as more avowedly Tory writers often did, Smollett alighted upon certain aspects of Druid society and used them to expose the failings of modernity. The Druids were 'uncorrupted by vice and luxury, weaned from all interested attachments, fitted by their education and experience for investigating the truth, and determining disputes according to the rules of equity...'[57] Although he allowed that 'in the dark ages of ignorance, religion and government could not well be divided', Smollett did not go so far as to attribute supreme power to the Druids alone; there was, he argued, a civil magistrate and a senate, although these bodies did nothing without the of the Druids.[58] Thus while Smollett argued for the Druids as a natural ruling class that was generally fair-minded, he did not attribute to them an active, executive role as his predecessor had.

Smollett's nuanced assessment of the Druids, however, was separate from his view of the Britons. Their pride and lack of discipline meant that the Britons were forever divided into warring tribes, and thus locked in a state of barbarism; only the Boudican rebellion gave them a common cause. Relating the events of the rebellion, Smollett wrote in a distinctive style reminiscent of his successful novels, and, although the pages of his history were peppered with references to classical sources, he took only the rudiments of the historical narrative from these sources and employed the flourishes of fiction in fleshing out the material at hand. Relating the plight of the ancient Britons under the Roman yoke, Smollett wrote:

> Nay, their miseries became the subject of ridicule to their oppressors, who insulted them on all occasions, so as to kindle a desperate spirit of resentment in a people naturally addicted to passion and revenge. Their minds being thus prepared, nothing was wanting but some remarkable outrage, to blow the embers into a dangerous flame of open rebellion...[59]

Here Smollett had set the stage for a battle between a desperate band of British tribesmen and a cruel but superior force. Of course, the outrage which eventually fanned the flames proved to be the mistreatment of Boudica and her daughters by the Roman troops. 'These shocking barbarities, added to the other motives of

---

[55] Smollett to Dr John Moore, 28 September 1758 in Melville, *Letters*, 163.

[56] By the early nineteenth century, Hume's and Smollett's histories, once in competition, had been combined into single works by a succession of editors, most successfully in 1835 by T.S. Hughes, *Hume and Smollett's History of England, from the invasion of Julius Caesar to the death of George II. With a continuation to the reign of William IV* (London, 1835).

[57] Smollett, *Complete history*, Vol. 1, 10.   [58] Ibid.   [59] Ibid., Vol. 1, 33.

discontent, exaggerated by the dowager, who was a woman of masculine spirit and irresistible eloquence, and inflamed by the remaining Druids, who had such influence over all the island, produced an universal revolt.'[60] Smollett accounted for the general insurrection by citing the unity of which the British tribes were capable when the threat was against the Druidic religion. The sudden death of Boudica, 'occasioned by the violence of her grief and despair, procured, as some alledge, by poison... disconcerted all their measures, and after having celebrated her funeral obsequies, the immediately dispersed...'[61] Based on his prose description of the event, Smollett's understanding of Boudica was that she was an esteemed commander, whose death, rather than defeat, brought an end to the rebellion. Indeed, Smollett's view harmonized with that of Rapin, who appeared to distrust the credulous ancient Britons, even as his depiction of Boudica remained one of a defeated hero-queen.

Smollett's determination to avoid controversy in the first volumes of his history invited a different but still revealing kind of criticism. An anonymous review attributed to Oliver Goldsmith suggests the problem with Smollett's history was not its bias or its fancifulness, but rather its restraint:

> Determined to avoid all *useless disquisition*... he steers wide indeed of that danger, and avoids all *disquisitions* as *useless*. A brief recital of facts is chiefly what the public is to expect from this performance. But, with submission, we think the ingenious Author might have afforded us something more. He has undoubted ability; and he well knows that a moderate interspersion of manly and sensible observations, must have greatly enlivened his work, and would hardly have been deemed superfluous by such Readers as have any turn for reflection.[62]

In this instance, Smollett's fame as a novelist worked against him, as his history failed to live up to the vigour of his earlier work in other genres, and yet also fell short of what was expected in lively historical writing. However, in a later review of the fourth volume, the same critic was forced to bend to another extreme, accusing Smollett of actively avoiding subjects that might reflect badly on Tory ministers of the recent past, even when they 'would have admitted all the colouring which he is so fond of lavishing upon almost every occasion...'[63] Indeed, the dull narration of bare facts contained in the first three volumes had culminated in the fourth with a portrayal of King William III that amounted to 'an assemblage of contrarieties which scarce ever met together but in the Author's imagination'.[64] Given the weight of such failures, the reviewer was forced to concede, 'this Writer's merit is rather that of an ingenious novelist than of an accurate historian. His imagination overpowers his judgment'[65]—and yet even as it condemned him to inaccuracy, it could not save him from being dull.

---

[60] Ibid.   [61] Ibid., Vol., 34.
[62] *Monthly Review*, xvi, (June 1757), 532. The attribution comes from P.-G. Boucé, 'A note on Smollett's *Continuation of the Complete History of England*', *Review of English Studies* (1969), 57–61. Boucé attributes another, longer review, published in the *Monthly Review*, xviii (April 1758) to Owen Ruffhead. However, the two reviews were almost certainly written by the same person.
[63] *Monthly Review*, xviii (April 1758), 289–305, at 299.   [64] Ibid., 303.
[65] Ibid., 305.

There was no detailed character sketch of Boudica comparable to that of William III in the *Complete history*; at least, not in prose. However, she did appear in an arresting new image which seemed to complicate the more measured prose discussion of the rebellion. New images of Boudica were still relatively rare in the mid-eighteenth century, although they were to increase in number as the market for printed histories expanded in the latter years of the century, when Boudica became quite a prevalent figure in book illustrations. The four original volumes of Smollett's *History*—as distinct from the penny numbers—were each published with only a single illustration, the frontispiece for each volume.[66] The image chosen to introduce Volume 1 was one of the first original images of Boudica to be produced since her appearance as a female worthy in the mid-seventeenth century (see Figure 4). The picture was the work of Smollett's friend, Francis Hayman RA, whose illustrations appeared in a number of Smollett's works.[67]

Judging by this image, Hayman's view of Boudica appears to have been somewhat different from Smollett's. The background scene of the frontispiece depicts a supplicant Briton at the feet of a Druid elder, likely an allusion to the undemocratic but engrossing nature of the order's authority and the powerlessness of the ordinary Briton. Meanwhile, in the foreground is a shaggy mongrel dog lapping at the spilled contents of an upturned barrel, one eye cast towards a man who appears to be sleeping, deaf to the fate of his burden. The foreground image is of Boudica, bare-breasted –an uncommon way of depicting her—in her chariot, unaccompanied by her daughters. She has employed a reluctant chariot-driver, whose stooped posture and shadowy features denote something less than a willingness to take on the role. This is hardly a picture of pristine bliss. Rather, it suggests a combination of despotism and anarchy, a king of organized chaos touched by absurdist humour. It is the latter that detracts somewhat from any sense that Hayman intended this as a serious critique of either past or present, and makes the image stand out as an interpretation independent of Smollett's text. While Smollett may have been content, or felt constrained, to adhere to the conventions of prose history, Francis Hayman was free to take a more engaging approach, rendering forms of barbarism both comic and toothless.

It is interesting to compare the light-hearted image of Boudica—probably the first instance of her as a figure of anything approaching fun—found in Smollett's history with others of the later eighteenth century, if only to suggest the subtle messages that could be conveyed through this medium in hands less inclined to comedy.[68] For instance, the political radical John Baxter's slightly later history of England cast Boudica as a symbol of liberty under threat. Despite being published

---

[66] The complete edition was sold with a promissory note exchangeable for the plates, which had not all been finished at that point; see, for example, *Whitehall Evening Post*, 21 July 1759.

[67] B. Allen, *Francis Hayman* (London, 1987), 145. The two were friends and correspondents for much of Smollett's career and Hayman provided illustrations for a number of his writings; see L.M. Knapp (ed.), *The letters of Tobias Smollett* (Oxford, 1970), 13 n. 1.

[68] Boudica was an increasingly common subject for illustrators in this period. Many of these eighteenth-century illustrations are discussed in S. Smiles, *The image of antiquity: ancient Britain and the romantic imagination* (New Haven, CT, 1994), 160–3.

Figure 4. Francis Hayman's ambiguous vision of ancient Britain in Tobias Smollett's *Complete History* (1757). The Bodleian Libraries, The University of Oxford, 13 THETA 190, Volume 1.

for the London Corresponding Society, a group which had been the subject of such intense government interest that spies were sent to infiltrate it and a number of its members were tried for treason, Baxter's history was somewhat implausibly billed as 'impartial', intended merely to satisfy the 'curious Politician' in his or her desire for historical information on which to base assessments of present circumstances. It sought to demonstrate the long historical fight for liberty, which began with Boudica's Britons and continued to the present day. Because it was simultaneously comprehensive, conveniently sized, and exceptionally cheap, Baxter hoped his history would encourage his fellow citizens to 'accelerate their exertions in the glorious cause of liberty'.[69]

In Boudica's case, this was articulated in an illustration which showed her being pulled along on a war chariot, in the act of delivering her moving speech and 'animating the Britons to recover their liberty' (see Figure 5). Her daughters are visible as two forlorn figures crouched behind her, their heads bowed in shame or sorrow, or both. Boudica herself is portrayed as unmistakably primitive in her dress, with a fur slung over her shoulder, one breast and leg exposed. A druid elder, identifiable by his bushy beard, gestures towards Boudica with open palms, suggesting either supplication or, perhaps, blessing. Her tribesmen are so numerous that they stretch off into the distance, a sea of spears. Most strikingly, in the foreground, a man holds aloft a pagan sun symbol, representing a hazily understood antique religion, as unfamiliar to the average reader as it probably was to the artist and to John Baxter himself. However, it gives a point for focus for Boudica's gaze, suggesting she may be praying to the goddess Andraste, as discussed by Dio.[70] But overall the image suggests unity, with Boudica and her children occupying a central position, flanked by religious and military might. While the image in Smollett's history implied there was no liberty to defend in ancient Britain, Baxter's vision was of an organized alliance intent on securing existing freedoms from foreign invasion.

These varying portrayals of the ancient Britons and of Boudica herself in the histories of course demonstrate that political and constitutional concerns lay beneath the surface of much eighteenth-century history writing, as well as visual imagery, about the ancient past. Although British antiquity could be and often was simply ignored as too unreliably documented, when it was discussed, it was in terms that harmonized with concerns around the present state of affairs in 'English'—as usual, a catch-all for 'British'—politics. So far so unsurprising, given the well-known intensity of political and historical debate in this period; the key difference was that, for many, the ancient past was insufficiently controversial compared to more recent periods.

However, what is less often pointed out is that despite such concerns, the need for politically useful history did not, in the main, detract from a general sense amongst even the most politically compromised of historical writers, such as Thomas Carte, that there were and must be strictures governing interpretations of even the least reliably documented of pasts. Furthermore, these strictures were discursively negotiated within the pages of prose histories and in reviews. The notion that historians must resist the temptation to 'novelize' their histories or to seduce readers with flourishes of invention and 'poetry'—to borrow a seventeenth-century form of

---

[69] J. Baxter, *A new and impartial history of England* (London, 1796).

[70] That said, the image is an amalgamation of the accounts by Dio and Tacitus—Dio has Boudica on a dais of raised earth (indeed, as she was depicted in the frontispiece to Edward Seymour's *Complete History of England* published in 1764), while Tacitus describes her as riding on a chariot amidst her tribesmen. Incidentally, the image in Baxter's history shows a chariot similar to that described by Julius Caesar in the *Gallic Wars*, and later made famous by Thomas Thornycroft in his statue on Westminster Bridge.

Figure 5. 'Boadicea, Queen of the Iceni, Animating the Britons to Recover their Liberty' in John Baxter's *New and Impartial History* (1796). The Bodleian Libraries, The University of Oxford, (OC) 226. I 245, illustration facing page 20.

words—would have been familiar to Thomas Heywood and Edmund Bolton. But, as Thomas Salmon lamented, the danger of such confected histories was all the more real when increasingly polarizing political arguments were at stake, and this, arguably, was far more relevant to eighteenth-century writers than to historians before the constitutional upheavals of the later seventeenth century. There also emerged during this period a sense that historians should distance themselves from the present, but while aligning themselves more firmly with the past; that is, they should look upon the past with eyes unclouded by present-day concerns. Proximity to the events of the past on its own terms was considered good historical method, while to be infected by the concerns of the present, and to allow these concerns to seep into interpretations of the past, was to invite inaccuracy and errors of judgement—or, at the very least, accusations of both.

DRAMA, HISTORY, AND HUMAN NATURE: RICHARD GLOVER'S *BOADICIA, QUEEN OF BRITAIN*

These debates were not dissimilar to those surrounding Richard Glover's new stage play, *Boadicia, queen of Britain* (1753). Politics and constitutional controversy once again sat in the background of Glover's work. As we have seen, Boudica's utility for party politics in prose histories was somewhat limited in the period, though it does seem that she was of most interest to critics of Walpole's government. However, the playwright, Richard Glover was more successful in articulating the political lessons to be learned from Boudica's story than prose historians, whose concern was not, for the most part, with her as an individual, but as part of the schema of ancient Britain. Yet this, I will argue, was not the most important connection between the play and the published prose histories. If anything, accuracy and the limits of interpretation were as great a concern, if not greater, for Glover's critics than for those commenting on prose histories. This was because Glover's play—and arguably all historical drama—was being judged on two different accounts: first, on its fidelity to the record of history, and second on its ability to stage some version of enduring, realistic human experience.

The writer and Member of Parliament Richard Glover (1712–85) was said to be 'a patriot of the most independent cast, and scorning to bind himself about any one political party, was by all alike neglected'.[71] But this was a somewhat rose-tinted view. For much of his political life, Glover was a well-known supporter of the 'patriot opposition' to Robert Walpole, a loose affiliation of disaffected Whigs who viewed the Prime Minister as corrupt and self-serving.[72] Glover's first major work, published in 1737, was the epic poem *Leonidas*, an extended paean to public spiritedness above party factionalism.[73] The work was an unabashed tribute to

---

[71] *Bell's British Theatre; consisting of the most esteemed English plays* (London, 1797), Vol. II.
[72] R. Anderson (ed.), *The works of the British poets, with prefaces, biographical and critical*, 14 vols (London, 1795–1807), Vol. 11, 467–82. See also P. Baines, 'Glover, Richard (1712–1785)', *ODN* (2004; online edn, Sept 2013), http://www.oxforddnb.com/view/article/10831, accessed 8 Aug 2017. One of Glover's early editors, Richard Duppa, believed him to have been the author of the *Letters of Junius*. Duppa published a volume, *An inquiry concerning the author of the Letters of Junius with reference to the memoirs by a celebrated literary and political character* (London, 1815) in an attempt to prove it. The real author of the *Letters* remains uncertain.
[73] For factionalism and disputes about its exact meaning, see P. Rogers, 'Swift and Bolingbroke on faction', *Journal of British Studies*, 9 (1970), 71–101. See also Q. Skinner, 'The principles and practice of opposition: the case of Bolingbroke versus Walpole', in N. McKendrick (ed.), *Historical perceptions: studies in English thought and society in honour of J.H. Plumb* (London, 1974), pp. 93–128, esp. 99–100; D. Armitage, 'A Patriot for Whom?: The afterlives of Bolingbroke's Patriot King', *Journal of British Studies*, 36(4) (1997), 397–418; B. Cottret (ed.), *Bolingbroke's political writings: the conservative*

Frederick, Prince of Wales, purportedly Glover's patron, who served as the inspiration for the eponymous hero.[74] *Leonidas* propelled Glover to the status of 'literary darling' of the Whig opposition.[75] However, the poet also had the backing of the metropolitan merchant class, by whom he was considered 'an able and steady patriot' with a zeal for commercial interests.[76] After an early flirtation with political agitation in the City, he eventually took a seat in Parliament for Weymouth and Melcombe Regis in the 1760s.[77]

But writing and literary society commanded Glover's attention in the 1740s and 1750s. He struck up a friendship with the most famous thespian of the day, David Garrick, in about 1741, and Garrick at least was led to believe that Glover was engaged in writing a new Boudica play as early as 1742, intending to stage it at the Theatre Royal, Drury Lane where Garrick regularly performed.[78] However, a period of financial difficulty at around this time meant that the play did not make its debut at Drury Lane until December 1753, by which time Garrick was manager as well as leading man. It was performed ten times throughout the month of December; a standard run for a new production.[79] One of Glover's benefit nights, 12 December 1753, was the same date on which the printed play was published.[80] Further printed editions appeared in 1754, 1776, 1791, 1797, and 1811.

Glover's work was entirely original and it dealt with themes which had been less evident in previous fictionalizations of Boudica's life, and which were particularly suited to the concerns of the patriot Whigs, specifically the problem of factionalism. In *Boadicia, queen of Britain* Boudica acts as a subversion of the ideal patriot leader who rises above factional disputes and petty personal rivalry. In the play, rather than uniting her countrymen, Glover's Boudica character succumbs to selfishness and pride, ultimately causing a rift between her own tribe and that of her general, Dumnorix, played by David Garrick.[81] This most unpatriotic of acts causes the

---

Enlightenment (Basingstoke, 1997). For a contemporary view, and one of the most significant, see D. Mallet (ed.), 'Remarks on the history of England', in *The works of the Right Honourable Henry St John, Lord Viscount Bolingbroke*, 5 vols (London, 1777), Vol. 1.

[74] Gerrard, *Patriot opposition*, 63.

[75] Ibid., 80. See also B. Dobree, 'The theme of patriotism in the poetry of the early eighteenth century', *Proceedings of the British Academy*, 35 (1949), 49–65. Anderson explains the relevance of *Leonidas* to contemporaries in *British Poets*, p. 469.

[76] Glover emerged from self-imposed obscurity following the death of Frederick.

[77] See Glover's entry in the Institute of History Research/History of Parliament database at http://www.historyofparliamentonline.org/volume/1754-1790/member/glover-richard-1712-85, accessed 27 Nov 2017. The entry originally appeared in *The History of Parliament: the House of Commons 1754–1790*, ed. L. Namier and J. Brooke (Woodbridge, 1964).

[78] David Garrick to Peter Garrick, 19 April 1742, *The letters of David Garrick*, ed. D.M. Little, G.M. Kahrl, and P. DeK. Wilson (London, 1963). Garrick refers to Glover as being in the process of writing a new play about Boudica's life.

[79] G.W. Stone (ed.), *TLS 1660–1800*, Part 4 (1747–76) (Carbondale, IL, 1962), cii.

[80] Stone, *TLS*, 394–7 and 409. There were 499 individual performances that season, with 192 in David Garrick's Theatre Royal Drury Lane. Ibid., 375.

[81] It is interesting that Glover chose this name, which was the same as one of Caesar's own generals. Caesar suspected that Dumnorix was conspiring to seize power in Gaul and has him killed. Whether Glover meant any of this potential treachery to be attached to Dumnorix in his play is uncertain. See Caesar, *Gallic Wars*, H.J. Edwards (trans.), *Loeb Classical Library Online* (Cambridge MA, 2014), Book V, 241–3.

downfall of the British rebellion against Rome. As a contemporary described it, the play was intended, quite simply, 'to shew the fatal Effects of Division between Commanders'.[82] Thus Glover portrayed the British defeat as being the unhappy but inevitable consequence of a personal rivalry. The play's Boadicia is hell-bent on taking revenge against the Romans, who had raped her daughters and beaten her, while Dumnorix spends much of the play trying to cajole the enraged Boadicia away from her bloodthirsty resolution and toward a policy of cool diplomacy. Of course the denouement was the same as in previous Boudica plays: the Romans eventually win the day, but not before a few piteous British suicides take place along the way. Not the least of these is Boadicia's fictional sister and Dumnorix's wife, the hopelessly docile Venusia—in every sense the diametric opposite of the formidable Boadicia. The factionalism that prevails amongst the Britons ultimately leads them to ruin, and it is Venusia who articulates this when she begs Boadicia to 'Yet let restoring union close our wounds…'[83]

However, for contemporary critics of the play, Glover's intended message of patriotism and factional unity, although acknowledged, was of little concern, and, tellingly, Boudica's femininity was not a matter for sustained discussion.[84] Critics instead focused on Glover's (in)accuracy as an interpreter of history and human nature—that is, they critiqued the playwright's ability to convincingly represent reality, both historical and experiential—and came to very different conclusions as to how successful his efforts had been. For some more generous reviewers, the ambiguity, even confusion, of Glover's historical characters was a true and accurate reflection of human beings under duress in difficult circumstances. Others claimed that the author had simply failed in his dual duty as historian and dramatist to portray Boudica and her contemporaries behaving as they had in the historical record, or as they might have done in a rationally imagined reality; instead, Glover presented his audience with a grotesque simulacrum of humanity.

To the first reviewer of the play, the physician and author Henry Pemberton (1694–1771), Glover's work was unique among plays of its day for its precise dissection of human passion and error. This, however, may not have been a disinterested opinion, since Pemberton was one of Glover's oldest friends and a consistent supporter of his literary efforts. In 1738 Pemberton had been vocally appreciative of the soon-to-be infamous *Leonidas*,[85] and his review of *Boadicia* nearly twenty years later continued this trend of public approbation for Glover's works. In *Some Few Reflections on the Tragedy of Boadicia*, published on 8 December 1753—very soon after, or possibly on, the play's opening night—Pemberton made superlative claims for the innovative nature of Glover's drama, but also, more tellingly, for its substance as a spectacle of historical and human reality. He remarked that, without resorting

---

[82] *Gentleman's Magazine*, 23 (December 1753), 576–8.
[83] R. Glover, *Boadicia, a tragedy* (London, 1753), 33.
[84] For alternative readings of the play, see Nielsen, 'Boadicea onstage' and Williams, 'Neo-classical embarrassment'. Glover drew on the familiar language of female/male dichotomy as an easy means by which he could create division between the titular character and the general Dumnorix, but it would seem that this was incidental than central to the work's message.
[85] See review quoted in Anderson, *British poets*, 475.

to an overly confected plotline, Glover's play gripped its audience's attention by 'imitating after the justest manner human actions and passions'.[86] This was high praise, possibly calculated to forego some of the criticisms that were emerging from other circles that the play was anything but imitative of humanity. However, Pemberton was suggesting that the play was a genuine reflection of the original— 'real life and manners'—which other playwrights sought in vain to imitate. In *Boadicia* the characters, he claimed, 'are made to speak and act, as men would actually do in the same circumstances'. Pemberton praised Glover's dialogue in particular as being shorn of unnatural embellishments such as would never be overheard in real conversation.

For Pemberton, Glover's exploration of the psychology of his characters was a success, serving to adorn the play with a more congenial complexity than mere intricacies of plot could afford:

> [The play's] excellence consists in the distinct representation of the effects the story in its several circumstances has upon the personages concerned according to their different situations in regard to the event, and the particular turn allotted to the mind and temper of each.[87]

Thus Pemberton made what some saw as a weakness into one of the play's great strengths. Glover's contradictory characters, whose behaviour appeared to some as irrational and inexplicable, in fact provided the substantive dramatic matter of the play, which might otherwise have been dictated by the artifice of events alone. This, Pemberton insisted, was the Aristotelean model of tragedy, 'where the catastrophe is brought about, not merely by the course of human affairs, but by some error in great and worthy characters' that condemns them to a fate ordained by their own flaws.[88] The fate Pemberton was referring to is Boudica's own part in her country's demise, which, compelled by his message of patriotic resistance to factionalism, Glover had explored in greater detail than previous playwrights. Pemberton's belief in the success of Glover's play lay in its portrayal of Boudica and accompanying characters in what the playwright thought to be a realistic manner, which ensured that they reflected 'true' human nature in all its occasionally contradictory guises. Thus the seeming oddities in characters' behaviour—such as Dumnorix's active encouragement of his wife's suicide, which does rather jar with his professed love for her—were interpreted by Pemberton as bold representations of the extremity of possibility that naturally occurred in the spectrum of human emotion and action. Thus Pemberton's appeal to human nature was to assert that it was in some sense unknowable to onlookers except through emotional exchanges in dialogue. These exchanges were not merely amenable to the conceit of the author, but in fact were utterly dictated by it. The author's imposition of a spectrum of human nature mattered far more than any imposed by convention or the expectations of the audience. However, it is worth noting that Pemberton's view of human nature, and the extent to which Glover's did or did not ring true to it, is not entirely clear in his discussion, so it is

---

[86] H. Pemberton, *Some few reflections on the Tragedy of Boadicia* (London, 1753).
[87] Ibid., 8–9. [88] Ibid., 9.

not possible to determine whether the two men shared a definition of human nature, or understood it to be constant or universal. Rather, Pemberton's view seemed to be that human nature constituted a spectrum of possibility rather than a predictable set of behaviours, and it was Glover's achievement to have made excursions to the extremes of that spectrum.[89]

But Pemberton's view of the play was not universally shared; most other critics were far less generous, and also much more rigid in their opinions about the latitude allowed for authorial dictation of 'natural' human behaviour. An anonymous reviewer in *The Spectator* was dismissive of the play and contemptuous of its title character, at least in the manner in which she was imagined by Glover. The play's 'Boadicia', the reviewer wrote, begins as one character and ends as another and, 'consequently, no one is under the least pain about what becomes of her, and begins to think the whipping she received was no more than what she deserved...'[90] This inconsistency of character was attributable to the failure of the author, and was not a judgement on the historical Boudica. It is also telling because, at least so far as *The Spectator* was concerned, the disparity between the Boadicia of the beginning and that of the play's end was not a conscious experiment in changing extremes, as Pemberton seemed to be suggesting, but rather a failure to properly understand the humanity of the character and, indeed, the sentiments of the audience. The reviewer was equally scathing in his commentary on the main male character, Garrick's Dumnorix, who suffered from the same inconsistency in behaviour, starting as 'a blusterer in the first part, a coward in the latter, and very weak in the last'.[91] Unlike Pemberton, the reviewer saw in the play an affront to human nature, not its apotheosis. 'It is in writing as in painting, often authors, with design to make the characters more striking, make them unnatural, as bad painters to give expression, communicate distortion; and thus to make Boadicea more savage and unforgiving, he [Glover] has terminated in making her an idiot.'[92] The reviewer's frustration was shared by the rest of the audience, who, he claimed, gave it a frosty reception.

There were more measured critiques. Pemberton's positive opinion was in part shared by Crisp Mills, who offered his review of the play in the form of a *Letter to Mr. Richard Glover* published in January 1754, soon after the negative review in *The Spectator*.[93] Mills cited what he took to be the approbation with which Glover's play had been received by audiences, contradicting the *Spectator* reviewer's assessment of audience reception as cold and critical. Upon viewing the play himself, Mills's own reaction was one of 'transport and rapture'.[94] While the reviewer in *The Spectator* had been appalled by the contrasts in Boadicia's character and actions and by her opposition to her fellow Britons—flaws which he attributed to

---

[89] The relationship between the historical 'science of man', as understood most famously by David Hume, and eighteenth-century historical drama demands further research. However, the notion of a 'spectrum' comes from S.K. Wertz, 'Hume, history, and human nature', *Journal of the history of ideas*, 36 (1975), 481–96; for debates on the 'constancy' and 'uniformity' of human nature in the period, see L. Pompa, *Human nature and historical knowledge: Hume, Hegel and Vico* (Cambridge, 1990), 42–9.
[90] *The Spectator*, 29 December 1753.   [91] Ibid.   [92] Ibid.
[93] Its publication was advertised in the *Whitehall Evening Post*, 12 January 1754.
[94] C. Mills, *A letter to Richard Glover on occasion of his tragedy of Boadicia* (London, 1754), 4.

the writer—Mills, like Pemberton, saw the portrayal of the titular character as one of Glover's greatest dramatic achievements. He described his own inner struggle to judge who the most virtuous character in the play was, and it was this appeal to his conscience that suggested Glover's triumph. Boadicia, he realized, had been wronged and maltreated, and thus her revenge was perhaps justified; but Venusia's gentle attempts to sway her sister to show mercy to Roman captives appealed equally.[95] 'These extraordinary effects on the mind of the very spectator of any sensibility, you, Sir, awaken by the artless language of the passions.'[96] A confused and confusing Boudica was a captivating character for the writer and the audience and had the potential to contribute to a positive reaction to the play. Pemberton and Mills both understood Glover's Boadicia character to have behaved in a manner that reflected the swaying passions of human life, and to capture this, they thought, was the ultimate aim of the dramatist.

These three reviews are all suggestive of preoccupations beyond the aesthetic and outwith the presumed necessity of historical accuracy. Rather they were embroiled in a discussion of the play as a spectacle of humanity, with the historical backdrop seemingly irrelevant to the more pressing question of Glover's portrayal of human action. Pemberton and Mills were in agreement that the contradictions inherent in Glover's characters were a conscious choice on the part of the playwright, and were intended to demonstrate to the audience the extremity of emotion that was possible under such violent circumstances. And, as Mills pointed out, even if contradictions were evident within individual personalities, the contrast between Boadicia and Venusia equally demonstrated how two different human beings could behave in starkly different ways under the same circumstances. The anonymous *Spectator* reviewer was not convinced, and found little but a failure of imagination in such conceits.

However, still other reviewers were less concerned with making any serious critique of the play as a representation of accurate history or reality, and were instead carried away by the play as an example of an emerging English form of drama. Yet Glover's unusual approach to characterization actually bolstered this view. In 1754 the historian William Rider (1723–85) claimed that the varied, even shambolic nature of English drama, which shunned the rigid conventions of the ancients, was itself a symptom of the innate 'love of liberty' to be found in the English nation at large. Thus it should be applauded as a virtue, and Glover's play, with its seemingly unpredictable characters, was the best example of its day. In Rider's opinion, even where English dramatists were been capable of conforming to rules, they should resist the tyranny of the ancients in favour of their own original forays into poetry and drama. 'Do we not admire the Height of Soul which has always characterized our Nation, and that Courage untamed by Oppression, for which Foreigners have so justly admired and applauded the English name.'[97] Yet by appealing to national pride, Rider was subtly commenting once again on the unusual behaviour of the play's characters. 'Rules' should be no bar to the creativity

---

[95] Ibid., 12.   [96] Ibid., 15.
[97] W. Rider, *A comment on Boadicia, with remarks on Mill's Letter* (London, 1754), 10.

of the author, whose message of patriotism trumped the constraints of human nature. This kind of exceptionalism legitimated Glover's experimental characterization as a patriotic act. However, Rider's call for the play to be revived was not heeded until 1800, when the play underwent extensive revisions before being restaged.

But the flurry of responses to Glover's play did not end with reviews of the staged version; the published text of the play occasioned the appearance of two new short histories focused on ancient Britain and Queen Boudica. Both were examples of the era's 'parasitical biography', a genre that fed off the growing market for history and exploited the ephemeral prominence of historical characters when they appeared on stage in order to sell short, cheap, biographies of the historical men and women thrust into the public eye.[98] The first in Boudica's case was the anonymous *Female Revenge*, a work '[c]alculated to instruct the Readers of this celebrated Tragedy, in that true History of one of the most memorable Transactions recorded in the British Annals; and to shew wherein Poetical Fiction has deviated from Real Facts'. The tract was part history, part review, and it offered a more detailed historic account than most examples of parasitical history or biography. The identity of the author is not known.

Like previous reviewers, the author of *Female Revenge* focused on two aspects of Glover's play: its historical accuracy and its portrayal of human nature. The critique of Glover's historical inaccuracies was subtle but damningly effective, because it took the simple form of an alternative 'true history' to that being performed on stage. The first fifteen pages of *Female Revenge* was a conventional retelling of Boudica's story, shorn of the embellishments present in Glover's drama. Much like a panoramic history, the events of the Boudican rebellion were set within the longer context of ancient British history, beginning with the first invasion of the island by Julius Caesar and including all the most notable occurrences prior to Boudica's uprising. This included a discussion of the British king and queen, Venutius and Cartiusmandua. The reviewer believed Glover's Dumnorix to have been based in part on the real Venutius, who was said to have divorced Cartismandua after a domestic quarrel. That Dumnorix, or Venutius, should remarry a new wife, called 'Venusia' by Richard Glover, 'herein varies from real History... However, it is not hard to imagine that Venutius, upon the Divorce between him and his Queen, might take another Wife, and that she supported the Character given her by the Poet. And therefore, as the Author's Invention has not exceeded the Bounds of Probability, we ought not to quarrel with him for a Licence which he has *decently assumed*.'[99] The fictionalization of history was not in itself objectionable, and the author acknowledged that the story of Boudica, even as 'truthfully' told by Tacitus and other reputable historians, 'furnish[ed] sufficient Materials for Tragedy', and the author pointed to instances in which Glover's play captured the liveliness

---

[98] D.A. Stauffer, 'A parasitical form of biography', *Modern Language Notes*, 55(4) (1940), 289–92. Pamphlet summaries of historical events had been given out at performances during the Restoration; see Woolf, 'From hystories to the historical', 63 n.103.

[99] Anon., *Female Revenge or the British Amazon: Exemplified in the life of Boadicia* (London, 1753), 7–8. Emphasis in original.

and horror of Boudica's battles. However, the dramatist had at times pushed the boundaries of credulity further than was probable or decent, demanding a corrective in the form of *Female Revenge*.

The inadequacy of Glover's interpretation, as judged by the author of *Female Revenge*, extended beyond mere historical inaccuracies towards the very questions that preoccupied Pemberton, Mills, and the anonymous *Spectator* reviewer. The author of *Female Revenge* was inexorably drawn to similar criticisms, particularly around the character of Boadicia herself, whose single-minded vengeance overtook all other concerns of duty or morality. The key question for the author of *Female Revenge* was whether 'any one [could] imagine such a Character in Nature?' The answer was resoundingly in the negative: Boadicia 'is a Contradiction to common Sense; and has no Foundation in Nature...', and, it followed, had no place on the stage. Neither was this simply a moral objection to the conduct of Glover's Boadicia; viciousness in fictional characters was perfectly acceptable, but only if 'copied from Examples or Practices daily observable among Mankind',[100] and thus in harmony with experience and consequently capable of imparting moral lessons. Glover's Boadicia was little better than an extravagance, not even believable enough to effectively illustrate the consequences of brutality. 'And if unnatural characters be inconsistent with the Rules of the Drama, which delights in pursuing Nature through all her variable shapes, I will be bold to say, that of Boadicia has no Title to a Representation on the Stage.'[101]

Thus Glover's disregard for the rules of drama, of nature, and of history blended together into one great failure of conceit:

> When a Piece of known History is converted into a Tragedy, the Poet constantly preserves a sacred regard to the Truth of the Characters of those great Personages whom he realizes upon the Stage... Has Mr. Glover done so with regards to Boadicea? I believe those who examine the antient Authors who give any Account of her, characterize her very differently from what he has done: Historians represent her as a Woman of undaunted Courage and Resolution, and of a Spirit and Magnanimity above her Sex; that she had suffer'd Injuries and Insults of the grossest Nature from the Hands of the Romans; for which she took a severe and just Vengeance on them as soon as it was in her Power. All this was agreeable to the Dictates of natural Justice. But no-where do we read, that she carried her Revenge to such an Extremity, as to sacrifice all Regards to Friendship, natural Affection, the Obligations of Honour and Justice, and her own, as well as the Interests of her People, to that implacable Passion; and therefore her Character is not only out of Nature, but without Precedent.[102]

Glover's dramatic blunder was simultaneously a blight on the character of the historical Boudica, an insult to recorded history, and an affront to human nature. For the author of *Female Revenge*, the anxiety around dramatic invention stemmed from the same source as that around novelized histories: the unwary might take them as impartial, accurate 'truth'. This critic of Glover had in mind the more heroic version of Boudica in the existing histories—a version which s/he evidently

---

[100] Ibid., 20.   [101] Ibid., 21.   [102] Ibid., 32.

took to be true. However, the problems ran deeper than inaccuracy. The reviewer seemed to be suggesting that Glover's play was not merely peddling untruths, it was also destabilizing the relationship between actions and their consequences. The actions of Glover's characters were so entirely outside of nature, or everyday experience, as to render inexplicable the relationship between their own human agency and the historical events that swirled around them.

Richard Glover did not, it seems, take all of this criticism lying down. Aside from *Female Revenge*, one other history of Boudica appeared at the same time as the play, but it was in a very different mould. *A Short History of Boadicia, Queen of Britain, being the story on which the tragedy is founded* was published in 1754, after *Female Revenge*, but if it was meant as a response it was hardly an effective one. It is entirely possible that this history was written by Richard Glover himself, or perhaps by his friend and enthusiastic reviewer, the historian William Rider, as a means of stemming the tide of animadversion. The opening paragraphs of the *Short History* are little more than a puff piece for Glover, calculated to attract the reading audience to a play that 'cannot but raise an eager desire in every English heart, to be warm'd by scenes which will bring before 'em the ancient heroism of our country'.[103] For the most part it drew on Tacitus for its account of the first half of Boudica's story, switching to Dio's atrocity stories only with the cautionary phrase 'as some authors say', suggesting that the writer of the *Short History* was not prepared to endorse the veracity of Dio's explicit account in full.[104] Yet the majority of the *Short History* coincided not with the known accounts by ancient or recent historical writers, but with the action of Glover's play. In the *Short History* the Boudica of this history is a textbook fomenter of faction, just as she had been in Glover's drama. In all probability, the *Short History* was published in the hope that it would indeed by bound with the play, thus insulating readers from the 'true' history related in the competing *Female Revenge* Such seamless intersection between factual and fictional history likely fed the anxiety expressed by some reviewers that Glover was playing a dangerous game with the public's understanding of the past, and perhaps even its moral character.

Glover's play was controversial in its day and the controversy continued to reverberate through the literary circles of the mid-eighteenth century; but the play did not travel well beyond its immediate context, and the overall view taken by posterity seems to have been rather more negative. Glover's claims to a public-spirited non-partisanship were well known to his contemporaries, and may even have encouraged men like Garrick to support the author's talents But even Garrick was not above reproach for his patronage. The author John Cleland, best known for the pornographic *Fanny Hill, memoirs of a woman of pleasure* (1748–9), wrote a haranguing letter to the theatre manager nearly twenty years after *Boadicia* was first seen on stage. Frustrated by Garrick's reluctance to perform his own dramas and

---

[103] Anon., *A Short History of Boadicea, The British Queen, Being the Story on which the new tragedy now in rehearsal at the Theatre Royal Drury Lane is Founded. Very proper to be bound with the play* (London, 1753), 6.

[104] *A short history of Boadicia*, 10.

intent on opening old wounds, Cleland remarked, 'You brought on *Boadicia*...only fit to make an ice-house of a summer-theatre, if there was such a thing as Taste existing.'[105] Garrick felt moved to defend himself: 'Why do You raise the Ghosts of *Boadicia*...to haunt me? If I had not perform'd [it], I should have been a very Shallow Politician.'[106] This suggests that Garrick was motivated by something other than the literary merit of Glover's play. Similarly, the novelist Tobias Smollett whose later success as a writer of prose belied his youthful struggles to promote himself as a dramatist, derided Glover's *Boadicia* as the latest in a glut of poor offerings at the theatre. The famously cantankerous Smollett poured scorn on theatre-goers 'that have not sense enough left to distinguish between Draff and Dainties'.[107]

Although Glover's political—or, more precisely, his purportedly apolitical—credentials meant that his play found its way onto the stage despite its many flaws, the play's instrumental message was to condemn it to oblivion after only a brief period. Yet the effect of the play was once again to bring Boudica to the fore in the theatre, as well as in readily available printed works such as *Female Revenge*, which were of a much more approachable stature than the panoramic histories in which Boudica's story was so often retold. But the critical reaction to Glover's play, especially when contrasted with the discussion around prose histories, reveals the unique set of concerns that the historical playwright had to take into account. Playwrights and historians were alike open to the accusation that they had violated the strictures of 'real' or 'true' history. Granted, these strictures were not precisely the same for historians as they were for playwrights, particularly in relation to the proximity of past and present. There is little sense from the response to Glover that his reviewers took particular issue with his wholly unsubtle message about the dangers of factionalism, which was, after all, very clearly influenced by the concerns of the present. By contrast, prose narrators such as Carte and Salmon saw their interpretations of the past castigated as a consequence of their perceived failure to distance themselves from contemporary events. Thus, although politics undoubtedly infused the historical production of the period, too overt an association between the past and the present in an individual historical work nevertheless provided firm ground for critical objection. Arguably, Thomas Carte's claim to have judged of the ancient past as if he had lived only in that time and not in the present suggests that a detachment from the present, as much as or more than detachment from the past, characterized an the ideal of history writing. This in itself is revealing of a contemporary perception that the distance between past and present should be policed with greater rigour than it was in practice.

Consequently, Glover's fictionalized ancient Britain was not deemed problematic in the sense that it was going to seduce unsuspecting readers to dangerous political beliefs. However, in a manner very similar to the less well-received histories, such as

---

[105] John Cleland to David Garrick, 22 May 1772 (Forster Collection. 28. 213. 48. F. 28. National Art Library). This was the second such letter Cleland had sent to Garrick, the first having been sent in 1754 and having much the same message.

[106] David Garrick to John Cleland, 24 May 1772, *The Letters of David Garrick*, Vol. II, Letter 689, p. 802.

[107] Smollett to Alexander Carlyle, 1 March 1754 in *Letters of Tobias Smollett*, 33–4.

that by Thomas Carte, Glover's play was subject to restrictions based on historical evidence; or at least, critics believed it should have been. This suggests that the very fact of taking the past as inspiration dictated writers' limits. That political debate, history, and narrative style abutted and occasionally permeated one another in this period is beyond doubt; but that critical commentary was often predicated on the idea that the permeability should be minimized in practice suggests that hardened boundaries between politics and history, fiction and fact, were the products of an ongoing discourse conducted between historians, dramatists, and critical audiences.

But the fate of Glover's *Boadicia* further suggests that the stage was seen as something of a laboratory for human subjects, testing the playwright's ability to convincingly re-enact 'real' human interactions against a historical background. Thus the battle for 'accuracy' had to be fought by the playwright on two fronts. The rigour applied to the playwright was based on an understanding of the latitude of believable human behaviour in given historical circumstances. As an imagined version of the past, Glover's failed to convince critics on the basis of its historical accuracy, as well as its approach to human sensibility, with his historical characters behaving in ways that were both historically unaccountable and contrary to conventional views of human experience.

But there are points that emerge from the critical discussion around Richard Glover's 1753 stage play, as well as the histories, that relate specifically to Boudica's story, namely, the story was in flux; a state of being which both contributed to and was reflected in the very fluidity of historical genres in the period up to the nineteenth century. Richard Glover's play had attracted a deal of controversy because of its unusual stance on dramatic convention, on historical accuracy, and on human behaviour. But at least one reviewer at the time—no less a figure than Thomas Herring, Archbishop of Canterbury—felt moved to defend Boudica herself against what he thought was Glover's unfair reproach. Referring to the play in a letter to a friend, Herring wrote, '...it is my opinion, that *Boadicea* is really not the object of crime and punishment, so much as pity; and notwithstanding the strong paintings of her savageness, I cannot help wishing she had got the better. She had been most unjustly and outrageously injured by those universal tyrants, who ought never to be mentioned without horror.'[108] Herring's view of the Romans was somewhat unusual, but he was clearly of the opinion that Richard Glover had unduly castigated Boudica, a wronged woman and queen.

Herring was not alone. In 1754, the year following the first production of Glover's play, a brief but telling piece appeared in *The Rational Amusement*, a volume comprised of five books of letters, each touching on a variety of light-hearted, entertaining but educative subject matter. Book V took the form of an imagined epistolary exchange between 'Florimund' and 'Phaon' on the subject of British heroes and history. In response to Phaon's request to describe the greatest hero from the British past, Florimund wrote a short piece, an original, affective, and edifying work, 'The History of Boadicea, a British Queen'. 'O! That Men would always think like this Woman, and believe that there is nothing just or unjust,

---

[108] Archbishop Thomas Herring, quoted in Anderson, *British poets*, 471.

beautiful or ugly, but as it stands in relation to the common Welfare of Society! No Guards could then preserve a Tyrant, or secure a successful Monster from the Hand of a true Patriot,' Florimund enthused on the subject of his hero. He continued:

> The intention of restoring freedom to her country, groaning under the load of a foreign Usurpation, ought to consecrate her Memory to all Posterity, and make her consider'd as a saint and martyr, by all free Britons of every Church...let eternal Honours wait on the Protectoress of British Freedom; and let this devout Reverence teach us, that the most cruel Death is preferable in the Cause of Liberty, to the best Life that can be led without it.[109]

Glover, well known for his devotion to the patriot Whigs and their shared notion of 'liberty', had used Boudica to illustrate the pitfalls of rivalry and factionalism, rather than to show her as an emblem of patriotism herself. Yet Florimund saw her as an unalloyed hero, with none of the ambiguity inherent in Glover's contemporaneous work. That such differing perceptions of Boudica could exist at almost precisely the same moment in time gives further weight to the idea that ambiguity was quite simply immanent in stories of ancient Britain, and, as a consequence, in Boudica's individual narrative. The next chapter will explore the proliferation of representations of Boudica that were sustained by the widespread culture of history that existed in nineteenth century. But, as this chapter has shown, any sense that the simultaneity of differing representations was only possible in the new 'popular history' of the modern period must be seen in light of the long discursive process, that, arguably, began with the disagreement between the versions of Tacitus and Dio.

---

[109] *The rational amusement: comprehending a collection of letters on a great variety of subjects, serious, entertaining, moral, diverting and instructive* (London, 1754), 342.

4
'Too strange to be popular'
Negotiating Past and Present in Early Nineteenth-century Historical Culture

> *We need not go out of England to seek heroines, while we have annals to preserve their illustrious names... let it suffice to name a Boadicea, who made the most glorious stand against the Romans in defence of her country, which that great empire was ever a witness to. And if her endeavours did not meet with the success of an Alexander, a Cesar, or a Charles of Sweden in his fortunate days; her courage and conduct were such as render'd her worthy to be consider'd equal, if not superior to them all, in bravery and wisdom; not to mention the nicer justice of her intentions.*[1]

The preceding chapters having grounded Queen Boudica's reputation in the early source material and later creative reception of the seventeenth and eighteenth centuries, this chapter goes on to explore nineteenth-century historical culture, drawing on the wide variety of historical genres that were available to audiences in the period. My emphasis here will be on the distinct degree of continuity that is evident in nineteenth-century iterations of Boudica when compared with those that came before. As I have sought to show, historical ideas are never created from nothing; in historical culture, creation is in itself an act of reception. However, this is not to deny change over time. The period that forms the focus of this chapter, that is to say the late eighteenth and early nineteenth centuries up to and including the early Victorian period, should be viewed with a degree of caution in Boudica's case: it was not a period of extreme or sudden change, and neither was it a period of stasis. 'Positive' and 'negative' views of Boudica had co-existed for centuries, and her actions were variously considered to have been just and unjust by different people at the same time: this is in the nature of historical culture, and indeed of human culture. That said, Boudica's emergence in new media and new genres in the period under discussion in this chapter undoubtedly contributed to a more widely understood view of her as a brave female hero. But this should not be attributed to a novel desire for a 'popular' form of history that did not exist before, and neither should it be dismissed as a predictable consequence of the 'age of heroism' that obtained during the reign of Victoria. It should be seen within the context of growth, not wholesale change.

[1] *Beauty's triumph or the superiority of the Fair Sex invincibly proved* (London, 1745), 54.

For many scholars of Boudica, one work in particular has been credited with establishing her 'acceptable' image amongst nineteenth-century audiences.[2] This was William Cowper's *Boadicea: an ode* (1782), the most famous lines of which are:

> Regions Cæsar never knew
>   Thy posterity shall sway,
> Where his eagles never flew,
>   None invincible as they.
> She, with all a monarch's pride,
>   Felt them in her bosom glow;
> Rush'd to battle, fought, and died;
>   Dying, hurl'd them at the foe.
> Ruffians, pitiless as proud,
>   Heav'n awards the vengeance due;
> Empire is on us bestow'd,
>   Shame and ruin wait for you.[3]

Much of the poem takes the form of a pronouncement by a Druid priest, a prophecy relayed to Boudica as she stands, 'bleeding from the Roman rods'. The Druid foresees the fall of Rome and the birth of a new empire in its place. The copyright on Cowper's poems expired in 1814, which allowed them to be reproduced at low cost and in vast numbers, and they were to become among the most widely read poems of the modern era.[4] *Boadicea: an ode* was reprinted over and over again in children's books and periodicals; it was later said that the poem became known to every schoolchild in England.[5]

Due in large part to the popularity of Cowper's *Ode*, the end of eighteenth century has been seen by scholars of Boudica's later reputation as a critical time for her emergence as a national heroine. This is contrasted in the literature with the early decades of the eighteenth century, when people were less actively engaged with Boudica's reputation, the suggestion being that it was only during the French Revolutionary and Napoleonic Wars that Boudica emerged from post-Elizabethan gloom to become 'a focus of literary endeavour and patriotic sentiment'.[6] The implication of this view is that Cowper's poem was the beginning of an upward trajectory for Boudica as an individual figure. However, it would be misleading to suggest that Cowper's romantic imagery single-handedly overthrew a widely held perception of Boudica as a villain, a madwoman, or a stubborn bulwark against civilization. What it did accomplish was the distillation and circulation of an idea of Boudica as a wronged woman and avenging heroine, indissolubly linked to the

---

[2] Williams, 'This frantic woman', 32.
[3] J.D. Baird and C. Ryskamp (eds), *The poems of William Cowper*, 6 vols (Oxford, 1980), Vol. I, 431–2.
[4] W. St Clair, *The reading nation in the Romantic period* (Cambridge, 2004), 207.
[5] When the poem was recited as part of the St Albans Pageant of 1907, '...a small, clearly defined cheer came from one corner of the audience, which evidently recognised an old friend of its school lessons', *Manchester Guardian*, 16 July 1907.
[6] MacDonald, 'Boadicea: warrior, mother, myth', 51.

Druids, but these, of course, were notions that had existed since Edmund Bolton's *Nero Caesar*, if not before. However, more so than any previous depictions of Boudica, Cowper's was to become an explicitly cited source in itself, almost on par with Tacitus and Dio in terms of its perceived historicity. Moreover, the poet's use of prophecy as a dramatic device was both novel and far-reaching, and it was pressed into service at various points in the ensuing decades.

But there is a larger point to draw out here. Connected with the notion of a late eighteenth- and nineteenth-century shift in Boudica's reputation is the wider sense evident among cultural historians that this period marked the emergence of a popular culture of history, best exemplified by the enormous popularity of Sir Walter Scott's historical fictions.[7] Roy Strong's assessment was that the early nineteenth century was the first era in which we can discern a commercial interest in the past, evidenced through the production of national histories, historical novels, and history painting.[8] Peter Mandler has similarly asserted the significance of national feeling in differentiating popular history after the early nineteenth century from that which came before, stating that, 'before the French Revolution, history neither needed nor wanted a popular audience'.[9] Elsewhere, Mandler has argued that between the years 1820–50, a 'popular and national tradition had to be recaptured, rescued from the dust of ages, and then revivified – continued in a modern, democratic idiom, confirming the commitment to progress and the future'.[10] Would-be popularizers of history were limited, Mandler argues, to the bequests of eighteenth-century antiquarianism and as a consequence developed a distinct interest in the 'olden times' of an imagined medieval England. Although Mandler also acknowledges the diversity of the period's historical genres and modes, there is nevertheless a widespread assumption that the story of historical culture begins in the nineteenth century—once again underscoring the implicit power of the 'invention of tradition' paradigm. Regarding the publication of history books before 1850, Leslie Howsam has argued that the popular idea of the British historical narrative prior to that date amounted to little more than a catalogue of kings and queens and a few picturesque anecdotes.[11] Billie Melman has stated that 'from about 1800 there developed an English popular culture of history', characterized

---

[7] S. Berger, 'Professional and popular historians', 18. For Scott's novels and their engagement with contemporary historical thought, see R. Maitzen, '"By no means an improbable fiction": *Redgauntlet*'s novel historicism', *Studies in the novel*, 25 (1993), 170–83, as well as M.S. Phillips, 'Macaulay, Scott, and the literary challenge to historiography', *Journal of the history of ideas*, 50(1) (1989), 117–33.

[8] R. Strong, *And when did you last see your father?: The Victorian painter and the British past* (London, 1978), 32. Strong goes on to say that the popularity of history was part of a 'deliberate attempt to create national mythologies strong enough to hold the minds of the masses who now made up and were necessary to the working of the modern state'.

[9] P. Mandler, *History and national life* (London, 2002), 11.

[10] P. Mandler, '"In the olden time": Romantic history and English national identity, 1820–50', in L. Brockliss and D. Eastwood (eds), *A union of multiple identities* (Manchester, 1997), pp. 78–92, at 81.

[11] L. Howsam, *Past into print: the publishing of history in Britain, 1850–1950* (London, 2009), 4.

by 'the production of segments of the past, or rather pasts' and 'the multiplicity of their representations'.[12]

Thus we might account for Boudica's later heroic persona by linking her to the emergence of a popular culture of history, cast as a uniquely nineteenth-century phenomenon. Along similar lines, one could also argue that any changes in Boudica's posthumous image might also be explained by the popular reaction against the Enlightenment-era view of history, which had been characterized by Thomas Carlyle as bloodless and detached from any real human feeling, and a turn to the more imaginative, appealing, and 'popular' historical modes characteristic of romantic historicism, and which were also more amenable to a burgeoning mass media.[13] But my argument here is that we could instead view the historical imaginary of the post-Enlightenment period as harmonizing with an enduring trend, namely the slow growth of the 'history market', which can be traced as far back as the Elizabethan chronicle.

Although a romanticized view of history undoubtedly did blur the historical and the imagined pasts in the early part of the nineteenth century, this blurring had existed for centuries, as had the connection between emotive and sensational language, 'hack' historical writing for a quick profit, and the appeal to new audiences. What Mark Phillips calls the 'imaginative identification with history'[14] evident in the romantic age was in fact inherent in all engagement with the past—and arguably continues to be. This imaginative engagement gave the past its power amongst non-specialist audiences in successive presents, far removed from the intellectual concerns of the Enlightenment, or the conventions of antiquarianism.

The truth lies somewhere between a complete disavowal of fundamental change and the position evident elsewhere in much of the existing scholarship. Rather than see this period as the beginning stage in the emergence of a 'popular' culture of history—and by extension of the move towards a separate, professionalized history—this period demonstrates the latest and perhaps the most recognizably 'modern' development in a long-term trend, in the role played by historical ideas in British culture. Those characteristics which distinguish 'popular' historical engagement from 'scholarly' or 'serious' historical work—for example, an emotive, imaginative, or fictionalized presentation, the co-existence of a multiplicity of representations, and a deep engagement with the past's direct relationship to the present, especially in the spirit of political debate—had all been essential to historical culture long before the nineteenth century. Indeed, the very act of producing historical work of any kind demands an admixture of some or all of these characteristics, and an attentiveness to previous depictions of the past; thus the sense of historical creation as an act of reception.

---

[12] Melman, *Culture of history*, 6–10. See also B. Melman, 'The power of the past: history and modernity in the Victorian world', in M. Hewitt (ed.), *The Victorian World* (London, 2013), pp. 466–83.

[13] A. Jarrells, '"Associations respect[ing] the past": Enlightenment and romantic historicism', in J. Klancher (ed.), *A concise companion to the Romantic age* (London, 2009), pp. 57–76.

[14] Phillips, 'Literary challenge to historiography', 119.

The emergence of professional and academic-institutional structures within and around the practice of history was of course an innovation of the later nineteenth century in Britain, but this should not lead us to the conclusion that the production of the past as an element of commercial and literary culture was similarly new. The history of historiography and historical scholarship is unabashedly 'Whiggish' in its assumption that, from the early modern period, there was a steady march towards the goal of ever greater objectivity culminating in 'scientific' or systematic history on the model of Leopold von Ranke. This may well be the case in the narrowly conceived intellectual history of history, but representations of the past have always has been distinguished by their relationship to some kind of 'truth', whether defined as authorial objectivity in regards to concerns of the present, or adherence to the extant record. This makes any attempt to separate scholarly and popular history before the nineteenth century—or indeed, to make either the product of the other—quite problematic. The form of history that has possessed intimate connections with imaginative or fictive genres, and has mapped onto commercial trends in, for instance, theatre attendance and reading, antedates 'professionalized' historiography by centuries. Indeed, even the most respected historians of the past had commercial goals: we have already encountered Thomas Heywood and Nathaniel Crouch, but even David Hume has been called 'the harbinger of the historical best-seller of our own day', and he was conscious of competing with Tobias Smollett for sales.[15]

With this in mind, this chapter will examine Boudica's appearance in various historical genres from the period around and after 1800. My rationale for choosing the examples in this chapter rests on the need to show the variety of representations current in the period, while bearing in mind their antecedents in previous periods, as well as the ways that representations of Boudica, following the shifting contours of historical culture, diverged from those that came before. Thus, despite its relative obscurity, I felt it was necessary to address the first nineteenth-century stage play about Boudica in order to understand its relationship to previous ones. Other examples serve to illustrate different trends. For instance, the interesting fillip in the years 1857–9, when, it has been argued, Boudica's imagined link with the rebellion against the British in India made her an inspiration for a surge in mid-Victorian versifying about her life and actions, furnishes a striking example of the congruity and incongruity between past and present. These focal points will be used to examine the changes and continuities, both in regards to Boudica's reputation, and to the nature of historical culture.

We can point to a number of shifts that take place in this period. Perhaps one of the most noticeable changes in Boudica's reputation is to be found in the drama and poetry discussed in the first and final sections of this chapter. As these works show, the morality or immorality of Boudica's actions became the subject of much more significant comment than had previously been the case. This was due in part to a second shift, more widely apparent in historical culture, which is explored in the section on women's histories: the increasing prevalence of female writers and

[15] Hay, *Annalists and historians*, 175.

readers, by and for whom Boudica was brought into the fold of moral education, especially in biographical collections. This emerging genre—which itself can be said to have an antecedent in seventeenth-century 'worthy women' literature—placed Boudica on a moral spectrum of feminine and queenly behaviour. Yet her deeds were not easily reconciled with this didacticism, as we will see.

A third shift, not unconnected with the debate around her didactic utility, is in the potential for Boudica's uprising to be imaginatively linked with events in Britain's empire, a connection that will be discussed here and in greater detail in Chapter 5. A surge of embellished versions of Boudica's life coincided—or nearly did—with the Indian Uprising of 1857, neatly illustrating her emerging importance in explicating the dangers of heathenism and resistance against civilizing powers during the nineteenth-century present. However, even these seemingly straightforward mirror-images of past and present belie a vision of Boudica as a victim of unjust cruelty, and thus the bearer of legitimate vengeance. These depictions also presage the difficulties inherent in celebrating Boudica as the harbinger of British imperial greatness, a view which will be discussed in greater detail in the next chapter.

THE PATRIOT QUEEN (1808): CREATION AS RECEPTION

Richard Glover's 1753 play was revised, given a new title—*Boadicea, or the British Amazon*—and a new staging at Sadler's Wells in 1800. Advertising in *The Observer*, the producers invited 'the admirers of splendid and classic Pantomime, the Historian, and the Patriot' to view 'a striking trait of national biography to be exhibited with all the fascination of superb costume'.[16] In return for such improving spectacle, the response from the same paper was little short of rapturous: 'We imagine it is impossible for any Briton to witness the exhibition of *Boadicea*, at Sadler's Wells, without experiencing the most forcible effects of that innate patriotism which reigns in every British breast, and which has tended so long to make Britannia the mistress of the world.'[17]

The glowing revival of this old play may have led the little-known author Thomas Rhodes to turn his own mind to the subject of Boudica. Indeed, there are similarities between Glover's stage play and *The Patriot Queen, or female heroism* (1808) by Thomas Rhodes, not least of which was a shared concern with patriotism and public duty. Indeed, in many ways the new play was a distillation of the themes present, sometimes implicitly, in previous plays about Boudica. For instance, the suffering of Boudica's children had been movingly explored by Charles Hopkins, and it was touched on to similar effect in Rhodes's work. However, Rhodes's play also gestured towards the interiority evident in Boudica's appearance in biographies later in the century. Rather than allow romantic themes to play out among the characters around Boudica, Rhodes focused on the queen's own suffering, as wife and mother. But by far the most significant addition to Rhodes's play was that

[16] *The Observer*, 13 April 1800.   [17] *The Observer*, 27 April 1800.

Cenulph—equivalent to Glover's Dumnorix and Fletcher's Caratach—is a Christian convert, prone to reflection on the barbarism engendered by the pagan religion in his native Britain. In another unusual turn, Rhodes cast the Druids as wholly inhumane and immune to reason. These characters were of course present in earlier dramatic retellings of the story, but Rhodes emphasized them against a background of Christian incursion into Britain.

The play was probably never performed before a large audience, and certainly not in any of the famous London playhouses, and little is known about Thomas Rhodes beyond the fact that he was working between 1808 and 1824.[18] However, I would like to consider Rhodes's play as a form of reception, bridging the eighteenth-century romantic Boudica evident in Cowper's poem, and the nineteenth-century version of Boudica presented in improving feminine literature; Rhodes's play encompasses elements of both. Interestingly, Rhodes also shared with Glover the sense that his play was its own form of patriotic resistance to the established rules of drama and thus a product of his national pride, of which Boudica was a succinct personification. Rhodes noted that the English—only one of the national identities Boudica was capable of embodying—were reverent to authority, but did not submit easily to arbitrary dogmas, including the conventions of drama. 'We love to be freed from constraint, and to think for ourselves; – a glorious characteristic!'[19] His words echo William Rider's assessment of Richard Glover's play more than fifty years earlier: the plays themselves were examples of the resistance they portrayed—ancient British and modern English.

The history of Boudica told by Richard Glover, both in his play and in the accompanying 'parasitical' biography, was not 'accurate' but it was nevertheless convincingly portrayed in the generic idiom of 'true' history. For his part, Rhodes distanced himself from any pretence that his work should be measured by the calculus either of historical accuracy or of the idiom of recorded truth; that is, he took a similar approach to that taken by Thomas Heywood in the 1640s. Although Rhodes allowed that '[a] Drama, taken from history, ought not certainly to deviate from facts as recorded by Historians; it is, however, allowed to be embellished with such incidents as, although not strictly true, are nevertheless highly probable: without those indulgences, indeed, an historical Play would be a dry, uninteresting narrative; an amplification, or an abbreviation of history...less calculated to convey instruction'.[20] Boudica's 'heroic virtue, and patriotic, undaunted spirit', had made her 'so conspicuous a figure in the history of our country' that there was simply no need for Rhodes remind his readers of the historical record, allowing him instead to focus attention on the potential for the story to teach its audience other kinds of lessons. Overshadowing the critical reaction to Glover's play had been a sense that the author had made his characters behave in improbable ways,

---

[18] J. Shattock (ed.), *The Cambridge Bibliography of English Literature* (Cambridge, 1999), Vol. 4, col. 426.
[19] T. Rhodes, *The patriot queen; or female heroism* (Coventry, 1808), Dedication, v.
[20] Ibid., iv–v.

but Rhodes headed such objections off by asserting the importance of probability while still making allowance for his own imaginative embellishments.

Rhodes's play is, at times, less straightforwardly moralizing than one might expect. His portrayal of Boudica never veers from the heroic, and he reserves judgement in reflecting on many of her more questionable actions. In previous plays about Boudica, the male generals—such as Fletcher's Caratach and Glover's Dumnorix—attempted to check Boudica's behaviour, and expressed horror at the violence of her interpretation of just vengeance. This was not the case in Rhodes's version. In fact, Boudica's pain and anger are here cast as unquestionable justification for war on the Roman invaders. The leader of one of the British tribes (the wholly fictional Cenessius of the Cangi) proclaims:

> In truth the Queen Boadicea's wrongs
> Demand exemplary, unusual vengeance;
> Had we no other motives for the war,
> They were sufficient to incite to arms...[21]

Rhodes is unusual among dramatists for this seeming acceptance, articulated through her followers, of Boudica's wrongs as justification for acts of vengeance against the Romans. Yet this stance, articulated by Cenessius, is fitting when seen in the context of Rhode's detailed exploration of the emotional landscape of the historical episode. Beginning with the aftermath of the rape of Boudica's daughters—here named them as Agatha and Anfleda—Rhodes shows the two young women in disagreement over how best to cope with their ordeal. Rhodes assured his audience that '...from the general tenor of what is related of them, it may fairly be inferred, that they were Ladies of the utmost greatness of mind'.[22] As in Charles Hopkins's own relatively unknown play, Rhodes makes a significant commentary on the horrors of sexual violence through this dialogue. Anfleda, to her sister, bemoans their fate:

> No, let keen anguish, like a canker worm,
> Gnaw our swol'n hearts, language must never tell
> What passes there; yet shall we strive in vain,
> Greatly I fear, our suff'rings to conceal;
> The far fetch'd sign, and the averted eye,
> Even in tears, will certainly betray us;
> In solitude alone we may be happy;
> Happy did I say? O, gracious heaven!
> Can we e're taste of happiness again?[23]

Wholly passed over by Richard Glover and trivialized by John Fletcher, Rhodes makes the original, unspoken sin committed against Boadicea's family—the rape of her daughters—the catalyst for war between two nations.

When Boadicea discovers what has befallen her children, she reacts as both a mother and a powerful queen. This conflation of royalty and motherhood has

---

[21] Ibid., 16.   [22] Ibid., v.   [23] Ibid., 12.

the effect of harmonizing Rhodes's concerns with those of earlier stage plays, foregrounding the same issues of private emotions and their consequences for public events. But, unlike Glover, who showed Boudica's pride as fatal to the public good, Rhodes explored the possibility that a queen's emotions might also be grounds for public acts of mercy. When a Roman family—father, mother, and child—are captured, the character of Boadicea proposes they be sacrificed to the pagan gods, but the Roman mother appeals on the grounds of their mutual experience of childbirth.

> Stay, Royal Madam: hear, for mercy's sake,
> A suff'ring, wounded, mother:- You, yourself,
> By that endearing, hallow'd name are known;
> You have endur'd those agonizing pangs,
> The which no tongue can tell, no pen describe:
> O, feel, then, for a mother! Whos fond soul
> Clings to her child so fast, that for to save
> His precious life she values not her own...[24]

The Roman mother's plea and the intervention of the Christian convert Cenulph convince Boadicea to set the family free and publicly denounce the practice of human sacrifice. The queen 'declaims all private hatred', vowing to forgo any form of private revenge and instead reserve her vengeance for the more appropriate place, the battlefield. Thus Rhodes attributed this single, perhaps most important, victory to Boudica: the victory of Christian sentiment over pagan blood rites.

Patriot Queen had powerful moral messages for the conduct of private individuals and public leaders, a message which had also been evident in plays about Boudica prior to this, most notably Glover's. In Rhodes's work, femininity and queenly duty to fight is a source of struggle for the character of Boadicea. She states:

> Women are best at home; performing well
> Domestic duties; acting well the parts
> Of duteous daughters, faithful virtuous wives,
> And fond, and tender mothers; but if once
> A sov'reigns pow'r is vested in a woman,
> Then let her govern as becomes a queen;
> Let her be steadfast, patriotic, brave,
> Skilful in politics, and even in war![25]

As Glover had done, Rhodes used the female/male dichotomy as a convenient idiom for exploring the demands of public duty. As a woman, Boudica's maternal instincts it is implied, render her naturally less inclined to understand her public duty. For Glover, this conceit had been to show that Boudica's inability to overcome her personal quarrels—a drawback for which her femininity was shorthand—led to national decline. Rhodes probed somewhat deeper, focusing on Boudica's own wish to retire and live without the demands imposed on her by her position. Later, after the Britons' defeat and as she lay dying from poison, Rhodes's Boadicea declares to her surviving daughter: 'If it be possible, live thou retir'd;/Pray to the Gods, possess a quiet spirit./

[24] Ibid., 40.   [25] Ibid., 18.

Meddle not thou with government or party.'[26] More than Glover, Rhodes's play brings to the forefront issues of women in government, but he gives his Boudica character far more self-awareness than Glover did his. Rather than make her an enemy of progress and peace, Rhodes made her a victim of circumstance, stripped to some degree of the negative agency that made Glover's Boudica so potentially dangerous. Rhodes's commentary in the play's epilogue echoes his Boudica's pitiable dying pronouncement. Women, Rhodes states, are to be esteemed by all, and are capable of resisting tyranny in their own right. However, it is the male duty to protect them from being forced to do so, and men must ensure that women and girls remain safe at home, where they can, as Rhodes memorably put it, 'give sweet nightly love'.

The foregrounding of Boudica's femininity is more evident in Rhodes's play than in any other before; the same can be said for the comparison Rhodes implied between paganism and Christianity. As he remarked in the preface to the published play in reference to the actions of Boudica and her daughters, 'It is true, that after they had been so inhumanely injured, they appear to have been wholly actuated by revenge; but let it be remembered, they were not Christians, and that the Religion of the Druids very much encouraged that baleful passion.'[27] However, Rhodes's willingness to see their actions in relation to the very different moral worlds of past and present allowed for other themes, especially the separation of public and private life and the fraught relationship between mother and children to come to the fore. For both Rhodes and Glover, Boudica's sex worked to their advantage in illustrating the nature of patriotism: with far greater demands placed on women in the private sphere, action in the public realm was rendered all the more difficult when the two forms of duty were in tension; a male protagonist simply could not have illustrated this point as powerfully as Boudica, the isolated widow and mother.

The next section explores the ways in which themes most clearly evident in Rhodes's work, especially duty, maternal love, and feminine propriety, were explored in greater details in collected biographies and histories of women. Like Rhodes, authors of such works were concerned with the implications of Boudica's paganism, and particularly her resort to suicide. Nevertheless, the ancient queen was held to be an exemplary figure for young women and girls, even if caveats were put in place to shield this impressionable audience from her more barbaric acts. The next section will also show that the didacticism of these works did not only encompass morality; historically, these were intended to teach women the story of their own past. As such, they were subjected to critical scrutiny, revealing interesting fissures between differing didactic intentions.

'PLEASANT, FEMININE, READABLE': BOUDICA IN WOMEN'S HISTORIES

Since the seventeenth-century accounts of 'worthy women', there had been some acknowledgement of women as not only subjects but also a distinct audience for history. Indeed, the production of histories aimed at a female audience increased

[26] Ibid., 68. [27] Ibid., v.

steadily as the number of general histories also increased.[28] The trend, inaugurated in the seventeenth century, continued in the eighteenth. Notable here is Charlotte Cowley's *Ladies History of England*, for instance, which appeared in 1780. It was published in sixty individual numbers which were then bound together and sold as a single volume. Cowley noted that it was 'the professed Design of this Work to interweave, in the Course of our History, the most striking Traits in the Characters of our most illustrious Women'.[29] When the time came to tell Boudica's story in the very first number of the *Ladies History*, Cowley broke off her narrative 'in pursuance of the plan I have proposed, of giving the most striking traits in the character of our most illustrious women' and proceeded to give a character sketch of Boudica using 'materials that are not to be met with in common Histories of England'.[30] This uncommon material was that compiled by none other than the antiquary Edmund Bolton, whom Cowley referred to as 'an old English author'.[31]

Not all historical works aimed at women were as learned as Charlotte Cowley's—her history was the first since Heywood's *Exemplary Lives* to draw on Bolton's work. Indeed, collected biographies especially were often judged, not on the merit of the scholarship involved in their production, but rather on the value of the moral instruction conveyed.[32] Their intended audience of young women and girls required—even if they may not have demanded—a very different version of Boudica's story to that found in many more general histories. Of course, it was sometimes the case that Boudica was simply left out. Many histories for women began their narrative of events after the Norman Conquest, while biographies might restrict themselves to the lives of only literary women, or Christian women, or the mothers of great men, and so on. Used in this way, the appellation 'history of women' could encompass highly specialized histories of small categories of women. These also took the form of collected biographies, which offered an alternative both to novels and to more scholarly forms of history writing, especially to female audiences for whom it was believed these alternatives were uniquely necessary.[33] But this body of historical works aimed at women was also, according to Rosemary Mitchell, the female response to Thomas Carlyle's definition of history as being made up of the lives and actions of Great Men.[34] Perhaps so; or perhaps the growing

---

[28] Burstein's estimate of 300 'histories of women' published in mid-nineteenth century might include both British and American examples, although it is not clear; see M.E. Burstein, 'From good looks to good thoughts: popular women's history and the invention of modernity, ca. 1830–1870', *Modern Philology*, 97 (1999), 46–75, at 48, and M.E. Burstein, 'Unstoried in history: early histories of women (1652–1902) in the Huntington Library collections', *The Huntington Library Quarterly*, 64(3/4) (2001), 469–500. N. Zemon Davies, 'Gender and genre: women as historical writers, 1400–1820', in P.H. Labalme (ed.), *Beyond their sex: learned women of the European past* (London, 1980), pp. 153–82, at 155, dates the cultivation of women as a specific audience for women to the middle of the eighteenth century, but see Woolf, 'A feminine past'.

[29] C. Cowley, *Ladies History of England*, First number (London, 1780). Very few of the individual numbers survive, but numbers 1, 2, and 5 can be found at the Kent Archives, U269Z26.

[30] Ibid., 13. [31] Ibid.

[32] Burstein, 'From good looks to good thoughts', 50.

[33] B. Caine, *Biography and history* (Basingstoke, 2010), 10.

[34] R. Mitchell, 'The red queen and the white queen', in G. Cubitt and A. Warren (eds), *Heroic Reputations and Exemplary Lives*, pp. 157–77. For women as historians, see Mitchell's *Picturing the past: English history in text and image, 1830–1870* (Oxford, 2000), esp. 141–4. For an overview of the genre in the Victorian period, see A. Booth, *How to make it as a woman: collective biography of women*

number of literate women catalysed the market for a different kind of historical work. But it is certain that female biography accounted for a growing number of didactic works in the late eighteenth century, and throughout the century following.[35]

There were other reasons Boudica may have been thought of as an uncomfortable subject for the moralizing biographer with a youthful audience in mind. The purview of female biography tended to be restricted to the inner life of the subject because the subject, more often than not, had led a life of relative inaction. Even those who did not were explained away as exceptional cases, women who did not, as women should, 'bravely live and die in the home'.[36] For their part, biographers did indeed have a difficult time reconciling Boudica as a woman of public action whose private life had left no trace, and from whose warlike deeds little could be learned by the average female reader. This is reflected in the fact that of the dozens of biographical collections published during the nineteenth century, Boudica only appeared in five of them.[37] This relatively low number cannot be fully explained by the assumption that authors disapproved of Boudica. To be sure, some may have balked at her actions and preferred to ignore her, but even authors who expressed misgivings about Boudica's conduct continued to publish accounts of her deeds as cautionary tales. Arguably it was the lack of known detail—a well-worn sticking point by this stage—about Boudica and her historical context that discouraged biographers from writing extensively about the ancient queen. But, as Rhodes noted in the preface to his stage play, very little was known about the details of Boudica's life, even if her name and actions were infamous, and thus the story was open to imaginative reading by intrepid authors.

The first author to include Boudica in a nineteenth-century work of collected biography was Mary Hays in 1803, five years before the dramatist Thomas Rhodes came to the subject. Hays was a woman of letters, and a friend to Mary Wollstonecraft, William Godwin, and their circle of radical and Dissenting friends. Like Wollstonecraft, Hays was an autodidact and something of a proto-feminist inheritor of the Enlightenment political ideal of equality and liberty, with a keen interest in female education.[38] She published her six-volume collection of *Female Biography; or memoirs of illustrious and celebrated women, of all ages and countries* in 1803, 'in the cause, and for the benefit, of my own sex'.

Rather than dwelling on the dangers of the fictional imagery of novels and plays—much castigated in the politicized histories of the previous century—Hays

---

from Victoria to the present (London, 2004); R. Maitzen, '"This feminine preserve": historical biographies by Victorian women', *Victorian Studies*, 38(3) (1995) 371–93; M. Vicinus, 'Models for public life: biographies of "noble women" for girls', in C. Nelson and L. Vallone (eds), *The Girl's Own: cultural histories of the Anglo-American girl, 1830–1915* (London, 1994), pp. 52–70.

[35] Phillips, *Society and Sentiment*, 134.

[36] J. Johnson, *Brave Women: who have been distinguished for heroic actions and noble virtues, etc.* (Edinburgh, 1875). Unsurprisingly, Johnson did not include Boudica in his collection.

[37] Alison Booth at the University of Virginia has created an indispensable online resource for surveying women's collected biography, mostly between 1830 and 1950. http://womensbios.lib.virginia.edu/, accessed 23 Nov 2017.

[38] For Hays's intellectual biography, see G.L. Walker, *Mary Hays (1759–1843): The growth of a woman's mind* (Aldershot, 2006).

instead proclaimed a new direction in historical literature for women: '... my book is intended for women, and not for scholars; that my design was not to surprise by fiction, or to astonish by profound research, but to collect and concentrate, in one interesting point of view, these engaging pictures, instructive narratives, and striking circumstances, that may answer a better purpose than the gratification of vain curiosity'.[39] That is, Hays did not intend to produce new research, or even to suggest, as Thomas Heywood had, that disquisitions on the methods of scholarly history were necessary window-dressing for what could, at its core, be merely an exercise in astonishing the ignorant with obscure tales of feminine doings. In this way, Hays's work was a generic departure from Heywood's *Exemplary Lives*. Even though *Female Biography* grew out of the same didactic tradition as the earlier work, it nevertheless represented an emerging genre of history made by and for women, and which was independent of the more patronizing, if well meaning, contributions of scholarly men.

As one might expect, Hays's *Female* Biography contains the first truly 'feminist' reading of Boudica's story. Hays's recitation begins with an implicit charge that Boudica's suffering was due to her husband's 'imprudent testament' that half of his kingdom should be granted to the Roman emperor. This was a veiled commentary on marriage, revealing Hays's own views of matrimonial inequity. Marriage had been—and by implication continued to be—an institution which exposed widows and children to the poverty, or far worse, upon the death of their male protector. The rest of Hays's Boudica story is an overtly emotive retelling of the conventional, and by this time familiar, narrative, but one which was centred solely on the 'heroic queen' and her actions. Hays makes no reference to the Roman general Suetonius Paulinus' movements on the Isle of Mona, which so often featured in previous works as the key turning point in the narrative, foreshadowing the final battle between the Romans and the Britons. This omission suggests that Hays had relatively little interest in the wider historical context of the events being related, setting hers apart from the generalist approach taken by Charlotte Cowley, as well as panoramic historians whose remit was far more diverse. Instead Hays's focus was on Boudica's conduct, the Britons' reaction to their queen's call to arms, and the manner in which 'Private and individual injury swelled the tide of public hatred.'[40] For Hays, there simply was no tension between private rage and public duty.

Hays's biography and Rhodes's play are both evidence of a shift in the nature and purpose of historical works which treated of individual lives. Both were intended for non-specialist—that is, non-scholarly— audiences made up of both sexes or, in Hays's case, probably one whose members were largely female. That heterogeneous audiences were engaged with historical culture is not novel to this period, but the fact that Boudica began to feature in instructive works, focused on celebrating individual reputations (rather than analysing success or failure) does present something of a development, especially as these works suited the

---

[39] M. Hays, *Female biography; or memoirs of illustrious and celebrated women, of all ages and countries*, 6 vols (London, 1803), Vol. I, 4.
[40] Hays, *Female biography*, Vol. II, 5.

improving impulses of female social reformers like Mary Hays, who brought these moral lessons to the fore of forms of historical culture that appealed to women and girls. This, arguably, was as a consequence of the greater diversity of authors now writing about Boudica, as much as it was to the changing demographics of audiences themselves. We have seen that Charlotte Cowley's history of 1780 took a distinctly scholarly view, encompassing research into the works of Edmund Bolton for the account of Boudica, and although Mary Hays, a woman writing for women, was similarly interested in Boudica as a prominent woman of the past, her own work was of a very different genre.

Hays was not the only author to view female biographies as a genre in need of authors. Boudica's womanhood also became newly important in this period because it qualified her for what Elizabeth Langland has called the 'comparative project' of British queens evident in popular literature, and especially in collected biographies that appeared throughout the long reign of Victoria.[41] Boudica had long been known by the title of 'queen', sometimes of her tribe, the Iceni, and occasionally of the whole of Britain.[42] However, like Hays, writers in this celebratory genre were primarily motivated by the didactic potential of historical lives, and, were only secondarily interested—if at all—in educating their readers in the methods or facts of general history. However, this didactic aim necessitated a confrontation with moral dilemmas that were much less problematic in, for instance, drama. Dramatic writers were free to choose which aspects of Boudica's story to investigate and which to overlook; they were not bound to justify or explain Boudica's actions in such a way as to legitimate her inclusion in an exemplary form. Earlier, writers like Thomas Heywood took it as a given that Boudica should be a part of a discussion of 'worthy women', with her heathenism provided a mitigating circumstance, but no such assurances greeted Boudica in the nineteenth century.

Thus authors of collected biographies of queens did not have an easy escape route from the demands of their genre, and, even when they disclaimed all pretences to 'scholarship', as was quite often the case, they were nevertheless bound by the strictures of history. The *Lives of the Queens of England Before the Conquest* (1854) by an author who called herself only Mrs Matthew Hall, presents one example of Boudica's appearance in a uniquely detailed account in a work of collective biography focused on queens. Indeed, the version of the Boudica story told in *Lives of the Queens* was so heavily confected as to have lost almost all resemblance to the conventional portrayal of Boudica in prose, except in that most crucial of particulars: Boudica's eventual descent into savagery. However, the contemporary comment surrounding Hall's account pointed to a degree of discomfort with

---

[41] E. Langland, 'Nation and nationality: Queen Victoria in the developing narrative of Englishness', in M. Homans and A. Munich (eds), *Remaking Queen Victoria* (Cambridge, 1999), pp. 13–32, at 28.

[42] There is little evidence for an imagined connection between Queen Boudica and Queen Anne. One reference comes from a poem written in honour of Anne's birthday in 1709, which included the telling line: 'And Boadicea's story/By the Admiring World so much renown'd/Can't parallel our Anna's glory', from J.S. Cousser, *A Sereneta to be represented on the Birth-day of the Most Serene Anne* (Dublin, 1709). However, Boudica was associated with later queens, particularly Queen Caroline. In 1820 a print circulated in London that cast the embattled Caroline in the role of Boudica, 'Boadicea, Queen of Britain overthrowing her enemies...'(1820) British Museum Satires. 1983, 0305.38.

such embellishment in a work which aspired to be 'historical'. The long-standing need—one which was often circumvented, for all it was repeatedly emphasized—for history to accurately reflect the sources simply did not accommodate a form of biography that aimed to improve its readers through examples.

Hall was in a difficult position with Boudica, who did not fit a mould of femininity that emphasized retiring domesticity, and the details she introduced were bound to be problematic for readers already familiar with Boudica's life. Thus in her prefatory remarks to the Boudica story, Hall stated that, 'The family details of Boadicea's history, of whom much has been written, have never before appeared in connection with her life, and without the knowledge of these it is impossible fairly to appreciate the exciting details of her sufferings as a woman, wife, and mother – in the delineation of *her* character, no fiction can arrive at the all-powerful force of simple truth.'[43] Such a remark was calculated to coax the reader into the sense that the history being related had simply been overlooked, and was being newly told in Hall's book; that is, Hall drew on a language of scholarship and yet sought to maintain the dignity of fictional and moral truth over mere historical accuracy. But there was little truth—or, more precisely, accuracy—in Hall's new assertions, and the idea that Boudica's family history had long been known but never acknowledged was not supported by any evidence. The assertion was made with the intention of rendering Boudica a more conventional inclusion in a collective biography of queens, and to prepare the reader for details that might seem unexpected.

A not-altogether-unsympathetic reviewer of Hall's book wrote in *The Spectator* that, 'As might be expected, Mrs. Hall is more at home in the mild and domestic than the heroic. The greatest of the British Queens, Boadicea, is not handled with the force and breadth which such a heroine required';[44] yet this was undoubtedly due, if only in part, to the demands of the genre in which Hall was working. Indeed, despite the appellation 'Boadicea the Warlike', Hall managed to weave together a Boudica story without its most violent but well-documented elements. Rather, Hall's version was embellished with ameliorative details of family life. Indeed, the biographer claimed to have excavated a whole filial and domestic world for Boudica. She named Caractacus as Boudica's brother, and provided details of her upbringing and education as a member of the British royal family. Hall claimed—probably on the authority of early Scottish histories—that Boudica was a princess of the Picts of Scotland, and that the ancient queen's childhood home had been located in present-day Edinburgh, indeed, at the top of Arthur's Seat.[45] There, according to Hall, Boudica and her companions were given some training in the art of war, but were more often employed in needlework and, most important for posterity, basket-weaving. British baskets, Hall asserted, were the envy of the Roman world. Thus Boudica grew up in a palatial, cosseted environment of genteel industriousness of the kind familiar to a Tudor noblewoman. The author went on to describe the young princess's subsequent marriage to the king of the Iceni,

---

[43] Mrs M. Hall, *The queens before the Conquest*, 2 vols (London, 1854).
[44] *The Spectator*, 23 September 1854.
[45] Hall, *Queens before the conquest*, 46. Emphasis in original.

transplanting her to the more familiar location of Norfolk. But then the story took a highly dramatic turn. After her marriage, Boudica's husband, called Arviragus by Hall, betrayed his new wife and switched his allegiance to the Roman side. A war then ensued between Boudica's vengeful, protective 'brother' Caractacus and his estranged brother-in-law, who had gained the backing of the Romans. In Hall's account, Boudica's pitiful plight—her husband had not only betrayed his country, but had also run off with a Roman princess—was a *cause célèbre* for the Britons, from Scotland to England. Boudica and Arviragus were able to reconcile after Arviragus abandoned his Roman life and, according to Hall, took the name of Prasutagus, which most previous writers agreed had been Boudica's husband's name all along.[46]

On the face of it, Hall's account of this period prior to the rebellion in AD 61 might seem to have been wholly fictionalized, but it was in fact a melding of several different stories of varying provenance. Arviragus, for instance, may have been an authentic person, corresponding roughly with Tacitus' documented Caractacus, King of the Silures. But Hall's version of events bore most resemblance to the disastrous marriage between the historical Venutius and the queen of the Brigantes, Cartismandua, discussed in detail by Tacitus. Their union ended in a manner similar to Hall's description of Boudica's to Arviragus. However, in the classical version of the story, Cartismandua remarried (to her husband's armour-bearer, no less) and allied with the Romans, to whom she betrayed Caractacus in the decade before Boudica's rebellion. Rather than imagine details and scenarios, Hall did turn to less familiar records, embroidering the familiar story of Boudica with details gleaned from a variety of places. But even if these were not wholly fictional, neither were they accepted parts of Boudica's history.

From this point Hall's narrative becomes more conventional, though still mitigated by slight additions intended to give the reader the impression that ancient Britain was a sophisticated, even civilized, society. Hall carved out a role for the Boudica as a campaigner against the moral corruption that had bred amongst the Britons as a result of the many vices imported by the Romans. Among these was the public theatre, used by the Romans to spread messages injurious to British independence. Hall claimed that Boudica not only abhorred such vices, she wrote encyclicals against them which were then circulated among neighbouring tribes. But this fanciful portrait could not withstand comparison with Tacitus' historical record, which Hall had either ignored or 'improved upon', and she was eventually forced to relate the slaughter of the Roman colonists which Boudica herself ordered. 'It is necessary to the veracity of history to add, awful as the picture is to contemplate, that the mandates of carnage were given by the stern Queen herself.' Even as Hall felt free to embellish upon those points for which there was no evidence, as an historical account, her heavily fictionalized version of the story had to reckon with the Boudica story as told in the classical sources. This meant addressing Boudica's savagery, and the ultimate destruction and death of the characters whose sophistication

---

[46] There is an interesting discussion of the variations on Boudica's 'family ties' in Williams, *Boudica and her stories*, Ch. 4.

and refinement Hall's narrative had done so much to establish in the reader's mind. This, perhaps predictably, made Hall's final point more powerful. No degree of refinement could be truly maintained without the embrace of true religion: '...nor can the horrors of Paganism appear in darker colours, than the picture of this revenge'.[47] Boudica's part in the narrative ended with her suicide, but Hall went on to relate a fictional account of the lives of the queen's two daughters. She said that one married a Roman general, in fact the very man who had raped her, and the other took the name Princess Boadicea and continued to campaign against the Roman occupiers until her death.[48]

Hall made claims for her work as a rigorous history, but she could not hoodwink her critics. As the *Spectator* reviewer put it, '...a person who took the trouble to bring together all such phrases as "we may imagine," "it may be presumed," "there is reason to think," "although no particulars have reached us," and so forth, would have a goodly collection of hypothetical terms'.[49] But Hall's work shows what it was that biographers wanted from the warlike figure of Boudica. By creating a private family life and a past filled with domestic trials through which the ancient queen could valiantly suffer, Hall's work demonstrates that Boudica's story could be fitted into these collected biographies, although with some difficulty. Even the life of a warrior queen, tinged as it was by savagery, could be adapted to teach moral lessons to girls and women. Hall's Boudica suffered in dignified silence when her husband abandoned her; she acted as a support to her father and brothers, stirred the hearts of her followers, and campaigned for the moral advancement of her people.

There were in fact two accounts of Queen Boudica published in 1854. The second was also written by a woman, Mrs Octavius Freire Owen, and entitled *Heroines of History* (1854). Owen's situation is somewhat better documented and her motivations somewhat easier to explain than Hall's, whose aims must by necessity be deduced from those of the genre as a whole. While Hall had noted paganism's evil consequences for Boudica and her people, who in so many other respects resembled the sophistication of the Victorians, Owen, the wife of the chaplain to the Duke of Portland, brought religion very much to the forefront of her account. Above all, it was Boudica's suicide that offended her:

> Contempt for death, and the reception of it with an exaggerated welcome, formed the grand basis of barbarian virtue; and the woman who fell by her own hand, was formerly an object of applause and example. Now the consolatory doctrine of Christianity teaches us a nobler lesson. The great principle of worldly probation, is the endurance of afflictions, which are 'but for a moment' by the exercise of a faith, constant and inviolate, in the unseen... He who is so much a coward, as to refuse to bow before the storms of adversity, will, upon moderate reflection, find in himself scarcely sufficient boldness to brave the anger at an offended Judge, when ushered... unsummoned, into the presence of his Maker.[50]

---

[47] Hall, *Queens before the Conquest*, 63.
[48] This genealogy of feminine resistance was also the basis for a later novel, *Voadica* (1928), in which Boudica's granddaughter continues the fight; it is discussed in detail in Chapter 5.
[49] *The Spectator*, 23 September 1854.
[50] Mrs O.F. Owen, *The heroines of history* (London, 1854).

However, this pronouncement against Boudica's religion and the conduct it inspired cannot be read as a straightforward condemnation on Owen's part. In fact, it is Boudica's portrait that serves as the frontispiece of the volume. Boudica appears tall and fearsome, with one arm raised above her head, the other gripping a spear, and a large gathering of bearded men clamours eagerly around her (see Figure 6). The most interesting addition to this image is the demure, wistful girl—pictured here almost as a phantom—representing one of Boudica's daughters seated at the edge of the noisy scene. Her eyes are cast down in a swooning display of shame, modesty, or both—an understated testimony to the cruel fate which the audience knows had befallen the blameless girl. The violated innocence of the daughter appears in stark contrast to the anger on the face of her mother and the violent energy of the crowd of men. On the whole, it is an emotional image, not unlike those which were being produced for histories written at the close of the eighteenth century.

Thus even for Owen, whose religious sensibilities were deep and genuine, there was a sense that Boudica's actions were if not justified, at least explained by the suffering she and her family had endured. As had long been the case, Boudica's savage actions did little to diminish the perception that her rage was understandable, nor did it negate her patriotism and bravery in the face of a superior hostile force. Her daughters, especially when portrayed in so sympathetic a light as Owen's illustrator has them, could only arouse pity for the young women and their mother. The sin of suicide could be condemned, but as an act born of ignorance rather than of wickedness or innate brutality.

Indeed, writers with a moralizing purpose were markedly reluctant to forsake Boudica, not least, it would seem, because her lifetime coincided with the earliest period of Christian history. Aside from her appearance in collected biography, Boudica's story was also distilled in magazines and periodicals aimed at a female audience, as well as an audience of young readers.[51] It was often told as part of a reduction of the full narrative of British or English history for readers whose primary interest was not in historical deeds, but in minor details such as historic dress.[52] However, such idle interest in Boudica could be coupled with very serious messages for young audiences. The *Ladies' Treasury* serialized 'An Hour with Mamma' in which readers were taught the history of Britain, including Boudica's story, through an imagined dialogue between a grandmother, her daughter, and her daughter's children. One child professes admiration for the ancient hero Caractacus, whom she sees an example of the 'true sublime'. Her mother agrees but points out that 'The queenly form of Boadicea "bleeding from the Roman rods," as the

---

[51] There are numerous examples one could point to, but see *The London Literary Pioneer*, 1 July 1848; *The Children's Treasury*, 1 March 1868; *The Children's Treasury*, 15 July 1876. A lengthy fictionalized account accompanied by an illustration, unique in featuring Boudica and her daughters taking an active part in battle (Boudica is wielding an axe) was printed in *Every Week*, 28 January 1880. She also featured in the *Girls Own Paper*, *Boys of England*, and the *English Illustrated Magazine*. For children's history, see M. Simpson, 'Telling lives to children: young versus new historicism in *Little Arthur's History of England*', in D.W. Davies (ed.), *Romanticism, history, historicism: essays on orthodoxy* (London, 2009), pp. 60–78.

[52] *La Belle Assemblée; or, Bell's Court and Fashionable Magazine*, 1 December 1823.

Figure 6. Queen Boudica portrayed as a heroine and leader of men, in Mrs O.F. [Emily] Owen's *The Heroines of History* (1854). The Bodleian Libraries, The University of Oxford, (OC) 210 M.688, frontispiece.

poet Cowper says, is, in its way, as touching and as fine.' But the mother ushers her children's narrative forward: 'I want to get on to the only really great and truly important event in the history of this – or indeed, of any other – country. I mean the introduction of Christianity.'[53]

A commentator in *The Lady's Newspaper* used Boudica as an example of an unpalatably fierce female hero: 'Somehow or other we never seem able thoroughly

---

[53] *The Ladies' Treasury*, 1 January 1859.

to swallow the idea of a fighting woman. It sticks in our throats like the husk of a horse chestnut. Boadicea and Joan of Arc are all very well as figures in the dim background of history, but we could scarcely tolerate them nearer our own times.'[54] In these snippets of history, tarrying too much on Boudica's story was not necessarily to be encouraged, but neither was she ignored. She was innately interesting, not least for being so unusual, but her story was also so deeply embedded in Britain's history that it was not possible to ignore her or pass over her unremarked.

'THAT BRAVE, MATERNAL, NOBLE, QUEENLY HEART': EMPIRE AND VERSE

As we have seen, the moral agendas of Victorian writers were not always conducive to strict adherence to the reality of Boudica's story. This was certainly true of works aimed at women and young people, whose educational needs were thought to be primarily of the moral kind, with factual knowledge a distant second. A similar agenda is evident in more imaginative work of the mid-nineteenth century, but there were other forces at play in these. The focus in this section will be on poetic works, most not at all well known, with only Tennyson's poem achieving much enduring fame. Most of these works were written and composed in a very short period of time, between the 1850s and 1860s. In Boudica's posthumous life, this flurry of activity was unprecedented, and may in some measure have been connected to the occurrence of the Indian Uprising in 1857. This was the beginning of what Hingley and Unwin have noted was an 'imperial cult' that flourished around Boudica in the late Victorian period.[55]

There were indeed direct and particular comparisons made at the time between Queen Boudica and the Indian women on both sides of the rebellion against British occupation. Commentators singled out Lakshmi Bai, the Rani of Jhansi, whose leadership was instrumental in the uprising.[56] The analogy was obvious: the Rani commanded a force against the British troops during the uprisings in 1857 and was thought to have committed suicide rather than be taken alive, although the manner of her death was disputed. At least one reporter made explicit the connection between the British warrior queen and the Rani, naming her as 'Boadicea of the Deccan'.[57] Another Indian princess, the Begum of Bhopal, was also the subject of comparison with Boudica, though somewhat after the fact and in a way that complimented rather than traduced the ancient queen and her present-day counterpart in India: 'The Bagum behaved nobly during the Mutiny, and, like Boadicea, harangued her troops', though she did not, as the Rani had, fight herself. Inspiring one's troops with words was acceptable, but the commentator drew the line at taking part in the fighting, noting that 'unlike the cruel Ranee of Jhansee, on the

---

[54] *The Lady's Newspaper*, 15 April 1863.
[55] Hingley and Unwin, *Boudica*, 155–8, have different readings of these works.
[56] For the life and reputation of the Rani of Jhansi, see J. Lebra-Chapman, *The Rani of Jhansi: a study in female heroism in India* (Honolulu, HI, 1986).
[57] *The Guardian*, 14 February 1859.

other side, she did not lead [her troops] into the field'.[58] It helped, of course, that the Begum of Bhopal had supported the British.

Boudica could and did act as a historical referent for present-day non-Christian queens, one of whom represented an uncivilized, even barbaric, woman rebelling against the superior military force of an occupying power. However, an exploration of Victorian verse reveals that even seemingly straightforward works are more complex than a simple comparison between ancient and contemporary 'barbarism' embodied in female military action. As in the work of Rhodes and Glover, the particular difficulties inherent in female leadership, with private and public duties in constant tension, remained a theme in mid-Victorian period. There was also a new emphasis on her individual psychological complexity. Boudica's emotional state had long been the subject of dramatic interpretation, some of it very moving in its vivid imagery and pathetic dialogue, but the authors in the mid-Victorian period focused on Boudica's femininity, motherhood, and religion in more detail and depth, suggesting messages that encouraged female decency and Christian piety.

These themes were abundantly evident in Sir Coutts Lindsay's *Boadicea: A tragedy*, which was printed privately in 1857.[59] Sir Coutts Lindsay (1824–1913) was the founder of the Grosvenor Gallery and an enthusiastic patron of the arts who wrote only a handful of dramatic works, all of which focused on well-known figures from British history, and all of which had a similar moralizing message centred around Christian conduct, in opposition to heathenism.[60] *Alfred* (1845) was a dramatization of the conversion of the Danes to Christianity, with the title character as an irreproachable paradigm of virtue; his opposite number, the King of the Danes, dies rather than become a Christian. *Edward, the Black Prince: a tragedy* (1846) told the story of the Prince's betrayal by Don Pedro of Castile, in which he compounded Pedro's known historical sins with fictional ones, not least the poisoning of Edward and his army. In Lindsay's play, Pedro was considered by his enemies to be the friend of 'heathen' Jews and Muslims. Edward was a principled dupe, drawn into the fight on Pedro's side by the instinct to defend the divine right of kings against illegitimate claimants. In being betrayed, Edward paid the price for trusting the friend of heathen peoples.

Lindsay's oeuvre of historical drama was shot through with covert criticism of non-Christian religions, but his *Boadicea* was a departure from his earlier work in its experimental and ambitious style. With the new play, Lindsay attempted to emulate the tragic plays of Greek antiquity. The action was accompanied by the vocal expressions of a chorus, complete with strophes and antistrophes at intervals. Although *Edward* had also been billed as a tragedy, Lindsay's *Boadicea* followed the rules of Greek tragic drama more overtly, with Boudica's character being overwhelmed by uncontrolled passion. In its blood-soaked exploration of maternal and filial feelings, it had echoes of *Medea*, making it very unlike the more mannered

---

[58] *The Manchester Guardian*, 28 December 1875.
[59] C. Lindsay, *Boadicea: a tragedy* (London, 1857).
[60] *New York Times* Obituary, 9 May Does this need an access date? http://query.nytimes.com/mem/archive-free/pdf?_r=1&res=9B0CE7D7173FE633A2575AC0A9639C946296D6CF.

depictions of British history in *Edward* and *Alfred*. As a performance, *Boadicea* would have depicted primal violence; the chorus is smeared with blood during the final scenes. Indeed, the play has a darkened aspect that is missing from even the most explicit dramatic portrayals of Boudica's circumstances, notably that of Charles Hopkins, which dealt in detail with the sexual violence of the historical record.

The play's atmosphere is in keeping with the titular character's deranged state of mind, which in turn accords with some of the flourishes of pagan barbarism Lindsay added to his imagined version of Boudica's ancient Britain. His detailed imagining of the Druid rituals, savage and strange, which attend the death and funeral of King Prasutagus, as well as the addition of a concubine and her illegitimate children—never before imagined as part of the story—added further pigment to the portrait of an unenlightened nation. But more substantively, Lindsay's version of Boudica's story is a painfully searching exploration of the character's femininity, and specifically her motherhood. Although Lindsay portrays Boudica as an ambitious, even acquisitive woman who used marriage to attain greater status, her cruel betrayal by the Romans early in the play casts a sympathetic light over even her most questionable actions. As her village is burned, she sinks into madness and remains a deranged figure throughout the play, as although she never quite loses her protective maternal instinct or her self-awareness as a powerful queen, both of cause her intense inner turmoil. The queen's pronouncement at the beginning of the play, upon learning that her children may have died, foregrounds the primacy of her relationship with her offspring as the focus of dramatic action. Speaking to one of her generals, she laments:

> Thou hast no daughters – never hadst a child
> Which sprang from forth the womb, – 'twas not for thee
> To feel thy heart beat when the callow thing
> Sought from the breast its food; thou hast not felt
> The dear delight to yield it nourishment;
> The first attempts at infant prattle made
> My grief's my own; how canst thou judge my pain?[61]

So profound is Boudica's grief that she is moved to wish that her children had died in infancy, saving her from her present pain. The impression given by Lindsay is of a queen with an almost animal instinct to protect her children. This instinct is challenged when the queen is betrayed by one daughter, Malvina, who falls in love with one of the Roman invaders. In the climactic scene, Lindsay's Boadicea and her army leave the Roman Temple of Jupiter in flames, allowing a number of wounded Roman soldiers to die within. Boudica stumbles upon Julius, who, it transpires, is Malvina's Roman lover. She watches Julius die, and she leaves the temple only to meet Malvina. Her thoughts of revenge momentarily forgotten, Boadicea embraces her child, taking on the voice of a mother once more:

> Little one, take rest;
> And I will once more rock thee in mine arms,

---

[61] Lindsay, 'Boadicea', 16.

> Close up thine eyelids with this tender kiss
> – I dream yet in this sudden happiness,
> And tremble for the waking, lest all fade
> Into the void of air. – Crown of my life![62]

But upon learning that her mother has effectively murdered her lover, Malvina rejects Boadicea's conviction that Julius had used magic or poison to entice her.

> Ah! kiss me not; I'll die without thy kiss.
> Here is my blood to dabble in, here his –
> Has thou shed both, thou cruel mother?
> – Thou shalt not keep me from him! What art thou?
> Gorgon, I'm not thy child![63]

Malvina runs back into the burning temple and dies alongside the body of her Roman lover.

Through the whole of the play, the queen persists in her mad desire for vengeance, and there is never a point at which Lindsay's Boadicea acknowledges the folly of her actions. Moments of mercy are relatively trivial, as when, finding Julius near death, she acquiesces to his plea for water, even as she mocks the dying man's devotion to the god Jove. Following the deaths of Julius and Malvina and the destruction of the British army, Lindsay's Boadicea casts herself off a cliff and drowns. In this case, the utter defeat of the British was mirrored by the complete destruction of Boadicea's family. What emerges most strongly from a close reading of the play is Lindsay's malignant vision of Boadicea's motherhood; the expression of maternal love by the queen is impregnated with the same violent, almost animalistic instinct that seems to pervade Lindsay's reading of ancient society as a whole.

As we have seen, the gaps in the historical record necessitated that narratives concerning Boudica's children be imagined anew by successive writers in a way that other relatively more well-documented aspects of the past could not be. Boudica usually carried with her the dignity of historical evidence, and an in-depth exploration of her interior life may well have been considered impertinent by authors prior to this period. Lindsay's play, which, even to the point of gratuitousness, exposed Boudica's intimate thoughts on motherhood and the tension between her public role as queen and her private role as mother, was unlike any work which had come before. What it revealed was a bloody, unheroic, but intensely gripping form of tragedy, shorn of the patriotic messages usually evident in plays that explored the dichotomy.

That said, it is difficult to map Lindsay's play onto issues prevalent in the present. It does not ring true as a comment on the recent uprising in India, nor indeed does it speak in any explicit way to any renewed contemporary interest in queenship. Although published in 1857, this was more than a decade after Lindsay's two other historical plays, and the author probably spent years rather than months writing it. It is nevertheless a significant work, representing a new and intense focus on Boudica as a mother, marking Lindsay out as author of a more purely imaginative stripe

---

[62] Ibid., 65.   [63] Ibid., 67.

than his contemporaries, most of whom had an overt didactic or moralizing agenda. Lindsay's play, in its empathetic exploration of Boudica's innermost thoughts, was an act of creative imagination. But given its reliance on the historical context of ancient Britain, and its distillation of themes evident in imagined versions of Boudica's story for years, it was also, in a sense, an act of reception.

Lindsay's contemporary, Francis Barker, presents a similar example of the author as receiver and creator. However, unlike Lindsay it seems certain that Barker's long dramatic poem *Boadicea* (1859) was indeed a response to contemporary events—an instance of the past presaging the present. As a commentary on the heathenism of the ancient Britons and their rebellion against the Romans, an invading force which, for illustrative purposes and with minimal historical rationale, Barker cast as a Christianizing civilization, the work was intended to be illustrative of the dangers of the wrong religion. There were, undeniably, moral anxieties inherent in the Christian Britain of the nineteenth century lionizing a Druid queen, but these were often overlooked, especially since most commentators seemed to accept the general conclusion that Christianity was not widespread in Britain during Boudica's lifetime and thus the possibility of salvation by that route had not been open to her.

The poem's 'good Christian sentiments' were praised by *The Baptist Magazine* in the winter of 1859 although, the reviewer noted, little could be said for the quality of the rhyme.[64] Despite its shortcomings, more than in many other works about Boudica, Barker's message was clearly evangelical. Indeed, the Christian religion was very much alive in the ancient Britain described by Barker. He portrayed Boudica's daughters as having been exposed to the Gospel by a family friend recently returned from Rome via Gaul, and even the British slaves taken as prisoners to the imperial capital make long disquisitions on the merits of Christianity. Whole pages of Barker's work were given over to the words of recently converted Britons who make explicit the stark contrast between the good work of the Christians and the brutality of the Druids. Tellingly, the religions of 'the East' are part of this commentary, with Boadicea's daughters expressing shock that the women in that part of the world are treated with such disrespect as to be placed in 'harems; cribbed and caged'.[65]

The action is fairly formulaic. As in Lindsay's play, the death of Boudica's husband and protector prompts her to fear for her family, not for her country, and she identifies with her role as mother more than with the duties of queenship. However, there is little of the harsh savage instinct in Barker's version of the queen. Instead, she describes her intense fear at the beginning of the poem, contrasting it with the domestic happiness she had experienced when the king was alive:

> Then in possession of each
> Varied joy, her heart could wish, she lived,
> A happy mother and a loving wife…
> She sees her daughters fatherless.

---

[64] *The Baptist Magazine*, March 1859.   [65] F. Barker, *Boadicea* (London, 1859), 44.

> Ye who have known a mother's anxious care,
> And seen her warm solicitude express,
> At shadow of a danger; ye can judge,
> Though faintly, of the feelings which oppressed
> Boadicea...[66]

Even the rousing speech she delivers before her troops prior to a decisive battle is couched in terms of loyalty to family, although in a form that extends to the entire nation. The children that the Britons must fight to protect are an imagined posterity whose future freedom is under threat.

> Men! Britons! Fathers!
> I appeal to you: for yourselves, your wives,
> Your children; and for the honour, of our
> Common country. I call upon you all,
> To arouse yourselves, and struggle for freedom,
> To the death. Soon, soon, then, will you enjoy
> The palm of victory; and your children,
> And your children's children, will bless you; as
> They boast themselves, the offspring of the free.[67]

The Boudica portrayed by Barker has fewer hints of brutality about her than that created by Lindsay. This was likely due to the author's desire to write Boudica into a narrative that claimed Christianity had a burgeoning influence in ancient British society. But the most striking divergence from previous accounts, both classical and fictional, is in Barker's imagined version of Boudica's death. Barker's Boadicea dies alone, slumped in her chariot, unaccompanied by her daughters, amongst the dead and dying soldiers of her defeated army:

> Down in the seat,
> She sank; her head reclining on her hands,
> Rested o'er the chariot back; appearing
> As if by grief bowed down. Alas! for ever,
> That brave, maternal, noble, queenly heart,
> Had ceased to beat.[68]

This rather more pathetic end was almost certainly an attempt by Barker to allay criticism of Boudica's purported final act of suicide. As was the case in Mrs Owen's biography, Boudica's Tacitean death had the potential to offend the sensibilities of Victorian commentators, and perhaps also an audience which looked to historical events for instruction and example. Rather than criticize the pagan Boudica, as Owen had, for taking her own life, Barker conjectured a more acceptable end for a self-sacrificing mother and queen: a heart broken by pain and defeat. Barker, the poet, had greater freedom to intervene in the historical record, while Owen the biographer could only reflect on the moral failings of her subject.

---

[66] Ibid., 4.   [67] Ibid., 163–4.   [68] Ibid., 190–1.

Yet this did not free Barker from any duty to the record itself. Aware that this ending contradicted the known facts of the story, Barker provided his readers with a reasoned historical explanation for his version of her death:

> Of course [Tacitus'] information would be obtained from some of his countrymen, returned from Britain; and these filled with prejudice, if not hatred, against the Britons, would naturally be led to ascribe her sudden death, to this with them not uncommon a cause. They would never conceive, of high feeling existing among a people, whom they had long endeavoured to debase, and bring into subjection; nor dream, that the spirit of Boadicea, even under the impulse of strong excitement-loved ones gone; friends falling around her; and hope lost – might in the inward struggle, burst its mortal coil; and thus find death, more instantaneously than by the most virulent poison in nature.[69]

Barker spun the facts of Boudica's story to suit his message, but he could not do so without an explanation; in spite of other demands, it remained necessary for the author to divide truth from dramatic embellishment, precisely because the poem was conceived of as both improving and entertaining. That Sir Coutts Lindsay felt no such need is telling, given his intense interest in aspects of Boudica's story that could never be knowable from the extant sources; neither did Lindsay render these details in a particularly improving fashion. That Barker felt the need to explain his reasons for embellishing the work, not by claiming poetic licence but by deducing that Tacitus had every reason to attempt to mar Boudica's reputation in the eyes of posterity, reveals a concern for his audience's prior knowledge, as well as for the message he intended to give them. In part, Barker was making an historical argument, inferring that the influence of Christianity was stronger in ancient Britain than the Roman historian had admitted. By undermining the facts recorded by Tacitus, Barker could make this argument more convincing, while also saving Boudica from one, but not all, of the worst sins of paganism.

One other poem is worthy of mention here, if only because of the fame of its author, the consequent scholarly attention it has received, and the conclusions reached about the work's significance. As previously noted, writers on the subject of Boudica in the nineteenth century have pointed in particular to Alfred, Lord Tennyson's poem about the queen as illustrative of a particular cultural moment. As Queen Victoria's Poet Laureate from 1850 until his death in 1892, scholars have argued that Tennyson was inspired by events in India when he wrote his 'Boädicea', published in 1864.[70] The poem has been read as a condemnation of the ancient queen which cast her as a rebellious barbarian, and implied a historic parallel between the ancient Britons and the Indian people who took up arms against the colonial occupiers in modern India. Such a reading of the poem seem, at least superficially, quite plausible, especially in light of what some have seen as the

---

[69] Ibid., 196.
[70] 'With the uprising in mind, Tennyson 'rediscovered the furious Boadicea of Dio, Fletcher, and others and reinterpreted her for a new imperial context' and thus she is portrayed as a 'patently barbaric and negative figure', Hingley and Unwin, *Iron age queen*, 156. V. Hoselitz, *Imagining Roman Britain: Victorian responses to a Roman past*, (Woodbridge, 2007), 36 reaches for a similar conclusion.

sometimes implicit imperialist discourse of Tennyson's poetry generally.[71] However, some Victorian commentators, not least Prince Albert, viewed Queen Boudica as an ancient predecessor, even an ancestor, of Queen Victoria, rendering it somewhat unlikely that the Queen's Laureate would have written a wholly negative poem about Boudica. Indeed, as previous examples attest, the Boudica discussed in mid-Victorian verse was rarely without saving graces. There are other ways of understanding Tennyson's work, suggesting once again the danger for historians in making reductive connections between a complex past and a complex present.

First, it may simply have been the poet's imaginative response to an engraving of Queen Boudica by Thomas Stothard, which Tennyson's friend, the sculptor Thomas Woolner, sent to him in February 1859 (see Figure 7).[72] There is no direct evidence that Woolner himself encouraged his friend to make Boudica the subject of poetry, though she had inspired a sculpture of his own in 1844.[73] Revealingly, the sculptor encouraged Tennyson to write an epic poem on the Indian Uprising some years after 'Boädicea'.[74] This, and the later publication of unmistakably jingoistic 'The defence of Lucknow' (1879), would suggest that the Uprising was either not treated in Tennyson's 'Boädicea' at all, or, if it was, the poet did not consider it a satisfactory treatment in itself. Moreover, Tennyson's unpublished verse experiments of the same period, which take a similar metre, focus on other subjects—notably the threat Russia posed to Europe—and other settings, specifically ancient Ireland.[75]

Aside from Stothard's image, Tennyson's work was a poetic realization of the classical accounts. Although Ricks cites Tacitus as Tennyson's main source, the riotous language evokes Dio's more sensational version. There are echoes of Dio's elaborated rendering, especially in Tennyson's reimagining of Boudica's speech inciting the Britons to war:

> Hear Icenian, Catieuchlanian, hear Coritanian, Trinobant!
> Me the wife of rich Prasutagus, me the lover of liberty,
> Me they seized and me they tortured, me they lash'd and humiliated,
> Me the sport of ribald Veterans, mine of ruffian violators!
> See they sit, they hide their faces, miserable in ignominy!
> Wherefore in me burns an anger, not by blood to be satiated...
> Burst the gates, and burn the palaces, break the works of the statuary,
> Take the hoary Roman head and shatter it, hold it abominable,
> Cut the Roman boy to pieces in his lust and voluptuousness,
> Lash the maiden into swooning, me they lashed and humiliated,

---

[71] For which, see D.G. Reide, 'Tennyson's poetics of melancholy and the imperial imagination', *Studies in English Literature, 1500–1900*, 40 (2000), 659–78. Boädicea is not discussed, but Reide's other readings are not entirely convincing.

[72] C. Ricks (ed.), *The Poems of Tennyson* (London, 1969), 1119.

[73] Woolner entered 'The Death of Boadicea' in the competition for art to decorate the new Houses of Parliament in 1844.

[74] L. Ormond, *Tennyson and Thomas Woolner* (Lincoln, 1981), 15.

[75] Ricks, *Poems of Tennyson*, 1119. Thorn also notes that Tennyson was occupied with the threat of war with France in 1859, which drove him to write patriotic verses for the press. Boädicea was completed in March of the following year. M. Thorn, *Tennyson* (London, 1992), 324.

142   *Queen Boudica and Historical Culture in Britain*

    Chop the breasts from off the mother, dash the brains of the little one out,
    Up my Britons, on my chariot, on my chargers, trample them under us.[76]

Dio's account of the atrocities, not recorded by Tacitus, is evident in Tennyson's version, with its allusion to the violent deaths of the very old and the very young,

Figure 7. Thomas Stothard's illustration of Queen Boudica for G.F. Raymond's *New, Universal and Impartial History*. The Bodleian Libraries, The University of Oxford, Antiq. C.E. 7, illustration facing p. 30.

[76] All excerpts from the poem are from 'Boädicea' in Ricks, *Poems of Tennyson*, 1118–22.

and the severed breasts of the suffering Roman mothers. However, although Tennyson portrays Boudica in all her extravagant anger, the poem ends not with her own death and defeat, but with the fall of the Roman colony of 'Cámulodúne', the poet's unusual rendering of Camulodunum, the ancient name for modern-day Colchester. The closing lines of the poem depict the fall of the Roman colony and its own realization that its end is in part its own doing:

> So the silent colony hearing her tumultuous adversaries
> Clash the darts and on the buckler beat with rapid unanimous hand,
> Thought on all her evil tyrannies, all her pitiless avarice,
> Till she felt the heart within her fall and flutter tremulously,
> Then her pulses at the clamoring of her enemy fainted away.
> Out of evil evil flourishes, out of tyranny tyranny buds...

Certainly, Tennyson used Boudica's rebellion as a means of criticizing the vice and decadence of the Romans, giving the reader the sense that he viewed their conduct as partially to blame for what ultimately became of their colonies in Britain. The message may have been a check on imperial ambitions, and a warning to those who would terrorize the oppressed that their methods might return on them—as, perhaps they had in India in 1857.

There is a more banal explanation. Tennyson's work on *Boädicea* may simply have been a comfort to him at a time when his wife and children were wracked by illness and the poet himself was enduring a period of depression. His friend, the Oxford don Benjamin Jowett, wrote in January 1861: 'I paid my annual visit to Tennyson last week... This year he has written nothing but a short piece called "Boadicea" in a very wild and peculiar metre, with long lines and innumerable short syllables. It is very fine, but too strange to be popular. He has been ill, and greatly suffering and depressed I fear.'[77] Jowett here seems to link the poem's bizarre structure with what he fears is Tennyson's own disordered state of mind. Tennyson himself was fond of the poem, referring to it with a kind of rueful affection: '"Boadicea"—no I cannot publish her yet—perhaps never, for who can read her except myself?'[78] Indeed, this would suggest that the poem was not intended to reflect on public events, to incite popular enthusiasm, or to honour the queen. Rather it was an experimental exercise, personal to the poet, whose troubled mind demanded an absorbing project at a trying time.

Of course it would be a relatively simple task to read Boudica's nineteenth-century reputation as hitched to any number of contemporary cultural concerns or events of public importance, rendering her story in the nineteenth century one of continuous reinvention. But this multiplicity of contradictory images of Boudica is simply reflective of the emergence over time of many varied presentations of the same person and event, all of which have been conceived by individual human minds influenced by a whole complex of concerns; not all of these concerns are easily recovered by historians. An awareness of previous depictions of Boudica; a sense of

---

[77] Benjamin Jowett to Margaret Elliott, January 1861 *The letters of Alfred, Lord Tennyson*, 3 vols, ed. C.Y. Lang and E.F. Shannon Jr (Oxford, 1987), Vol. II, 270–1.
[78] Tennyson to Argyll, 10 November 1861, *Letters of Tennyson*, Vol. II, 283.

narrowing generic boundaries; assumptions about the needs and desires of new audiences; and, of course, Boudica's utility for contemporary moral and cultural discourses all provide possible contexts in which her image can be embedded. Although such a story can best be recovered in a chronologically linear way, we should resist any temptation to seek a single narrative trajectory in Boudica's posthumous life. I have sought to show that Boudica was a complex mixture of identities, which could change depending on who was doing the imagining, and for what audience, but which never succeed in wholly contradicting one another, or indeed cancelling one another out.

As I have argued, conceiving of the study and production of history as part of a field of culture means we can move beyond a simplistic view of Boudica's reputation that reads the late eighteenth to the nineteenth century as the beginning of an upward trajectory, the point at which she began to transform from female savage to patriotic icon. The historical-cultural approach makes it possible to embrace the complexity and variety of recitations of the past. While the period from about 1800 is usually seen as the starting point for the popularization of history, and it undoubtedly was a period of unprecedented publicity for historical ideas, this avalanche of material should not be mistaken for a new or more urgent impulse to consume historical products, nor for the entire novelty of the substance of popular history. As the example of Boudica shows, most of the substantive content of her story and elements of her character were in circulation long before the nineteenth century. Thomas Heywood brought her into the fold of women's history in the seventeenth century, and she had been a mainstay of the history market—both print and theatrical—throughout the eighteenth century. While there is of course much to set the nineteenth century apart from the period before, not least in the professionalization of the study of the past, modern historians should nevertheless be cautious in attributing the 'invention' of popular history to that period.

I have argued here that multiple understandings of Boudica could, did, and do coexist, and that this simultaneity of multiplicity amounts to integrity and, in a sense, continuity. It does so by acknowledging that the past itself was not—and is not—epiphenomenal to any present, and that any refraction through later events, personalities, or prejudices, while certainly revealing of those later events, personalities, or prejudices, does not entirely strip the past of its past-ness. Any reading of historical reputations that privileges the present over the past can lead us to overlook instances of continuity, not only in regards to Boudica's image, but also in the ways that people—historians and imaginative writers alike—engaged with her as an element of the historic, or, revealingly, failed to do so, thereby inviting the criticism of their contemporaries.

As this chapter and those preceding it have shown, the culture of history has been comprised of many genres, authors, and audiences, whose concerns were indeed occasionally linked to the immediate present. But even these harmonized with an overarching and shared understanding of history, in all its guises, as malleable by its very nature, at least within certain constraints. The fluidity of generic boundaries made this possible, and even fictions could be measured against a scale of probability, evidence, and accuracy and, as we have seen, were occasionally thought to come up short.

In other words, historical culture, factual and fictional, is interpretive by nature and so can never yield a single version of Boudica. Boudica—or any historical idea—is, of course, a moving target, but not a changing one. This means that Boudica was and is amenable to contradiction insofar as the limits of historical interpretation and fictionalization allow for it. The works, lives, and opinions discussed in this chapter, and those that came before it, have suggested, that any sense that Boudica's reputation was reliant on the changing views of successive generations in regards to femininity, queenship, or imperialism, must be complicated by the multiplicity of ways that images of truth could and did coexist. The next chapter pursues this argument into the end of the Victorian era, when Boudica is thought to have reached an apotheosis as an 'imperial icon'.

5
'A great deal of historical claptrap'
Heroine of Empire

Although biographers and to some extent poets and dramatists of the mid-nineteenth century struggled with the details of Boudica's story, their engagement with her was nevertheless an articulation of the 'collective emotional investment' in individual figures typical of the 'age of heroism' that spanned the Victorian and Edwardian periods. Geoffrey Cubitt and others have explored heroic reputations as they were circulated through commercial literature, news, and images, and propagated through more formal institutional channels.[1] Perhaps the most obvious, though often overlooked, means of public celebration was through the placement of public sculpture. There were at least five known statues of Boudica created before the end of the First World War. All but one, which once stood in the so-called People's Palace in Mile End, East London, are extant.[2]

Despite these monuments to her deeds and person, there has been surprisingly little scholarly work on the subject of Boudica in the nineteenth century. What little there is has reached for a single resounding conclusion: by the second half of the nineteenth century Boudica had been reinvented as an 'imperial icon', an image of Victorian triumphalism. In her eloquent study of allegory and femininity, Marina Warner argues that Queen Boudica presented the Victorians with a convenient encapsulation of this newly imperialist character.[3] More recently, Virginia Hoselitz has argued that Boudica had undergone a series of transformations culminating in the vision of her held by the Victorians: she was a patriotic heroine in the late eighteenth century, subsequently falling into a period of unpopularity during the early nineteenth century when she came to represent the savagery of conquered peoples—exemplified in the work of Tennyson. This state of affairs, Hoselitz suggests, changed again by the turn of the twentieth century, when Boudica

---

[1] G. Cubitt and A. Warren (eds), *Heroic reputations and exemplary lives* cited in the Introduction, n. 18, is the most comprehensive study of the phenomenon. See also A. Yarrington, *The commemoration of the hero, 1800–1864: monuments to the British victors of the Napoleonic Wars* (London, 1988); M. Jones, *The last great quest: Captain Scott's Antarctic sacrifice* (Oxford, 2003); J. Price, *Everyday heroism: Victorian constructions of the heroic civilian* (London, 2014).

[2] Opened in 1887 by Queen Victoria, the People's Palace housed the Queen's Hall, in which sculptures of twenty-two queens, from all times and places, were on display. Queen Boudica, the only queen to be shown bearing arms, was located next to the biblical Queen Esther. A diagram of the arrangement of the statues is found in *The Handbook to the People's Palace* (1887) held in the Queen Mary University Archives. The People's Palace was destroyed in a fire in 1931. The other sculptures of Boudica will be discussed in due course.

[3] Warner, *Monuments and maidens*, 51.

won the hardened hearts of the British public and became a celebrated heroine of a triumphant empire. In short, she was reconstructed 'to best suit the symbolic requirements of contemporary events'.[4] These contemporary events, it is agreed, revolve around the expansion of the British Empire in the late Victorian period and particularly the South African Wars.

The view of Boudica as an imperial heroine is based in large part on a single, quite literally monumental, source: Thomas Thornycroft's huge bronze 'Boadicea group', which stands on the north-east corner of Westminster Bridge, across the road from the Houses of Parliament (Figure 8).[5] Scholars have pointed out the statue's relevance as a symbolic homologue to Queen Victoria, whose presence on the throne legitimated a view of Queen Boudica as a prototype of British unity and triumphalism, an association that Hoselitz argues was emphasized by Thornycroft at the behest of Prince Albert.[6] That the statue was used by the historical novelist Marie Trevelyan for the cover of *Britain's Greatness Foretold: the prediction fulfilled* has led scholars to conflate Thornycroft's own motivations with those of Trevelyan and her co-author, Edwin Collins. Both the novel and the statue are seen as articulating the same late Victorian burst of imperial fervour, which inaugurated the

Figure 8. Thomas Thornycroft's massive 'Boadicea group' on Westminster Bridge. Image copyright Michael Ciancia.

---

[4] Hoselitz, *Imagining Roman Britain*, 37.
[5] I have told this story somewhat differently elsewhere; see M. Vandrei, 'A Victorian invention? Thomas Thornycroft's Boadicea group and the idea of historical culture in Britain', *Historical Journal*, 57 (2014), 485–508.
[6] Hoselitz, *Imagining Roman Britain*, 36 n. 34. Hoselitz does not provide a source for this report.

revival and wholesale reconstitution of Boudica as an imperial heroine, or even as the embodiment of an 'imperial cult'.[7]

This chapter will begin with a detailed account of the evens that surrounded the creation and placement of Thomas Thornycroft's famous statue. It will work to separate and thickly contextualize events that have too often been collapsed into each other: the lengthy gestation of the statue in Thornycroft's studio, its years of neglect in a warehouse following the artist's death, the excavation in 1894 of 'Boadicea's grave' in Hampstead Heath, and finally, the statue's placement, after much to-ing and fro-ing between local and national governments, on Westminster Bridge in 1901. These events took place over the course of nearly thirty years, making it difficult to directly link Thornycroft's creative process with the work's erection at the behest of the London County Council, largely through the labours of Sir William Bull MP. The story is complicated yet further when we take into consideration the unrelated decision in 1894 to excavate the tumulus known locally as 'Boadicea's grave' on Parliament Hill Fields in Hampstead Heath, North London. The London County Council brought in the archaeologist Charles Hercules Read of the British Museum to undertake the work, but they did so in response to what was little more than a popular local tradition. The excavation became the immediate motivating factor behind the decision to erect Thornycroft's statue in its current position, a circumstance brought about by the public interest generated in the press. Thus Read's own enthusiasm for bringing archaeology and the distant past to a wide audience can be seen, indirectly, to have been of considerable significance to the story.

The second part of this chapter gets to the heart of the connection between Boudica and Victorian imperialism by exploring some of the ways that engaged audiences—in this case, book reviewers—responded to the link. Thomas Thornycroft's statue was used by Marie Trevelyan as the frontispiece to her historical novel *Britain's Greatness Foretold*, and, arguably, cemented the statue's perceived link with the author's own irrefutable jingoism. However, the critical response to the novel is revealing of the discomfiture aroused by the notion of Boudica as a predecessor of Victoria, and, more to the point, by the use of the distant past as a legitimating power for the present. While Thomas Thornycroft's reaction to Prince Albert's insistence that the 'Boadicea group' should echo the real Victoria is one instance of this, the critical reaction to Marie Trevelyan's work reveals an even greater reluctance to make hard and fast links between events so far apart in time, in spite of—or perhaps because of—the language of prophecy, borrowed from William Cowper, that was employed by the novelist. While scholars of ancient Britain have insisted that Boudica was a figure of cultish imperial enthusiasm, or perhaps a female barbarian of the dark ages both opposing and presaging the civility of modernity, there is a more complex story to tell around the relationship between the ancient past and the Victorian present.

---

[7] R. Hingley, *Roman officers and English gentlemen: the imperial origins of Roman archaeology* (London, 2000), 77.

UNITY OF PURPOSE? THOMAS THORNYCROFT'S 'BOADICEA GROUP' AND LATE VICTORIAN EMPIRE

Thomas Thornycroft's massive Boadicea group is the most visible tribute to Queen Boudica in London, or indeed in the United Kingdom; it is also probably the artist's most famous work. However, Thomas Thornycroft was by no means the most well-known, or even one of the more talented, sculptors of his day, and he is perhaps best known as the father of the far more successful and prolific late Victorian sculptor Hamo Thornycroft (1850–1925).[8] Unlike his celebrated son, Thomas struggled to obtain the commissions which were the lifeblood of all artists, but especially of sculptors, whose works were expensive in terms of time, money, materials, and sheer artistic energy.[9] Although the statue known to its creator as the 'Boadicea group' was to become his most successful, even it had roots in failure: the Boudica statue was created as a conscious response to professional disappointment, as well as to a broader concern for the state of British sculpture in the mid-Victorian period. To understand this we must look to the events of 1851, and the Great Exhibition of that year, for which Thomas had produced an equestrian statue of Queen Victoria.

The sculptor harboured high hopes for his Victoria statue; these hopes were encouraged by the Prince Consort's evident enthusiasm for the work. Thornycroft dared to believe that a coveted royal commission was imminent. 'My fortune', Thornycroft wrote to his friend and mentor, the sculptor W.B. Dickinson, shortly before the Great Exhibition, 'vibrates in the balance.'[10] But no commission came and in some powerful critical circles, opinion was against Thornycroft's Victoria. A review published in *The Times* asserted that the equestrian statue was 'not sufficiently ideal' for its majestic subject,[11] an especially painful assessment for the artist. He had portrayed Victoria in a close-fitting riding habit, which marked the statue as adhering to strictures of portraiture rather than to the 'ideal' or imagined, classical approach which, in *The Times* reviewer's opinion, would have been more appropriate for the sovereign.[12] Thornycroft saw this not merely as an attack on his Victoria statue, but on his entire artistic world view. He sensed, rightly or wrongly, that his work has been condemned because it did not conform to classical, and thus 'foreign' characteristics. He wrote to Dickinson shortly afterward: 'It would be folly

---

[8] E. Manning, *Marble & bronze: the art and life of Hamo Thornycroft* (London, 1982).

[9] B. Read, *Victorian sculpture* (London, 1982), 49ff, relates the difficulties of working as a sculptor in Victorian Britain. Sculptors' materials were expensive and a sculptor could waste years modelling figures that never saw the light of day, let alone received commissions.

[10] All letters refer to Leeds Museum & Galleries (Henry Moore Institute Archive), Papers of the Thornycroft family (collection reference: 1986.4). Thomas Thornycroft (TT) to W.B. Dickinson (WBD), undated, but certainly written in March or early April of 1851, T II-C (TT) 2.

[11] TT to WBD, 15 Nov. 1851, T II-C 152/1-2. The original review appeared in *The Times*, 15 April 1851. Thomas Thornycroft's reading of its subtext may or may not have been accurate, but the review itself was excoriating.

[12] This is discussed in M. Stocker, 'Thornycroft, Thomas (1815–1885)', *ODNB* (2004; online edn, Oct 2006), http://www.oxforddnb.com/view/article/27369, accessed 8 Aug 2017.

to shut one's eyes to the fact that sculpture illustrating our own history and poetry is coldly received; that English opinion and English art as yet exists not...'[13]

Thomas was not alone in his alienation. The mid-Victorian period was a fraught one for sculpture in Britain, as many British practitioners of the art perceived themselves being shunted aside in favour of continental competitors, of whom the Italian Baron Carlo Marochetti was the most reviled among British artists.[14] Thornycroft and others like him condemned the practice of awarding public commissions to foreign sculptors.[15] When Thornycroft received the news that Marochetti had been awarded the commission for a statue of Queen Victoria (erected 1854) in Glasgow—the very commission, it seems, that he had dreamed of for his equestrian Victoria—Thornycroft vented his anger to Dickinson: '...English art has been sacrificed to foreign interests; and a most successful agent in that offer is Baron Marochetti, a second rank artist, but one of mighty pretension and consummate intrigue'.[16] Even so, Thomas professed to believe that 'There is in England, nevertheless, the germ of a more hopeful state; there are men who believe that art may grow here, founded on our age and philosophy, accepting the Greek only as its keynote, its tone...'[17]

It was in the aftermath of this frustrating episode that Thornycroft conceived of his statue of Queen Boudica and her daughters. He began work on a plaster model, which was housed in his studio and only occasionally shown to the public.[18] He approached his subject as a work of historical portraiture intended to express the character of the nation to whom the warrior queen Boudica belonged, rather than as a classicized or 'idealized' figure.[19] The group exemplifies what W.M. Rossetti called at the time 'national character' sculpture, or:

> ...the rendering of whatever is beautiful, suggestive, and sculpturally available in the character, type, costume, employment, or intellectual purposes of the various nations of the earth. This has truth, like portraiture; an open field for all differences of feeling and perception in the sculptors; no restriction as to the number or quality of phases of beauty which it may include; and a real demand upon the artist's mind in seizing and presenting his subject. This range of the art is much more pursued by foreign sculptors, and especially the French, than by our own.[20]

---

[13] TT to WBD, 15 November 1851, T II-C 152/1-2.

[14] Read, *Victorian sculpture*, 297–8. See also Ormond, 'Tennyson and Thomas Woolner', 15, who notes Marochetti's popularity with the aristocracy, which likely provoked some jealousy.

[15] E. Thornycroft, *Bronze and steel: The life of Thomas Thornycroft, sculptor and engineer* (Long Compton, 1932), 53. A 'Memorial of British sculptors' appeared in the *London Daily News*, 31 May 1856, which expressed dismay at the perceived prejudice against British sculptors and pleaded that public commissions be granted only after fair, open, public competitions had been held. Thomas Thornycroft was among the signatories.

[16] TT to WBD, 15 Nov. 1851, T II-C 152/1-2. [17] Ibid.

[18] The 'bold, colossal head of Boadicea' displayed by Thomas Thornycroft at the Royal Academy in May 1864 almost certainly came from his model for the statue group. *The Observer*, 8 May 1864.

[19] D.J. Getsy, 'Introduction', in D.J. Getsy (ed.), *Sculpture and the pursuit of the modern ideal in Britain, c. 1880–1930* (Aldershot, 2004), 1–10. Others have shown this tension between the ideal and the real, characteristic of 'national' sculpture in Britain, as early as 1840; see M. Greenwood, 'Victorian ideal sculpture', DPhil thesis (Courtauld Institute of Art, 1998), Ch. 1.

[20] W.M. Rossetti, 'British sculpture: its conditions and prospects', *Fraser's Magazine* (April 1861), 493–505, at 503. See also F.T. Palgrave, 'Historical art in England', *Fraser's Magazine* (June 1861), 773–80.

In other words, sculpture of a 'national character' allowed for both faithful, realistic representation, and imaginative or reflective elaboration. This was the area of sculpture which Thornycroft intended to appropriate for his own national version of the art.

Even in an atmosphere perceived as potentially unfriendly to British sculptors, Thornycroft's efforts did not go unnoticed. By 1860 the large plaster model of Boudica had begun to garner wide attention. In June of that year, Thomas wrote to Dickinson that 'Boadicea' 'has been much talked of at the Court this last week and I feel confident if providence grants me health to finish the work, that I shall have their countenance in a public subscription for erecting it'.[21] Indeed, Prince Albert himself took a personal interest in the work as early as 1859, and the two horses shown careering in advance of Boudica's chariot are modelled on the Prince's own, which he had lent to the artist for the purpose. The Prince even suggested that the finished statue might fittingly adorn the top of the arch at Hyde Park Corner.[22] Given the extensive interaction between Prince and sculptor, it is unsurprising that historians have assumed that Albert had a degree of influence on substantive matters of representation, but Thornycroft's correspondence is revealing of the artist's true feelings on the subject. The Prince's influence was limited, and there is no evidence that the two men were of one mind as to the group's appearance.

Thornycroft's discomfiture in the face of persistent royal meddling is clear from his many letters to Dickinson. He described one occasion when the Prince Consort pronounced that Boudica's chariot should be 'the throne upon wheels';[23] a conscious evocation of modern royalty; he had even, Thornycroft professed with horror, suggested adding a third horse. Thornycroft fretted to Dickinson that doing so would 'absolutely condemn, nay destroy my composition'.[24] But this disparity in opinion reflected deeper disagreements between the artist and the Prince Consort. Thomas reported a conversation in which the two had discussed 'the comparative advantages of realistic treatment...against artistic and poetic views; and [Prince Albert's] decision was decidedly to the latter'.[25] But despite Albert's efforts, Thornycroft did not intend the group to be a tribute to Queen Victoria; not, at least, to the extent or in the manner that the Prince would have liked. Nor was the sculptor willing to assent to royal interpolations which contravened his own vision for the statue, or his values as an artist. To make too explicit a connection between the ancient and contemporary queens would, in the artist's opinion, amount to bowdlerizing the past, as and the destruction of his attempt at realism.

Thus, contrary to the Prince's suggestions, Thornycroft concerned himself with modelling a chariot that corresponded to the qualities of the object which could best be determined by research into the classical sources. Thornycroft consulted Julius Caesar's account of ancient Britain in the *Gallic Wars* in which detailed descriptions of British chariot warfare could be found. In light of the information he gathered, the sculptor rejected the Prince's majestic, throne-like chariot in favour of a plain,

---

[21] TT to WBD, 26 June 1860, T II-C(TT) 22.
[22] L. Priddle, *The history of the 'Boadicea group'* (London, 1902).
[23] Manning, *Marble & bronze*, 38.   [24] TT to WBD, 10 June 1859, T II-C (TT) 21.
[25] TT to WBD, 26 June 1860, T II-C (TT) 22.

flat platform on wheels: '...the advantage of a different form of car has grown upon me. Caesar says the British ran along the pole of their charrriots [*sic*] [and] leaped down in front of their horses[.] [H]ad there been a high point to the vehicle this would have been inconvenient. A flat platform is the probable shape and this suits me best as it permits the figure to be seen down to the feet.'[26] This question continued to occupy him a month later, when Thornycroft wrote to Dickinson: 'With regard to the war chariot of Boadicea Caesar's description supplies as much as I want to know. It warrants the view I <u>want</u> to take.'[27] In this instance, historical accuracy and artistic intent were in harmony.

In addition to designing a British war chariot based on classical descriptions, Thornycroft concerned himself with the spectrum of feeling which his three human subjects might conceivably have experienced. He discussed this with Dickinson, writing to his constant friend, 'I am pleased that you concede the justness of the emotion by which young barbarians would be moved, in the circumstances of Boadicea's Daughters. Further the necessities of art composition demand that the majestic fury of the Queen should be supplemented in the daughters. The vehemence of her movement would be impotent did it not excite sympathetic disturbance in the figures clinging to her garment. Unity of purpose, is the grand element of the quality described as breadth in art.'[28] In a manner not unlike some writers of historical drama, the sculptor reflected deeply on the emotional beings his subjects may have been, and by doing so, added another facet of historical and human realism to the work. Thornycroft's own sense of the possibilities and limitations of human action and emotional response in a given circumstance are evident here, but many others had made similar interpretative statements in the preceding centuries, on paper and on stage.

Despite Albert's initial support, Thornycroft never received a commission for the group; one wonders whether the artist's persistence in his design was a factor. But Thornycroft continued to work on the 'Boadicea group' well into his old age, never losing sight of it as a response to an earlier failure. His past disappointment was somewhat ameliorated when, in 1871, a critic visited Thomas's studio unannounced and published a review of the 'Boadicea group' in *The Times*, the same newspaper which had caused the artist so much distress twenty years before. The reviewer enthused that the group was 'the most successful attempt in historical sculpture of this barren time...which we would fain hail as the hope of better things and better days for an art which, on English soil at least, is sadly degenerate'.[29] Thomas was delighted with the praise, though he could not resist, in his letter to the paper, making reference to the group's antecedent circumstances: 'I rejoice very much to find my aim in the treatment of this subject so completely understood and appreciated by a critic entertaining more realistic views of sculpture than I have found practicable. Twenty years ago I made a realistic equestrian statue. This was

---

[26] TT to WBD, n/d (March 1861), T II-C (TT) 102.
[27] TT to WBD, 9 April 1861, TT464. Emphasis in original.
[28] TT to WBD, n/d (March 1861), T II-C (TT) 102.   [29] *The Times*, 21 July 1871.

condemned by the "Times". But you have now made ample amends.'[30] The aim Thornycroft was referring to here was the resuscitation of the art of sculpture in Britain in the face of competition from continental Europe, especially in so far as the British art was characterized by the kind of realistic treatment that he esteemed. Any notion of a symbolic connection between his ancient queen and the reigning one had faded entirely with the death of Prince Albert, and the artist embraced his statue as a response to professional frustration.

Thomas Thornycroft did not live to see his model cast in bronze, however. After his death in 1885, the plaster 'Boadicea group' became the property of the sculptor's elder son, John Isaac (1843–1928), whose success as a naval engineer was one of the great joys of his father's latter years—the old man was often seen cruising up and down the Thames on his narrowboat, the *Waterlily*. But the colossal model of Boudica in her primitive war chariot was left to repose, incongruously, amidst the experimental motorized vehicles at John Isaac Thornycroft & Co.'s Chiswick workshop for almost a decade, until the 1890s, when events began to turn, quite by accident, in the statue's favour.[31]

ENTER THE ARCHAEOLOGISTS

The story of the statue's creation is one of personal difficulty and, belatedly, something like triumph, or at least consolation. But the story behind the statue's eventual placement is one of institutional machinations, which linked Boudica with the formal, professional structure of the British Museum, with metropolitan government, and with the public's interest in her as a local London heroine. This marks something of a departure; art and literature in various forms had been the primary means by which Boudica had entered into and reflected the public imagination from the seventeenth century onward. Aside from the appearance of navy ships bearing her name,[32] there had been little overlap between public bodies—whether civic or national—and the celebration of Boudica's legacy. However, in the later nineteenth century, change was afoot in the form a growing interest in popular antiquarianism and archaeology, especially on a local level, and the intersection between nascent bodies of professional archaeologists and local and national governance.[33]

---

[30] Quoted in Manning, *Marble & bronze*, 62.
[31] E.I. Carlyle, 'Thornycroft, Sir John Isaac (1843–1928)', rev. Alan G. Jamieson, *ODNB* (2004), http://www.oxforddnb.com/view/article/36512, accessed 8 Aug 2017. A. Townsin, *Thornycroft* (Hersham, 2001), gives a history of Thornycroft's engineering firm and Boudica's small part in it.
[32] The first was in 1797. There were to be three more HMS Boadiceas in the service. The last, a destroyer finished in 1930, was struck by a torpedo and sunk in Lyme Bay in 1944; see J.J. Colledge and B. Warlow, *Ships of the Royal Navy* (London, 2003), 53–4.
[33] The most comprehensive study remains P. Levine, *The amateur and the professional: antiquarians, historians and archaeologists in Victorian England, 1838–1886* (Cambridge, 1986), but see also K. Hudson, *A social history of archaeology: the British experience* (London, 1982); and S.J. Speight, 'A gentlemanly pastime: antiquarianism, adult education and the clergy in England, c. 1750–1960', *History of Education*, 40 (2011), 143–55.

Organizations such as the British Museum, founded in 1753, reflected the notion that collections of antiquities would be to the benefit of future generations, but there was little sense of connection between this large, unwieldly body and the small, amateur endeavours undertaken by groups of local antiquaries whose interests tended to be close to home. It was only in 1866 that the Museum created a Department of British and Medieval Antiquities and Ethnography, 'a tardy recognition of the interest and importance of the products of the ancient Britons, who until that time had been rashly and hastily dismissed as mere savages'.[34] Whether this truly was the view taken by the British Museum, it was an attitude certainly not shared by the many individuals whose research appeared in antiquarian journals. The general journal of antiquity, *Archaeologia*, founded in 1770, represented the catholic tastes of its many subscribers and contributors, with ancient British topics, as well as Roman remains found in Britain, often featuring. By far the most active bodies in the discovery of archaeological remains in Britain were the local antiquarian societies, many of which were keenly interested in the items to be found within easy reach of their meetings.[35]

By the late nineteenth century, archaeological research into British antiquity had begun to benefit from the patronage of local and central government, not least in the passage of the Monuments Protection Act of 1882.[36] For Boudica this was a significant development because it made possible the first organized archaeological investigation into one of the purported sites of her death and burial: Hampstead Heath's Parliament Hill Fields in north London. In the autumn of 1894, the London County Council (LCC) approved a decision to excavate a raised barrow of earth there, which had come to be known locally as 'Boadicea's Mound' or 'Boadicea's Grave'.[37] The impetus to open the tumulus came from the LCC's Parks and Open Spaces Committee, specifically the Northwest District Subcommittee, the body responsible for the parks and commons of north-west London, including the location of the tumulus.[38] Although there were other sites in London that could lay claim to being the site either of Boudica's final camp, or of the fatal battlefield, the Northwest District Subcommittee was in a position to take action, since it had only just acquired responsibility for the land on which the barrow sat.[39] The

---

[34] A.B. Tonnochy, 'Four keepers of the Department of British and Medieval Antiquities', *The British Museum Quarterly*, 18 (1953), 83–8, at 84.

[35] A full list of mid-Victorian county antiquarian societies can be found in P. Levine, *The amateur and the professional*, Appendix IV. Virginia Hoseltiz also emphasises the importance of the local dimension to antiquarianism, *Imagining Roman Britain*, Ch. 3. This antiquarian interest extended well beyond the mid-Victorian period which has been the focus of much scholarly work; see P. Readman, 'The place of the past in English culture, c. 1890–1914,' *Past and Present*, 186 (2005), 147–99, at 160.

[36] A useful overview can be found in G. Clark, 'Archaeology and the state', *Antiquity*, 32 (1934), 414–28.

[37] The suggestion was first raised in July 1894, see London Metropolitan Archives (LMA), London County Council, Presented Papers, LCC/MIN/08818, 11 July 1894.

[38] LMA, Parks and Open Spaces Committee, Northwest District Subcommittee Minutes, LCC/MIN/08738, 3 October 1894.

[39] For instance, some believed that what appeared to be the remains of a camp or stronghold around Ambresbury Banks, in Epping Forest, might have been the site of Boudica's final, fatal encampment. Two obelisks in the area lent some credence to the idea, but commentators remained divided on the exact location of Boudica's final battle, let alone where her body might have been

Subcommittee engaged the services of an ambitious archaeologist, Charles Hercules Read (1857–1929), who waived any claim to a fee. A self-taught archaeologist and ethnologists, Read was a close friend of Sir Augustus Wollaston Franks, who, as the first Keeper of the British Museum's Department of British and Medieval Antiquities, was responsible for cementing the importance of the new section in the Museum's activities.[40] Read eventually replaced Franks as head of the collections when the latter retired in 1896; notably, Read was also President of the Royal Institute of Anthropologists.

But all of this was in Read's future. In 1894, as ever, Queen Boudica did not fail to attract attention. As early as the summer of that year, some months before the Subcommittee came to a decision to permit the excavation, word had already got around that the tumulus was to be opened. Even as the proposal was under discussion, the Subcommittee received letters from interested members of the public, like C.E. Fagan, an ornithologist at the Natural History Museum. Fagan enquired whether it was indeed true that the 'London County Council have given directions to examine the tumulus in Parliament Hill, which tradition marks as the burial place of Queen Boadicea? If so, may I ask if you can give me any idea of when the work will be commenced?'[41] Fagan may have wanted, out of interest, to attend the excavation and be among the first witnesses of Boudica's exhumation; this was certainly the case with one professional archaeologist who wrote to express a desire to be present at the opening of the barrow.[42] Another archaeologist, this one an enthusiastic amateur, a Mr Kennedy, wrote in July to express his anxiety that the site's integrity might be compromised, and request that the barrow not be 'seriously interfered with'.[43] A photographer for *Strand Magazine* also offered his professional services if any objects of interest were to be uncovered.[44]

Public knowledge of the proposed excavation was also apparent in the press, though it seemed to some that the Parks Committee was indulging popular ignorance rather than acting on expert opinion: 'The reported proposal to open and excavate Parliament Hill for the sake of seeing what it contains, and particularly whether it contains in its dark recesses the tomb of Boadicea, is an excellent illustration of the hold which tradition has on the human mind. For, except in vague, shadowy legend, there is not a particle of evidence that the British "Warrior Queen," who lives rather in the verse of Cowper and Tennyson than in the pages of veritable history, lies in this spot.'[45] Despite this disclaimer, the paper's report went on to describe the history recorded by Tacitus, noting the likelihood that the battle had indeed taken place in or near London; it was the proposal to dig in

buried. See discussion in E. Walford, *Greater London: a narrative of its history its people and its places* (London, 1894), Vol. I, 418–23.

[40] T.W. Potter, 'Later prehistory and Roman Britain: the formation of the national collections', in M. Caygill and J. Cherry (eds), *A.W. Franks; Nineteenth-century collecting and the British Museum* (London, 1997), pp. 130–5.

[41] LMA, Papers presented to Parks and Open Spaces Subcommittees, Letter from C.E. Fagan, 16 August 1894. LCC/MIN/8819.

[42] Letter from H.W. Mengedoht, 26 July 1894, LCC/MIN/8819.

[43] Letter from Mr Kennedy, 22 July 1894, LCC/MIN/8819.

[44] Letter dated 30 July, LCC/MIN/8819.   [45] *The Standard*, 20 July 1894.

the precise location at Parliament Hill Fields that lacked credibility, at least from the point of view of many scholars.

By the time work began on 29 October 1894, public interest was most definitely aroused. The proceedings of the dig were reported in newspapers across the country while, on site, Read and his team of helpers were watched 'with an interest so keen that it may almost be called feverish... there is undoubtedly a fascination even for the untutored mind in respect to the places of sepulchre, whether authentic or suppositious, of historic personages whose deeds have been handed on to us...'[46] This interest must indeed have been intense, perhaps even obstructive; Read wrote in his final report that 'the presence of large numbers of the public somewhat hamper[ed] operations'.[47]

The excavation of 'Boadicea's Grave' lasted a week, from 29 October to 6 November. But despite Read's thorough search, nothing was found bar a few bits of china and a soil horizon of relatively recent origin, suggesting that additional layers had recently been added.[48] There was disappointment that nothing indicative of Boudica's burial or any relic at all of ancient Britain was found but, as one newspaper report admitted, her association with the tumulus was 'essentially latter-day folklore', counter to the 'known facts and the natural presumptions of history', and to professional opinion.[49]

The overall sense in the press was that there had been only the vaguest hope that something of the period would be revealed by the excavation. Ever the professional, Read had searched the tumulus with all the assiduity of conviction, but in truth he undertook the dig with little hope of finding anything connected to the ancient queen. In his final report on the excavation, Read described to his assembled colleagues at the Society of Antiquaries his careful study of the exposed mound and the few meagre items he was able to locate, mostly from the previous two centuries. He also addressed the popular tradition associating Boudica with the area. With an air of apology, Read allowed that 'It is scarcely necessary... to bring forward evidence to prove that popular nomenclature is seldom supported by historical fact... but the tradition now seems so wide spread that it would be impossible not to refer to it.'[50] But his downbeat attitude to the dig was not due to the questionable origin of the myth in popular opinion; rather, from the outset, he had every reason to doubt the existence of a tomb for Boudica on Hampstead Heath.

In his paper to the Society of Antiquaries, Read noted that Dio had described how the Britons gave Boudica a splendid funeral with many of her compatriots in attendance; he speculated that Dio would not have made such a statement without some authority for it, and that such a momentous occasion was unlikely to have been allowed under the watchful eyes of the Romans so near to London. Although he felt that such a level of detail was unnecessary before his present audience, Read

---

[46] *Morning Post*, 2 November 1894.
[47] C.H. Read, 'Account of the opening of..."Boadicea's Grave"', *Proceedings of the Society of Antiquaries of London*, 15 (22 November 1894), 233–55, at 241.
[48] *Birmingham Daily Post*, 5 November 1894.   [49] *Morning Post*, 7 November 1894.
[50] 'Account of the opening of..."Boadicea's Grave"', 241.

addressed the tradition in his report precisely because it was so prominent in non-specialist circles. Indeed, given the nature of the excavation—popularly understood to be the search for the ancient queen's remains and watched with great anticipation—he could hardly have ignored it.

Read's career combined a professional concern with recovering, preserving, and cataloguing antiquities, while also arguing for the relevance of these remains for public life in the present He did much to further the collections of the Department of British and Medieval Antiquities, and in his later capacity as Keeper, Read oversaw the creation of a series of catalogue guides to the collection, intended to introduce amateur enthusiasts and non-specialists to the items held at the museum.[51] Read continued to lobby for increased support for archaeological training for interested amateurs, and for government support for Britain's antiquities. In an anniversary address delivered at the Society of Antiquaries in April 1911, Charles Read, by now the Society's president, expressed the need for archaeologists and antiquaries to engage the public with the past, to work with universities and government bodies, and to safeguard artefacts by petitioning for funds. He was firmly of the opinion, expressed some years after the dig at Hampstead Heath, that '...such intellectual enterprises as ours add to the intellectual food of the nation, and the mere fact that such tasks are being carried on in the country helps to arouse and quicken the intelligence of the oft-quoted man on the street; they provide him with sane subjects of conversation; they help to revive in his mind long forgotten scraps of history or tradition; they finally assume the form of crystallised fact and fill the gaps in school histories, and thus eventually, if not at first, they become directly helpful in education and an essential part of it'.[52]

The excavation at Hampstead Heath was not a resounding success from an archaeological point of view, but it was the beginning of what Read hoped would be an ongoing commitment on behalf of the LCC to undertake similar works in the future. It also succeeded in arousing public interest in Boudica's place in the history of London, demonstrating the productive continuum that existed between the public's historical imagination, an active antiquarian establishment, and willing public bodies. The Subcommittee's decision to allow the excavation was to bear fruit in other ways, setting into motion the placement of Boudica's likeness on Westminster Bridge.

THE QUEEN IN BRONZE

As it happened, one of the interested members of the public to see coverage of the excavation in the newspapers was John Isaac Thornycroft, whose steam-powered

---

[51] Tonnochy, 'Four keepers', 85.

[52] 'Anniversary Address', *Proceedings of the Society of Antiquaries*, 27 April 1911, 428–47, at 443. It is also worth noting that as President of the Royal Anthropological Institute, Read presided over the first public Huxley Memorial Lecture and the publication of the first number of the Institute's new monthly journal, *Man*, in 1900 and 1901 respectively, both with the aim of 'obtaining recruits' for anthropology; see 'Presidential Address', *The Journal of the Anthropological Institute of Great Britain and Ireland*, 31 (4 February 1901), 10.

van had met with such great success that he would require the whole of his Chiswick shed for the second, larger model.[53] This left no room for Boudica and her daughters. Rather than discard the plaster statue, however, it was the younger Thornycroft's hope to see it cast in bronze and presented to the public. He approached his near-neighbour, Sir William Bull (1863–1931)[54] with the suggestion that Thomas's statue might serve as an appropriate gravemarker if the ancient queen's resting place was indeed uncovered during the course of the excavation in north-west London.[55]

William Bull could not have been better placed to advocate on behalf of the Thornycrofts. In addition to being MP for the constituency of Hammersmith and Fulham, Bull was a member of the LCC, and sat on the Parks and Open Spaces Committee's North-west District Subcommittee. He was enthusiastic about the statue, and brought Thornycroft's offer before the London County Council. Indeed, such was his enthusiasm that, without waiting for his colleagues' approval, he ordered the plaster model to be taken to the bronze foundry of John W. Singer and Sons in September 1896. The foundry agreed to keep the model until the money could be raised to complete the bronze work, at last freeing John Isaac from his unwieldy burden.[56] However, the LCC rejected Bull's pleas for the Council to raise funds for the statue on the grounds that no tomb had been found in Parliament Hill Fields, which had been the proposed home of the finished piece. In addition, casting the bronze model was estimated to cost a hefty £6000.[57] Bull's own estimate for the whole project—from casting to placement—was £3000, and he promptly formed the Boadicea Fund Committee to appeal to the public for subscriptions.[58]

Aside from the crucial question of how to pay for the 'Boadicea group', there was the equally pressing matter of where to place the finished work. As the LCC had pointed out, Hampstead Heath no longer seemed appropriate given that the tumulus had been proven once and for all to have no recoverable connection to Boudica. Various alternatives were debated, but the north-eastern corner of Westminster Bridge, across from parliament's clock tower, eventually won the day. In large part due to Bull's efforts, the funds were finally assembled, and the LCC agreed to provide a pedestal.[59] But the many delays to the project, coupled with the prominence of the site, led to the LCC's decision that the plaster model should be temporarily placed on the proposed site to undergo a trial period during which the public could voice its opinion on both the site and the work itself.[60]

---

[53] Townsin, *Thornycroft*, 9.

[54] There is no biography, or even *ODNB* entry, for William Bull, but his son wrote an entertaining memoir of his father's later career as MP and *paterfamilias*: P. Bull, *Bulls in the Meadows* (London, 1957).

[55] This story is related in a letter to *The Times* from William Bull, 2 March 1896, as part of an appeal for public subscriptions.

[56] Letter from Singer and Sons to William Bull, 28 September 1896, Bull Papers, 2/12, Churchill Centre, Cambridge.

[57] LMA, General Purposes Committee, Presented Papers, LCC/MIN/06323, 22 December 1896.

[58] *The Times*, 2 March 1896; it was also printed in *The Globe*, 29 July 1896. The real figure was in fact much less, although still substantial at £1995, by the foundry's calculation. Singer and Sons to William Bull, 28 September 1896, Bull papers, 2/12.

[59] *The Echo*, 19 January 1898.   [60] *The Morning Post*, 19 January 1898.

'A great deal of historical claptrap' 159

The arrival on Westminster Bridge of the 10 foot tall mock bronze warrior queen created some stir. A week after the its placement, it was reported that 'thousands have made a pilgrimage to the Embankment, and submitted Mr. Thornycroft's great work to critical examination... an observer would be justified in pronouncing the general verdict a favourable one'.[61] Even the elderly and reclusive Queen Victoria was driven to the site to observe the newest proposed addition to London's public statuary.[62] The positive public response to the statue prompted the LCC to agree that, when it was finished, the bronze 'Boadicea group' should indeed be placed on Westminster Bridge. But the passage of almost four years between the trial period and the completion of the bronze meant that the LCC rejected Bull's pleas for a formal unveiling in 1902, citing the numerous delays to the project.[63]

Prophetic lines from Cowper's poem were hastily chosen for the plinth, probably by Bull himself: 'Regions Caesar never knew/Thy posterity shall sway'. But even these lines, although they have provided an enduring context in which the statue continues to be read, have the ring of special pleading in light of the general lack of enthusiasm in 1902 for a formal unveiling. As popular attention drifted and the archaeological work sank into the ever more distant past, it was left to William Bull at the London County Council to push the project limpingly to its end. In 1898 Read's excavation had been fresh enough in the popular memory to be viewed as a significant impetus behind the statue's proposed endorsement. As one newspaper commented at the time: 'The vain search made a few years ago by the London County Council for the grave of Boadicea, was productive of much interest and amusement, and now the almost forgotten quest is brought to the memory of the public by the erection on the embankment of a model of a statue of this queen.'[64] However, by 1902 the fervour which had surrounded the excavation in 1894 had lost all immediacy, and even the public's enthusiastic reception of the plaster model, as the only tangible result of the excavation, was a distant memory.

Previous accounts of the Boudica statue have collapsed Thornycroft's design of the statue into the moment of its placement on Westminster Bridge, casting two distinct efforts as a single example of the Victorian impulse to celebrate the surpassing of one great empire by an even greater one. The story related here—from Thomas Thornycroft's disappointment in 1851 to John Isaac's space allocation problems and the lucky coincidence of this with the excavation on Hampstead Heath in 1894—seems somewhat bathetic in light of arguments that map the statue's significance onto Victorian or Edwardian ideas of empire. However, it is a revealing instance of the importance of understanding, in fine detail, the processes behind the creation of individual historical products.

---

[61] *The London Argus*, 22 January 1898.
[62] An artist's impression of the meeting between the two queens appeared in *Black & White*, 5 March 1898.
[63] LMA, Highway Committee, signed minutes, LCC/MIN/06726, 10 June 1902.
[64] *The Irish Independent*, 18 January 1898.

The moment of the statue's permanent placement was separated from Thornycroft's painful process of creation by the passage of nearly three decades. The sculptor's sense of rejection and frustration had driven him to take up the subject of the wronged queen, and although he appreciated the interest and moral support of Albert, the Prince Consort's insistence on making the statue a direct tribute to Queen Victoria did not sit easily with the artist. Thornycroft's individual artistic sensibilities demanded his work have grounding in the realness of the documentary record, which Julius Caesar's account provided. Indeed, the classical record was also at the root of Boudica's connection with the history of London, which, on detailed examination of the individuals involved, emerges as the most significant impetus for the statue's placement. The decision by the Parks Committee and the British Museum to excavate the tumulus was a response to what amounted to little more than local speculation, but even that speculation was not ruled out as evidence by Charles Read. 'Popular nomenclature' might in this case have been opposed to 'historical fact', but measuring one against the other was by no means considered wasted effort for the archaeologist. Indeed, he concluded that the barrow was almost certainly of Bronze Age origin, even if any bodies that had once been interred there had long since disintegrated. The antiquity of the site, then, had never been in question.

In the same year the statue was erected, it appeared as the frontispiece to Marie Trevelyan's historical novel, *Britain's Greatness Foretold*, an unapologetically imperialist book. Yet, as we shall see in the next section, even this source is a problematic one; its reception by reviewers was far from straightforward, and it was precisely Trevelyan's apparently cynical use of an imperialist discourse that brought into question her fictionalization of the ancient past. The extensive fictionalization of the work did not invite as much criticism as Trevelyan's imagined continuum: from Boudica's vain resistance against Roman invasion to the later glory of Queen Victoria. Trevelyan's jingoistic novel will be compared with Ian C. Hannah's *Voadica* (1928), which carries Boudica's story into the third century. Voadica was embedded in archaeological research—Hannah himself was a practising archaeologist. Like Trevelyan's, Hannah's novel explores the implications of Roman imperialism through the eyes of ancient—and by extension, contemporary—Britons. However, Hannah did so through a much more critical and moralizing lens, challenging the notion that Romano-British archaeology masked a pro-imperialist bias within the archaeological profession in the early twentieth century.[65] However, critical commentary on the novel raised questions about where, in a work claiming to be fictional, one should draw the line between conscious untruth and thoughtless inaccuracy.

---

[65] See R. Hingley *Roman officers and English gentlemen*. Hingley has been criticized for making what some see as too reductive a link between Victorian and Edwardian classical studies and pro-imperialist views; see E. Adler, 'Late Victorian and Edwardian views of Rome and the nature of "defensive imperialism"', *International Journal of the Classical Tradition*, 15 (2008), 187–216, at 190. See also M. Beard, 'Officers and gentlemen? Roman Britain and the British Empire', in A. Swenson and P. Mandler (eds), *From plunder to preservation: Britain and the heritage of empire, c. 1800–1914* (Oxford, 2013), pp. 49–62.

NOVELIZING BOUDICA

From very early in her posthumous career, Queen Boudica has been most at home in a dramatic setting. The speeches and prayers gleaned from Tacitus and Dio were easily tailored to set-piece confrontations between Briton and Roman, while Boudica's daughters, along with an accompanying cast of malleable pseudo-historical characters could be transposed onto traumatic scenes of innocence lost or love denied. Even the most emotive prose histories could not never attain climactic heights of stage dramas, constrained as the former were by the pattern of the classical sources. Thus, given their open reliance on fictionalization, we might expect to find Boudica in the genre of historical novels more often than we do. After all, ancient Roman subjects were highly popular in the genre before the First World War,[66] and ancient Britain occasionally cropped up in this context. However, there were relatively few novels that took Britain's distant past as its sole subject; even more rare were novels in which Queen Boudica was the main character.

In fact there was only a single full-length novel about Queen Boudica's rebellion published in the first decade of the twentieth century—or, indeed, in Boudica's entire posthumous career before the later twentieth century—that garnered any significant readership or attention. This was Marie Trevelyan's *Britain's Greatness Foretold: The Prediction Fulfilled* (1901) and indeed in this book Boudica herself was not even the protagonist. Instead, she is a distant, albeit heroic presence in the novel, while a young British woman, 'Golden Beauty', is the main character around whom Marie Trevelyan weaves a rousing romantic adventure story. There is little trace of the more brutal, disturbing, or otherwise unsuitable elements of the rebellion which serve as a schematic backdrop. As the story unfolds, Golden Beauty distances herself from Queen Boadicea, the heroine of her youth, whose increasingly irrational decisions and obsession with revenge are seen by many as presaging national ruin. As the Romans and Britons prepare to do battle, Golden Beauty realizes that Boudica's cause is lost and, having failed to convince the deluded yet kindly queen of the advisability of surrender, the young Briton leaves the field, marries her Christian lover and lives a quiet life of propriety and domestic contentment.

The plot and overall scheme of the Trevelyan work is familiar from earlier dramatic and poetic treatments, in which one of Boudica's daughters often played an ameliorative role analogous to that of Golden Beauty, shielding the reader from Boudica as the protagonist in a story that must inevitably end in death and defeat. The appearance of a love interest to complete the severance between the younger generation and Boudica's vain resistance was by now a familiar trope. However, there were important differences between Trevelyan's novel and earlier dramatic treatments. Significantly, Golden Beauty was not bound to commit suicide, while

---

[66] S. Goldhill, *Victorian culture and classical antiquity*, Chs 5 and 6. American educationalists of the later twentieth century were especially interested in these works as resources for Latin teachers. H.S. Beall, 'Historical fiction on classical themes: revised list, 1967', *The Classical World*, 61 (1967), 53–66. Beall lists another novel about Boudica, Ernest Protheroe's 1909 *For Queen and Emperor*, but it seems to have attracted very little attention at the time it was published.

Boudica's daughters usually died, willingly or unwillingly, alongside their mother. Thus Golden Beauty's much more distant kinship allowed for a happier ending than was usual, and had the effect of orienting the story towards the future: Golden Beauty, now a Christian woman, would live on, conscious of the memory of the heroic Queen Boudica, but with every intention of building a more civilized Britain. This extensive and explicit discussion of the prophetic nature of Boudica as a direct predictor of Victoria's reign is the most original aspect of the book. Cowper's use of the Druids to voice Britain's coming triumphs had become a common device by the nineteenth century, but Trevelyan's story was by far the most explicit and sustained attempt to link British antiquity with modernity.

Trevelyan was very clearly using Boudica to articulate jingoistic imperialism during the South African War. Much of this effect was achieved, not by the novel itself—a rather pedestrian romance in the guise of epic—but by the prefatory material. Thomas Thornycroft's monumental sculpture provided the frontispiece, while the front cover was adorned with the Union Jack—based on a design, Trevelyan noted with more than a hint of self-importance, that had been supplied by the Heralds' College and was thus indisputably correct. The already rather long novel was preceded by the author's preface and a second introductory meditation on the growth and nature of British imperialism by the minor writer Edwin Collins, grandly titled 'The Prediction Fulfilled'. These addenda make abundantly clear the relevance of the ancient to the modern: Queen Boudica's defeat was the necessary antecedent to Queen Victoria's imperial triumph 1800 years later.

Of course, Trevelyan's factual basis for any such assertions was slim-to-non-existent. She overcame this by treating William Cowper's poem as an historical source in itself, an outline skeleton which her novel fleshed out in detail. She gave Cowper's druid seer a name, Arianrod, and referred to his prophecy as if it was nothing less than documented history. The druid's prophecy, spoken 1800 years ago, was, she claimed, coming to fruition in the Victorian present. But Trevelyan and Collins made little attempt to engage with the original source material for Boudica, basing their assertions of factual accuracy on contemporary events rather than distant ones. In his introductory essay, Collins detailed some of the recent triumphs of Victoria's empire which, he claimed, 'by their realisation, in solid fact, of a prediction uttered over eighteen centuries ago, [...] show how close is the relation between imagination and history'.[67] Here, Collins lapsed into a kind of mystical, though not wholly unfamiliar, defence of the authorial imagination as inspiration for the retelling of history:

> Without that inspired insight which, by enabling us to understand the true relations and the subtle meaning of the events we witness, and their causes in character and in the eternal and unchangeable nature of things, also enables us with unerring vision to pierce the veils that hide the future and the past, history would be dull and useless. It would present nothing but a collection of unrelated facts, incapable of being explained in relation to their causation and antecedents, and meaningless and uninstructive for our future guidance.

---

[67] M. Trevelyan, *Britain's greatness foretold: the prediction fulfilled*, with introduction by E. Collins (London, 1901), lxiv.

In his fifty-page introductory essay, Collins belaboured the similitude between Boudica and Victoria, between national and imperial greatness, and between past and present. Presided over by Queen Victoria as the new Queen Boudica, the empire would be a beacon of hope for future generations of Britons. Collins's essay was ponderous with statistics—imports, exports, demographics; this and its length made it an unwieldly, portentous appendage to what purported to be an entertaining historical novel for all ages.

Reviewers were unconvinced, either by Trevelyan's approach to history or to what seemed to some to be her cynical deployment of the present in order to market a version of the past. One tongue-in-cheek review pointed out the implausibility of this 'juvenility' ever making it into the classroom, since no part of the story so much as resembled the classical accounts with which teachers and students would be familiar. Nevertheless, 'its cover and its title will cause it to be bought for good little loyal boys and girls, and they will hear how Boadicea's "Druid, hoary chief" prophesied truly about many things – principally Imperial. They will perhaps prefer the British warrior queen by the name of "Buddig," pronounced "Bythig." These things are a matter of taste.'[68] The humorous tone of this review was echoed in others, most of which found the work both pompous and absurd. They also expressed uncertainty about the authors' intentions with their work and its presentation:

> We cannot say we are in the least taken with the idea, nor that Mr Collins as a patriotic pamphleteer greatly impresses us. We fancy his services have chiefly been enlisted in order that they might beguile us into taking Miss (or Mrs) Marie Trevelyan and her story as seriously as he and she take both, and we are, as a consequence, treated to a great deal of historical clap-trap. At the very outset we have an amusing instance of the author's idea of the supreme seriousness of her book.[69]

Although, like many others, this review was leavened with humour, it was making a serious point. The anomaly of Collins's prefatory essay, grafted onto a fairly conventional historical romance, raised suspicions that Trevelyan was making instrumentalist use of imperialist sentiments in order to attract greater attention to her book. Nor was this reviewer alone. Another was more explicit:

> We should like to speak kindly of this book, its intention is so excellent, but, to tell the truth, it is crude and sorry stuff... An unfortunate literary style and a lack of any sense of humour render it, however, always unconvincing and occasionally ridiculous.... We give Miss Trevelyan and Mr. Collins the benefit of the doubt and ascribe this curious production to a genuine desire to propagate patriotism and not to any intention of using 'Imperialism' as a stalking horse.[70]

These reviewers were unpersuaded by the book's imperialist project, and, quite possibly, by Boudica as an imperial heroine. A review in the *Daily News* echoed much of the dismissiveness of earlier commentaries, but went further in pointing out the inaccuracy of Cowper's earlier prediction, and thus of Trevelyan's new version,

---

[68] *St James Gazette*, 9 January 1901.   [69] *Glasgow Herald*, 6 December 1900.
[70] *Manchester Courier and Lancashire General Advertiser*, 26 December 1900.

which rendered Boudica's place in a particularly English past questionable. Even the much-admired Cowper was the subject of derision:

> Most of us have become familiar with the outline of that prediction. Cowper's version of it has long been a stumbling block and an offense to children who are visited with what is called 'repetition'. We cannot, however, agree with either Cowper or Mr. Collins in thinking that the Englishmen who have made the power of Britain can properly be regarded as Boadicea's 'posterity'... It is a contention among historians whether the Anglo-Saxon conquest left any Britons in England or not. But it is agreed among them that if any remained they were but a remnant; and if the Arch Druid meant the English race when he alluded to 'thy posterity' it strikes us as very careless or decidedly cool.[71]

This reviewer took the unusual step of engaging with Trevelyan on the terms of her own history, arguing, on the solid basis of contemporary historiography, that Boudica's Celtic blood made her an unlikely heroine for the Anglo-Saxon empire. Similarly, a reviewer in the Cardiff-based *Western Mail* questioned the notion that Christianity had spread to Britain during or immediately before the era of Queen Boudica's uprising, noting the complete lack of evidence to warrant such a conclusion.[72] The commentator allowed that in a work of romance, rather than history, 'fidelity to facts is not of great importance', but the difficulty arose from the controversial nature of the historical debates into which the author was irresponsibly wading. '... it is well for the authoress not to allow herself to be carried away by the crude notions which have obtained credence in this country for many years in regard to Druidism, the early British Church, and other debatable points'.[73] The reviewer was a sceptic when it came to the recent revival of Welsh cultural nationalism that traced the origin of Christianity in ancient Britain to Wales. Trevelyan was wholly ignorant of, or at the very least she ignored, the traditional classical source base for Boudica, and instead chose to present Cowper's poem as the historical source for her own prophetic fiction. But, her fatakl mistake was to intervene in a record of the past that had yet to be settled definitively, whether it was the extent to which there remained any Celtic presence in Britain after the invasion of the Anglo-Saxons, or the date at which Christianity reached mainland Britain.

But more problematic still was Trevelyan's blatant—and some thought cynical—use of the present to legitimize her imagined version of the past that came under critical scrutiny. The *Western Mail* review concluded damningly:

> Marie Trevelyan looks upon Britain eighteen centuries or more ago through eyes which are too modern, a proof of defective imagination.[74]

There are a number of possible reasons critics took such issue with her use of the Boudica story, ranging from a disdain for the author's self-important promotion of her historical novel as a document of her own times, to a genuine discomfort

---

[71] *London Daily News*, 1 March 1901.
[72] There was, in the shape of Gildas's history, but nothing conclusive.
[73] Boudica's place in Welsh historical culture is discussed in Chapter 6.
[74] *Western Mail*, 21 December 1900.

'A great deal of historical claptrap' 165

with the naked jingoism of the work. But it is clear that Trevelyan's novel was not received by contemporaries as a convincing endorsement of Boudica as a predecessor to Victoria or to imperial glory. Critics were forthrightly sceptical of the deployment of historical argumentation in the service of the present, even in the context of conscious, avowed and largely unapologetic fictionalization.

Thus critics objected to the facile similitude Trevelyan created between past and present, and the debatable nature of the past in question. It may be that by this late stage only the most well-worn of recorded pasts could be freely fictionalized, lest the fiction be taken for fact. Or, paradoxically, perhaps the more settled nature of the overall narrative of the past left the details vulnerable to misuse. Trevelyan, with a smattering of learning in Celtic myth and a desire to trumpet the past as a twisted mirror of the contemporary world, presented a dangerous foil to serious historical debate.

Matters were somewhat different where historical novels based in sound research were concerned, and it is interesting to compare Trevelyan's novel with a somewhat later one: Ian C. Hannah's *Voadica* (1928). Hannah's novel could almost be a sequel to Trevelyan's prophetic one, were it not for the marked difference in their approach to using the past as inspiration, and to the different reception with which each was greeted. There is little doubt that Hannah was qualified to make scholarly judgements about the ancient past. Born in Scotland, Hannah was a Fellow of the Society of Antiquaries of Scotland and a prolific author of scholarly works on subjects ranging from Christian monastic communities to the history of Asia.[75] Aside from an enthusiasm for medieval architectural remains, he was also a well-respected authority on Roman Britain, evidently with similarly popularizing tendencies to Charles Read's at the British Museum. His career in education brought him to an American theological college and, after returning to Scotland from Oberlin, Ohio, Hannah was active in the University Extension Scheme, giving a series of lectures on 'The Romans in Britain' in provincial villages like Braunton in North Devon. Tellingly, advertisements for this lecture series noted *Voadica* as proof of Hannah's learned credentials.[76]

Voadica is an interesting mix of antiquarian learning and romantic invention. The book's main character is the titular Voadica, so named because she is the great-great-granddaughter of Queen Boudica herself and suggesting that one or both of Boudica's children survived the fate ascribed to them by the classical historians. Boudica is a presiding presence, prayed to as a goddess by the ancestor-worshipping Voadica. Like her illustrious ancestor, this young woman leads an army against the Romans of Emperor Hadrian's day. She is ultimately captured and imprisoned by the young Roman officer Cato, who swiftly falls in love with the brave, free-spirited Briton. He is forced to take her to Rome, where she meets the kindly Emperor

---

[75] He eventually became an MP. There is little reliable biographical information on Hannah, aside from that in J. Venn and J.A. Venn (eds), *Alumni Cantabrigienses* (Cambridge, 2011 [first edn 1947]), Vol. II, Part 3, p. 227. See also the obituary of his wife, Edith Brand Hannah in *The Oberlin Alumni Magazine*, May 1948, p. 28, http://www.oberlin-high.org/obits/ohs_obits_ha-he.html, accessed 10 Aug 2016.
[76] *North Devon Journal*, 6 September 1928.

Hadrian. Hadrian repudiates the actions of his own predecessor, Nero, proclaiming that he would have 'made a friend of Queen Boudicca', and, like Golden Beauty in Trevelyan's earlier novel, Voadica is soon convinced of the superiority of the Romans and their more civilized ways.

But, perhaps unexpectedly, the novel does not end with the acceptance of Roman civility over the rudeness of her native Britain. Instead, the reader accompanies Voadica as she is gradually introduced to the more unseemly side of Rome and the Romans. The gladiatorial games fill her with a 'Celtic sympathy with suffering' and a horror at blood spilled 'in no great cause'.[77] In a silent prayer to her illustrious ancestor Boadicea, Voadica vows to defeat the Romans from within; she marries Cato and the couple return to Britain, where the newly Roman wife proceeds to plot the demise of the interlopers. Despite her genuine love for her husband and the birth of children, Voadica is bound by a sense of duty to her secret rebellion, and she is eventually forced to meet her own husband in battle. Cato is certain he will die during this confrontation with his wife's forces, but Voadica pleads with her army to make peace. Even Cato prays to his wife's ancestor when he realizes the battle is over before it has begun: 'Great Boudicca, thy image shall be placed among the gods of Rome.'[78] Voadica returns to Cato, declaring that she loves him above all else, and even she will be loyal for his sake. The book ends with Voadica's oath to her husband, which is itself an apology to her ancestor, delivered in the Celtic language: 'The noble Boudicca will understand. She would have made her peace with such as thee.'[79] The couple are reconciled in mutual respect and affection and, contrary to Trevelyan's novel, without the benefit of an historically questionable Christianity.

In contrast to Trevelyan's work, Hannah's novel was well-received by critics, who praised it for what many took to be engaging but realistic portrayals of ancient Britain and Rome, as well as for its merits as a romance. For many, it was Hannah's antiquarian detail that gave the novel its air of historic realism. One reviewer noted that 'interesting and well-studied pictures are given of the Roman prisons and of the splendours of Hadrian's villa at Tibur... The work holds its archaeological and historical learning lightly in hand, and makes its romantic interest all the keener because Voadica is all along successfully portrayed as at once a formidable Amazon and a resolute champion for peace.'[80] Another pointed to Hannah's depiction of the Emperor's villa, 'the ruins of which are to-day a rendezvous of tourists'.[81] The lively evocation of a place visible to the present only in ruins was a seductive element of the story when told by an archaeologist with what was believed to be a firm grasp of the evidence for the long-vanished sites. It is striking that the book was reviewed in a number of scholarly journals, including the *Scottish Historical Review*, and the American *Classical Journal*, neither of which primarily concerned themselves with fictional works, although the latter did take an interest in educational matters

---

[77] I.C. Hannah, *Voadica, a romance of the Roman Wall* (London, 1928), 191.
[78] Hannah, *Voadica*, 271.   [79] Ibid., 273.
[80] *The Scotsman*, 28 May 1928.   [81] *Western Daily Press*, 11 April 1928.

and the challenge sometimes posed by historical fictions.[82] Both reviews noted the usefulness of the work as an educational tool and as a spur to the young to visit sites of archaeological interest. As the anonymous reviewer in the *Scottish Historical Review* noted, 'No doubt a critic who was disposed to be censorious might take exception to some of the colouring... But these are details, and we all know what medievalists in their sterner mood are inclined to say of Ivanhoe.'[83]

That censorious voice emerged in the pages of *The Classical Review*, an organ not usually associated with reviews of works of fiction.[84] Furthermore, the voice belonged to the philosopher and archaeologist of Roman Britain, R.G. Collingwood, whose antiquarian father, W.G. Collingwood, was himself a writer of swashbuckling works of fiction about the Vikings in the Lake District. Hannah's engagement with documentary source material had been limited, but his much-admired evocation of historic environments was based on his archaeological knowledge, and there were few people, Collingwood being a very notable exception, capable of finding inaccuracies in such recherché source material. And find inaccuracies Collingwood did. He disparaged Hannah's scholarship and hinted at, but did not pursue, criticism of Hannah's merit as a novelist: 'The writing of an historical romance sets himself an exceedingly difficult task. He has to meet two separate problems: he has to prove himself at once a competent historian and a competent novelist. Mr. Hannah does not quite satisfy either test.' It is interesting that although Collingwood himself distinguished between the novelist and the historian, he nevertheless applied the same methodological criteria to both aspects of Hannah's work. According to Collingwood, the historian of Rome would be 'appalled', 'scandalised', and 'puzzled' by what might appear to be slight inaccuracies in spelling and chronology, but which Collingwood took to be far from minor. Collingwood clearly viewed Hannah's novel, not as an innocent work of fiction, but as a vehicle for archaeological supposition.

Collingwood took particular umbrage with Hannah's 'misleading' description of the building of Hadrian's Wall, a topic on which Collingwood himself was something of an expert. Collingwood had provided his own detailed sketch of the building of the wall in his *Roman Britain* (1923), and in doing so put forth the view that Wall had been an elevated sentry post, not a fighting platform.[85] Hannah, speaking in the internal voice of the Emperor Hadrian rather than in the voice of the expert, claimed that the wall was to be 'a frontier line against barbarian hordes' formed of a barrier built between a series of pre-existing forts; as they built it, Hadrian's men were constantly under attack from the tribes around them, further emphasizing the wall's defensive necessity.[86] But, for Collingwood, the wall was 'not in an ordinary sense a military work' for defence against invasion, but was rather

---

[82] For instance, F.S. Dunn, 'The un-historical novel', *The Classical Journal*, 22 (1927), 345–54, which is little more than a catalogue of the slight inaccuracies in recent historical novels.

[83] 'M', Book review: I.C. Hannah, *Voadica: a romance of the Roman Wall*, Scottish Historical Review, 25 (1928), 368. See also E. Preston, Book review: I.C. Hannah, *Voadica: a romance of the Roman Wall*, *The Classical Journal*, 24 (1928), 143–4.

[84] R.G. Collingwood, 'Review: *Voadica: a romance of the Roman Wall*', Classical Review, 42 (1928), 151.

[85] R.G. Collingwood, *Roman Britain* (London, 1923), 30–2.   [86] Hannah, *Voadica*, 52–5.

a deterrent against lesser, and less exciting, activities which were nevertheless detrimental to the Roman Empire, particularly smuggling.[87]

Published alongside a review of a new edition of a fourteenth-century manuscript, Collingwood's dissection of the inaccuracies of what was in essence a work of fiction seems curmudgeonly. Although he claimed that *The Classical Review* was unconcerned with the work as fiction, Collingwood was unable or unwilling to suspend his disbelief, even if doing so would have released aspects of the debatable past into the realm of plausible fiction. But the line between deliberate fictionalization and thoughtless mistake was difficult to draw; Collingwood pointed to an incongruity in Hannah's description of the passage of the seasons as an example both of the novelist's poor story-telling and the historian's lack of attention. In spite of his attempts to argue that the two were separate, Collingwood's criticism of the fiction seems always to collapse into his criticism of the history.

In his much more well-known work on the philosophy of history, Collingwood did not by any means object to the fictionalization of history in and of itself, but his views suggest that the historical novelist did, in the philosopher's mind, share many of the same responsibilities as the historian and was thus bound to the strictures that applied in historical narrative. True, the historian must aim to achieve three 'rules of method': adherence to real times and places, consistency with itself, and finally, to maintain its 'peculiar relation to something called evidence'.[88] But Collingwood also noted that both the novelist and the historian were reliant on their imagination. Thus while one might ask then whether it was Ian C. Hannah the historian and archaeologist who was writing this work of fiction, or Hannah the novelist, the answer, at least according to Collingwood, was irrelevant: the rules applied to both in equal measure. What Collingwood called the a priori imagination—that is, the necessary intervention of the historian's imaginative faculties in order to interpolate what was unrecoverable in the historical record—formed the basis of all historical creativity, as well as criticism, and the historical novelist was as indebted to that faculty as the historian. This capacity to imagine was the means by which the historian could achieve the continuity and coherence that were the essence, Collingwood thought, of historical truth.[89] But the historical novelist, in attempting to recreate a past universe, submitted him- or herself to the same rigours. Hannah, by misjudging chronology, allowing passing inaccuracy, and committing himself to questionable archaeological positions, was as guilty as any historian of flouting the rules. Or this, it seems, was Collingwood's position.

Historical novels, even at this late stage, were not seen as simple acts of fictionalization They were read, in varying degrees, with the gravity of expectation that seems to attend all engagement with historical subject matter. Authors of historical fiction were not without political or ideological motives, nor could their works be consumed or valued purely as entertainment. At times authorial motives were explicit, with significant implications for the moral or political message of a work, as was the case with Trevelyan's imperialistic *Britain's Greatness Foretold*. Other

---

[87] Collingwood, *Roman Britain*, 31.
[88] R.G. Collingwood, *The idea of history* (Oxford, 1978 [first edn 1946]), 246.
[89] Collingwood, *Idea of history*, 240–1.

fictions, like Hannah's *Voadica*, were not widely viewed as problematic, at least in the sense of conveying an ideological message, and indeed could be seen as wholly beneficial to educationalists. However, they could invite criticism from interested experts who—perhaps wilfully—misread their didactic aims. After all, Hannah had not cast his work as a treatise offering new readings of Hadrian's Wall to experts; its educational value, as the reviewers in the *Classical Journal* and *Scottish History Review* pointed out, lay in its imaginative excavation of vanished worlds, which encouraged the curious to look elsewhere for historical reality. Collingwood's review might seem at first glance to be out of keeping with his tolerant attitude towards history as engaging the imagination, but there is in fact no contradiction. Collingwood's view was merely that the imagination, as an indispensable part of historical work of all kinds, must play by the rules.

I have sought to show in this chapter that the sheer variety of Boudica's roles in the later nineteenth century make it possible to contextualize her within the discourse of popular enthusiasm for imperial ventures. This chapter has sought to foreground some of the other possible contexts for Boudica's celebration in the period. Trends in Victorian art; an increasingly organized archaeological profession and its relative popularity with the public; the prominence of antiquarianism at a local level; and the popular exposure made possible by press coverage—all of these can cast a different light on Boudica's nineteenth-century image. I have sought to show that Victorians were not seeking 'to create a historical ancestry for British national pedigree and imperial greatness'[90]—or, at least, not all of them were. Cynical uses of the ancient past could be and often were met with incredulity and even hostility.

My aim therefore in questioning Boudica's straightforward association with imperialism in the late Victorian period is not simply to refute earlier readings. There is a more salient point to be made here regarding the relationship between past and present, and between those who represent the past and those who consume or receive it, whether specialists or not. There was a far more diverse conversation around Boudica and the ancient past she represented, even in this era of imperialism, than might perhaps be assumed. Thornycroft's statue is misleading in its monumentality, suspended as it is in a single moment without narrative context, only the palimpsest of statue, plinth, and inscription to guide the viewer. Thus the viewer of the statue would not know that it was once thought that this denizen of Westminster might have been more at home in the rural–urban liminality of Parliament Hill Fields; neither would the viewer realize that its maker was a thwarted realist in an age of idealism, for whom the statue was an act of resistance, not of conformity. The dignified corporeality of the bronze will never knowingly reveal how its plaster original had languished for decades in a warehouse, nor how a burst of institutional enthusiasm for a scrap of 'popular nomenclature' would be the impetus that led to its casting. The statue can speak only to the heroic scene it depicts, which undoubtedly cemented Boudica as a Victorian heroine for the ages, even if it was not, as has been claimed and the next chapter will explore, the sole site of Boudica's 'cult'.

---

[90] Hingley and Unwin, *Iron age queen*, 173.

6

'That ubiquitous monarch'
Boudica from Wales to Essex

It has been said that the trouble with Boudica is that she has no 'site of memory'; that is, she has no particular place where her commemoration makes undeniable sense.[1] She has no Winchester like King Alfred, no Tintagel like King Arthur, no central site of celebration, like Lord Nelson's column in Trafalgar Square.[2] That, at least, is the claim made by those who would end her story with the abortive attempt to find her final resting place in Hampstead Heath and the begrudging, belated placement of her likeness on Westminster Bridge. Richard Hingley has argued that without a single, specific locality or physical trace to be found, Boudica's 'cult' simply could not take root; her womanhood made widespread celebration even more difficult, especially after the death of Queen Victoria, when she reverted to that ambiguous realm of suspicion reserved for warrior women in Western culture.

Aside from noting a few comical comparisons with famously intransigent female politicians, Boudica's reputation in the twentieth century has not undergone systematic study or thorough contextualization.[3] This is, arguably, due at least in part to a widespread misconception about the nature of historical culture in the later nineteenth and twentieth centuries, and only secondarily due to any real misreading of Boudica's place within it. As ever, assumptions about which discourses were and were not relevant to Boudica's reputation remain problematic, but, as we have seen, such is the nature of Boudica's multifarious identity that evidence can usually be found to support multiple conclusions. For instance Boudica's occasional association with Margaret Thatcher can be seen as part of a long-running convention, beginning with the reign of Elizabeth I, that saw Boudica linked to prominent women, sporadically and when necessity dictated.[4] But beyond this conventional narrative, the ubiquitous, multimedia nature of twentieth-century mass historical culture makes finding any single story to tell about Boudica in the period even more daunting, inviting a return to the chronicle genre: that is, a list of instances of Boudica's appearance, with little or no contextual discussion or useful general reflection.

There most certainly is a story—or multiple stories—to tell about Boudica in the period from the reign of Victoria up to the twentieth century. As in previous periods, these stories can reveal something of the nuance of modern historical

---

[1] Hingley, *Roman officers*, 77.
[2] For the celebration of King Alfred, see S. Heathorn, '"The highest type of Englishman": gender, war, and the Alfred the Great commemoration of 1901' and Readman, 'Place of the past', 175–82.
[3] The period serves as the epilogue to Frenée-Hutchins, *Boudica's odyssey*, in Ch. 5.
[4] Ibid., 190.

culture beyond the superficial or suppositious. Boudica's identity in the period was not rootless, nor was she sporadically recrudescent. Rather her story was written, performed, and celebrated as part of community histories across Britain. Ranging from the cultural-nationalist narrative that grounded her in Welsh history, to the unlikely story of her having once passed over a precise spot in Lincolnshire, Boudica was part of multiple narratives of the past that went beyond national and imperial utility. Indeed, far from clinging to an association with an abstract notion of an eroding empire, or even straightforward articulations of either a predominating 'English' or overarching 'British' nationhood, Boudica has had many sites and physical places that can, did, and do lay claim to her life, death, and burial, and whose inhabitants—at least some of them—identify her as their own native daughter. These articulations of historical exceptionalism were, I would argue, typical of regional and local historical culture in the late nineteenth and twentieth centuries in a way that has too rarely been acknowledged. Boudica's story presented an opportunity for communities, small and large, to explore and assert their place in antiquity and the durability of their identity over time. Historical pageants, public sculpture, and enthusiastic, even gymnastic, antiquarianism were all brought to bear in the articulation and celebration of local historical culture.

The places that laid claim to Boudica did so through the interpretation of different forms of evidence, from the classical source base to local archaeology and community tradition; this is shown to have been the case in Hampstead Heath, but it was equally true in many other places. But nowhere was this more evident, important, and arguably interesting, than in the case of Boudica's unique place in Welsh historical culture and in articulations of Welsh cultural identity.[5] From the eighteenth century, to the reign of Victoria, and into the early twentieth century, Boudica played a part in Welsh history through the work of historians, antiquaries, poets, and artists. However, I argue here that this was not a case of wholesale appropriation or 'invented tradition' in any crude sense. Rather, by appealing to obscure antiquarian evidence, aspects of Boudica's story could be convincingly reinterpreted—or, at least convincingly enough for those willing to be convinced—in a manner that transplanted her from England to Wales. Most notably, the antiquary, Welsh cultural nationalist, and Arch-Druid Owen 'Morien' Morgan (1836–1921) was the most prolific writer on the subject of Boudica's Welshness.[6] He based his claims on a new interpretation

---

[5] The most comprehensive study of Welsh identity and history in fact conceives of its subject as 'historical culture'; see N. Evans and H. Pryce, 'Introduction: Writing a small nation's past: states, races and historical culture', in N. Evans and H. Pryce (eds), *Writing a small nation's past: Wales in comparative perspective, 1850–1950* (Farnham, 2013), pp. 3–30. See also, of course, P. Morgan, 'From a death to a view: The hunt for the Welsh past in the Romantic Period', in Hobsbawm and Ranger (eds), *The invention of tradition*, pp. 43–100.

[6] I make reference to 'cultural nationalism' throughout this chapter. I do so advisedly, and not to suggest any separatist tendencies on the part of the writers and commentators I mention; indeed, quite the opposite. For the useful distinction between 'political' and 'cultural' nationalism, see J. Hutchinson, 'Cultural nationalism', in J. Breuilly (ed.), *The Oxford handbook of the history of nationalism* (Oxford, 2013), pp. 75–94. Krishnan Kumar has also argued that the 'growing sense of nationhood' as early as the fourteenth and fifteenth centuries must be distinguished from the 'ideological nationalism' of the nineteenth century, or the shared political community that characterizes modern nation-states; see K. Kumar, *The making of English national identity* (Cambridge, 2003), 59. Although my own view

of the classical sources, as well as on archaeological evidence. However, as we will see, her celebration occurred at many levels of society, including local *eisteddfodou*. The richness of this story demands a lengthy re-telling, which this chapter is in large part devoted to providing.

That said, similarly tailored narratives of the ancient past were also evident in other parts of the country, particularly in the English localities mentioned in the classical source base. We have already seen how London locations were thought to have special relevance to Boudica's story, but the two other towns mentioned by Tacitus and Dio—Colchester and St Albans—were not content to be left behind in celebrating Queen Boudica. These places were neither static not definitive: the locations named in classical sources rarely corresponded neatly with their modern-day equivalents, but the imprecision of place names such as Villa Faustini—somewhere near present-day Bury St Edmunds—gave locals interpretative latitude. Others places were somewhat more specific. St Albans in Hertfordshire had been Verulamium to the Romans, and was said to have been sacked and burned during the course of Boudica's rebellion. The response from the town has been to make Boudica a prominent part of its historical pageantry and local museum since the early twentieth century.

Similarly, Colchester, or Camulodunum, is situated outside of the traditional heart of the Iceni homeland in Norfolk, but Boudica has nevertheless been associated with the town, giving rise to the popular notion that she was the first 'Essex girl'. Colchester is home to two statues of Boudica: one on the façade of the Edwardian town hall and the other erected in the late twentieth century in the centre of an unprepossessing roundabout. She is featured in a stained-glass window, and even in graffiti in the local multi-storey car park. Boudica's associations also spread further north, into Suffolk and Norfolk, where the Iceni flourished. She made prominent appearances in historical pageants in these counties, notably Bury St Edmunds in 1907 and Norwich in 1926. Indeed, historical pageants were one of the main ways in which the local past was retold, celebrated, and embedded in a national narrative in the twentieth century. The historical pageant movement was nothing short of a phenomenon, maintaining popularity through the period up to the late twentieth century, and involving thousands of volunteer participants as performers, organizers, designers, and craftspeople.

Nor was the localized celebration of Boudica confined to towns mentioned by the classical sources as having been 'visited' by the ancient queen. In the early 1960s it was claimed that the town of Stamford, Lincolnshire, sat on the spot where,

---

is that of a cautious modernist when it comes to political nationalism, literary scholarship has gone some way to recovering the power and variety of forms of collective identity that persisted throughout early modernity, and which provide a useful foil to political or sociological definitions of nationhood and nationality. Illuminating work on Wales has been done by P. Schwyzer, *Literature, nationalism, and memory in early modern England and Wales* (Cambridge, 2004), and there is a very good discussion of this and similar literature in the introduction to S. Mottram and S. Prescott (eds), *Writing Wales from the Renaissance to Romanticism* (Abingdon, 2012). Ultimately, the constituent matter of a shared British (or at least Anglo-Welsh) identity is grounded in elements of historical culture that have endured for centuries—and, as previously noted, the importance of the very notion of a 'Briton' requires further research.

1900 years before, Boudica had chased Paulinus' Roman legionaries northward. The assertion was taken so seriously by the Borough Town Council that they erected a memorial at Stamford Meadows, complete with an inscription explaining how Boudica has pursued the Roman troops across it. The story was wholly unsupported by evidence and was likely to have been spurred by a desire on the part of the town to take advantage of the 1900th anniversary of Boudica's rebellion; after the passage of a few decades, the story looks decidedly suspect, even to locals.[7] Nevertheless, the 1900th anniversary was celebrated with great gusto in Stamford, with a local woman taking on the role of Queen Boudica and riding at the head of a procession through the town.[8]

The raw material to make and maintain links between Queen Boudica and various locations in Britain could be found in the classical sources, but historical pageants and other localized commemorative activities—processions and statues, for instance—cemented her connection to these places. This location-specific nature of historical culture in the period was echoed in the first film to be made about Boudica: H. Bruce Woolfe's *Boadicea* (1926), a lavish production in the historical-romantic mode familiar from the earliest historical dramas of the seventeenth century. In their use of crowd scenes and detailed costume, the films also echoed the more recent craze for historical pageants, which, as we will see, employed armies of volunteer performers to create large-scale spectacles. The film was also shot on location in places that had associations in the popular imagination with Boudica's rebellion. Although a national medium, the film-makers nevertheless foregrounded locality, a decision which, in this instance, acted as a marker of authenticity, a key criteria, according to Anthony Smith, which renders appeals to the past a powerful constituent of identity.[9] This link between authenticity and locality was a further feature of historical culture in the period, particularly evident in pageants, in which local ruins and ancient sites often acted as backdrops to the pageant festivities.

This chapter will proceed first to tell the story of Boudica's association with Wales, beginning with her early appearance in a Welsh panoramic history of 1716, up to what some would see as her direct lineage with Queen Victoria, and her commemoration, in the form of a marble statue, in the early twentieth century. Crucial to this story will be the efforts of the Welsh antiquary known as Morien to prove, using historical and archaeological evidence, that Boudica had died and been buried in Wales. Colchester, St Albans, and Bury St Edmunds, the site of the major pageants that featured Boudica, were bound by no such necessity. Her role in these places, and the importance of pageants to her twentieth-century reputation, will be the focus of the second section of this chapter. The third section will focus on the 1926 film, drawing links between forms of dramatic production old and new, from seventeenth-century romance to the twentieth-century pageant. The importance of community histories, albeit connected to larger, national stories, unites all of

---

[7] I am indebted to Gwyneth Gibbs of the Stamford Civic Society for this information.
[8] *The Times*, 23 May 1961.
[9] A.D. Smith, *The nation in history: historiographical debates about ethnicity and nationalism* (Cambridge, 2000), 64, and the discussion of 'historical authenticity' in A.D. Smith, *The antiquity of nations* (Cambridge, 2004), 86–90.

these depictions of Boudica, showing how local historical narratives could challenge and sometimes supplement mainstream views of the past.

'BOADICEA REDIVIVA': BOUDICA IN WALES

Thomas Thornycroft's 'Boadicea group' was not the first statue of Boudica to be erected in Britain, even if it remains the most visible. John Thomas (1813–62), the architectural sculptor responsible for overseeing the exterior decoration of the new Houses of Parliament, can in fact be credited with creating the first full-size statue of Boudica and her daughters. The statue was probably a private commission for Sir Morton Peto's house at Somerleyton Hall, Suffolk. Thomas completed the statue in 1855 and exhibited it at the Royal Academy in 1856.[10] It shows Queen Boudica face upraised, holding a sword aloft as if swearing an oath, as her two daughters crouch by her side, huddled in what looks like either lamentation or supplication, or both. According to one reviewer, the statue was meant to show Boudica just as she had finished delivering her moving speech to the assembled host of British troops, pleading with them for their help, but expressing a willingness to die without it. Working from the account given by the eighteenth-century historian Paul Rapin de Thoyras, the reviewer related the last words of Boudica's speech as: 'It is much better to fall honourably in defence of liberty, than be again exposed to the outrages of the Romans.' Yet, despite these warlike words he attributed to Boudica, the review noted that, 'Mr. Thomas has assumed, as he had a right to do in the absence of contrary evidence, that the queen of the Iceni and her daughters were cast in nature's fairest mould...'[11]

Although John Thomas's own 'Boadicea group' was completed at the same time as he was supervising the decoration on the new Houses of Parliament, there is no evidence to suggest that there was any intention of placing the statue within the confines of the building even if, previous to Peto's commission, Boudica had been considered as a possible subject in the Houses of Parliament: as we have seen, Thomas Woolner proposed a statue of 'The Death of Boadicea', and no fewer than five paintings of the queen were submitted to the Westminster Hall cartoon competition in 1843, held to decide which figures would appear in the decorated building. H.C. Selous's painting, a picture busy with fleshy figures, won him a prize.[12] However, none of these works made it into the finished building. On the face of it this seems odd given that the Houses of Parliament were effectively designed to tell the history of the nation through art and architecture. But the history presented in the Houses of Parliament was thoroughly Anglo-Saxon, and took a view of the constitution as being of Teutonic origin and particularly English significance,

---

[10] *The Art Journal*, 29 May 1857. [11] Ibid.
[12] T.S.R. Boase, 'The decoration of the New Palace of Westminster, 1841–1863', *Journal of the Warburg and Courtauld Institutes*, 17(3/4) (1954), 319–58, at 330. There were at least five depictions of Boudica entered in the cartoon competition according to T.J.L. Prichard, *The heroines of Welsh history; comprising memories and biographical notices of the celebrated women of Wales...* (London, 1854), 93–4.

leaving out much of the ancient, 'Celtic' past.[13] Only the King Arthur myth—told in carved oak scenes—appeared, in the Queen's Robing Room. Thus departing from the eighteenth-century debates around Druidism and ancient British government, the late Victorian interpretation rendered early British history irrelevant to the task of explaining the origins of government, and even of Christianity—at least in England. This was a view evident in the works of E.A. Freeman, whose account of the distant past focused almost exclusively on the Saxon and Norman periods (though he was hardly alone in this).[14] Boudica and the ancient Britons had little place in what Freeman called 'strictly English history'.[15]

But, in an irony almost too neat to be credited, the English John Thomas's Boudica statue, created in the shadow of his work on the Anglo-Saxon Houses of Parliament, and for a very English country house, was to find its way to Wales, where it now sits in the grounds of the Brecknock Museum at the edge of the Brecon Beacons. This was because, until recently, the bronze group was thought to have been the work of the Welsh sculptor John Evan Thomas, and so it was moved to his hometown of Brecon, from its previous position in (for reasons that still remain unclear) the town centre of Birmingham. Between Birmingham and Brecon, the statue had been neglected in a scrap yard for a number of years, echoing the ignominious fate of Thornycroft's plaster model.[16] It was only in the 1980s that the first statue of Boudica was definitively determined to have been the work of John Thomas, whose early death (a result, it was thought, of his exertions during the rebuilding of the Palace of Westminster) and relative obscurity even in his lifetime has made his work less easily traceable. Nevertheless, it remains in the museum grounds as a representative of that period beyond Freeman's 'strictly English history'.

The circuitous journey of Thomas's Boudica statue to the fringes of the Brecon Beacons is the latest in a series of coincidences that infuses the whole fabric of Boudica's Welsh narrative. No geographic link—at least, none directly evidenced by

---

[13] R. Quinault, 'Westminster and the Victorian constitution', *Transactions of the Royal Historical Society*, 6th series, 2 (1992), 79–104. There were also aesthetic objections to ancient and even classical subjects. During the course of debates around art in the new Houses of Parliament, the art historian Henry Hallam asked his fellow committee members: 'Would there not be something ridiculous in covering the walls of our Houses of Parliament with Caesar or Caractacus?'; see the Third Report of the Royal Commission on the Fine Arts, 'Observations on the principles which may regulate the selection of subjects for painting in the palace at Westminster, By Mr. Hallam', 22. Parliamentary Archives, HL/PO/RO/1/25.

[14] This view was best exemplified in the work of the first 'professional' Victorian historians; see E.A. Freeman, *The history of the Norman Conquest of England*, 6 vols (Oxford, 1867–79), Vol. 1, especially 8–21 for the effect of the Anglo-Saxons on Celtic peoples. Many historians have examined this trend in Victorian history writing; see: J.W. Burrow, *A liberal descent: Victorian historians and the English past* (Cambridge, 1981); H.A. MacDougall, *Racial myth and English history: Trojans, Teutons, and Anglo-Saxons* (Hanover, NH, 1982); P. Mandler, *The English national character: the history of an idea from Edmund Burke to Tony Blair* (London, 2006), Ch. 3.

[15] E.A. Freeman, 'Colonia Camulodunum', *Macmillan's Magazine*, 36 (1877), 119–34, at 119.

[16] The sculpture is like to be a copy of the marble original, said to have been at Somerleyton Hall, but which it has proved impossible to locate. The sculpture's strange history has been reconstructed by Abigail Kenvyn at the Brecknock Museum and Art Gallery, to whose correspondence I owe this information. See also Read, *Victorian sculpture*, 145–6.

the works of the classical historians—rooted her physically in Wales, yet nineteenth- and twentieth-century Welsh commentators were able to build and maintain an antiquarian and historical claim to Boudica. This claim was then articulated in a variety of historical-cultural contexts, some of the earliest of which were the local *eisteddfodou*, of which she was a documented part as early as the 1820s.[17] Although John Thomas's statue was not, in fact, a Welsh tribute to a Welsh heroine, she was eventually commemorated in a new sculpture by James Havard Thomas in Cardiff in the early twentieth century, an effort which is discussed below. But the creation of these two statues was separated by decades, during which a fevered discussion of Boudica's place in Wales and Welsh history took place among keen antiquaries and modern-day Druids; this discussion had begun in the eighteenth century (possibly even earlier), and encompassed prose history, imaginative literature, and antiquarian research. Indeed, Havard Thomas's statue of Boudica was the culmination of many years, and many different individual contributions, to Boudica's Welsh identity and her place in Welsh historical culture.

Boudica made her first appearance in a history of Wales for a Welsh-speaking audience as 'Buddug' in *Drych y prif oesoedd* or *The Mirror of Past Ages* (also sometimes translated as *The Mirror of Primitive Ages*) in 1716. This was the work of then-23-year-old Theophilus Evans (1693–1767), a native of Brecon and later Bishop of St Davids. Evans's was the first history of Wales in the Welsh tongue, but it fit the mould of a typical eighteenth-century panoramic history. Like many of its popular English-language counterparts, *Drych y prif oesoedd* ran to multiple editions, with a total of five published before the close of the eighteenth century and a further sixteen in the nineteenth century, making it the most popular history book in Welsh before 1900.[18] In common with other panoramic histories of the period, Evans's 'Buddug' story mirrored that found in Tacitus. However, later Welsh writers, under the influence of eighteenth-century scholarly research into Celticism and Druidism and the romantic medievalism of self-proclaimed arch-Druid, Iolo Morganwg (1747–1826), began to excavate the history of 'Buddug' in order to reinter her in a specifically Welsh past.

In particular, antiquarian writers worked to associate the historical/classical Buddug with a figure unique to Welsh history, a shadowy woman known as 'Aregwedd Voeddig'. This Welsh princess was said to have been referred to in the 35th Triad of the Island of Britain,[19] a collection of ancient Welsh manuscript poems which had been embellished with modern verses by Iolo Morganwg. Drawing on the Triads, the Welsh author William Owen Pughe, in the *Cambrian Biography* (1803), had attempted to combine Aregwedd Voeddig with not one, but two of

---

[17] *The North Wales Chronicler and Advertiser for the Principality*, 25 September 1828, reports on the Denbigh Eisteddfod, at which a medal struck with her image was awarded to the best poem on the subject of 'Buddug'.

[18] G.H. Jenkins, *The foundation of modern Wales, 1642–1780* (Oxford, 1987), 248.

[19] This attribution comes from H.A. Bruce, *Gwent and Dyfed Eisteddfod, 1834; the prize translation of the Welsh ode on the British Druids by Taliesen Williams* (London, 1835). A later author gives the relevant place as the 21st and 22nd Triad; see B.B. Woodward, *The history of Wales from the earliest times to its final incorporation with the kingdom of England* (London, 1853), 63.

Tacitus' queens: 'the Cartismandua and the Boadicea of the Romans'.[20] Pughe must have been working from the first, confused testimony of Tacitus, who had made the two queens, Boudica and Cartismandua, the same person in the *Agricola*. Pughe claimed that these two queens were not only one in the same with each other, but also with the Aregwedd Voeddig of the Triads. It was not an elision made by others, but it did do the work of drawing together the accepted classical source base with the more ambiguous, in part fraudulent, but very firmly Welsh, Triads. The link was made more successfully in 1854, when T.J.L. Prichard clarified that Boudica had indeed originally been called by the name 'Aregwedd Voeddawg' but that she had been granted a new name, 'Buddug', by her grateful countrymen after her initial triumphs against the Romans in Camulodunum and Verulamium. He indignantly denied Pughe's assertion that Boudica, the heroine, and Cartismandua, the unalloyed villain, could possibly have been the same person.[21]

The debate about the identity of 'Aregwedd Voeddig' was peculiar to Welsh commentators, and it foregrounded the essential question of Boudica's name. This was to become a very important background to the most intriguing coincidence of all: that the Welsh 'Buddug' translated loosely to 'Victory' or 'Victoria'. Queen Victoria's accession undoubtedly prompted Prichard to clear up the confusion caused by the pre-Victorian Pughe, but this was not an instance of 'invented tradition' any more than Thomas Thornycroft's reliance on Julius Caesar's description of British war chariots had been. The translation of 'Buddug' to 'Victory' pre-dated the birth of the nineteenth-century monarch, but this useful coincidence was exploited with enthusiasm by Welsh cultural nationalists. One of the earliest explicit reference to Boudica and Victoria as namesakes occurred earlier, in 1853 at the *eisteddfod* held in Abergavenny. John Williams ab Ithel, Anglican priest and enthusiastic antiquary, proclaimed, 'Victoria is peculiarly our Queen—Boadicea *rediviva*—our Buddug the Second... We can address our English friends: "We have... more right in Victoria than thee", a larger quantity of Celtic than of Saxon blood flowing through her royal veins.'[22] It was no great leap to draw a connection between two reigning queens: one at the beginning of history and one in the glorious present; the first the prophecy and the second the fulfilment. This honour was not reserved for the queen only; it extended to another royal Victoria. When Victoria's daughter, Princess Victoria, visited the National Eisteddfod in Caernarfon in 1894, she was honoured with the name 'Buddug Boadicea' by her hosts.[23]

As had been the case before Queen Victoria came to the throne, *eisteddfodou* continued to be a means whereby Boudica could become a part of an embedded

---

[20] W. Owen Pughe, *The Cambrian biography or historical notes of the celebrated men among the ancient Britons* (London, 1803), 11.
[21] Prichard, *Heroines of Welsh history*, 86.
[22] J. Davies, 'Victoria and Victorian Wales', in G.H. Jenkins and J.B. Smith (eds), *Politics and Society in Wales, 1840–1922. Essays in Honour of Ieuan Gwynedd Jones* (Cardiff, 1988), 14.
[23] *Western Mail*, 12 July 1894.

tradition of poetry and drama.²⁴ At the 1858 is 'A Poem of English Sympathy with Wales', presented at the *eisteddfod* in Llangollen:

> The Roman came, and saw, but conquered not
> Till Fraud and Discord had oppressed the land,
> Victoria's*²⁵ curse and red avenging hand—
> Vain the doomed Legion this last shock to quell
> Colonia Victrix <Camalodunum> sank, dirged by the conquerors yell!²⁶
> There rose, alas! the tide of blood and turned
> Back on the hapless Princess; utter woe
> Consumed her, but the heroic heart that spurned
> Forlorn and crownless life, and Roman show,
> Lived yet again and laid the Armada low,
> Spurning for Tudor England threats and chains—
> Lives quenchless yet, and may it quenchless glow
> In her, our new Victoria, who reigns
> Invincible and free o'er ancient hills and plains!²⁷

As the poem makes clear, the Buddug/Victoria coincidence was a useful one. It allowed Welsh commentators to use the character of Boudica to celebrate the exceptional place of Wales in British history, and of Britain in the world, while simultaneously proclaiming unique loyalty to Queen Victoria. Indeed, Boudica was far more likely to be used as an assertion of Welshness in a jocular gesture of superiority over Englishness than she was to be part of a narrative of Welsh separatism, past, present, or future. Boudica instead signified a link between England and Wales, while also encapsulating a narrative of monarchy with uniquely Welsh roots. After all, as one patriotic commentator put it, 'Wales is really the cradle of the English crown, for before a man can be King of England, he must be Prince of Wales.'²⁸

This link between Boudica and Victoria was recognized at the local and national level—which is to say, it became part of celebrations of Welsh nationhood—through the *eisteddfod*, but this message was also evident in relations between England and Wales at a diplomatic level. In 1893 Boudica's place in the narrative of British history became part of an overt gesture of loyalty to the monarchy by members of the Welsh cultural establishment. It was announced in that year that the Duke of York, the future George V, would marry Princess Victoria Mary of Teck, the Welsh National Presentation Committee was formed for the purpose of arranging a suitable gift for the occasion, to be presented to the couple from the people of Wales. The chairman and treasurer of this Committee was one of the most eminent Welshmen in late

---

²⁴ A total of seven dramas on the subject of 'Buddug (Boadicea)' were submitted to the National Eisteddfod in Carnarvon in 1886, though none were considered of high enough quality to be awarded a full prize. *Carnarvon and Denbigh Herald and North and South Wales Independent*, 17 September 1886.

²⁵ The asterisk alerts the reader to a note on the alternative spellings '*Boadicea (Vuddig)'.

²⁶ The interpolation is in the original.

²⁷ 'Elfynydd' [James Kenward], '*A poem of English sympathy with Wales*', written for the Great National Eisteddfod of 1858 and 'Llangollen', a Poem, upon the same occasion (Birmingham, 1858). The attribution to Kenward comes from C. Reilly, *Mid-Victorian poetry, 1860–1879, an annotated bibliography* (London, 2000), 254.

²⁸ 'Griffith', *The Welsh question and Druidism* (London, 1887), 33.

nineteenth-century London, Sir David Evans (1849–1907), formerly Lord Mayor of London. He was also one of very few Welshmen to hold the office and, at only 42, he was among the youngest Lord Mayors in the City's history. What was more, his love of his native Wales was said to be 'of a sterling type, not that pseudo-patriotism of the Welsh nationalist sort... [he is], in every sense, a most worthy son of Wales...'[29]

This dual identity was reflected in the gift itself, which was paid for by subscription, taking the form of a large boat-shaped centrepiece cast from silver, silver gilt, gold, and enamel.[30] Flanked by two equestrian figures (one of Henry V and the other George's father, the future Edward VII, then Prince of Wales) the central portion of the centrepiece was decorated with gold reliefs depicting scenes from Welsh geography and history, including 'Queen Boadicea Repelling the Romans AD61'. The scene is a conventional rendering, showing Boudica atop her chariot urging her troops onward amidst a scene busy with horses, soldiers, and spear points. Its inclusion is far more striking than its unoriginal imagery: there were no other scenes illustrating ancient Britain, and even Caractacus was excluded in favour of Boudica as sole representative of ancient Wales (and Britain). In this instance, Boudica's dual Englishness and Welshness worked in her favour. Caractacus, king of the Silures, was more overtly and exclusively Welsh and would have borne less meaning as part of an object intended to illustrate the shared history of England and Wales.

However, as has so often been the case in Boudica's history, she was not easily cast as a monodimensional symbol, and not everyone accepted the version of Boudica that saw her Welshness as at least equal to her Englishness. There were some Welsh historians who went so far as to omit any mention of her from their narratives. This was the case in O.M. Edwards's new history, originally published in Welsh as *Cymru* (1891) and then in English as *Wales* (1901). Edwards described the events surrounding Boudica's rebellion, such as the massacre of the Druids in Mona, the collapse of the statue of the goddess Victory in Camulodunum and the destruction of the city of London. Yet he did not see fit to make any mention of the woman herself throughout his record of events, a strange and surely purposeful omission, considering she was otherwise universally acknowledged as the commander-in-chief of the mutinous British tribes. Rather than relate Boudica's place in Welsh history, Edwards, who was certainly aware of her, chose to focus his attentions on Caractacus, king of the Silures and indisputably a Welshman, geographically speaking.

Edwards's point of view was implicit, but the rationale for his position was articulated quite clearly by Robert Scourfield Mills, or Owen Rhoscomyl (1863–1919), who showed a similar disregard for Boudica in his work. Rhoscomyl was a great popularizer of Welsh history, one of the architects of the National Pageant of Wales in 1909, as well as the author of a number of novels and histories.[31] He had been

---

[29] *Western Mail*, 1 August 1892.
[30] The centrepiece is on public display at the National Museum of Wales, Cardiff.
[31] There has yet to be a full biography of Rhoscomyl, but see H. T. Edwards, *The National Pageant of Wales* (Llandysul, Ceredigion, 2009); J.S. Ellis, 'Outlaw historian: Owen Rhoscomyl and popular

raised for a time in Lancashire, but went to live with his grandmother in Tremeirchion at the age of six, after the death of his mother, where he absorbed from his grandmother's storytelling a sense of the romance of the Welsh past. When he grew older, Rhoscomyl lived a life intrepidity and adventure: he crossed the Atlantic to South America, was a cowboy in the Wild West, fought with Theodore Roosevelt's Rough Riders in Cuba, and then went to South Africa to fight in the Boer War. Eventually, Rhoscomyl returned to his grandmother's native Wales and began to enthusiastically promote, in a series of novels and histories, a nationalistic—at least in a cultural sense—view of Welsh history. He published a history of Wales under the title *Flame-bearers of Welsh History* (1905), and it is in this work that we find his opinion of Boudica, and that of some others, stated most explicitly:

> Boudicca, the widow of the King of the Eceni (whose name, anciently distorted into Boadicea, you see in a famous poem)[32] roused the revolt... So the struggle went on. Prince after prince, people after people, come to the front in the desperate struggle against Rome. But as the descendants of the people Boudicca roused are now part of the English people, their deeds do not come into this book in detail.[33]

Neither did Rhoscomyl include Boudica in his script for the National Pageant of Wales in 1909. Ancient Welsh history was instead personified by Caractacus and his Silures, the opposite of what had been the case in the 1893 wedding gift to the future George V. Similarly, the 1913 Pageant of Gwent used Caractacus (or Caradoc, as he was more usually known in Wales) to illustrate the early history of Wales, and there was no mention of Boudica at all.[34] Boudica was a near-constant presence in English pageants, where her local identity was far more well evidenced.

But despite outliers like Rhoscomyl who forsook Boudica, the mainstream view, exemplified by the wedding gift to the Prince of Wales, was that she embodied Celtic and English reconciliation, uniting the geography of England with the chronology of Welsh (or British) history. Boudica's story was a source for cultural compromise and internal unity through diversity, in a similar fashion to the ceremony surrounding the investiture of the Prince of Wales.[35] Nevertheless, it remained important to Welsh cultural nationalists to do more than simply claim Boudica through assertions of shared language and blood.

The full weight of antiquarianism was brought to bear on the question, an endeavour performed most effectively by Owen 'Morien' Morgan. Like Rhoscomyl, Morien was immersed in a romantic and somewhat sensationalist view of Welsh

---

history in Edwardian Wales', in N. Evans and H. Pryce (eds), *Writing a small nation's past*, pp. 111–26. For the tension between 'scientific' and 'popular' approaches to Welsh history, see in particular H. Pryce, 'J.E. Lloyd's History of Wales (1911): publication and reception', in N. Evans and H. Pryce (eds), *Writing a small nation's past*, pp. 49–64; M. Löffler, 'Failed founding fathers and abandoned sources: Edward Williams, Thomas Stephens and the young J.E. Lloyd', in N. Evans and H. Pryce (eds), *Writing a small nation's past*, pp. 66–81.

[32] That is, Cowper's.
[33] O. Rhoscomyl, *Flame-bearers of Welsh history* (Merthyr Tydfil, 1905), 24.
[34] *Book of the Pageant of Gwent* (Abergavenny, 1913).
[35] J.S. Ellis, 'Reconciling the Celt: British national identity, empire, and the 1911 investiture of the Prince of Wales', *Journal of British Studies*, 37(4) (1998), 391–418.

history heavily influenced by Edward Williams or Iolo Morganwg.[36] Morganwg had done much to revive the sense that Wales had deep associations with a sacred Druidic antiquity, and thus could lay claim to rites and ceremonies derived from this mystical past. His literary forgeries and picturesque reimagining of the *gorsedd* ceremony yielded tangible results in the revivification of the *eisteddfod* movement in the last decade of the eighteenth century. The first national *eisteddfod*, as distinct from the older local ones, took place in 1861 and was heavily indebted to Morganwg's laudanum-laced teachings.[37]

After Morganwg's death, it was up to Morien and his compatriots to maintain and promote Morganwg's view of the Welsh nation in the late nineteenth and early twentieth centuries. Morien himself took the title of 'Archdruid' after the death of his friend Evan Davies aka Myfyr Morganwg (1801–88), who had inherited the title from Iolo Morganwg's son Taliesen Williams (1787–1847). As Arch-druid, Morien was at the forefront of Welsh historical and cultural nationalism but, unlike Owen Rhoscomyl, he embraced Boudica as a Welsh heroine, and claimed that she had been wrongly appropriated by the English. 'It is true,' wrote Morien, taking on the imagined voice of an English interlocutor, 'that Caractacus, Arviragus, &c., were Welshmen; that the heroic Boadicea was a Welshwoman. You don't mind our referring to them occasionally as Englishmen, and to Boadicea as an Englishwoman? We do not want to lay claim to Queen Cartismandua, who betrayed General Caractacus? You shall refer to her exclusively as a Welshwoman.'[38]

The revival of Druidism in modern-day Wales by Iolo Morganwg and his successors also encouraged the rehabilitation of the Druids of the past, which could be accomplished by asserting a lineage between Druidism and modern Welsh resistance to Anglican conformity. For William Richards, writing in 1820, the Druids represented the predecessors of those who would resist a corrupt and amoral church.[39] While the ancient Christian churches increasingly acted against their professed principles of peace and goodwill, the Druids continued to '...worship[...] the true God in simplicity'—the spirit of Christianity over the letter.[40] Richards denied all allegations of human sacrifice and professed the Druids to have been pacifists, a claim later repeated by Morien, as well as by others. According to 'Griffith' who frequently contributed articles to the Welsh press on the subjects of revived

---

[36] For Iolo Morganwg and his legacy, see P. Morgan, *Iolo Morganwg* (Cardiff, 1975); G.H. Jenkins, A rattleskull genius: the many faces of Iolo Morganwg (Cardiff, 2005); M. Löffler, *The literary and historical legacy of Iolo Morganwg 1826–1926* (Cardiff, 2007).

[37] For the *eisteddfod*, see P. Morgan, 'Early Victorian Wales and its crisis of identity', in L. Brockliss and D. Eastwood (eds), *A union of multiple identities*, pp. 93–109, esp. 103–5; and H.T. Edwards, *The Eisteddfod* (Cardiff, 1990). Wales presents an interesting case study for Anthony D. Smith, who views the *eisteddfod* as an example of an 'invented tradition' that in fact corresponds so closely to its historic original that any notion of 'invention' seems inadequate. He repeats this in various places, but see Smith, *Nation in history*, 55, and A.D. Smith, 'The nation: invented, imagined, reconstructed?', *Millennium: journal of international studies*, 20 (1991), 352–68, at 357–9.

[38] *Western Mail*, 10 July 1891.

[39] This argument could cut both ways, with detractors viewing the Druids as originators of that corruption; see Kidd, 'Wales', 221–4, and discussion in Chapter 3 above.

[40] W. Richards, *The Welsh nonconformists memorial; or Cambro-British biography...*, ed. J. Evans (London, 1820).

Druidism and English arrogance, the Druids had worshipped only the rudest monuments in order to avoid any temptation to idolatry, and they acknowledged the supremacy of God, not his agents on earth, in all spiritual matters. Once again, Boudica was never far from these stories of ancient religion. Although 'Griffith' stopped short of directly addressing the role Boudica played in organizing Druid resistance as part of his defence of the Druids, he claimed that Boudica could not have been merely Queen of the Iceni in Norfolk: such a small district could not possibly have supplied the 230,000 men which the Roman sources reported as having made up Boudica's rebellious troop. 'The improbabilities of the whole story are enormous; we are told that these Britons were infuriated, and had already slaughtered 70,000 Romans, that they had swept the country from Anglesea to Colchester; but when Suetonius, who had only 10,000 men, attacked the infuriated army of 230,000, they slew 80,000 Britons, with the loss of 400 Romans only. If this be not a cooked account, we never saw one; yet such, as a rule, are the accounts we find in Roman and English Histories, when speaking of the Britons and the Welsh.'[41] This opinion further complicates Boudica's association with the modern-day triumph of British imperialism in the mould of the Roman; the Welsh Boudica was a rebel against such oppressive monoliths as Rome—and England. And Griffith seemed to be suggesting that either she, the Druid religion, or a combination of both, commanded far greater power than English or Roman chroniclers cared to admit.

Morien took a similar view to 'Griffith' but he drew Boudica into the history of the Druid religion in Wales in a much more direct manner and professedly as a means of reclaiming her from the English who had, he thought, unfairly monopolized her. It was Morien's purpose to historicize and authenticate Boudica's geographical connection to Wales, and to transform her into a figurehead for a version of Druidism that was historically plausible and yet embedded in the moral traditions of Wales. Morien first asserted the link between Boudica and revenge for the destruction of the Druids' sacred isle in his history of ancient Druidism, *The Light of Britannia* (1893). The dedication blatantly reappropriates the ancient past by appealing to:

> ...the sacred memory of those of our ancestors, who, a vast multitude of aged and young Druids and Druidesses, were massacred in A.D. 61, on the Mona side of the Menai Straights [*sic*], by the Roman legions under the command of General Paulinus Suetonius.... The slaughter of the British priests and priestesses, all of whom were non-combatants, was, however, speedily avenged, for the British nation uprose in arms and slew scores of thousands of the Romans, and, commanded by Queen Victoria I. (Buddug – Boadicea), marched, with fire in their eyes, towards Mona.

The Druids, Morien pointed out, were, 'like our present clergy', innocent pacifists massacred by the marauding Romans, and it was left to the heroic Queen Boudica and her followers to avenge the native religion. They did so, in fact, on their native Welsh soil: 'At New Market, Flintshire, the British and Roman armies met in

---

[41] 'Griffith', *The Welsh question*, 105.

deadly conflict. According to Tacitus, who erroneously describes the scene of battle as near London, the Britons were eventually defeated in the battle. That Queen Victoria I perished seems certain, for her grave is still shown near the said New Market, in the midst of many a heap of bones of warriors slain.'[42] Morien once again subverts the notion that Boudica—here emphatically linked to Victoria—could possibly be an English heroine, when she had died in Wales. Moreover, while Victoria remained on the throne, Welsh cultural nationalists like Morien rarely passed up the opportunity to refer to Boudica as the first of that name.

The following year, Morien watched Charles Read's excavation at Hampstead Heath with interest, and even claimed to have inspected the tumulus himself. Having done so, the Arch-Druid took the opportunity to write to the London press to express his own deduction that the tumulus was not a grave at all—and certainly not Boudica's—but a sort of Druidic pulpit, a 'Gwyddva'. After expounding on the significance of these mounds to ancient Druidic thought, Morien concluded that all the work of English archaeologists was in vain. Celtic scholars, at least, were in agreement 'that the greatest of British Queens was buried in North Wales'.[43] This was a line of argument that almost certainly originated from Morien's own prejudice, but it was a natural conclusion to draw if one accepted his earlier assertion that Boudica was held in the highest esteem by the ancient Britons precisely because she had led the movement to avenge the murder of the Druids on Mona. It followed quite logically that Boudica's battles and eventual death would have occurred closer to the site of the massacre itself, not, as had been argued since the time of Tacitus, near London or East Anglia. Even Edmund Bolton's long-dead belief that her body lay in Wiltshire would have put her much too far to the east for Morien.

Although he had held this conviction since the reign of Victoria, Morien continued doggedly to pursue his line of argument at greater length, producing three separate works in the early decades of the twentieth century. This included Morien's own attempts at a panoramic Welsh history, of which Boudica's battles formed an early chapter. His *History of Wales from the earliest period, including hitherto unrecorded antiquarian lore* (1911) was republished in a slimmed down version titled *The battles of Wales, the unconquered country of the empire* (1920). However, Morien clearly thought the Boudica story worth pursuing in a separate work; he consolidated his research and voluminous speculations on her life and death in a small pamphlet, *Queen Boadicea: Her Life, Battles, and Death Near Rhyl* (1913).[44] Morien used much the same evidence to make the same argument in these three works, but the 1913 pamphlet provides the most detailed account of his rationale. For all three, Morien drew on the story of the massacre of the Druids given in Tacitus' *Agricola*; this was written, Morien thought, with the vividness of an eyewitness account, which gave it a greater air of authenticity than other classical sources. However, Morien, somewhat predictably, took issue with Tacitus' interpretation, if not his

---

[42] O. Morgan 'Morien', 'Dedication', *The light of Britannia: the mysteries of ancient Druidism revealed* (Cardiff, 1893).
[43] Morien wrote to the *Sun*, but his letter also appeared in *Western Mail*, 1 December 1894.
[44] O. Morgan, 'Morien', *Boadicea: her life, battles, and death near Rhyl* (Pontypridd, 1913) bears Thomas Thornycroft's statue as its frontispiece with the caption 'Boadicea rushing through Chester to the front'.

general overview of the facts. First, the Roman historian was wrong about the Druids, who were far from the savage brood described by Tacitus. The modern antiquary deduced that the invasion of Britain in AD 43 had in fact driven the Druid priests, as pacifists and non-combatants, to flee to the distant Isle of Angelsey, along with their defenceless wives and daughters. There they were tracked down by the Roman general Suetonius Paulinus, who used flat-bottomed boats to cross the Menai Straits and attack the confused group of women, girls, and pacifist priests that he found there. Tacitus' assertion that these blameless people somehow were 'ranged in order with hands uplifted invoking the gods, and pouring forth horrible imprecations' was entirely mistaken. According to Morien, it was far more probable that the inhabitants of the islands were appealing for mercy in the Welsh tongue, which no Roman would have understood.[45] It was as he was going about the grim work of exterminating this helpless group of people that Suetonius received word of the uprising in the south.

Morien proclaimed a wholly patriotic stance for Boudica, whose outrage he cast as due entirely to the insult to her native religion. Morien acknowledged that she had been personally wronged by the Romans, but her private wrongs were not the primary reason she began her bloody uprising. Instead 'it is perfectly clear that the revolt was due entirely to the massacre of the Druids on the Menai Straits'. Her anger was felt across the country, and, in Boudica, 'frenzied Britain discovered a leader'. Morien stopped short of claiming that Boudica had been born within the contemporary Welsh borders, instead acknowledging her traditional homeland of East Anglia, but he conjectured that after she had put down what little resistance there was in the Roman colonial towns of the south and east, Boudica intended to intercept the bulk of the Roman forces, who had interrupted their mission to exterminate the Druids on Mona in order to put down the uprising on the mainland. In order to achieve this end, she would have had to turn her army north-westward and ride at full speed toward modern-day Chester. She met the Roman troops in Flintshire, near Newmarket (present-day Trelawnyd), just outside Rhyl, and the final destructive battle ensued. Morien himself surveyed the terrain in the area through his 'binocular glasses', noting the presence of a forest through which the Romans were likely to have come, emerging 'into high, open, sloping fields', where Boudica and her troops would have gathered in anticipation.[46]

Drawing on the long tradition of Welsh linguistic scholarship evident in the 'Aregwedd Voeddawg' controversy, Morien cited copious archaeo-philological evidences for Boudica's presence in the area, especially in place names around Flintshire. He asserted that a hill known locally as Bryn Sion had been considered sacred long before the introduction of Christianity to north Wales and that the biblical name was in fact an allusion to its enduring sanctity as the very spot where the great queen had fallen. A golden torque was said to have been found there in 1816 by a miner working in a limestone quarry and this, Morien argued, was likely

---

[45] O. Morgan, *The battles of Wales* (Liverpool, 1920), 3.
[46] Morien, *Boadicea...near Rhyl*, 15. The site described by Morien might be 'Gop Hill' on which a cairn of stones can still be seen.

to have belonged to Boudica or one of her daughters.[47] Furthermore, the road near the Bryn Sion was known locally as 'The Road that is Harrowed' suggesting a 'Passage where the Britons harrowed the Romans', which Morien believed to be the derivation of the earliest name for Newmarket, 'Rhiw Lyvnwyd'.[48]

Extant antiquarian remains were also brought to bear. There was, Morien noted, a stone monolith called Maen Achwynfan or the 'Stone of Lamentation' that stood close to the road. The stone marked what Morien believed to be the site of Boudica's death. Convinced by his own mounting store of evidence, Morien departed from the classical accounts by claiming that neither sickness nor suicide (a mere 'rumour' of Tacitus') had caused Boudica's death, but rather that the mother and her two daughters had died of wounds sustained during battle:

> In this hideous confusion Romans and Britons mixed during a distance of about three miles, going to the South-east from the first point of contact, when either Boadicea's horse was slain or fell on the slippery declivity, and she and her two daughters received mortal sabre cuts on their heads.

This disaster occurred near the Maen Achwynfan, where the three women were found before being moved to a nearby cottage. There they succumbed to their wounds and, 'when dead, the three Royal ladies were taken from the cottage and placed on the green sward, then lovingly covered over, and finally hidden underneath the soil of Wales, drenched with the blood of brave men'.[49] According to Morien's investigation, a stone known to locals as the 'Careg Bedd Buddug', which he translated as 'Boadicea's Gravestone' served as definitive proof that Boudica had died in the area. Morien's account thus had Boudica and her two children literally subsumed under Welsh soil, where her people, the Britons—past and present—dwelled.

All of this, picturesque as it undoubtedly was, was of course conjecture on Morien's part, though not uninformed conjecture. His account, generously peppered with the language of speculation, was nevertheless grounded in antiquarian and philological research. The Maen Achwynfan, for example, had stood on the spot for centuries; it had been the subject of speculation by Thomas Pennant in *The history of the parishes of Whiteford and Holywell* (1796), although that author made no mention of Boudica and suspected that the monument was of late and likely Christian origin. Watkin Williams made an illustration of the Maen Achwynfan in 1759 for Sir Roger Mostyn, the owner of the property on which it sat, but again no mention was made of a link to the ancient queen.[50]

Morien had only the slimmest factual basis for his story, but it was crucial for him to establish that his own account was at least plausible. Rather than 'inventing' a Welsh past for Boudica, Morien reinterpreted existing evidence and 'corrected'

---

[47] Morien had made this assertion some time before in the *Western Mail*, 6 September 1892, once again suggesting the longevity of his project.
[48] Morien, *Boadicea...near Rhyl*, 21.   [49] O. Morgan (Morien), *Boadicea...near Rhyl*, 24.
[50] An interesting footnote to this history was the discovery in the 1990s of the subsumed remains of a cottage, probably built in the nineteenth century, known as Pant y Fechwan. The site forms part of an archaeological walk curated by the Clwyd–Powys Archaeological Trust; see 'Graig Fawr to Gop Cairn', http://www.cpat.org.uk/walks/gopcairn.pdf , accessed 30 Nov 2017.

misinformed conclusions. He adhered to the language of authenticity and historical argument, asserting the prejudicial nature of Roman historians in regards to ancient British practices. Morien's purpose in doing so was to assert the equality of Wales with other parts of Britain, but most particularly and pointedly, England. No other historical person could have done the same work as Queen Boudica in Morien's antiquarian writings: Caractacus, as we have seen, was simply too Welsh already; King Alfred was much too English. King Arthur was widely accepted as a fiction and did not carry the legitimacy of 'authentic' history. Boudica was chronologically British (or Welsh), geographically English (according to most accounts), and carried the additional gravitas of being Queen Victoria I. Morien had once stated, somewhat implausibly, 'England and Wales mutually agreed to the union of the two countries, and the union will ever continue to respect the proud national spirit of the Welsh people.'[51] Thus it was precisely because Boudica's identity was contested that she served Morien's unionist purpose; she was a heroine capable of being venerated for both her Welshness and her Englishness. As Morien himself put it, 'we are all Britons now',[52] and he was perfectly willing to share his heroine with the English, providing the English showed equal magnanimity.

Boudica was a singularly useful figure for Morien the antiquary: much as she had done for Edmund Bolton in the distant past, Boudica provided Morien with a means of asserting the power of antiquarian research to challenge and overthrow conventional opinion, starting with the still-controversial Tacitean account. Morien and the many other, more mainstream Welsh figures who argued in favour of Boudica as a Welsh heroine were eventually rewarded with an institutional tribute to Queen Boudica in Wales. James Havard Thomas's statue of 'Buddug/Boadicea' in Cardiff City Hall marks an intriguing apotheosis for Boudica in Wales (see Figure 9). Although intended as a local authority building, Cardiff City Hall was constructed in 1906 with the attendant purpose of locating a national centre.[53] The ambitious nature of the project is testified to by the grandeur of the building's exterior and the splendour of its interior design, in particular the grand Marble Hall. This room was conceived of as a 'national Valhalla for Wales' in which the heroes of Welsh history would be immortalized in a series of marble statues.[54] James Havard Thomas, RA (1854–1921) was best known for his controversial 'Lycidas' of 1905, a figure that was heralded as the 'most modern in Britain' at the time of its exhibition.[55] This controversial sculptor was brought in from the Royal Academy in London to oversee this spatial and material recreation of Welsh national history through its heroes.

After a public vote, the result of which determined a shortlist of candidates to be housed in the new Welsh Valhalla, a panel of three judges made the final decision.

---

[51] Quoted in Edwards, *National Pageant of Wales*, 59.   [52] Morien, *Queen Boadicea*, 15.

[53] P. Lord, *Imaging the nation: the visual culture of Wales* (Cardiff, 1998–2003), 337.

[54] A. Gaffney, 'A National Valhalla for Wales: D.A. Thomas and the Welsh historical sculpture scheme', *Transactions of the Honourable Society of Cymmrodorion*, New Series, 5 (1999), 131–44.

[55] See D. J. Getsy, 'The Lycidas "scandal" of 1905: James Havard Thomas at the crux of modern sculpture in Britain', in D. J. Getsy (ed.), *Sculpture and the pursuit of a modern ideal in Britain, c. 1880–1930* (Aldershot, 2004), pp. 167–90.

Figure 9. 'Buddug and her daughters' by John Havard Thomas in Cardiff City Hall. Image copyright Rob Watkins.

The subjects chosen for inclusion were for the most part unsurprising: St David, Hywel the Good, Llewelyn ap Grufydd, Owain Glyn Dŵr, and Harri Tewdwr (Henry VII) were all granted a place in the Marble Hall, along with some more recent heroes of the Welsh nonconformist movement. At some point in the proceedings, it was decided that the Welsh Valhalla should house at least one woman and two close contenders emerged: Ann Griffiths (1776–1805), the poet and hymn writer, and Queen Boudica.⁵⁶ Although Boudica was a figure of popular myth, the Welsh public was as incredulous as any other when it came to the antiquarian notions of men like Morien, which, in the absence of classical evidence, were necessary to ground her in Wales. She received very few votes in the national competition, and the Committee had to intervene in order to secure the eleventh plinth for the ancient queen, which had been added in order to balance out the positioning of the statues in the Hall.⁵⁷

James Havard Thomas himself may have played some part in securing a place for 'Buddug', probably with the assistance of D.A. Thomas, Lord Rhondda, the coal baron and principal financial backer for the project, who had insisted that Havard Thomas contribute a statue to the Marble Hall pantheon. The sculptor had initially refused, noting his position as assessor, but eventually acquiesced to his benefactor's request. His choice of Boudica as an addition to the Cardiff City Hall scheme might also have been the culmination of his personal artistic investment in Boudica as a subject. Although a native of Bristol, the 20-year-old Havard Thomas had won the £15 15s prize in the 1874 Bangor Eisteddfod for a plaster bas relief of 'Boadicea at the head of her army';⁵⁸ Havard Thomas returned to a subject that had captured his youthful imagination as a tribute to Wales. Along with the ten Welsh heroes, Havard Thomas's 'Buddug' was duly unveiled by then Secretary of State for War, David Lloyd George in October 1916.

According to a posthumous review, the group was 'only respectable',⁵⁹ but the modern-day viewer is arrested by one powerful detail: Boudica's daughters are depicted as adolescent children. Nearly every narrative description of Boudica's life included a reference, however veiled, to the rape of her two daughters, but their ages were rarely commented on in prose accounts. Dramatic authors were the most inclined to speculate on the circumstances of the sexual violence mentioned in the ancient works. We have seen how Charles Hopkins (see Chapter 2) imbued the incident with pathos: when Boudica's gentle daughter Camilla is overcome by Decius, she cuts a heart-breaking figure, all too conscious of the bleak future before her. But, in the Cardiff statue, Boudica's daughters are too young, it would seem, to understand fully what is happening. In Havard Thomas's version of the story—here told in a single mute and static scene—one daughter, who even when standing upright is much smaller than her mother, looks up to her in a state of confusion, while the other is huddled against Boudica, as if more shy than scared. The look on the face of the older woman, however, is one of disbelief, as if she has only just realized that no mercy will be forthcoming from her interlocutors. The viewer is struck by the same sense of cruel inevitability that is dawning on Boudica but from which her daughters are shielded by their innocence. This only makes their mother's fear all the more powerful: the worst has not yet happened, but the narrative is what it is and cannot be changed. In this single sculpture group, James Havard Thomas accomplished with much greater success the unity of emotional purpose sought decades earlier by Thomas Thornycroft.

---

⁵⁶ Lord, *Imaging the nation*, 337.
⁵⁸ *The Bristol Mercury*, 29 August 1874.
⁵⁷ Gaffney, 'National Valhalla for Wales', 139.
⁵⁹ *The Manchester Guardian*, 25 April 1922.

With Havard Thomas's statue, Queen Boudica was cemented as a heroine of a particularly Welsh view of the historical narrative, which emphasized Wales as the preserve of an original British identity. The Welsh narrative ran in parallel to other ways of envisioning Boudica's significance in particular places and within particular interpretations of the past, and only rarely was it suggested that Boudica belonged solely to the Welsh or to Welsh history. For the most part, Boudica was used to assert the importance of the Principality in the national story. Similar narratives were prevalent in other parts of Britain. Although none of these were freighted with the same powerful cultural nationalism that Boudica was capable of articulating in Wales, nevertheless, these narratives of place show how wide-ranging Boudica's story could be, taking her from the mountains of Wales to the cobbled streets of English market towns.

LOCALITY AND PAGEANTRY

In Wales, Boudica played an important part in connecting regional and national histories. Agile antiquarian deduction and supposition were necessary to make the pieces fit, but men like Morien, driven by a belief in the exceptionalism of Welsh history and immersed in a wealth of semi-mythical stories, were more than equal to the task. The case was different in the parts of England where links with Boudica were well supported by documentary evidence, ranging from the classical source base to the growing collection of archaeological finds relating to ancient Britain which was coming to light during the interwar years.[60] Small market towns in Essex, Norfolk, and Suffolk made Boudica part of their town fabric, literally through monuments and commemoration, and figuratively by giving her a key part in the dramatic re-enactment of local history in historical pageants held throughout the east of England and beyond.

For all their huge popularity in Britain in the twentieth century, it is only recently that historians have begun to study the pageant movement in detail.[61] Each historical pageant took the form of a scene-by-scene retelling of local history,

---

[60] *The Times* had a dedicated archaeological correspondent who wrote about the many finds that were made between the First and Second World Wars. Digs in London, St Albans, and Colchester often yielded evidence of ancient British habitation, with Boudica's rebellion acting as a key chronological reference point; see P. Ottoway, *Archaeology in British towns: from the Emperor Claudius to the Black Death* (London, 1996), 9–10.

[61] The research of the Arts and Humanities Research Council-funded project 'The redress of the past: historical pageants in Britain, 1905–2020', forms the basis of much of my discussion of historical pageantry. The project database, which is by no means comprehensive, records many hundreds of pageants performed in Britain between these dates. However, many small-scale pageants are not recorded in this number and the real count was likely to be higher. I am grateful to the project team—Angela Bartie, Paul Caton, Linda Fleming, Mark Freeman, Tom Hulme, Alex Hutton, and Paul Readman—for allowing me pre-publication access to their findings. The full pageant database can be accessed here: A. Bartie, P. Caton, L. Fleming, M. Freeman, T. Hulme, A. Hutton, and P. Readman, *The Redress of the Past*, http://www.historicalpageants.ac.uk/pageants/, accessed 30 Nov 2017. For earlier work on the subject, see P. Readman, 'The place of the past', 168–75; A. Yoshino, *The Edwardian historical pageant: local history and consumerism* (Tokyo, 2010); M. Freeman, '"Splendid display; pompous spectacle": historical pageants in twentieth-century Britain', *Social History*, 38 (2013), 423–55.

embedded in a schematic vision of the national past—it was, in a sense, a panoramic history play, performed by local community volunteers. The 1905 Sherborne Pageant, in Sherborne, Dorset, is considered to be the first 'modern' pageant, distinct from the historical processions that had become popular in the later nineteenth century. These earlier spectacles shared with later pageants a reliance on volunteer participation, both in performance and in activities such as the making of costumes and sets, but they did not feature dialogue or any discernible story, instead representing historical 'epochs' through an exhibition of its 'celebrities' and their entourage in lavish historic dress.[62] Modern pageants, such as that held in Sherborne, were managed by semi-professional Pageantmasters—Louis Napoleon Parker was the most successful—whose task it was to marshal local volunteers, choreograph crowd scenes, and ensure the performances went smoothly. Pageant scripts—sometimes reproduced in 'Books of Words' that were available for purchase on the day of performance—were often the work of local writers, many with historical and antiquarian leanings. Pageants were performed outdoors, in the grounds of castles, ruined abbeys, or other sites of significant antiquity, rooting them definitively in the local community.

The pageant movement—enthusiasts were said to suffer from 'pageantitis'—relied upon popular appeal and often popular participation, with the number of cast members sometimes soaring into the hundreds or even thousands.[63] As one contemporary noted in report on the 1907 Bury St Edmunds pageant:

> The pageant is the latest and most picturesque development of civic life. One may fairly claim it as a manifestation of all that is best in the new democracy, made possible by the broadening and refining influences of popular education, and successful only so far as it is able to command the aid of all classes of society in the task of setting forth those great deeds of old days which have made our cities what they are.[64]

Pageants soon became a phenomenon, with local pageants held in towns and cities across Britain. By the summer of 1914, the subject matter of pageants had become somewhat predictable with Boudica featuring often enough to attract comment. One newspaper noted that '... no pageant would deserve the name without scenes in which Boadicea and her Ancient Britons, the Romans, and Queen Elizabeth might figure'.[65] Another had, even earlier, cast Boudica as the '... ubiquitous monarch who has appeared in nearly every pageant throughout the length and breadth of England'.[66] But even if Boudica was a 'ubiquitous monarch' in Edwardian pageantry, her role was most evident in pageants staged in towns and regions in whose history she had played an active part.

One of the first major pageants to feature Boudica was that held in St Albans, on the grounds of Verulamium Park, the site of the Roman centre of the town, in

---

[62] For instance, the report on the Ripon Historic Festival was revealingly titled 'From Boadicea to Victoria', *The Manchester Guardian*, 19 August 1896. The festival was held in celebration of the community's thousandth year and featured, among other amusements, a game of whist played with 'living cards'.
[63] Readman, 'Place of the past', 169.   [64] *The Manchester Guardian*, 16 July 1907.
[65] *The Observer*, 28 June 1914.   [66] *The Times*, 22 August 1910.

July 1907.[67] Boudica's rebellion formed the basis of Episode II, in which the emphasis was on the importance of St Albans to the events of the uprising and its strategic importance to the Britons. According to the souvenir booklet, Boudica was a competent general who understood the strategic necessity of capturing Verulamium. This glorified Boudica's position as a leader, not often taken very seriously, and emphasized St Albans as central to the events of her story:

> It was generalship, not merely desire for plunder, which led Boadicea to post her forces at St. Albans. The capture of St. Albans cut Suetonius's line of communications, left him all the marching to do through a thickly wooded and hostile country, and placed a formidable barrier in his way. With the advantage of perspective that time has given us, it is easy to say that the whole Insurrection was short-sighted and a mistake... At all events, the very utmost was made of their chances by fighting men and fighting women.[68]

The writer noted, wryly, that Boudica's efforts were 'British, almost English, in the combination of courageous pluck, cool judgment, and contempt of odds', exposing once again the tension that existed between Boudica's two identities: one ethnic, the other geographic.

The official Book of Words, filled with its own historical notes, bears a somewhat different interpretation of events, seeming to foreground the town's wealth rather than its strategic value to a canny general. This historical note on the Boudica episode summarizes how she took advantage of the absence of General Suetonius Paulinus in Anglesey to lay waste to Camulodunum and Londinium. Afterward, 'passing by other places, [Boudica] hastened to Verulamium, being attracted by the riches and importance of the city. The same fate befell it, and over 70,000 persons suffered death and torture in the three places. Suetonius Paulinus avenged this by a decisive victory, in which 80,000 Britons are said to have fallen; Boadicea, to prevent capture, put an end to her life by poison.'[69] This interpretation emphasized the economic power of the town of Verulamium, but at the expense of Boudica's character, who seems to have been driven by greed.

The writers of the St Albans pageant itself were not very original in their interpretation of the events of the story. William Cowper's famous poem formed the core of Boudica's rallying speech to the assembled Britons, for instance, meaning there was little opportunity for original composition. The Romans made quick work of the Britons and Boudica is given a queenly burial before the pageant moves swiftly on to the martyrdom of St Alban in Episode III. The whole message of the Boudica episode, the book claimed, was to 'accentuate the difference between

---

[67] Boudica has less of a presence in the fabric of the town of St Albans than in Colchester. There are no statues of Boudica in St Albans, nor does she feature in civic architecture. However, there are sections devoted to her in the Verulamium Museum, and she also appears on interpretive displays at the town's Roman ruins.

[68] E.W. Townson et al., 'St Albans and its Pageant, being the official souvenir of the pageant held July, 1907, With contributions by the Very Rev. Dean Lawrence, Rev. J.V. Bullard, Mr. C.H. Ashdown, and Mr. W.G. Marshall. The whole arranged by Ernest W. Townson' (London and St Albans, 1907).

[69] C.H. Ashdown, 'The St Albans Pageant.' July 15th to July 20th 1907. Book of the words and lyrics. Text and Lyrics by Charles H. Ashdown' (St Albans, 1907).

the easy control of the country under Rome, and the difficulty of controlling it all during the Middle Ages, when Roman authority was gone', though this is not self-evident.[70]

This sparing take on the Boudica story in 1907 can be compared to the St Albans pageant of 1953, presented as a 'Masque of the Queens' in celebration of the coronation of Elizabeth II. Here Boudica featured along with ten other British queens up to Queen Victoria. However, each queen's story was linked with that of St Albans. Episode VII, for instance, shows Anne Boleyn and Henry VIII meeting at Sopwell, near St Albans, during their courtship. Boudica's connection to St Albans, however, would have been far more well known. The 1953 pageant foregrounded the cruelty of the Romans and the injustices suffered by the Britons. Boudica's speech was original this time, though it was based on Dio:

> The Roman tribes have treated us with scorn,
> Extorted cruel taxes,
> Taken away the nobles of my court as slaves,
> Stripped us of our possessions, outraged my daughters,
> And me, they have scourged with whips.
> Let us avenge our freedom that is lost,
> That we may live again in peace.[71]

The writers of the St Albans pageant in 1907 were clearly unsure about how to cast Boudica. The tension between the two versions of the story presented in the Book of Words and the souvenir booklet were only resolved in the 1953 pageant.

By contrast, the West Suffolk town of Bury St Edmunds, a place to which Boudica made no documented visit, was willing from the start to cast her as a great heroic figure. In doing so, the writers of the pageant made the Boudica episode into a newly imagined dramatic conceit. The scene takes place at a feast in the 'Villa Faustini', the name of Roman site mentioned in ancient Roman itineraries as being somewhere in present-day Norfolk, but not definitively located.[72] The link with Bury was thus somewhat tenuous. But for the purposes of the pageant, the villa belonged to the imagined Roman general Faustinus, a drunken, decadent figure with echoes of the Roman Emperor Nero. The Romans lounge around while the Britons act as their servants, complaining how their own people go hungry while the Romans feast. They discuss their queen in hushed tones. Faustinus commands an entertainment, in which a Briton dressed as 'Barbarity' is brought to his knees by a Roman girl representing 'Civility' to the cheers and applause of the assembled Romans. As the entertainers dance, there is a bustle in the crowd and, like a bolt from the blue, Queen Boudica enters at full speed on a horse-drawn chariot, the

---

[70] 'St Albans and its pageant', 34.
[71] A. Bartie, L. Fleming, M. Freeman, T. Hulme, A. Hutton, and P. Readman, 'St Albans Pageant 1953: A Masque of the Queens', *The Redress of the Past*, http://www.historicalpageants.ac.uk/pageants/1205/, accessed 30 Nov 2017.
[72] Local antiquaries had long been interested in the idea; see E. Gillingwater, *An historical and descriptive account of St. Edmund's Bury* (London, 1804), 3–8.

crowd paring in panic and disarray. She exposes the scars on her back, rallying her fellow Britons to attack the Romans. Faustinus is killed, as are many others.[73]

It is possible to get a very good sense of this scene from the impressive silent film of the pageant.[74] The Britons are dressed in skins and furs, carry clubs, and appear hunched, making strange and striking figures next to the upright Roman dancing girls dressed in flowing white robes. As Boudica's chariot clatters onto the scene, panic ensues and dancers scatter in all directions. The local woman, Mrs Aylmer, who played the part of Boudica, possessed the height, stature, and dignified features corresponding to an idealized heroic woman, and her hair flows loose; in colour photographs, it is has a red tinge that contrasts with the vibrant green of her dress (see cover image). This is the old description by Dio—that long ago flummoxed Edmund Bolton—here translated into a living, moving person. The chariot of war in which she rides is impressively large and she cuts an imposing figure as she comes galloping at speed onto the scene, using one hand to control her two horses as they career across the field. In the other hand she holds a tall spear that towers over her head. Her daughters appear belatedly, though they do not speak.

The dramatic conceit created in the Villa Faustini scene foregrounds Boudica's grievances and the Romans' decadence and insensate treatment of a grieving widow. When Boudica descends from her chariot, she is jeeringly offered wine by a drunken Faustinus. Boudica refuses, and the company mock her grief for her husband, Prasutagus, and her protestations of cruelty are met with derision. This contrast between the injured dignity of the British queen and the Romans' brutality forms the central dichotomy of the ancient British story. By setting the episode in the Villa Faustini, a real Roman settlement in East Anglia, the writers asserted the antiquity of Bury St Edmunds, interpolating the connection between the site and the beginning of Boudica's rebellion against Rome. As in all pageants, the assertion of local importance in national affairs drove most of the dramatic action in individual episodes, and formed the pageant's central point. But even so, the Boudica scene in the Bury St Edmunds pageant of 1907 suggests that, to an audience of ordinary people Boudica's story was a spectacular one, redolent with dramatic and aesthetic potential. Visually, little in the pageant could rival Boudica's astonishing entry in the first scene. Her defeat and death were implied but not shown, leaving the audience not with a sense of failed purpose, but with the impression of Boudica's bravery and heroism.

Yet if there is one town that has truly embraced Boudica as its own it is Colchester, where she was being celebrated before the pageant movement took off, in the form of civic decoration. In 1898, the same year that the plaster model of Boudica was undergoing its trial period on Westminster Bridge in London, the foundation stone was laid for the new town hall in Colchester, described by David Cannadine

---

[73] Described in *St Edmundsbury Pageant, July 8th to 13th, 1907, Book of Words* (Bury St Edmunds, 1907). See also Bartie et al., 'The Bury St Edmunds Pageant', *The Redress of the Past*, http://www.historicalpageants.ac.uk/pageants/1017/, accessed 20 Nov 2017.

[74] 'The Bury St Edmunds Pageant', East Anglian Film Archive, cat. no. 527, http://www.eafa.org.uk/catalogue/527, accessed 30 Nov 2017.

as 'a secular shrine to civic antiquity'.[75] John Belcher, the architect who oversaw the project, left niches for decorations on the exterior of the building, which could be fitted with statues of Colchester's heroes. In 1901, a likeness of Boudica was placed on the West Stockwell Street façade of the building, next to Edward the Elder. In the same year, a stained-glass window was donated to the town hall by the Ladies of Colchester, a committee formed by Mrs Edwin J. Sanders, the town's Mayoress.[76] The stained-glass window was one of a triptych of such windows adorning the Moot Hall, each of which illustrated some aspect of the history of Colchester. The one in which Boudica appeared was dedicated to queens and shows a dignified, even majestic, head and shoulder view of Boudica.

Boudica's appearance in the Colchester pageant further reiterated this link with the town. The pageant, a huge affair involving 3000 performers, was held in the grounds of Castle Park in June 1909, in keeping with Pageant-master Louis Napoleon Parker's belief that locating pageants in sites of local historical importance lent the whole spectacle greater authenticity. Like neighbouring Bury St Edmunds—with which the Essex town had a friendly rivalry—Colchester's pageant was one of Parker's great successes, proving both popular and profitable. It was a distinctive and original pageant, especially insofar as it dwelt longer in the ancient past than many others. Beginning with the story of Kymbeline, Shakespeare's Cymbeline, who was based on a pre-Roman king of Britain known as Cunobelinus, the story moves to AD 43, bending the chronology slightly in order to include the invasion of Britain by Claudius, who is shown taking over Colchester and leaving it in the hands of Suetonius Paulinus. The locals are forced to build a temple for the Emperor, but Paulinus soon grows bored with his assignment and marches off with his troops to terrorize the inhabitants of Mona. This marks a departure for Suetonius who, in many dramas for the stage, is often cast as a hero, or at least a reluctant villain. But his impetuous departure leaves the Britons to abandon their work and seek help from well-known rebel queen, Boudica. In the next scene, which takes place some twenty years later, Boudica and her troops defeat the Romans and are last seen marching off to London. The ensuing battle and defeat are not shown, once again leaving the audience with a more uplifting version of events than the sources could justify.

Once again, Colchester's prominent role in ancient history formed the central message. The temple, abandoned by the Britons, was mentioned in the works of Tacitus and Dio, and was said to have collapsed as an ill omen witnessed by the Romans stationed in Camulodunum. As for Boudica, she is held in great reverence by the Britons. Her somewhat distant presence reinforces this sense of reverence by making her the subject of prophetic chatter before her eventual arrival in AD 61.

---

[75] D. Cannadine, 'The transformation of civic ritual in modern Britain: the Colchester Oyster Feast', *Past & Present*, 94 (1982), 107–30, at 118. See also W. Marriage and W.G. Benham, *The New Town Hall and municipal buildings for Colchester* (Colchester, 1900); D.T.D. Clarke, *The Town Hall Colchester* (Colchester, 1973). For civic architecture and its significance in the period, see I. Morley, *British provincial civic design and the building of Late-Victorian and Edwardian Cities, 1880–1914* (Lampeter, 2008); P. Waller, *Town, City, and Nation* (Oxford, 1983).

[76] Marriage and Benham, *New Town Hall*, 23.

Like the temple of Claudius, Boudica is a unifying figure for these ancient episodes in the pageant. In response to Bury's claim to be the site of the beginning of Boudica's rebellion, the Colchester pageant transplanted it back to the temple at Camulodunum. The Bury pageant was even cited as evidence for Boudica's role in Colchester's history: 'Sainted Edmund's town used her Boadicea in such a way as to suggest that the noble queen would find her "life's fulfilment" on your [Colchester's] classic soil...'[77]

Queen Boudica's relationship with Colchester has proved the most enduring and affectionate of all her local affinities. The town's identification with Camulodunum had been established by appealing to the works of Tacitus and Dio and reiterated over centuries of local historical studies and antiquarianism. Certainly when contrasted with Bury St Edmunds, whose connection to Villa Faustini was largely supposition, Colchester had a more legitimate claim a historical link with Boudica. But this alone does not explain her local heroism. More significant is that Roman Camulodunum had been a colonial settlement peopled by veterans of the Roman army and the location of a cult dedicated to the victories of Emperor Claudius. According to Tacitus in the *Annals*, the military veterans who lived there behaved like petty tyrants towards the native population, who looked to Claudius's temple as 'a citadel of perpetual tyranny'.[78] Thus Boudica's rebellion liberated Colchester, a point made clear in the dialogue of the third scene if the pageant, in which Boudica declares Colchester's freedom before rushing towards London. The battle at Camulodunum, then, could be considered a triumph for Boudica on behalf of the beleaguered Britons, which goes some way towards explaining the esteem with which she is held there. Female pageanteers in Colchester were given medals struck with Queen Boudica's image, and the ceremonial chain of the Mayoress includes a depiction of the famous queen.[79]

Essex and East Anglia remained a stronghold for Boudica during the interwar period. The Pageant of Essex, staged in Ilford in 1932, spread Boudica's story across the county and beyond, placing her in Colchester, a camp outside Verulamium (probably near the Hertfordshire/Essex county border), and to Loughton, in the west of Essex, near Epping Forest. But aside from its studied inclusivity of the entire county, perhaps the most interesting aspect of this pageant is its return to the older conventions of the dramas in which Boudica had appeared in previous centuries. In a departure from the usual pageant mode, the Essex pageant tells the Boudica story over successive episodes, allowing time for a level of characterization and plot development not seen in earlier pageants, and yet familiar in other dramatic forms. It was a history play in miniature, in which the elements of historical romance were somewhat occluded by the weightier historical matter integral to pageants. Boudica's daughters are not named, nor are they a significant element of the story itself. In large part, the story is driven by Boudica's suffering after petitioning the

---

[77] L.N. Parker, *Souvenir book of words of the Colchester Pageant* (Norwich and London, 1909).
[78] Tacitus, *Annals*, 338. See also Ottoway, *Archaeology in British towns*, 46–55.
[79] I owe this information to Ellie Reid of the Ellie Reid Collection, a private collection dedicated to pageant ephemera and the material culture of the pageant movement.

Romans for justice; there are druid seers and Roman priests in the background, predicting victory or defeat for one side or the other. Thus while the ancient British context is fully fleshed out, and Boudica herself is cast as a heroic figure, the dramatic elements are historical far more than they are romantic.

This reflected the unique medium of the historical pageant as educative and entertaining. Of the 1926 Norwich Pageant, and of pageants in general, one newspaper correspondent had complained that 'Cynics may sometimes wonder how it is that nearly every important incident in English history seems to be claimed for its own by every locality that produces a pageant.'[80] However, the liberties taken by local pageant organizers could not dilute the heady blend of factual evidence based on classical sources, local antiquarianism, and, increasingly, archaeological finds, with a varying quality and degree of drama. The combination drew in the crowds and, some Pageantmasters believed, had the effect of educating audiences in their own local and national pasts. The Pageantmaster Nugent Monck said that the aim of the Norwich Pageant of 1926 was to:

> bring home to the citizens of Norwich a sense of continuity with the past. I think the pageant will help us not only to visualise those citizens of former ages, but will make us more appreciative of the beauty of the buildings and of the other relics they have left us. In a word, I hope that no one will be able to witness it without a quickened sense of beauty and a deepened historic understanding.[81]

Figures like Boudica were memorable devices for imparting this combination of aesthetic, historic, and civic education and, even as cynics could and did deride the pageant movement, it was undeniably popular. Moreover, the movement maintained its popularity throughout the twentieth century, challenging the view that the culture of history became less robust after the First World War.[82] As local events of a somewhat ephemeral nature—although they live on in the memories of participants, as well as in more concrete ways, such as public amenities built with pageant funds[83]—they have been overlooked as a demonstration of the phenomenal interest that people took in their local history. Figures like Boudica, who represented antiquity, heroic resistance, and, in the case of Colchester, liberation, were frequent focal points for celebration in the medium. But Boudica's story, and indeed history generally, had long been mined by dramatists, whether for traditional theatrical productions or civic pageantry. As technology moved on, the long reciprocal relationship between drama and history persisted and adapted. Just as pageants, like the 1932 Essex pageant, which pursued dramatic conceit and character development over successive scenes, had many commonalities with older forms of staged history, so too did the new medium of historical film. Arguably, the apotheosis of

---

[80] *The Manchester Guardian*, 19 July 1926.   [81] *The Observer*, 18 July 1926.

[82] See T. Hulme, '"A nation of town criers": civic publicity and historical pageantry in inter-war Britain', *Urban history*, 44(2) (2015), 1–23; A. Bartie, L. Fleming, M. Freeman, T. Hulme, and P. Readman, '"And those who live, how shall I tell their fame?" Historical pageants, collective remembrance, and the First World War, 1919–1939', *Historical research*, 90 (2017), 636–61.

[83] The first modern pageant at Sherborne gave birth to the town's Pageant Gardens, which remain a focal point for community life.

Boudica's appeal to the dramatist and to a mass audience was in her first appearance in the new medium of historical film.[84]

'THE SOUL OF ENGLAND ON THE SCREEN': BOUDICA IN THE AGE OF FILM

Like pageants, historical films were known for their crowd scenes, a spectacle thought to capture the attention of audiences like few others. Battle scenes were also a favourite, and Boudica's story afforded scope for both. The first and only film to be made about Boudica before the Second World War was simply entitled *Boadicea*, a silent film produced by Sinclair Hill and directed by H. Bruce Woolfe. After a production period of nearly a year, it appeared in cinemas in November 1926, accompanied by much fanfare in the press.[85] It starred some of the most prominent actors of the period, including Phyllis Neilson-Terry in the title role, and two younger actresses, Lillian Hall-Davis and Sybil Rhoda, as her daughters.

Unfortunately, the film itself has not survived, but there is extensive promotional material, including a detailed summary of the storyline.[86] The film is of interest for a number of reasons, not least because it shares so much in common with the historical-romantic vision of Boudica's story that had been in circulation since John Fletcher's *Bonduca*. Indeed, promotional material for the films looks very much like the printed plays common in the past: a cast list is divided between Britons and Romans, as in Hopkins's play of 1697. Even names used in previous plays crop up in the film: Caradoc, who had appeared in Fletcher's *Bonduca*, was a 'British Yeoman' in the film. One of Boudica's daughters had been called 'Emmeline' by Richard Glover; in the 1926 *Boadicea*, we find 'Emmelyn'. It is impossible to say whether the writers of the film had looked at any of the published plays of the past, but there are also tantalizing similarities in the film's storyline.

Of course, many of these similarities can be attributed to the historical source base, but there are also interpolations familiar from earlier dramas. In the film, as in the histories, Boudica and her family are left defenceless, though in the film her husband's death is a slow process, portrayed in the early scenes.[87] As Prasutagus lay dying, Suetonius Paulinus' troops descend on Mona, leaving only a handful of its inhabitants alive. One Druid priest, Badwallon—a character likely meant to echo

---

[84] For the origins of film in Victorian popular culture, see J. Kember, *Marketing modernity: Victorian popular shows and early cinema* (Exeter, 2009), though pageants are not discussed.

[85] Dyer notes that the film was a 'rare excursion into the spectacular' in British film, but was eclipsed by the Hollywood epic *Ben-Hur*, released in the same year; see P.J. Dyer, 'From Boadicea to Bette Davis', *Films and Filming*, 5 (1959), 13–33 (non-consecutive), at 14.

[86] This 'press book' is held at the British Film Institute's Reuben library in microfiche slides. The press book contains a detailed plot summary and a list of suggested music for each scene, along with a selection of promotional material, including an array of 'Catch Lines' and 'Preliminary pars' to be used as summaries by individual cinemas. There were also a number of film stills and posters available to order. The material is not paginated. All quotes are from the microfiche copies.

[87] The plot summary derives from 'Boadicea, the story of the film', Boadicea press book, BFI Reuben Library.

Cowper's druid seer—escapes eastward, secure in the belief that he will be able to convince the newly crowned Queen Boudica to help him have revenge on the invaders. As her coronation takes place, her daughter's lover, Marcus, is discovered and accused of spying. Here, as in Fletcher's and Glover's works, Boudica has the opportunity to show mercy on a captured foe; she does so, but only because Emmelyn declares that she loves the Roman soldier. A similar scene also took place in the 1932 Essex pageant, though in that version Boudica's intention to execute her captives is interrupted by the arrival of Suetonius.

The film's scene is familiar from Dio's interpretations of the events, which saw the Romans extract punitive taxes from the Britons, provoking resistance. However, the film, like the dramas, makes this a climactic scene. Boudica is shown slapping the Envoy of Imperial Rome and, at this insult, 'the savage lust and violence' of the conquerors is unleashed. Boudica is ordered to be flogged—a scene the stalwart actress Neilsen-Terry is said to have performed without protection from the blows, in order to achieve a more realistic effect—and her youngest daughter, Blondicca, is dragged away by the Roman soldier, Burrus. Marcus is able to save Emmelyn, but this is little comfort to the horrified queen. As the plot summary describes it, 'a nameless horror' has fallen upon the younger daughter, and an 'awful rage sweeps over the half fainting Queen, as she goes out with her two daughters to face her people'. She delivers a haranguing speech, her daughters at her side, as the Druid priest Badwallon looks on. This, he realizes, is the moment at which 'suffering Britain can bear no more' and, echoing the words of Tennyson, 'is about to hurl its forces into the cause of revenge'.

Fights and crowded battle scenes dominate this latter part of the film. As in the 1907 pageant in Bury St Edmunds, at Colchester, Boudica's troops interrupt a decadent Roman feast, taking their enemies by surprise. After the colony's destruction, Marcus rides to Mona to summon the forces of Suetonius Paulinus eastward. Meanwhile, the audience is treated to the sacking of London by Boudica's troops, before Suetonius arrives on the scene. Ignoring the advice of her more experienced generals (as she often had in the dramas) she pursues her vengeance to its bitter, determined end. As in historical romances of old, Boudica and her daughters drink poison together. Blondicca, who has had enough of suffering, accepts death willingly, while Emmelyn does so reluctantly, and only after witnessing the deaths of her mother and sister—again employing a dynamic familiar from earlier plays. She dies in the arms of her lover, Marcus, who finds her too late. Upon discovering the bodies, the Roman general 'acknowledges courage, and commands his officers to salute the woman who, although an enemy, had died as bravely as she had lived'.

On the whole, the film was well-received by critics, who praised its accuracy, but noted that the film-makers' reluctance to indulge in the more gratuitous excesses made possible by the story did render it somewhat bland:

> This is, we hope, a forerunner of a series of British historical films on a large scale. It sets a good example by keeping close to tradition and making no serious attempt to improve upon history with studio contrivances. The slender love story of a Roman officer and one of Boadicea's daughters does not receive a disproportionate emphasis; the examples of Roman oppression, which in many films would have made an excuse

for elaborate tortures, are given with reasonable restraint; and even the flogging of Boadicea is harmless enough. The picture is, in short, altogether unobjectionable, but that does not save it from being a little dull.[88]

As a presentation of accurate history, the film was on par with most dramatic interpretations of the story, doing little imagining beyond the bounds of what was conventionally accepted in the theatre.

However, there is an additional layer to the film that sheds light on its perceived appeal: that of mass marketing. This material reveals the potential reach of the story, as imagined by the people who made and marketed it. In order to appeal to as large an audience as possible, the makers of *Boadicea* produced a large amount of press material that cast the story in a wide variety of lights, giving cinemas a choice of programme text and imagery. Catch lines—sentence-long summaries for the film's release—were numerous. Some framed the action in general terms, ranging from 'A picture of intense patriotic interest' to 'A dramatic story with a fascinating love romance'. Some focused on Boudica as the film's heroine, such as 'An epic picture of a Warrior Queen's endeavour to defeat oppression' and 'Poignant story of a proud woman and a great Queen'. Others were about national pride: 'Moving drama of a growing nation's fight for freedom', or, somewhat less inspiring, 'An early revolt against unjust taxation'. Yet others focused on the romantic subplot, such as, 'A love story that threads its way through treachery and deceit'.[89] It is striking that these catch lines, written to market the 1926 film, could easily have been applied to Boudica's story as it had been interpreted since Tacitus.

Boadicea was a 'location film', with most scenes shot outside using sets constructed to resemble specific historical locations.[90] This was often emphasized in potential marketing material: 'Boadicea...is a picture of intense interest, in that it was filmed around Colchester, St Albans, London, Dunstable and Tring.'[91] The makers of the film were at pains in this marketing material to show how accurately placed the scenes were. For instance, it was noted that during the filming, 'a complete Roman camp was reconstructed on the Edgware Road, on a site which must have been used by the Legions which defeated Boadicea'. This defeat was filmed 'on the exact site of the historical conflict', an area around the Dunstable downs known as Ivinghoe Valley. To the north-west of St Albans, the downs had never been specifically associated with Boudica in antiquarian literature before the twentieth century, but it was a plausible enough location. Ivinghoe Valley, the pressbook claimed, was located on the old Icknield Way, a Roman road that supposedly ran through the Iceni lands. Indeed, the poet Edward Thomas's book on the ancient road notes that the Icknield Way might have been the avenue of escape taken by the Iceni who fled

---

[88] *Capitol Theatre*, 14 December 1926.
[89] 'Catch lines', 'Boadicea (1926)', Press book, BFI Reuben Library.
[90] R. Low, *The history of the British film, 1918–1929* (London, 1971), 244.
[91] 'Preliminary Pars', 'Boadicea (1926)', Press book, BFI Reuben Library. These were summaries of a few sentences in length, emphasizing various aspects of the film. 'Catch Lines' were effectively shorter versions of 'Preliminary pars'.

after Boudica's defeat, though he did not make any claim to know where the battle was fought.[92] The pressbook, however, provided the film-makers' rationale:

> Ivinghoe Valley completely answers to the description of the battlefield found in the works of the Roman historian, Tacitus, who is our main and only source of information about the life of Boadicea. It is also a gateway from London to the country of the Iceni. Therefore it may well be that this is the actual battle-ground, a surmise strongly reinforced by the fact that many graves of ancient Britons have been found around this valley.[93]

The makers of *Boadicea* were as keen as any pageant committee to set their film in locations legitimated by history and archaeology, but much too was made of the film as a national story. Evidently, there was no perceived contradiction in casting Boudica as both English and British, and claiming the film itself as a triumph of 'national' film-making.[94] Andrew Higson has discussed the emergence of 'heritage film', defined as 'a genre of film which reinvents and reproduces...a national heritage for the screen', as a key component of a particularly British form of cinema.[95] *Boadicea* could be considered an early example of such a film, though the specific subject matter—the ancient Britons—had long invited reflection (or knowing omission of such) on the nature of a 'British' past. So, more precisely, *Boadicea* was the latest example of an old genre—historical drama—in a new medium.

But even the film's appeal to a sense of nationhood owed much to its embeddedness in identifiable locations with which Boudica was bound up. Indeed, it is possible that the film was even intended to appeal directly to audiences in those locations: one catch line, presumably meant for cinemas in Essex, claimed the film was 'The tale of Roman Colchester depicted in a mighty, moving drama'.[96] Even in the most 'national' and wide-reaching of modern media, identification with locality lent greater authenticity to the subject matter, and thus it remained an integral feature—perhaps even gained greater significance. With the possibilities presented by civic organizations, married to a growing awareness of local identity, coupled with the reach of new media, Boudica's story could return to the places to which she had been bound by Tacitus, multiplying and magnifying her significance in the age of mass communication and culture.

Scholarly interpretations of Boudica's nineteenth-century image have been dominated by the belief that she articulated imperial triumphalism or a sense that it was Britain's national destiny to rule entire continents. But this was only one possible interpretation and one which failed to convince all comers. I have sought

---

[92] E. Thomas, *The Icknield Way* (London, 1911), 82.
[93] 'The story of the film', 'Boadicea (1926)', Press book, BFI Reuben Library.
[94] See A. Higson, *Waving the flag: constructing a national cinema in Britain* (Oxford, 1995). Higson, p. 8, notes that this assertion of nationhood in interwar cinema was especially important in light of Hollywood's international standards. For national comparisons, see Dyer, 'Boadicea to Bette Davis'.
[95] Higson, *Waving the flag*, 26. See also S. Harper, *Picturing the past: the rise and fall of the British costume film* (London, 1994). Harper's study begins in 1933, after *Boadicea* was in cinemas. Interestingly, Low notes that a two-reel educational film, *Roman Britain*, was released to accompany *Boadicea*. Low, *British film*, 292.
[96] 'Catch Lines', 'Boadicea (1926)'.

in this chapter to highlight some of the different narratives that Boudica could be and was a part of in the nineteenth and twentieth centuries, and to understand the contrived and yet learned ways in which those localities staked their claims. Historical evidence could be employed and interpreted to place Boudica in Wales, to assert her special importance in Colchester, or to create an authentic and widely appealing screen presence. Although post-nineteenth-century portrayals of Boudica are far from being well-understood—the proliferation of possibilities for contextualization is overwhelming—it is important to recognize how geographically specific her story could be, based on the classical sources and antiquarian interpretations.

By far the most thoroughly realized and significant of these alternative narratives was that which prevailed among some Welsh cultural nationalists, exemplified most powerfully by Morien. The coincidence whereby Queen Boudica could be understood as the first Queen Victoria was particularly appealing to Welsh commentators, who used it to proclaim the significance of Britain's Celtic past, and to challenge the predominance of Anglo-Saxon priority in the period. But even beyond her association with Victoria, Boudica was a figure of unique utility to the Welsh. To lay claim to Boudica was to lay claim to the authentic British antiquity contained in the Tacitean histories—histories which nevertheless provided material for counterarguments. This assertion of Welsh priority was driven simultaneously by a sense of cultural and historical exceptionalism and, to a degree, by the seemingly contradictory desire to reinforce a shared British past. Indeed, Boudica's Welshness was at its most powerful when it was founded on philological and antiquarian evidence and used as a means of asserting unity and equality between the Principality and its neighbour. As much as Morien might try, there was no getting away from Boudica being at least a little bit English.

Meanwhile, even Boudica's identity in England was fragmented, especially as twentieth-century historical culture became much more closely tied to locality, and to the diverse narratives of place that thrived on local traditions. Historians still have much to learn about the importance of the past to a sense of place and identity below the much-examined layer of the nation, whether Welsh or English or otherwise.[97] But Boudica possessed a particular appeal for certain English localities. This is especially evident in pageants, which drew on local historical knowledge, tradition, and archaeology to construct and celebrate locality-specific versions of the national past. For the citizens of Colchester, Boudica was nothing less than a liberator, while in St Albans, left in ruins by the Britons, she was celebrated with somewhat less bombast, at least until recently. This degree of difference suggests a subtle, sustained, and inquisitive engagement with the local past. These variations

---

[97] There is no equivalent in Britain to studies of German states and the idea of nationhood, such as C. Applegate, *A nation of provincials: the German idea of Heimat* (Oxford, 1990) and A. Confino, *The nation as a local metaphor: Wurttemberg, imperial Germany, and national memory, 1871–1918* (London, 1997). Brockliss and Eastwood, *A union of multiple identities*, investigates Irish, English, Welsh, and Scottish forms of cultural nationalism, but has little to say on more localized interpretations of the past. Boudica's Welsh story could be as varied as that of Caractacus, whose name is associated with a number of specific locations in Wales.

in what might be termed the 'national' paradigm of historical culture deserve greater attention than they have hitherto had, especially insofar as they challenge the wholesale dominance of any single 'national canon' in the twentieth century.[98]

But while pageants were produced by and for a local audience, it is striking that even the first film of Boudica's life *Boadicea* (1926) repeatedly asserted its embeddedness in landscapes and localities found in the classical source base. Location filming, even as the specific sites chosen were based in large part on supposition and wishful thinking on the part of the film-makers, gave the story its authenticity. Indeed, all of the cases discussed above—Boudica's identity in Wales, her appeal for English towns, and her appearance in film—all point to the supremacy of authenticity in historical narratives, including through associations with physical locations. As ever, there were different ways of establishing the parameters of historical truth, and, as ever, different genres demanded varying degrees of supporting evidence. Morien, writing his antiquarian tracts, read the landscape as documenting Boudica's presence in Flintshire, dispensing with a verbatim reading of the classical source base. But it was the documentary source base that mattered most for the residents of Verulamium and Camulodunum, where historical pageants were employed to simultaneously entertain and educate. The makers of the Boadicea film employed the notion of authenticity somewhat differently. Rather than make sustained historical argument about their choice of settings, they allowed the settings to speak for themselves. That is, their ability to shoot on location at all gave the Boudica story a greater realism than it could have had on stage. Only historical pageants, with their lavish sets and costumes, could come close to the realistic spectacle of film, but they lacked the narrative depth, shared by both film and drama, which had done much to sustain Boudica in the popular imagination since the seventeenth century.

---

[98] Readman, for instance, suggests that 'historic continuity functioned as an essential repository – perhaps the essential repository – of English (or British) conceptions of nationhood', 'Place of the past', 198. See also M. Grever, 'Plurality, narrative and the historical canon', in M Grever and S. Stuurman (eds), *Beyond the canon: history for the twenty-first century* (Basingstoke, 2007), pp. 31–47.

Conclusion

Every limit is a beginning as well as an ending.[1]

I have waited until this late stage to admit—to myself as much as to the reader—that this book has been something of an experiment. It brings together two ideas that could, perhaps more easily and with greater clarity, have been pursued separately: one, the idea of history as historical culture, and the other, the sustained study of representations of Queen Boudica over four centuries and more. By conducting this experiment, I have in part sought to persuade historians of history to look beyond the discipline to the ways historical knowledge percolated outside its confines. Simultaneously, and perhaps more urgently, I have attempted to put the case to cultural historians that they should look beyond mere 'representations' and their immediate function as part of hegemonic discourses, to the more thoughtful human stories behind cultural production, and the subtle interplay between fact and fiction in narratives of history. Moreover, this study has sought to move between and beyond genres and disciplines without losing sight of the unique methodologies and vocabularies that have made up the idea of something called 'history'. In this way, I have tried to tell a story that gives due regard to continuity as much as to change. Boudica's example has acted as a constant refrain, but it cannot be convincingly argued that because she is an inheritance from an historical source base she has been portrayed the same way and for the same reasons everywhere at all times. And yet it would be equally unconvincing to say that historical representations are so ever-changing and so distant from historical originals that they do not share an essence or echo across time.

It has become clear to me that in order to tell one story—that of historical culture—it is necessary that the other story—that revolving around Boudica's representation—must remain in a state of irresolution. There is no way of reconciling with each other all the different individual images or portrayals of Boudica without imposing a degree of order which would render the whole exercise synthetic in the most negative sense of the word. Yet even if a single monumental idea of Boudica remains elusive, there are nevertheless conclusions we can draw about Boudica *qua* Boudica. One is that she had a greater role in early modern political culture than has previously been acknowledged—which is to say she most certainly had one, albeit minor. Edmund Bolton's extensive study of her as a dangerous rebel shows

---

[1] G. Eliot, *Middlemarch* (Oxford, 1996), 779.

her utility as an historical example for the early modern present, but one which nonetheless required extensive framing and bolstering through Bolton's antiquarian tinkerings. Related to this is another important point, that her origin in Tacitus' histories lent her a much greater significance in the period than has hitherto been suggested. This, I have argued, challenges previously held views of Boudica as a mere synecdoche for female power, whose fame rose and fell with the life and death of Elizabeth I.

Indeed, her femininity made her more rather than less prominent in British historical culture. She did not disappear from public view in the early modern period; rather, she entered the pantheon of 'great women' in the work of popularizing historians such as Nathaniel Crouch and Thomas Heywood, and her femininity made her story a powerful parable for the perilousness of partisanship in the historical culture of the eighteenth century. The demands imposed on her by motherhood were in tension with her public duty as a queen and it was in this dichotomy that playwrights and poets found a most fruitful area for dramatic exploitation—one which ensured that Boudica remained a consistent presence on stage. Her motherhood and the harrowing experiences of her daughters were also, as we have seen, aspects of the story on which historical writers could elaborate in order to infuse their narratives of ancient Britain with pathos and emotional interest, in an attempt, I think, to draw in the same audiences for reading as for watching history on stage.

Finally, I have sought to question the notion that Boudica was a Victorian 'imperial icon' in the straightforward or monolithic sense of being 'iconic'. Even if we have been left with only the most mute and solid of testimonies to her Victorian identity, she was, in fact, a palimpsest. For Thomas Thornycroft she represented a personal struggle against the domestic artistic establishment and the creative influences he considered 'alien'. Boudica's placement on Westminster Bridge also reflected a longer relationship that the queen had had with London and with various outlying areas of the city, especially in the north and east. Indeed, although Victorian imperialism is one significant context in which Boudica can be read, that this was the only or even the predominant context for Boudica's popularity in the later nineteenth century is worth questioning, especially in light of her posthumous life as a Welsh heroine, and as an illustrious figure in St Albans, Colchester, and the county of Essex, among other places.

Thus while we could see this dissolution of Boudica's iconicity into multiplicity as a limitation, or even a failure of the approach taken here, there is another way of viewing matters. Boudica has indeed been depicted in disparate ways, some of them contradictory, many ambiguous, but rather than see this as problematic or as demanding the imposition of a rigid framework or trajectory, we might reframe it as an immanent part of the iterative and dialogic nature of history-making: that is of, history as a form of broad-based, organic cultural production. Interpretations of the past derive meaning from their identification with an idea of 'history', which is itself an elusive concept but one which possesses enough integrity to have been employed by generations of human beings as a means to both critique and legitimate representations of the malleable-because-interpretable past. We have seen that even very different forms of historical representation—drama and factual narrative prose, for instance—shared, and often were expected to share, a common approach to their subject matter. This was evident even—indeed, especially—when the fictive and factual elements of historical representation were in tension; that tension was fruitful, forming what we might think of as a contradictory but nevertheless harmonious whole: an idea of history.

The shifting definitional and descriptive limits of what is and was recognized and recognizable as 'history' are set and challenged and set again by generations of human actors. But these limits, I have argued, have retained a degree of similarity over time and across various forms of cultural production, from chronicle to film. Some of these invite further research. In particular, notions of human nature—put simply, what humans are likely to do in given circumstances—have emerged as a common concern of historical writers in both drama and prose. This is, I think, an important point, but one which requires further study and elucidation in regards to works of popular history, especially in the eighteenth century, a time when human nature itself was a potent preoccupation. Indeed, in a general sense, our understanding of history's long-standing relationship with drama remains somewhat murky and overshadowed by the significance of the novel. Moreover, market forces in historical production in the same period demand further investigation. 'Serious' Enlightenment histories have garnered a huge amount of scholarly attention, but we know far less about the way the average reader engaged with the very large number of lesser-known histories written from the late seventeenth century to the end of the eighteenth. In fact, we have yet to fully grasp the historical culture of the eighteenth century in any degree of fine-grain detail, especially compared to our knowledge of earlier and later periods.

In short, by acknowledging the malleability of the past, but bearing in mind the constraints on interpretative latitude that are immanent in historical production—be it 'hack' history, historical drama, or 'parasitical' biography—we open up new areas of research that could shed light on the depth, breadth, and character of historical knowledge in the past, especially amongst the wider public. This, I have argued, requires a different way of approaching the history of history. What might be termed a question of discipline—is Queen Boudica rightly the subject of literary studies, history, antiquarianism, political thought?—is also a problem of chronology: the latter gives rise to the former as the realness of time's passage chafes against the artifice of vocabulary and intellectual fashion. The further back in time one goes, the less familiar, and less rigidly distinguished, the disciplinary terrain becomes. This renders the history of ideas both difficult and necessary. Disciplines, especially when moored to institutional structures, delineated by funding bodies, and enshrined in practice as well as theory, have a tendency to shrink rather than expand the fields in which scholars are comfortable doing their work. Ideas, however, float across chronological, disciplinary, generic, and even geographic boundaries, and the scholar who wishes to keep up must be constantly dashing in all directions, infringing on territory that might rightfully belong to another tribe. Such free-range wandering and the incidental foraging that goes with it is not, I think, to be discouraged, nor seen as inherently less rigorous. An idea of history persists, and it is as valid in a history department as it is in—to take a random example—a department of fashion design; it belongs to the family historian as much as it does the telly-don.

But this shared notion of history should not allow us to lose sight of what makes history unique among the kinds of stories human beings tell. This brings us to a current debate in historical studies, which centres on the place of history and the historical profession in contemporary public life. Recently, Jo Guldi and David Armitage issued *The History Manifesto*, a call for historians to embrace the large time spans and momentous questions that have been lost in the face of what they see as the profession's overall short-termism; such an approach, they argue, is made more manageable by the use of 'big data'. Furthermore, the historian who takes this expansive viewpoint would be better placed to advise governments, NGOs, and the voluntary sector on the direction of public policy.[2] Thus *The History Manifesto* admits that the historical profession is in need of some rehabilitation, a position which echoes a much earlier, and in some ways more challenging claim made by Hayden White in 2005:

> the salvation of professional historiography – if it deserves salvation at all... consists in reversing or rather amending our notions of history's importance as a field of study, the revision of history's so-called 'methodology,' and most importantly a return to the intimate relationship it had with art, poetry, rhetoric, and ethical reflection prior to professionalization and embarkation on the impossible task of becoming 'scientific' in the modern sense of the term.[3]

White's provocative statement here echoes to a degree the argument of his earlier work, in which he suggested that '...the current generation of historians will be called upon to...expose the historically conditioned character of the historical discipline, to preside over the dissolution of history's claim to autonomy among the disciplines, and to aid in the assimilation of history to a higher kind of intellectual inquiry which, because it is founded on an awareness of the similarities between art and science, rather than their differences, can be properly designated as neither.'[4]

Yet despite the hand-wringing of White, Guldi, and Armitage, it is a matter of debate whether the historical profession is suffering so badly that it demands saving (and indeed, the nature of its malady is somewhat unclear). But salvation, if it is required, need not be achieved solely on the basis of slavering enthusiasm for engaging with policymakers, or the fashionable new orthodoxy of 'big data' and number crunching. Rather, history's salvation—or renewal, or simply maintenance—could come as a consequence of extant but too-often overlooked relations with the imaginative arts, poetry, rhetoric, and dramatic re-enactment—not, or not only, as

---

[2] J. Guldi and D. Armitage, *The history manifesto* (Cambridge, 2014). Also see the response from D. Cohen and P. Mandler, 'The history manifesto: a critique', *American Historical Review*, 120 (2015), 530–42.
[3] H. White, 'A reply to Dirk Moses', 335. The exchange was published in 'The public relevance of historical studies', *History and Theory*, 44 (Oct 2005), 333–8.
[4] H. White, *Tropics of discourse*, 29.

subjects of historical study, but as consciously integrated aspects of historical production, of teaching, and of writing.

It is almost certainly necessary, I think, for professional historians to expand their notion of 'history' in the present, and acknowledge its fluidity today, while perhaps rolling back on some of the more extreme consequences of postmodernism. Hayden White elsewhere hints at another way in which historians can contribute to present society, by 'humaniz[ing] experience'. My own sense is that part of humanizing experience lies in acknowledging the complexity of human actors, in the past and in the present, rather than persisting in ascribing simplistic motivations or passive modes of reception to people in the past. My appeal to White then is highly selective. I cannot agree with him that 'we require a history that will educate us to discontinuity more than ever before; for discontinuity, disruption, and chaos is our lot'.[5] Chaos may well be our lot, but the historian's desire for order is merely a human one, and it seems impossible to 'humanize experience' while somehow existing outside it. There is something to be gained from taking a more mature attitude to continuity, and to the individual's place in culture and its history.

Although scepticism is natural and necessary, continuity is not, as inventors of tradition might argue, specious by its very nature. Historical interpretations are not created in a vacuum, nor are they created equally. As we have seen, critical opinion tended to note inaccuracy, whether in factual history or fictive depictions of human behaviour; imaginative licence was by no means a blanket defence, and the outright politicization or manipulation of the past to suit the present has long been looked on with disdain. But even that tense conversation is just that: a conversation, and only one of many. These conversations between and about past and present are, to some extent, recoverable, and insofar as it is possible there is value in attempting to recover them and in attempting to understand them both within and outwith their immediate societal context. As R.G. Collingwood put it in his masterful *Speculum Mentis*: 'My mind is obviously a product of society, and conversely the society I know is the product of my mind... The absolute mind, then, unites the differences of my mind and other people's, but not as the abstract universal unites: rather as the concrete universal of history unites... It lives in its entirety in every individual and every act of every individual, yet not indifferently... expressing itself in every individual uniquely and irreplaceably.'[6] Whatever one might think of Collingwood's more idealist (one might even say mystic) sensibilities, the spirit of the remark is worth reflecting on, not least for historians of culture.

Narratives of continuity should remind us of the individuals that populate them, and of the long human story that preceded ours. An allowance for the possibility of continuity steels us in our duty—if that is not too strong a word—to understand each other as individuals, not as ciphers for a cultural moment, or stereotypes of

---

[5] Ibid., 50. See also S. Cohen, *Historical culture: on the recoding of an academic discipline* (London, 1989), for a radical interpretation, but one typical of a cultural moment in late twentieth-century academia.

[6] R.G. Collingwood, *Speculum Mentis, or the map of knowledge* (Oxford, 1970 [first edn 1924]), 299.

a recognizable set of rarefied identities; surely that is an exercise worth performing in our everyday lives, as much as in our work. In short, a sense of the possibility of continuity encourages us to attempt, as Collingwood long ago argued we should, to think the thoughts of others. This empathy with the past might in turn help to instil in us a degree of caution and humility in the face of our unasked-for grandeur as rulers of the transient present. It could help us not only to humanize the past and present, but to think in the long term about our own role in time.

Bibliography

ARCHIVAL SOURCES

British Film Institute, Reuben Library
British Library, Addisson MS
British Library, Harley MS
British Library, Lansdowne MS, Hicks Collection
British Library, Royal MS
Churchill Centre, Cambridge, Bull Papers
East Anglian Film Archive
Forster Collection, National Art Library, Tate Gallery
Kent County Council Archives, Coll. U269Z26
Leeds Museum & Galleries (Henry Moore Institute Archive), Papers of the Thornycroft family (collection reference: 1986.4)
London Metropolitan Archives, General Purposes Committee
London Metropolitan Archives, Highway Committee
London Metropolitan Archives, London County Council, Presented Papers
London Metropolitan Archives, Parks and Open Spaces Subcommittees
Parliamentary Archives, Fine Arts Commission

PUBLISHED SOURCES

Anderson, R., *The works of the British poets, with prefaces, biographical and critical*, 14 vols (London, 1795–1807), vol. 11, 467–82.
Anon., *Memories of Venutius and Cartismandua, extracted from the most authentic accounts, and explaining the Historical parts of the Tragedy called The Briton* (London, 1723).
Anon., *Beauty's triumph or the superiority of the Fair Sex invincibly proved* (London, 1745).
Anon., *A Short History of Boadicea, The British Queen, Being the Story on which the new tragedy now in rehearsal at the Theatre Royal Drury Lane is Founded. Very proper to be bound with the play* (London, 1753).
Anon., *Female Revenge or the British Amazon: Exemplified in the life of Boadicia* (London, 1753).
Anon., *The rational amusement: comprehending a collection of letters on a great variety of subjects, serious, entertaining, moral, diverting and instructive* (London, 1754).
Anon. review of Tobias Smollett's *History of England, Monthly Review*, June 1757, XVI, 530–6.
Anon., *Book of the Pageant of Gwent* (Abergavenny, 1913).
Ashdown, C.H., 'The St Albans Pageant.' July 15th to July 20th 1907. Book of the words and lyrics. Text and Lyrics by Charles H. Ashdown' (St Albans, 1907).
Aske, J., *Elizabethan Triumphans* (London, 1588).
Aubrey, J., *Brief Lives*, ed. R. Barber (Woodbridge, 2004).
Barker, F., *Boadicea* (London, 1859).
Baxter, J., *A new and impartial history of England* (London, 1796).
Bell's British Theatre; consisting of the most esteemed English plays, Vol. II (London, 1797).
'Boadicea, Queen of Britain overthrowing her enemies…'(1820), British Museum Satires. 1983, 0305.38.

Bolton, E., *Nero Caesar, or monarchie deprav'd* (London, 1624, 1627).
Bolton, E., *Hypercritica, or a rule of judgement for writing or reading our histories*, published in N. Triveti, *Annalium Continuatio ut et... Edmundi Boltoni Hypercritica* (Oxford, 1722).
Bruce, H.A., *Gwent and Dyfed Eisteddfod, 1834; the prize translation of the Welsh ode on the British Druids by Taliesen Williams* (London, 1835).
Caesar, *Gallic Wars*, trans. H.J. Edwards, Loeb Classical Library Online (Cambridge, MA, 2014).
Carte, T., *A Collection of Several Papers published by Mr Thomas Carte in relation to his History of England* (London, 1744).
Carte, T., *A General history of England*, 2 vols (London, 1747), Vol. I.
Coley, W.B. (ed.), *The Jacobite's Journal and related writings* (Oxford, 1974).
Collingwood, R.G., *Roman Britain* (London, 1923).
Collingwood, R.G., 'Review: *Voadica: a romance of the Roman Wall*', *Classical Review*, 42 (1928).
Cousser, J.S., *A Sereneta to be represented on the Birth-day of the Most Serene Anne* (Dublin, 1709).
Cowley, C., *Ladies History of England* (London, 1780).
The poems of William Cowper, 6 vols, ed. J.D. Baird and C. Ryskamp (Oxford, 1980), Vol. I.
'Epitome of Book LXII', *Dio's Roman History*, ed. E. Cary (London, 1961).
Dio: the Julio-Claudians. Selections from books 58–63 of the Roman History, ed. J. Edmonson (London, 1992).
Dunn, F.S., 'The un-historical novel', *The Classical Journal*, 22 (1927), 345–54.
Echard, L., *History of England* (London, 1707).
'Elfynydd' [James Kenward], *'A poem of English sympathy with Wales', written for the Great National Eisteddfod of 1858 and 'Llangollen', a Poem, upon the same occasion* (Birmingham, 1858).
Evans, T., *Drych y prif oesoedd (The mirror of past ages)* (Shrewsbury, 1716).
Freeman, E.A., *The history of the Norman Conquest of England*, 6 vols (Oxford, 1867–79).
Freeman, E.A., 'Colonia Camulodunum', *Macmillan's Magazine*, 36 (1877), 119–34.
The Letters of David Garrick, ed. D.M. Little, G.M. Kahrl, and P. DeK. Wilson (London, 1963).
'G.L.', *A compendious history of the monarchs of England from King William I* (London, 1712).
Giles, J.A. (ed. and trans.), *The works of Gildas and Nennius* (London, 1841).
Gillingwater, E., *An historical and descriptive account of St. Edmund's Bury* (London, 1804).
Glover, R., *Boadicia, a tragedy* (London, 1753).
Granville, C., *A synopsis of the troubles and miseries of England during the space of 1800 years* (London, 1747).
'Griffith', *The Welsh question and Druidism* (London, 1887).
Gurdon, T., *History of the high court of parliament* (London, 1731).
Guthrie, W., *A general history of England from the invasion of the Romans under Julius Caesar...* (London, 1744).
Hall, Mrs M., *The queens before the Conquest*, 2 vols (London, 1854).
Hannah, I.C., *Voadica, a romance of the Roman Wall* (London, 1928).
Hays, M., *Female biography; or memoirs of illustrious and celebrated women, of all ages and countries*, 6 vols (London, 1803).
Heywood, T., *The two most worthy and notable histories which remaine unmained to posterity; the Conspiracie of Cateline, undertaken against the government of the Senate of Rome, and The warre with Jugurth* (London, 1608).

Heywood, T., *Gynaikeion or, Nine bookes of various history. Concerninge women inscribed by ye names of ye nine Muses* (London, 1624).

Heywood, T., *Exemplary lives and memorable acts of nine of the most worthy women of the world* (London 1640).

Higgins, B., *A short view of the English history* (London, 1723).

Holinshed, R., *The firste volume of the Chronicles of England, Scotlande, and Irelande* (London, 1577).

Hopkins, C., *Boadicea, Queen of Britain, a tragedy, as acted by His Majesty's Servants at the Theatre in Lincolns-Inn-fields* (London, 1697).

Hume, D., *History of England, from the invasion of Julius Caesar to the revolution in 1688*, 6 vols (London, 1762).

Johnson, J., *Brave Women: who have been distinguished for heroic actions and noble virtues, etc.* (Edinburgh, 1875).

Lindsay, C., *Boadicea: a tragedy* (London, 1857).

Lipsius, J., *Two books Of Constancie written in Latine by Iustus Lipsius*, trans. J. Stradling (New Brunswick, NJ, 1939).

'M', Book review: I.C. Hannah, *Voadica: a romance of the Roman Wall*', *Scottish Historical Review*, 25 (1928).

Mac Carte, Duncan, *A Letter to John Trot-Plaid, Esq. Author of the Jacobite Journal, concerning Mr Carte's General History of England, By Duncan Mac Carte, a Highlander* (London, 1748).

Marriage, W., and W.G. Benham, *The New Town Hall and municipal buildings for Colchester* (Colchester, 1900).

Massinger, P., T. Middleton, and W. Rowley, *The Old Law, together with an exact and perfect catalogue of all the playes... more exactly printed then ever before* (London, 1656).

Mills, C., *A letter to Richard Glover on occasion of his tragedy of Boadicia* (London, 1754).

Complete prose Works of John Milton, 8 vols, ed. D.M. Wolfe et al. (London, 1953–82).

Morgan, O. (B.B.D.), 'Morien', 'Dedication', *The light of Britannia: the mysteries of ancient Druidism revealed* (Cardiff, 1893).

Morgan, O., *Boadicea: her life, battles, and death near Rhyl* (Pontypridd, 1913).

Morgan, O., *The battles of Wales* (Liverpool, 1920).

Owen Pughe, W., *The Cambrian biography or historical notes of the celebrated men among the ancient Britons* (London, 1803).

Owen, Mrs O.F., *The heroines of history* (London, 1854).

Parker, L.N., *Souvenir book of words of the Colchester Pageant* (Norwich and London, 1909).

Pemberton, H., *Some few reflections on the Tragedy of Boadicia* (London, 1753).

Pennant, T., *The history of the parishes of Whiteford and Holywell* (London, 1796).

Powell, G., *Bonduca or, the British heroine, a tragedy, etc. [Altered from the play generally attributed to Beaumont and Fletcher, but more probably by Fletcher alone]* (London, 1696).

Preston, E. 'Review of I.C. Hannah, *Voadica: a romance of the Roman Wall*', *The Classical Journal*, 24 (1928), 143–4.

Prichard, T.J.L., *The heroines of Welsh history; comprising memories and biographical notices of the celebrated women of Wales...* (London, 1854).

Priddle, L., *The history of the 'Boadicea group'* (London, 1902).

Rapin de Thoyras, P. de, *The History of England from the invasion of the Romans to the end of the reign of William the Conqueror*, trans. N. Tindal (London, 1725).

R.B. [Nathaniel Crouch], *Female Excellency, or the Ladies Glory, illustrated in the worthy lives and memorable actions of Nine Famous Women, who have been renowned either for Virtue or valour in several Ages of the world* (London, 1683).

R.B. [Nathaniel Crouch], *England's monarchs* (1685).
R.B. [Nathaniel Crouch], *A natural history of the principality of Wales* (1695).
R.B. [Nathaniel Crouch], *History of the Kingdom of Scotland* (1696).
Read, C.H., 'Account of the opening of…"Boadicea's Grave"', *Proceedings of the Society of Antiquaries of London*, 15 (22 November 1894), 233–55.
Read, C.H., 'Presidential Address', *The Journal of the Anthropological Institute of Great Britain and Ireland*, 31 (4 February 1901).
Read, C.H., 'Anniversary Address', *Proceedings of the Society of Antiquaries* (27 April 1911), 428–47.
Rhodes, T., *The patriot queen; or female heroism* (Coventry, 1808).
Rhoscomyl, O., *Flame-bearers of Welsh history* (Merthyr Tydil, 1905).
Rider, W., *A comment on Boadicia, with remarks on Mill's Letter* (London, 1754).
St John, H., and D. Mallet (eds), 'Remarks on the history of England', in *The works of the Right Honourable Henry St John, Lord Viscount Bolingbroke*, 5 vols (London, 1777), Vol. 1.
Salmon, T., *Modern History or the present state of all nations* (London, 1732), Vol. XVI.
Seller, J., *The History of England* (London, 1696).
Sidney, P., *An apology for poetry (or the defence of poesy)*, ed. R.W. Maslen (Manchester, 2002).
Smollett, T., *Complete history of England*, 5 vols (London, 1757).
Smollett, T., *Plan of the Complete History of England* (London, 1757).
Life and letters of Tobias Smollett (1721–1771), ed. L. Melville (London, 1926).
The letters of Tobias Smollett, ed. L.M. Knapp (Oxford, 1970).
Speed, J., *The history of Great Britaine* (London, 1611).
Squire, S., *Remarks upon Mr. Carte's Specimen of his General History of England very proper to be read by all such as are Contributors to that great Work* (London, 1748).
Tacitus, *The Annals*, trans. A.J. Church and W.J. Brodribb (Mineola, NY, 2006 [first edition 1869]).
Tacitus, *Agricola and Germania* (London, 2009).
The letters of Alfred, Lord Tennyson, 3 vols, ed. C.Y. Lang and E.F. Shannon Jr (Oxford, 1987).
Thomas, E., *The Icknield Way* (London, 1911).
Todd, H., *A sermon preach'd before the honourable House of Commons* (London, 1711).
Townson, E.W. et al., 'St Albans and its Pageant, being the official souvenir of the pageant held July, 1907, With contributions by the Very Rev. Dean Lawrence, Rev. J.V. Bullard, Mr. C.H. Ashdown, and Mr. W.G. Marshall. The whole arranged by Ernest W. Townson' (London and St Albans, 1907).
Trevelyan, M., *Britain's greatness foretold: the prediction fulfilled*, with introduction by E. Collins (London, 1901).
Walford, E., *Greater London: a narrative of its history its people and its places* (London, 1894), Vol. I.
Williams, R., *The Welsh nonconformists memorial; or Cambro-British biography…*, ed. J. Evans (London, 1820).
Woodward, B.B., *The history of Wales from the earliest times to its final incorporation with the kingdom of England* (London, 1853).

NEWSPAPERS AND PERIODICALS

The Art Journal
The Baptist Magazine

La Belle Assemblée; or, Bell's Court and Fashionable Magazine
Birmingham Daily Post
Black & White
Boys of England
The Bristol Mercury
Carnarvon and Denbigh Herald and North and South Wales Independent
The Children's Treasury
Daily Courant
Daily Post
The Echo
English Illustrated Magazine
Every Week
Fraser's Magazine
Girl's Own Paper
Glasgow Herald
The Globe
The Guardian
The Irish Independent
The Ladies' Treasury
The Lady's Newspaper
The London Argus
London Daily News
The London Literary Pioneer
Manchester Courier and Lancashire General Advertiser
The Manchester Guardian
Monthly Review
The Morning Post
The New York Times
North Devon Journal
The North Wales Chronicler and Advertiser for the Principality
The Oberlin Alumni Magazine
The Observer
St James Gazette
The Scotsman
The Spectator
The Standard
The Times
Western Daily Press
Western Mail
Western Mail
Whitehall Evening Post

SECONDARY LITERATURE

Adler, E., 'Late Victorian and Edwardian views of Rome and the nature of "defensive imperialism"', *International Journal of the Classical Tradition*, 15 (2008), 187–216.

Adler, E. *Valorizing the barbarians: enemy speeches in Roman historiography* (Austin, TX, 2011).

Allen, B., *Francis Hayman* (London, 1987).

Allan, D., *Philosophy and politics in later Stuart Scotland: Neostoicism, culture, and ideology in the age of crisis, c. 1540–1690* (East Lothian, 2000).

Anderson, E.H., *Eighteenth-century authorship and the play of fiction: novels and the theatre, Haywood to Austen* (New York, 2009).

Ankersmit, F., 'Finding meaning in memory: a methodological critique of collective memory studies', *History and theory*, 41 (2002), 179–97.

Ankersmit, F., 'The Three levels of Sinnbildung in historical writing: language and historical experience', in J. Rüsen (ed.), *Meaning and representation in history* (Oxford, 2006) pp. 108–22.

Ankersmit, F., *Meaning, truth and reference in historical representation* (Ithaca, NY, 2012).

Applegate, C., *A nation of provincials: the German idea of Heimat* (Oxford, 1990).

Arber, E. (ed.), *The term Catalogues, 1668–1709* (London, 1903), vol. I.

Armitage, D., 'A Patriot for Whom?: The afterlives of Bolingbroke's Patriot King', *Journal of British Studies*, 36(4) (1997), 397–418.

Assmann, A., *Cultural memory and western civilization: functions, media, archives* (Cambridge, 2012).

Atkins, G. (ed.), *Making and remaking saints in nineteenth-century Britain* (Manchester, 2016).

Avery, E.L. (ed.), *The London stage, 1660–1800*, Part II (1700–29) (Carbondale, IL, 1962).

Axon, W.E.A., 'Burton, Robert or Richard (1632?–1725?), miscellaneous author', *Oxford Dictionary of National Biography Archive* (1886), http://www.oxforddnb.com/view/olddnb/52645, accessed 23 Nov 2017.

Backscheider, P.R., 'Powell, George (1668?–1714)', *Oxford Dictionary of National Biography* (Oxford, 2004), http://www.oxforddnb.com/view/article/22647, accessed 8 Aug 2017.

Baines, B., *Thomas Heywood* (Boston, MA, 1984).

Baines, P., 'Glover, Richard (1712–1785)', *Oxford Dictionary of National Biography* (Oxford, 2004; online edn, Sept 2013), http://www.oxforddnb.com/view/article/10831, accessed 8 Aug 2017.

Baker, G.P., *Tiberius Caesar: Emperor of Rome* (New York, 1928).

Baldwin, E., L.M. Clopper, and D. Mills, *Cheshire including Chester vol. I, Records of Early English Drama* (London, 2007).

Barczewski, S., *Myth and national identity in nineteenth-century Britain: the legends of King Arthur and Robin Hood* (Oxford, 2000).

Bartie, A., P. Caton, L. Fleming, M. Freeman, T. Hulme, A. Hutton, and P. Readman, *The Redress of the Past*, http://www.historicalpageants.ac.uk/pageants/, accessed 10 Aug 2017.

Bartie, A., L. Fleming, M. Freeman, T. Hulme, A. Hutton, and P. Readman, 'St Albans Pageant 1953: A Masque of the Queens', The Redress of the Past, http://www.historicalpageants.ac.uk/pageants/1205/, accessed 10 Aug 2017.

Bartie, A., L. Fleming, M. Freeman, T. Hulme, and P. Readman, '"And those who live, how shall I tell their fame?" Historical pageants, collective remembrance, and the First World War, 1919–1939', *Historical research*, 90 (2017), 636–61.

Beall, H.S., 'Historical fiction on classical themes: revised list, 1967', *The Classical World*, 61 (1967), 53–66.

Beard, M., 'Officers and gentlemen? Roman Britain and the British Empire', in A. Swenson and P. Mandler (eds), *From plunder to preservation: Britain and the heritage of empire, c. 1800–1914* (Oxford, 2013), pp. 49–62.

Berger, S., 'Professional and popular historians, 1800–1900–2000', in B. Korte and S. Paletschek (eds), *Popular history now and then, international perspectives* (London, 2012).

Bergeron, D.M., *Thomas Heywood's pageants: a critical edition* (London, 1986).
Biddiss, M., and M. Wyke (eds), *The Uses and Abuses of Antiquity* (New York, 1999).
Black, J., 'Ideology, history, xenophobia and the world of print in eighteenth-century England', in J. Black and J. Gregory (eds), *Culture, politics and society in Britain, 1660–1800* (Manchester, 1991), pp. 184–216.
Blackburn, T.H., 'The date and evolution of Edmund Bolton's *Hypercritica*', *Studies in Philology*, 63(2) (1966), 196–202.
Blackburn, T.H., 'Edmund Bolton's The Cabanet Royal: a belated reply to Sidney's Apology for Poetry', *Studies in the Renaissance*, 14 (1967), 159–71.
Blair, A., *The theatre of nature: Jean Bodin and Renaissance science* (Princeton, NJ, and Chichester, 1997).
Boase, T.S.R., 'The decoration of the New Palace of Westminster, 1841–1863' *Journal of the Warburg and Courtauld Institutes*, 17(3/4) (1954), 319–58.
Booth, A., *How to make it as a woman: collective biography of women from Victoria to the present* (London, 2004).
Booth, A., *Collective Biographies of Women*, University of Virginia Library, http://womensbios.lib.virginia.edu/, accessed 23 Nov 2017.
Boucé, P.-G., 'A note on Smollett's *Continuation of the Complete History of England*', *Review of English Studies* (1969).
Boucher, D., 'Ambiguity and originality in the context of discourse', in W.J. Van der Dussen and L. Rubinoff(eds), *Objectivity, method and point of view: essays in the philosophy of history* (Leiden, 1991), pp. 22–46.
Bradford, A.T., 'Stuart absolutism and the "utility" of Tacitus', *Huntington Library Quarterly*, 46 (1983), 127–55.
Braund, S. (ed.), *Seneca: De Clementia* (Oxford 2009).
Brook, D., *From playhouse to printing house* (Cambridge, 2000).
Brooke, C., *Philosophic pride: Stoicism and political thought from Lipsius to Rousseau* (Princeton, 2012).
Bryden, I., *Reinventing King Arthur: the Arthurian legends in Victorian culture* (Aldershot, 2005).
Bull, P., *Bulls in the Meadows* (London, 1957).
Burgess, G., *Absolute monarchy and the Stuart constitution* (London, 1996).
Burke, P., 'Tacitism', in T.A. Dorey (ed.), *Tacitus* (London, 1962), pp. 149–71.
Burke, P., 'A survey of the popularity of ancient historians, 1450–1700', *History and Theory*, 5 (1966), 135–52.
Burrow, J.W., *A liberal descent: Victorian historians and the English past* (Cambridge, 1981).
Burstein. M.E.,'From good looks to good thoughts: popular women's history and the invention of modernity, ca. 1830–1870', *Modern Philology*, 97 (1999), 46–75.
Burstein, M.E., 'Unstoried in history: early histories of women (1652–1902) in the Huntington Library collections', *The Huntington Library Quarterly*, 64(3/4) (2001), 469–500.
Butterfield, H., *Man on his past: a history of historical scholarship* (London, 1969).
Caine, B., *Biography and history* (Basingstoke, 2010).
Cannadine, D., 'The transformation of civic ritual in modern Britain: the Colchester Oyster Feast', *Past & Present*, 94 (1982), 107–30.
Cannadine, D. (ed.), *What is history now?* (Basingstoke, 2002).
Carlyle, E.I., 'Thornycroft, Sir John Isaac (1843–1928)', rev. Alan G. Jamieson, http://www.oxforddnb.com/view/article/36512 accessed 8 Aug 2017.
Carr, D., 'The reality of history', in J. Rüsen (ed.), *Meaning and representation in history* (Oxford, 2006), pp. 123–36.

Carr, E.H., *What is History?* (London, 1961).
Cassirer, E., *The logic of the humanities*, translated with foreword by C. Smith Howe (New Haven and London, 1961).
Clark, A.M., *Thomas Heywood, playwright and miscellanist* (Oxford, 1931).
Clark, G., 'Archaeology and the state', *Antiquity*, 32 (1934), 414–28.
Clarke, D.T.D., *The Town Hall Colchester* (Colchester, 1973).
Clegg, C.S., 'Renaissance play-readers, ordinary and extraordinary', in M. Straznicky (ed.), *The book of the play: playwrights, stationers, and readers in early modern England* (Boston, MA, 2006), pp. 23–38.
Cohen, D., and P. Mandler, 'The history manifesto: a critique', *American Historical Review*, 120 (2015), 530–42.
Cohen, S., *Historical culture: on the recoding of an academic discipline* (London, 1989).
Colledge, J.J., and B. Warlow, *Ships of the Royal Navy* (London, 2003).
Collingwood, R.G., *Speculum mentis, or the map of knowledge* (Oxford, 1970).
Collingwood, R.G., *The idea of history* (Oxford, 1980 [first edn1946]).
Collini, S., 'Seeing a specialist: the humanities as academic disciplines', *Past & Present*, 229 (2015), 271–81.
Confino, A., *The nation as a local metaphor: Wurttemberg, imperial Germany, and national memory, 1871–1918* (London, 1997).
Cooper, T. 'Bolton, Edmund Mary', *Oxford Dictionary of National Biography* (Oxford 1885).
Corbett, M., and M. Naughton, *Engraving in England in the sixteenth and seventeenth centuries. Part III, The Reign of Charles I, compiled from the notes of A.M. Hind* (Cambridge, 1964).
Cottret, B. (ed.), *Bolingbroke's political writings: the conservative Enlightenment* (Basingstoke, 1997).
Craddock, P., 'Historical discovery and literary invention in Gibbon's "Decline and Fall"', *Modern Philology*, 85 (1988), 569–87.
Crawford, J., '"The Tragedie of Bonduca" and the anxieties of the masculine government of James I', *Studies in English Literature, 1500–1900*, 39 (1999), 357–81.
Cressy, D., *Bonfires and bells: national memory and the Protestant calendar in Elizabethan and Stuart England* (London, 1989).
Cubitt, G., and A. Warren (eds), *Heroic reputations and exemplary lives* (Manchester, 2000).
Curran, J.E., *Roman invasions: the British History, Protestant anti-Romanism, and the historical imagination in England, 1530–1660* (Newark, DE, 2002).
Davies, D.W. (ed.), *Romanticism, history, historicism: essays on orthodoxy* (London, 2009).
Davies, J., 'Victoria and Victorian Wales', in G.H. Jenkins and J.B. Smith (eds), *Politics and Society in Wales, 1840–1922. Essays in Honour of Ieuan Gwynedd Jones* (Cardiff, 1988).
Davis, A., *Renaissance historical fiction: Sidney, Deloney, Nashe* (Cambridge, 2011).
Dean, L.F., 'Bodin's Methodus in England before 1625', *Studies in Philology*, 39 (1942), 160–6.
de Groot, J., *Consuming history: Historians and heritage in contemporary popular culture* (London, 2009).
Dobree, B., 'The theme of patriotism in the poetry of the early eighteenth century', *Proceedings of the British Academy*, 35 (1949), 49–65.
Doran, S., 'Tudor King's and Queens', in P. Kewes, I.W. Archer, and F. Heal (eds), *Oxford Handbook to Holinshed's Chronicles* (Oxford, 2013), pp. 475–90.

Dyer, P.J., 'From Boadicea to Bette Davis', *Films and Filming*, 5 (1959), 13–33 (non-consecutive).
Edwards, H.T., *The Eisteddfod* (Cardiff, 1990).
Edwards, H.T., *The National Pageant of Wales* (Llandysul, 2009).
Ellis, J.S., 'Reconciling the Celt: British national identity, empire, and the 1911 investiture of the Prince of Wales' *Journal of British Studies*, 37(4) (1998), 391–418.
Ellis J.S., 'Outlaw historian: Owen Rhoscomyl and popular history in Edwardian Wales', in N. Evans and H. Pryce (eds), *Writing a small nation's past: Wales in comparative perspective, 1850–1950* (Farnham, 2013), pp. 111–26.
Eliot, G., *Middlemarch* (Oxford, 1996).
Evans, N. and H. Pryce, 'Introduction: Writing a small nation's past: states, races and historical culture', in N. Evans and H. Pryce (eds), *Writing a small nation's past: Wales in comparative perspective, 1850–1950* (Farnham, 2013), pp. 3–30.
Fabel, R., 'The patriotic Briton: Tobias Smollett and English politics, 1756–1771', *Eighteenth-century studies*, 8(1) (1974), 100–14.
Feingold, M., 'The Humanities', in N. Tyacke (ed.), *The History of the University of Oxford*, vol. IV, *Seventeenth-century Oxford* (Oxford, 1997), pp. 327–58.
Finkelpearl, F.J., 'Beaumont, Francis (1584/5–1616)', *Oxford Dictionary of National Biography* (Oxford, online edn, Oct 2006), http://www.oxforddnb.com/view/article/1871, accessed 20 Nov 2012.
Finlayson, J.C., 'Thomas Heywood's Panegyric to London's "University" in *Londini Artium & Scientiarum Scaturigo: or, Londons Fountaine of Arts and Sciences* (1632)', *The London Journal*, 39 (2014), 102–19.
Forster, B., 'Popular history, gender and nationalism', in B. Korte and S. Paletschek (eds), *Popular history now and then, international perspectives* (London, 2012), pp. 149–68.
Fox, A., and D.R. Woolf (eds), *The spoken word: oral culture in Britain, 1500–1850* (Manchester, 2002).
Franklin, J.H., *Jean Bodin and the sixteenth-century revolution in the methodology of law and history* (New York, 1963).
Freeman, M., '"Splendid display; pompous spectacle": historical pageants in twentieth-century Britain', *Social History*, 38 (2013), 423–55.
Frenée-Hutchins, S., *Boudica's odyssey in early modern England* (Farnham, 2014).
Fussner, F.S., *The historical revolution in English historical writing and thought, 1580–1640* (London, 1962).
Gajda, A., *The Earl of Essex and late Elizabethan political culture* (Oxford, 2012).
Gajda, A., 'Essex and politic history', in A. Connolly and L. Hopkins (eds), *Essex: the cultural impact of an Elizabethan courtier* (Manchester, 2013), pp. 237–59.
Gaffney, A., 'A National Valhalla for Wales: D.A. Thomas and the Welsh historical sculpture scheme', *Transactions of the Honourable Society of Cymmrodorion*, New Series, 5 (1999), 131–44.
Getsy, D.J. (ed.), *Sculpture and the pursuit of the modern ideal in Britain, c. 1880–1930* (Aldershot, 2004).
Getsy, D.J., 'The Lycidas "scandal" of 1905: James Havard Thomas at the crux of modern sculpture in Britain', in D. J. Getsy (ed.), *Sculpture and the pursuit of a modern ideal in Britain, c. 1880–1930* (Aldershot, 2004), pp. 167–90.
Gerrard, C., *The patriot opposition to Walpole: politics, poetry, and national myth, 1725–1742* (Oxford, 1994).
Glassberg, D., 'Public history and the study of memory', *The Public Historian*, 18 (1996), 7–23.

Goldhill, S., *Victorian culture and classical antiquity: art, opera, fiction, and the proclamation of modernity* (Princeton, NJ, 2011).
Goldstein, D.S., 'The organizational development of the British historical profession, 1884–1921', *Bulletin of the Institute of Historical Research*, 55 (1982), 180–93.
Goldstein, D.S., 'The origins and early years of the *English Historical Review*', *English Historical Review*, 101(398) (1986), 6–19.
Goy-Blanquet, D., *Shakespeare's early history plays: from chronicle to stage* (Oxford, 2003).
Grafton, A., *What was history: the art of history in early modern Europe* (Cambridge, 2007).
'Graig Fawr to Gop Cairn',http://www.cpat.org.uk/walks/gopcairn.pdf, accessed 10 Aug 2017.
Grafton, A., and L. Jardine, *From humanism to the humanities: education and the liberal arts in fifteenth- and sixteenth-century Europe* (London, 1986).
Green, P.D., 'Theme and structure in Fletcher's *Bonduca*', *Studies in English Literature 1500–1900*, 22 (1982), 305–16.
Greenwood, M., 'Victorian ideal sculpture', unpublished DPhil thesis (Courtauld Institute of Art, 1998).
Grever, M., 'Plurality, narrative and the historical canon', in M. Grever and S. Stuurman (eds), *Beyond the canon: history for the twenty-first century* (Basingstoke, 2007), pp. 31–47.
Griffin, B., *Playing the past: approaches to English historical drama, 1385–1600* (Woodbridge, 2001).
Griffin, M., *Nero: the end of a dynasty* (New York, 2001).
Griffiths, A., *The print in Stuart Britain, 1603–1689* (London, 1998).
Griffiths, A., 'Delaram, Francis (*fl.* 1615–1624)', *Oxford Dictionary of National Biography* (Oxford, 2004).
Guldi, J., and D. Armitage, *The history manifesto* (Cambridge, 2014).
Hacking, I., *Historical ontology* (Harvard, MA, 2002).
Harper, S., *Picturing the past: the rise and fall of the British costume film* (London, 1994).
Hay, D., *Annalists and historians: western historiography from the eighth to the eighteenth centuries* (London, 1977).
Heal, F., 'What can King Lucius do for you? The Reformation and the early British Church', *English Historical Review*, 120 (2004), 593–614.
Heal, F., 'Readership and reception', in P. Kewes, I.W. Archer, and F. Heal (eds), *Oxford Handbook to Holinshed's Chronicles* (Oxford, 2013), pp. 356–72.
Heathorn, S., '"The highest type of Englishman": gender, war, and the Alfred the Great commemoration of 1901', *Canadian Journal of History*, 37 (2002), 459–84.
Helgerson, R., 'Murder in Faversham: Holinshed's impertinent history', in D. Kelley and D.H. Sacks (eds), *The historical imagination in early modern Britain: history, rhetoric, and fiction, 1500–1800* (Cambridge, 1997), pp. 133–58.
Henderson, K.U., and B.F. McManus, *Half humankind: contexts and texts of the controversy about Women in England, 1540–1640* (Chicago, 1985).
Herendeen, W., 'Later historians and Holinshed', in P. Kewes, I.W. Archer, and F. Heal (eds), *Oxford Handbook to Holinshed's Chronicles* (Oxford, 2013), pp. 235–50.
Hicks, P., *Neoclassical history and English culture: from Clarendon to Hume* (Basingstoke, 1996).
Higson, A., *Waving the flag: constructing a national cinema in Britain* (Oxford, 1995).
Hill, R., *Stonehenge* (London, 2008).
Hill, T., *Mors ambitiosa: suicide and self in Roman thought and literature* (London, 2004).
Hingley, R., *Roman officers and English gentlemen: the imperial origins of Roman archaeology* (London, 2000).

Hingley R., and C. Unwin, *Boudica, Iron Age queen* (London, 2000).
History of Parliament, 'Glover, Richard (?1712–85), of Exchange Alley, London', http://www.historyofparliamentonline.org/volume/1754-1790/member/glover-richard-1712-85, accessed 12 June 2017.
Hobsbawm, E., and T. Ranger, *The invention of tradition* (London, 1983).
Hoffer, P., *Clio among the muses: essays on history and the humanities* (New York, 2013).
Hogan, P.C., *The mind and its stories: narrative universals and human emotion* (Cambridge, 2003).
Hopkins, L., 'The false domesticity of *A Woman Killed with Kindness*', *Connotations*, 4 (1994–5), 1–7.
Hoselitz, V., *Imagining Roman Britain: Victorian responses to a Roman past* (Woodbridge, 2007).
Howsam, L., *Past into print: the publishing of history in Britain, 1850–1950* (London, 2009).
Hudson, K., *A social history of archaeology: the British experience* (London, 1982).
Hulme, T., '"A nation of town criers": civic publicity and historical pageantry in inter-war Britain', *Urban history*, 44(2) (2015), 1–23.
Humphreys, R.A., *The Royal Historical Association, 1868–1968* (London, 1969).
Hunter, J., 'An account of the scheme for erecting a Royal Academy in England in the reign of King James I', *Archaeologia*, 32 (1847), 132–49.
Hunter, J.P., 'Protesting fiction, constructing history', in *The historical imagination in early modern Britain: history, rhetoric, and fiction, 1500–1800* (Cambridge, 1997), pp. 298–317.
Hutchinson, J., 'Cultural nationalism', in J. Breuilly (ed.), *The Oxford handbook of the history of nationalism* (Oxford, 2013), pp. 75–94.
Hutton, R., *Blood and mistletoe: the history of the Druids in Britain* (London, 2009).
Jackson, K., 'Queen Boudicca?', *Britannia*, 10 (1979), 255.
Jarrells, A., '"Associations respect[ing] the past": Enlightenment and romantic historicism', in J. Klancher (ed.), *A concise companion to the Romantic age* (London, 2009), pp. 57–76.
Jenkins, E. (ed.), 'Introduction: Eighteenth-century British historians', *Dictionary of Literary Biography*, vol. 336 (London, 2007).
Jenkins, G.H., *The foundation of modern Wales, 1642–1780* (Oxford, 1987).
Jenkins, G.H., *A rattleskull genius: the many faces of Iolo Morganwg* (Cardiff, 2005).
Jenkins, K., *'What is history?': from Carr and Elton to Rorty and White* (London, 1995).
Jones, M., *The last great quest: Captain Scott's Antarctic sacrifice* (Oxford, 2003).
Jones, M., *The print in early modern England: an historical oversight* (London, 2010).
Jordanova, L., 'Public history', *History today*, 50 (2000).
Jordanova, L., *History in Practice* (London, 2006).
Jowitt, C., 'Colonialism, politics, and Romanization in John Fletcher's "Bonduca"', *Studies in English Literature 1500–1900*, 43 (2003), 475–94.
Kamps, I., *Historiography and ideology in Stuart drama* (Cambridge, 1996).
Kansteiner, W., and C. Classen (eds), *Historical representation and historical truth* (Middletown, CT, 2009).
Kelley, D.R., 'What is happening to the history of ideas?', *Journal of the history of ideas*, 51(1) (1990), 3–25.
Kelley, D.R., and R.H. Popkin (eds), *The shapes of knowledge from the Renaissance to the Enlightenment* (Dordrecht, 1991).
Kelley, D.R., and D.H. Sacks (eds), *The historical imagination in early modern Britain* (Cambridge, 1997).

Kember, J., *Marketing modernity: Victorian popular shows and early cinema* (Exeter, 2009).
Kendrick, T.D., *British antiquity* (London, 1950), Ch. 6.
Kewes, P., 'The Elizabethan history play: a true genre?', in R. Dutton, and J.E. Howard (eds), *A companion to Shakespeare's Works, vol. 2, The Histories* (Oxford, 2003), pp. 170–93.
Kewes, P., 'Henry Savile's Tacitus and the Politics of Roman History in Late Elizabethan England', *Huntington Library Quarterly*, 74(4) (2011), 515–51.
Kewes, P., I.W. Archer, and F. Heal (eds), *Oxford Handbook to Holinshed's Chronicles* (Oxford, 2013).
Kidd, C., *British identities before nationalism: ethnicity and nationhood in the Atlantic world, 1600–1800* (Cambridge, 1999).
Kidd, C., 'Wales, Enlightenment and the new British history', *Welsh History Review*, 25 (2010), 209–30.
Klein, K.L., 'On the emergence of memory in historical discourse', *Representations*, 69 (2000), 127–50.
Klein, U., and W. Lefèvre, *Materials in eighteenth-century science: a historical ontology* (Cambridge, MA, 2007).
Knowles, R., *Shakespeare's arguments with history* (Basingstoke, 2002).
Korte, B., and S. Paletschek (eds), 'Introduction', *Popular history now and then, international perspectives* (London, 2012).
Kumar, K., *The making of English national identity* (Cambridge, 2003).
Kusch, M., 'Hacking's historical epistemology: a critique of styles of reasoning', *Studies in History and Philosophy of Science*, 41 (2010), 158–73.
LaCapra, D., *Rethinking intellectual history* (London, 1983).
Lambert, P., and B. Weiler (eds), *How the past was used: historical cultures, c. 750–2000* (Oxford, 2017).
Langland, E., 'Victoria in the developing narrative of Englishness', in M. Homans and A. Munich (eds), *Remaking Queen Victoria* (Cambridge, 1999), pp. 13–32.
Lebra-Chapman, J., *The Rani of Jhansi: a study in female heroism in India* (Honolulu, HI, 1986).
Lesser, Z., *Renaissance drama and the politics of publication* (Cambridge, 2004).
Levine, J.M., *Humanism and history: origins of modern English historiography* (Ithaca, NY, 1987).
Levine, J.M., *The autonomy of history: truth and method from Erasmus to Gibbon* (London, 1999).
Levine, J.M., 'Fact and the English revolution', *Journal of the history of ideas*, 64 (2003), 317–35.
Levine, P., *The amateur and the professional: antiquarians, historians and archaeologists in Victorian England, 1838–1886* (Cambridge, 1986).
Levy, F.J., *Tudor historical thought* (San Marino, CA, 1967).
L'Hoir, F.S., *Tragedy, rhetoric, and the historiography of Tacitus's Annales* (Ann Arbor, MI, 2006).
Löffler, M., *The literary and historical legacy of Iolo Morganwg 1826–1926* (Cardiff, 2007).
Löffler, M., 'Failed founding fathers and abandoned sources: Edward Williams, Thomas Stephens and the young J.E. Lloyd', in N. Evans and H. Pryce (eds), *Writing a small nation's past: Wales in comparative perspective, 1850–1950* (Farnham, 2013), pp. 66–81.
Looser, D., *British women writers and the writing of history, 1670–1820* (London, 2000).
Lord, P., *Imaging the nation: the visual culture of Wales* (Cardiff, 1998–2003).

Lorenz, C., 'Historical knowledge and historical reality: a plea for "internal realism"', *History and theory*, 33 (1994), 297–327.
Low, R., *The history of the British film, 1918–1929* (London, 1971).
Lowenstein, D., *Milton and the drama of history: historical vision, iconoclasm, and the literary imagination* (Cambridge, 1990).
McCrea, A., *Constant minds: political virtue and the Lipsian paradigm in England, 1583–1650* (London, 1997).
MacDonald, S., 'Boadicea: Warrior, mother and myth', in S. MacDonald, P. Holden, and S. Ardener (eds), *Images of women in peace and war: Cross-cultural and historical perspectives* (Basingstoke, 1987), pp. 40–55.
MacDougall, H.A., *Racial myth and English history: Trojans, Teutons, and Anglo-Saxons* (Hanover, NH, 1982).
McElroy, T.A., 'Genres', in P. Kewes, I.W. Archer, and F. Heal (eds), *Oxford Handbook to Holinshed's Chronicles* (Oxford, 2013), pp. 267–83.
McMullan, G. (ed.), 'Introduction' to William Shakespeare and John Fletcher, *King Henry VIII, all is true* (London, 2000), pp. 161–74.
McMullan, G., 'The colonisation of early Britain on the Jacobean stage', in G. McMullan and D. Matthews (eds), *Reading the medieval in early modern England* (Cambridge, 2007), pp. 119–42.
Maitzen, R., '"By no means an improbable fiction": *Redgauntlet*'s novel historicism', *Studies in the novel*, 25 (1993), 170–83.
Maitzen, R., '"This feminine preserve": historical biographies by Victorian women' *Victorian Studies*, 38(3) (1995), 371–93.
Maley, W., '"That Fatal Boadicea": depicting women in Milton's *History of Britain*, 1670', in D. Loewenstein and P. Stevens (eds), *Early modern nationalism and Milton's England* (London, 2008), pp. 305–30.
Mandler, P., '"In the olden time": Romantic history and English national identity, 1820–50', in L. Brockliss and D. Eastwood (eds), *A union of multiple identities* (Manchester, 1997), pp. 78–92.
Mandler, P., *History and national life* (London, 2002).
Mandler, P., *The English national character: the history of an idea from Edmund Burke to Tony Blair* (London, 2006).
Manning, E., *Marble & bronze: the art and life of Hamo Thornycroft* (London, 1982).
Mayer, R., 'Nathaniel Crouch, bookseller and historian: popular historiography and cultural power in late seventeenth-century England', *Eighteenth-Century Studies*, 27 (1994), 391–419.
Mayer, R., *History and the early English novel: matters of fact from Bacon to Defoe* (Cambridge, 1997).
Melman, B., *A culture of history: English uses of the past, 1800–1953* (Oxford, 2006).
Melman, B., 'The power of the past: history and modernity in the Victorian world', in M. Hewitt (ed.), *The Victorian World* (London, 2013), pp. 466–83.
Mendell, C.W., *Tacitus: the man and his work* (London, 1957).
Mikalachki, J., *The Legacy of Boadicea: Gender and nation in early modern England* (London, 1998).
Miller, P., 'Nazis and Neostoics: Otto Brunner and Gerhard Oestreich before and after the Second World War', *Past and Present*, 176 (2002), 144–86.
Mink, L.O. 'Change and causality in the history of ideas', *Eighteenth-century studies*, 2 (1968), 3–25.

Mitchell, R., *Picturing the past: English history in text and image, 1830–1870* (Oxford, 2000).
Mitchell, R., 'The red queen and the white queen', in G. Cubitt and A. Warren (eds), *Heroic Reputations and Exemplary Lives* (Manchester, 2000), pp. 157–77.
Momigliano, A., *Essays in ancient and modern historiography* (Oxford, 1977).
Momigliano, A., *The classical foundations of modern historiography* (Oxford, 1990).
Morford, M., *Stoics and neostoics: Rubens and the circle of Lipsius* (Princeton, NJ, 1991).
Morgan, P., *Iolo Morganwg* (Cardiff, 1975).
Morgan, P., 'From a death to a view: The hunt for the Welsh past in the Romantic Period', in E. Hobsbawm and T. Ranger (eds), *The invention of tradition* (London, 1983), pp. 43–100.
Morgan, P., 'Early Victorian Wales and its crisis of identity', in L. Brockliss and D. Eastwood (eds), *A union of multiple identities* (Manchester, 1997), pp. 93–109.
Morley, I., *British provincial civic design and the building of Late-Victorian and Edwardian Cities, 1880–1914* (Lampeter, 2008).
Mottram, S. and S. Prescott (eds), Writing Wales from the Renaissance to Romanticism (Abingdon, 2012).
Myrone, M., and L. Peltz (eds), *Producing the past: aspects of antiquarian culture and practice 1700–1850* (Aldershot, 1999).
Nelson, C., and L. Vallone (eds), *The Girl's Own: cultural histories of the Anglo-American girl, 1830–1915* (London, 1994).
Nielsen, W.C., 'Boadicea on stage before 1800: a theatrical and colonial history', *Studies in English Literature 1500–1900*, 49 (2009), 595–614.
O'Brien, K., 'The history market', in I. Rivers (ed.), *Books and their readers in eighteenth-century England: new essays* (London, 2003), pp. 105–33.
O'Brien, K., 'History and the novel in eighteenth-century Britain', in P. Kewes (ed.), *The uses of history in early modern England* (San Marino, CA, 2006), pp. 389–405.
Oestreich, G., *Neostoicism and the early modern state* (Cambridge, 1982).
Okie, L., *Augustan historical writing: histories of England in the English Enlightenment* (Lanham, MD, 1991).
Ormond, L., *Tennyson and Thomas Woolner* (Lincoln, 1981).
Osmond, P., 'Edmund Bolton's Vindication of Tiberius Caesar: A "lost" manuscript comes to light', *International Journal of the Classical Tradition*, 11 (2005), 329–43.
Ottoway, P., *Archaeology in British towns: from the Emperor Claudius to the Black Death* (London, 1996).
Paletschek, S., 'Introduction: why analyse popular historiographies?', in S. Paletschek (ed.), *Popular historiographies in the 19th and 20th centuries: cultural meanings, social practices* (Oxford, 2010).
Parker, C., *The English idea of history from Coleridge to Collingwood* (London, 2000).
Parker, J., *England's Darling: the Victorian cult of Alfred the Great* (Manchester, 2007).
Parry, G., *The trophies of time: English antiquarians of the seventeenth century* (Oxford, 1995).
Patterson, A., *Reading Holinshed's Chronicles* (London, 1994).
Paul, H., 'Hayden White and the crisis of historicism', in F. Ankersmit, E. Domańska, and H. Keller (eds), *Re-figuring Hayden White* (Stanford, 2009), pp. 54–73.
Peardon, T.P., *The transition in English historical writing, 1760–1830* (New York, 1966).
Phillips, M.S., 'Macaulay, Scott, and the literary challenge to historiography', *Journal of the history of ideas*, 50(1) (1989), 117–33.
Phillips, M.S., *Society and sentiment: genres of historical writing in Britain 1740–1820* (Princeton, NJ, 2000).

Phillips, M.S., 'Rethinking historical distance: from doctrine to heuristic', *History and theory*, 50 (2011), 11–23.
Phillips, M.S., *On historical distance* (New Haven, CT, 2013).
Pittock, M.G.H., 'Enlightenment historiography and its legacy: plurality, authority and power', in H. Brocklehurst and R. Phillips (eds), *History, nationhood and the question of Britain* (Basingstoke, 2004), pp. 33–44.
Plumb, J.H., *The death of the past* (London, 1969).
Pocock, J.G.A., *The ancient constitution and the feudal law: a study of English historical thought* (Cambridge, 1957).
Pocock, J.G.A., *The ancient constitution and the feudal law: a study of English historical thought in the seventeenth century* (Cambridge, 1987).
Pocock, J.G.A., *Barbarism and religion*, 6 vols (Cambridge, 1999–2015).
Pocock, J.G.A., *Political thought and history: essays on theory and method* (Cambridge, 2009).
Pompa, L., *Human nature and historical knowledge: Hume, Hegel and Vico* (Cambridge, 1990).
Popper, N., *Walter Ralegh's 'History of the World' and the historical culture of the Renaissance* (London, 2012).
Potter, T.W., 'Later prehistory and Roman Britain: the formation of the national collections', in M. Caygill and J. Cherry (eds), *A.W. Franks; Nineteenth-century collecting and the British Museum* (London, 1997), pp. 130–5.
Portal, E.M., 'The Academ Roial of King's James I', *Proceedings of the British Academy, 1915–1916* (1916), 189–208.
Pratt, A.T., and D.S. Kastan, 'Printers, publishers and the *Chronicles* as artefact', in P. Kewes, I.W. Archer, and F. Heal (eds), *Oxford Handbook to Holinshed's Chronicles* (Oxford, 2013), pp. 21–42.
Price, C.A., *Henry Purcell and the London stage* (Cambridge, 1984).
Price, J., *Everyday heroism: Victorian constructions of the heroic civilian* (London, 2014).
Pryce, H., 'J.E. Lloyd's History of Wales (1911): publication and reception', in N. Evans and H. Pryce (eds), *Writing a small nation's past: Wales in comparative perspective, 1850–1950* (Farnham, 2013), pp. 49–64.
Quinault, R., 'Westminster and the Victorian constitution', *Transactions of the Royal Historical Society*, 6th series, 2 (1992), 79–104.
Raymond, G.F., *A new, universal, and impartial history of England* (London, 1790).
Read, B., *Victorian sculpture* (London, 1982).
Readman, P., 'The place of the past in English culture, c. 1890–1914', *Past and Present*, 186 (2005), 147–99.
Reide, G., 'Tennyson's poetics of melancholy and the imperial imagination', *Studies in English Literature, 1500–1900*, 40 (2000), 659–78.
Reilly, C., *Mid-Victorian poetry, 1860–1879, an annotated bibliography* (London, 2000).
Rheinberger, H., 'A plea for a historical epistemology of research', *Journal for the general philosophy of science*, 43 (2012), 105–11.
Ribner, I., *The English history play in the age of Shakespeare* (Princeton, NJ, 1957).
Richardson, R.C., *The debate on the English revolution* (Manchester, 1998).
Ricks, C. (ed.), *The Poems of Tennyson* (London, 1969).
Rogers, P., 'Swift and Bolingbroke on faction', *Journal of British Studies*, 9 (1970), 71–101.
Rowland, R., *Thomas Heywood's theatre, 1599–1639, Locations, translations, conflict* (Farnham, 2010).
Rüsen, J. (ed.), *Meaning and representation in history* (Oxford, 2006).
Rüsen, J., 'Tradition: a principle of historical sense generation and its logic and effect in historical culture', *History and Theory*, 51 (2012), 45–59.

St Clair, W., *The reading nation in the Romantic period* (Cambridge, 2004).
Salmon, J.H.M., 'Stoicism and Roman example: Seneca and Tacitus in Jacobean England', *Journal of the History of Ideas*, 50 (1989), 199–225.
Salmon, J.H.M., 'Seneca and Tacitus in Jacobean England', in L.L. Peck (ed.), *The mental world of the Jacobean court* (Cambridge, 1991), pp. 169–88.
Sayer, F., *Public history: a practical guide* (London, 2015).
Schelling, F.E., *The English chronicle play: a study in the popular historical literature environing Shakespeare* (London, 1902).
Schelling, F.E. (ed.), *Francis Beaumont and John Fletcher* (New York, 1912).
Schwyzer, P., *Literature, nationalism, and memory in early modern England and Wales* (Cambridge, 2004).
Seaward, P., 'Clarendon, Tacitus, and the Civil Wars of Europe', in P. Kewes (ed.), *The uses of history in early modern England* (San Marino, CA, 2006), pp. 268–83.
Shapiro, B., *A culture of fact: England, 1550–1720* (Ithaca, NY, 2000).
Shattock, J. (ed.), *The Cambridge Bibliography of English Literature* (Cambridge, 1999).
Shifflett, A., *Stoicism, politics, and literature in the age of Milton: war and peace reconciled* (Cambridge, 1998).
Simpson, M., 'Telling lives to children: young versus new historicism in *Little Arthur's History of England*', in D.W. Davies (ed.), *Romanticism, history, historicism: essays on orthodoxy* (London, 2009), pp. 60–78.
Skinner, Q., 'History and ideology in the English Revolution', *The Historical Journal*, 8 (1965), 151–78.
Skinner, Q., 'The principles and practice of opposition: the case of Bolingbroke versus Walpole', in N. McKendrick (ed.), *Historical perceptions: studies in English thought and society in honour of J.H. Plumb* (London, 1974), pp. 93–128.
Skinner, Q., *The foundations of modern political thought*, 2 vols (Cambridge, 1978).
Smiles, S., *The image of antiquity: ancient Britain and the romantic imagination* (New Haven, CT, 1994).
Smith, A.D., 'The nation: invented, imagined, reconstructed', *Millennium: journal of international studies*, 20 (1991), 325–68.
Smith, A.D., *The nation in history: historiographical debates about ethnicity and nationalism* (Cambridge, 2000).
Smith, A.D., *The antiquity of nations* (Cambridge, 2004).
Society of Antiquaries, *Making history: three hundred years of antiquaries in Britain, 1707–2007* (London, 2007).
Speight, S.J., 'A gentlemanly pastime: antiquarianism, adult education and the clergy in England, c. 1750–1960', *History of Education*, 40 (2011), 143–55.
Sprague, A.C., *Beaumont and Fletcher on the Restoration Stage* (Cambridge, MA, 1926).
Spufford, M., *Small books and pleasant histories: popular fiction and its readers in seventeenth-century England* (London, 1981).
Stauffer, D.A., 'A parasitical form of biography', *Modern Language Notes*, 55(4) (1940), 289–92.
Stocker, M., 'Thornycroft, Thomas (1815–1885)', *Oxford Dictionary of National Biography* (Oxford, 2004; online edn, Oct 2006), http://www.oxforddnb.com/view/article/27369, accessed 8 Aug 2017.
Stone, G.W. (ed.), *The London Stage 1660–1800*, Part 4 (1747–1776) (Carbondale, IL, 1962).
Strange, S.K., and J. Zupko, *Stoicism: traditions and transformations* (Cambridge, 2004).
Strong, R., *And when did you last see your father?: The Victorian painter and the British past* (London, 1978).

Sullivan, M.G., 'Rapin de Thoyras, Paul de (1661–1725)', *Oxford Dictionary of National Biography* (Oxford, 2004), http://www.oxforddnb.com/view/article/23145, accessed 21 Nov 2012.
Sweet, R., *The writing of urban histories in eighteenth-century England* (Oxford, 1997).
Sweet, R., *Antiquaries: the discovery of the past in eighteenth-century Britain* (London, 2004).
Thorn, M., *Tennyson* (London, 1992).
Thornycroft, E., *Bronze and steel: The life of Thomas Thornycroft, sculptor and engineer* (Long Compton, 1932).
Tonnochy, A.B., 'Four keepers of the Department of British and Medieval Antiquities', *The British Museum Quarterly*, 18 (1953), 83–8.
Townsin, A., *Thornycroft* (Hersham, 2001).
Trevor-Roper, H., 'A Huguenot historian: Paul Rapin', in I. Scouloudi (ed.), *Huguenots in Britain and their French background, 1550–1800* (London, 1987), pp. 3–19.
Trevor-Roper, H., *History and enlightenment*, ed. J. Robertson (New Haven, CT, 2010).
Tuck, R., *Philosophy and government, 1572–1621* (Cambridge, 1993).
Turner, J., *Philology: the forgotten origins of the modern humanities* (Princeton, NJ, 2014).
Vance, N., 'Roman heroism and the problems of nineteenth century empire: Aeneas and Caractacus', in G. Cubitt and A. Warren (eds), *Heroic reputations and exemplary lives* (Manchester, 2000), pp. 142–56.
Vandrei, M., 'A Victorian invention? Thomas Thornycroft's Boadicea group and the idea of historical culture in Britain', *Historical Journal*, 57 (2014), 485–508.
Vandrei, M., '"Britons, strike home": politics, patriotism, and popular song in British culture, c. 1696–1900', *Historical Research*, 87(238) (2014), 679–702.
Vandrei, M., 'Claudia Rufina', in G. Atkins (ed.), *Making and remaking saints in nineteenth-century Britain* (Manchester, 2016), pp. 60–76.
van Lennep, W. (ed.), *The London stage, 1660–1800*, Part I (1660–1700) (Carbondale, IL, 1962).
Venn, J., and J.A. Venn (eds), *Alumni Cantabrigienses* (Cambridge, 2011 [first edn 1947]).
Vergo, P. (ed.), *The new museology* (London, 2000 [first edn 1989]).
Vicinus, M., 'Models for public life: biographies of "noble women" for girls', in C. Nelson and L. Vallone (eds), *The Girl's Own: cultural histories of the Anglo-American girl, 1830–1915* (London, 1994), pp. 52–70.
Walker, G.L., *Mary Hays (1759–1843): The growth of a woman's mind* (Aldershot, 2006).
Waller, P., *Town, City, and Nation* (Oxford, 1983).
Warner, M., *Monuments and maidens: the allegory of the female form* (London, 1985).
Webster, G., *The British revolt against Rome AD 60* (London, 1999).
Wertz, S.K., 'Hume, history, and human nature', *Journal of the history of ideas*, 36 (1975), 481–96.
White, H., *Metahistory: the historical imagination in nineteenth-century Europe* (Baltimore, 1973).
White, H., *Tropics of discourse: essays in cultural criticism* (London, 1978).
White, H., 'A reply to Dirk Moses', 335. The exchange was published in its entirety as 'The public relevance of historical studies', *History and Theory*, 44 (October 2005), 333–8.
White, H., *The practical past* (Evanston, IL, 2014).
Widmayer, A.F., *Theatre and the novel, from Behn to Fielding* (Oxford, 2015).
Williams, C.D., '"This Frantic Woman": Boadicea and English Neo-Classical Embarrassment', in M. Biddiss and M. Wyke (eds), *The Uses and Abuses of Antiquity* (New York, 1999), pp. 19–35.

Williams, C.D., *Boudica and her stories: narrative transformations of a warrior queen* (Newark, DE, 2009).
Williams, C.D., '"On Boadicea think!": In search of a female army', in C.D. Williams, A. Escott, and L. Duckling (eds), *Woman to woman: female negotiations in the long eighteenth century* (Newark, DE, 2010), pp. 204–24.
Womersley, D., 'Against the teleology of technique', in P. Kewes (ed.), *The uses of history in early modern England* (San Marino, CA, 2006), pp. 91–104.
Woolf, D.R., 'Edmund Bolton, Francis Bacon, and the Making of the *Hypercritica*', *Bodleian Library Record*, 11 (1983), 162–8.
Woolf, D.R., 'Genre into artifact: the decline of the English chronicle in the sixteenth century', *Sixteenth Century Journal*, 19 (1988), 321–54.
Woolf, D.R., *The idea of history in early Stuart England: erudition, ideology, and the 'Light of Truth' from the accession of James I to the Civil War* (London, 1990).
Woolf, D.R., 'The dawn of the artefact: antiquarian impulse in England, 1500–1730', *Studies in Medievalism*, IV (1992), 5–35.
Woolf, D.R., 'A feminine past? Gender, genre, and historical knowledge in England, 1500–1800', *American Historical Review*, 102 (1997), 645–79.
Woolf, D.R., 'Disciplinary history and historical discourse; a critique of the history of history: the Case of Early Modern England', *Cromohs*, 2 (1997), 1–25.
Woolf, D.R., 'Little Crosby and the horizons of early modern historical culture', in D.R. Kelley and D.H. Sacks (eds), *The historical imagination in early modern Britain* (Cambridge, 1997), pp. 99–132.
Woolf, D.R., *Reading history in early modern England* (Cambridge, 2000).
Woolf, D.R., *The social circulation of the past: English historical culture, 1500–1730* (Oxford, 2003).
Woolf, D.R., 'Bolton, Edmund Mary (*b*. 1574/5, *d.* in or after 1634)', *Oxford Dictionary of National Biography* (Oxford, 2004), http://www.oxforddnb.com/view/article/2800, accessed 8 Aug 2017.
Woolf, D.R., 'From hystories to the historical: five transitions in thinking about the past, 1500–1700', in P. Kewes (ed.), *The uses of history in early modern England* (San Marino, CA, 2006), pp. 31–67.
Woolf, D.R., *A global history of history* (Cambridge, 2011).
Worden, B., 'Historians and poets', in P. Kewes (ed.), *The uses of history in early modern England* (San Marino, CA, 2006), pp. 69–90.
Wright, L.B., 'Heywood and the popularizing of history', *Modern Language Notes*, 43 (1928), 287–93.
Wright, L.B., 'The Elizabethan middle-class taste for history', *The Journal of Modern History*, 3(2) (1931), 175–97.
Wright, L.B., 'The reading of plays during the Puritan Revolution', *Huntington Library Bulletin*, 6 (1934), 72–108.
Yarrington, A., *The commemoration of the hero, 1800–1864: monuments to the British victors of the Napoleonic Wars* (London, 1988).
Yoshino, A., *The Edwardian historical pageant: local history and consumerism* (Tokyo, 2010).
Zemon Davies, N., 'Gender and genre: women as historical writers, 1400–1820', in P.H. Labalme (ed.), *Beyond their sex: learned women of the European past* (London, 1980), pp. 153–82.
Zimmerman, E., *The boundaries of fiction: history and the eighteenth-century British novel* (London, 1996).

Index

Note: Page numbers in italics refers to figures.

Agripinna [known as the Younger] 29, 38–40, 47
Albert [Prince Consort] 141, 147, 148–9, 151, 152, 153, 160
almanacs 54
ancient Britain 7, 25, 41, 45, 50, 62, 64, 65, 66, 84, 101, 112, 114, 130, 136, 138, 166, 175–6, 179, 186, 194, 196
  Archaeology of 154, 160, 189 n. 60
  Boudica as representative of 7, 37, 100, 109, 148, 169, 201
  focus of civic pride 171, 172, 190, 193–4
  in Caesar's *Gallic Wars* 151
  in panoramic histories 67, 73, 74, 79, 101
  subject of political debate 84–103
Ancient Constitution 18 n. 63, 82–6, 90, 94, 174
Andraste [Druidic goddess] 4, 88, 101
Anglesey [Isle of Mona] 2, 43, 44, 87, 93, 127, 179, 182–3, 191, 197
Anglo-Saxons 3, 45, 86, 88–9, 164, 174, 175, 201
antiquarians and antiquarianism 14, 22, 49, 54, 56, 67, 75, 77, 93 n. 41, 117–18, 199, 205
  local historical culture and 153–5 n. 35, 171, 190, 195, 196, 200–1
Archaeologia 154
archaeology 1 n. 2, 44, 50, 148, 153–7, 160, 169, 185 n. 50
Aregwedd Voeddig 176–7, 184
Armitage, David 206
Ars historica 34 n. 40, 53, 58, 60, 63
Aviragus, *See* Prasutagus
Aske, Jonathan 19
audience 8, 11, 16, 18, 50, 53, 56, 62, 64–7, 79, 80, 96, 107, 117, 118, 128, 148, 176, 196, 200, 204
  female 55 n. 15, 58–9, 124, 125 n. 28, 128, 132
Augustus [first Roman Emperor] 27

Barker, Francis 138–40
Baxter, John 101–2
Begum of Bhopal 134
Beroaldus 27
biography
  collective 124, 125–32, 146
  'parasitical' 109, 121, 205
Boadicea, *see* Boudica
Boadicea (1926) (film) 173, 197–202
Bodin, Jean 34–6, 54, 58

Methodus translated by Thomas Heywood 60–2, 65–7, 79
Bolton, Edmund 3, 9, 22, 25, 31, 32
  Academic Roial 33 n. 36, 54
  ancient Britain in works 37 n. 49, 45
  antiquarianism 23–6, 32, 37, 45, 48–9, 53, 204
  devotion to monarchy 26, 32, 35 n. 41, 41
  early interest in Boudica 25–6, 31, 46
  historical method 26, 32–7, 47–8
  Hypercritica 9, 34–5
  Nero Caesar 22, 37–47, 117
    1627 afterword 37 n. 50
    1627 frontispiece *39*
    British Museum annotation 37
    Boudica's rebellion 41–4
    Seneca's hypocrisy 42
    Nero's early life 38, 40–1
    Stonehenge 37–8, 45–6
    referred to by Heywood 61–2
    referred to by Cowley 125
  Roman Catholicism 25, 31–2, 35
  Stoicism and 26, 31, 36–7, 40, 44–5
  Tacitus and 25, 35 n. 41, 36
Bonduca, *see under* Boudica; Fletcher, John
Burke, Peter 28
Bury St Edmunds 172, 194–5
  1907 pageant 190–3, 198
Blair, Ann 36
Bradford, Alan 49
Britons, *see* Ancient Britain
Brooke, Christopher 30
Bull, Sir William 148, 158 n. 54, 159
Burton, Richard
  See Crouch, Nathaniel
Burton, Robert 59, 63
Boudica
  alternative names
    Bonditia 51
    Bonduca 19–20, 61, 68–70, 197
    Boadicea 1 n. 1, 23, 37, 70, 72, 77–9, 85, 90, 107, 113, 116–17, 120, 122, 129, 132, 134–40, 147, 155, 161, 163–4, 166, 180–1, 185, 186, 190, 191, 195, 199, 200
    Buddug 163, 176–78 n. 24, 182, 185–6, *187*, 188
    Voada 18
  See also Aregwedd Voeddig
  atrocities committed by 4, 77, 91, 142
  battle 2–4, 26, 45, 76–7, 91, 97–8, 123, 127, 132 n. 51, 139, 154–5, 183, 194–5, 197–8, 200

Index

Boudica (cont.)
  possible location of final
    Epping Forest 154 n. 39
    Ivinghoe Valley 199
    Rhyl 183–5
    River Wylye 45
  Commanders and princes named in
      fiction 121–2, 136
    Caratach (Fletcher) 19, 122
    Caratach (Powell) 69
    Caradoc (film) 197–8
    Cassibelan, (Hopkins) 71–2
    Cennessius (Rhodes) 122
    Cenulph (Rhodes) 121
    Dumnorix (Glover) 104 n. 81, 105–7,
      109, 121–2
    Venutius (powell) 69
  daughters 1, 2, 19, 40, 57, 61, 68–9, 75, 78,
      137, 152, 161, 198
    Agatha and Anfleda (Rhodes) 122
    believed escaped 131
    Blondicca and Emmelyn (film) 197
    Camilla and Venutia (Hopkins) 71–2
    Claudia and Bonvica (Powell) 69
    converted to Christianity 138
    Emmeline (Glover) 197
    images of 101, *102*, 132, *133*
    in sculpture *147*, 152, 174, *187*, 188
    Malvina (Lindsay) 136–7
    other fictional counterparts
      Golden Beauty (Trevelyan) 161–2, 166
      Voadica (Hannah) 165–9
    rape of 2, 19, 69–72, 76, 78–9, 105, 122,
      131, 188, 198
  death
    in 73AD 65
    sadness 94, 139
    sickness 4, 46
    suicide 2, 4, 19, 46, 65–6, 70, 78, 89,
      105, 124, 131–2, 137, 139
    wounds 185
  final resting place 171, 191
    London 148, 154–6
    Wales 173, 183–5
    Stonehenge 45–6, 49
  justness of her actions debated 75, 89, 108,
      110, 182
  oratory 2, 4, 70, 74, 79, 89, 91, 101, 139,
      141, 161, 174, 191–2, 198
  original story 1–4
  physical description 47, 61–2, 75, 101
      n. 70, 193
  rebellion 1–4, 17, 22, 26–30, 37, 42–4,
      48–50, 64, 72, 77–8, 87, 89–93,
      97–9, 109, 134, 138, 143, 161, 173,
      179, 195
Boudica's daughters, *see under* Boudica
Britannicus [Nero's step-brother] 40
Bruce Woolfe, H. 173, 197
Bryn Sion 184–5

Camden, William 15 n. 56, 50, 54
Camulodunum 2, 44, 89, 143, 172, 177, 179,
    191, 194–5, 202
  See also Colchester
Cannadine, David 193
Caractacus/Cardoc 1, 77, 180, 201 n. 97
Cardiff City Hall 164, 176
  Marble Hall competition 186–7
  statue of Boudica *187*
Carlyle, Thomas 118, 125
Carr, E.H. 9
Carte, Thomas 84, 92–6, 101, 112, 113
Cartismandua 1, 2 n. 66, 77, 109, 130, 177, 181
Cassius, Dio
  See Dio Cassius
Caesar, Julius 1, 37, 101, 109,
  Gallic Wars 87, 151, 160, 177
Cecil, Robert, first earl of Salisbury 36
Celts 87, 164–6, 175–7, 180, 183, 201
  See also Ancient Britain
Cerealis [or Cerialis, Roman administrator] 41
chapbooks 54
Charles I 25, 32
children's literature 132–3
Christianity 60, 124, 135, 138–40, 164, 166,
    175, 181, 184
  Boudica and 123–4, 131, 132, 138–40
chronicle genre 16, 18, 20, 55, 67, 73, 76,
    118, 170
chronology 15, 21
Cicero [Marcus Tullius] 27
Classicus, Julius [Roman commander] 41
Claudius [Roman Emperor] 1, 28, 40, 194–5
Cleland, John 111–12
Colchester 2, 44 n. 71, 81, 143, 172, 182, 189
    n. 60, 201
  1909 pageant 173, 195–6
  Town Hall 172, 193–4
  See also Camulodunum
Collingwood, R.G. 8 n. 25, 9, 167, 207–8
  on historical novels 167–9
Collins, Edwin 147, 162–4
Colman, George 68
continuity 8, 15
Cowley, Charlotte 125, 127–8
Cowper, William 116–17, 121, 133, 148, 155,
    162, 164, 180, 191, 198
Crouch, Nathaniel 56, 62–7
cultural nationalism 171 n. 6, 173
  See also under Wales

Danes 45
daughters, Boudica's, *see under* Boudica
Delaram, Francis 38
de Montaigne, Michel 29
Dio Cassius 20, 61, 44, 74–7, 79, 91, 114,
    117, 161, 172, 195
  account dismissed
    by Milton 74
    by Salmon 91

Index

audience appeal 18
Bolton and 41–3, 61
Boudica's physical appearance in 61, 75, 101 n. 70, 193
Carte and 94
compared to Tacitus 3–4, 46, 88, 111
Holinshed and 17–18
Rapin and 88–9
Read (C.H.) and 156
Seneca's culpability 42–4, 46
Tennyson and 141–2
use in historical pageants 192–5
use in film 198
disciplines 4, 12, 24, 204–5
see also under historical culture
Dickinson, W.B. 149–52
Druids and Druidism 2, 43–4, 84, 124, 131, 136, 179
Boudica and 88, 94, 116, 162–4, 182
Christianity and 121, 131, 138, 164
in political discourse 86–7, 88–99
massacre on Mona 2, 87, 184
as cause of Boudica's rebellion 87–8, 93–4, 179
named in fiction,
Arianrod (Trevelyan) 162
Badwallon (film) 197–8
Wales 171, 176, 181–4

Edwards, O.M. 179
Eisteddfod 172, 176 n. 17, 177, 181, 188
See also Wales
Elizabeth I 26, 49, 52, 58
Empire, *see* imperialism; Rome and Romans
England 20, 26, 30, 62–3, 66, 73, 82, 108–9, 117, 130, 164, 175, 178–9, 182, 186, 189–90, 201
See also national identity; national narrative; Wales
Enlightenment 79, 83, 118, 126
Essex 189, 194, 200, 204
See also under historical pageants
'Essex girl', Boudica the first 172
Essex second earl of 30–1
Evans, Theophilus 73 n. 64, 176

fact 5, 17, 24–5, 34–5, 56, 59–60, 73, 78, 93, 98, 109, 111, 113, 121, 128, 134, 140, 156–7, 160, 162, 164, 203, 205, 207
See also historical accuracy
factionalism 30, 48, 103–6, 112, 114
femininity 20, 24–5, 46, 105, 121, 123–4, 129, 135–6, 145, 147, 170, 204
Boudica's 25, 45, 60, 123–4, 129, 204
patriotism and 104–6, 114, 116, 120, 124, 204
modern scholars and 127, 146
biographers and 51, 59–60, 62, 135–8

fiction 5, 10, 12, 18–19, 24, 49, 54–5, 60, 73, 77, 90–7, 102, 109–11, 113, 126–31, 135, 144–5, 160–9, 203
See also poetry
Fielding, Henry 95
Fletcher, John 19 n. 69, 31, 49
Tragedie of Bonduca 19–20, 57, 121, 122, 197
anti-Catholicism 20 n. 72
influence on Powell's *Bonduca* 68–70
Foucault, Michel 6 n. 16, 10
Franks, Sir Augustus Wollaston 155
Freeman, E.A. 175
Frenée-Hutchins, Samantha 19, 25

Galgacus [ancient Scottish hero] 2
Gallic Wars
see under Julius Caesar
Garrick, David 103–4, 107, 111–12
Gauls 65, 87, 91
Geoffrey of Monmouth 3, 65–6
George V, wedding 178
Gerrard, Christine 82
Gibbon, Edward 81
Glorious Revolution 82
Glover, George, portrait of Boudica 51–4, *52*, 60
Glover, Richard 103–4, 112–14
Boadicea, queen of Britain 85, 104–5, 120
and *Boadicea* (film) 197–8
and Rhodes's *Patriot Queen* 121–4, 135
reviews of 105–12
Goldsmith, Oliver 98
Granville, Charles 79
Great Exhibition of 1851 149
Guldi, Jo 206
Gurdon, Thornhagh 90
Guthrie, William 78–9

Hacking, Ian 10 n. 32
Hadrian [Roman Emperor]
in fiction 165–6
Hadrian's Wall 168–9
Hall, Mrs. Matthew 128–30
Hampstead Heath 148
excavation 154–7, 159, 169–70, 183
Hannah, Ian C. 160–9
Hayman, Francis 99–100
illustration of Boudica *100*
Hays, Mary 126–8
Herring, Thomas [Archbishop of Canterbury] 113
heroism 6, 65, 75, 113–14, 146–7
Heywood, Thomas 22, 56–62, 63
Bodin's *Methodus* 58, 60–1
Gynaikeion 58–9
Exemplary Lives 59–62, 66
illustration of Boudica in *52*
Higgins, Bevill 77–8
Higson, Andrew 200
Hingley, Richard 134, 160 n. 65, 170

historical accuracy 98, 113, 145, 199, 207
　in drama 103, 105, 108, 110, 113, 121, 129
　in novels 101, 160, 162, 168, 199
　in sculpture 152, 199
historical culture 5, 12–16, 18, 25, 49, 73, 79–80, 83, 117, 144–5, 205–8
　allows for contradictory views of the past 115, 143–4, 170, 171–2 n. 6, 204
　creation as reception in 11, 21, 118, 115, 120–4, 138
　cross-cultural dialogue 14–15
　early modern 20, 24–5, 32, 48–9
　eighteenth-century 82–4
　growth and continuity 48, 118
　history of history 5, 9, 11–12, 15, 119, 205
　history of ideas 4 n. 15, 8 n. 25, 10 n. 31, 12, 14, 205
　intellectual history 9 n. 29, 119
　literary studies 21, 25, 53, 172–3 n. 6, 204–5
　memory studies 14
　nineteenth-century shifts in 117–20, 127
　philosophy of history 5, 10
　　and historians 10 n. 35
　popular history 9, 57, 114, 117, 119, 144, 205
　　history of 13–14 n. 48
　public history 5, 14, 15
　　as media studies 13
　See also past and present
historical drama 5, 11–14, 22, 26, 50, 54, 55, 113, 121, 128, 205
　Boudica's suitability to 161, 202, 204
　chronicles and 18 n. 66
　film and 173, 198, 200
　human nature and 85, 105–10
　narrative histories and 55 n. 17, 56–7, 74–7, 80
　rules of 108, 110, 121
　relationship to sculpture 152
historical figures 6–7
historical film 173, 197, 200
historical imagination 13
historical knowledge 11
historical method 9, 25, 34, 35, 47–9, 53–4, 67, 74, 82, 88, 103, 127–8, 167–8, 203, 206
historical novels 160–1, 168–9
　see also novels
historical pageants 51 n. 3, 189–90, 196
　Bury St Edmunds (1907) 172, 190, 192–3
　Colchester (1909) 193–5
　Essex (Ilford, 1932) 195–6
　Gwent (1913) 180
　Norwich (1926) 196
　St Albans (1907; 1953) 191–2
　Welsh National Pageant (1909) 179–80

historical truth 8, 12, 22, 96, 145, 168, 202
　See also under historical culture
history,
　a cultural process 7–8, 12
　and authenticity 173
　definition 9
　didactic potential 53, 56, 67
　idea of 7–9, 15
　knowledge of 11
　malleability 6
　popular 13–14
　professional 9 n. 29, 10–15, 118–19, 175 n. 14, 206
　public 13–14
　see also historical culturee
History Manifesto, The 206
'history market' 55, 79, 118, 144
Hobsbawm, Eric 6
Holinshed, Raphael, Chronicles 16–19, 20, 49
　ancient constitution and Boudica 18 n. 63
　panoramic histories and 73
Hopkins, Charles 57, 70, 76
　Boadicea, Queen of Britain, a tragedy 70–3, 78, 122, 136, 188, 197
Hoselitz, Virginia 147–8
Houses of Parliament 174–5 n. 13
Howsam, Leslie 117
human nature 85, 105–10, 205
Hume, David 81, 86, 97, 107 n. 89, 119
Hyperboreans 93

Iceni, see Boudica; Ancient Britain
idealism
　in art 169
　and the past 207
imperialism 6, 116, 120, 134, 138, 140 n. 70, 143, 145–48, 159–64, 169, 171, 182, 200, 204
Indian Rebellion of 1857 134, 140, 143
individuality
　as focus of historical culture 7, 8 n. 25, 11,
　influence on historical events 36, 46–7
interpretation 8, 12
invented tradition 5–7, 117, 146, 171, 177, 181 n. 37, 207

James I and VI 31, 33, 38, 45, 49 n. 85
Johnson, Samuel 63
Jones, Inigo 45
Jonson, Ben 33
Jowett, Benjamin 143

Kennett, White 86
King Arthur 3, 170, 175, 186
knowledge and knowing 7, 11

Langland, Elizabeth 128
Livy [Titus Livius] 26–7
Lindsay, Sir Coutts 135–8

Index

Lipsius, Justus 29, 30, 31, 36
Lloyd George, David 188
local history 26, 54, 67, 80, 148, 154, 160, 169–74, 176, 178, 180, 189, 195, 200–2
   See also historical pageants
London 18, 26, 31, 37, 50, 57, 70, 76–7, 81, 121, 146–9, 154–60, 172, 179, 183, 186, 193–5, 198, 200, 204
   See also Londinium
Londinium 38, 44
   See also London
London County Council (LCC) 148, 154–9
London Corresponding Society 100
Looser, Devoney 81

Maitland, William 81
Mandler, Peter 117
Masculinity 16, 19–20
   See also under Boudica, generals and allies
Mayer, Robert 66
McCrea, Adriana 30
Maen Achwynfan 185 Marble Hall (Cardiff), *see* Cardiff City Hall
Marochetti, Carlo 150
Melman, Billie 7
Memory studies 13–14
   See also historical culture
metahistory 10
Mikalachki, Jodi 16–17
Mills, Crisp 107–10
Mills, Robert Scourfield, *see* Rhoscomyl, Owen
Milton, John 65–6, 73–6, 86
misogyny 58, 71, 74
modernity 97, 117 n. 8, 118, 144, 148, 162
Moore, John 96
Morant, Philip 81
Morford, Mark 29
Morgan, Owen, *see* Morien
Morien 171, 173, 181–9, 201–2
Morganwg, Iolo 176, 181
Mossman, Judith 18
motherhood 19, 22, 41, 75, 120–4, 129, 135–9, 185, 188, 204
museums 13 n. 47
   Brecknock Museum 175
   British Museum 148, 153–5, 157, 160, 165
   National Museum of Wales 179 n. 30
myth 12

national history 3, 16, 26, 53, 49–50, 53–4, 56, 62–3, 67, 73, 79, 81–3, 86, 108, 117 n. 8, 121, 171–2, 200–1
national identity 6, 101, 121, 150–1, 169, 173, 176, 178–9, 186, 189, 200–1
   Boudica's 63, 171, 178–9, 181, 186, 200–1
   See also cultural nationalism; Wales
nationalism,
   See cultural nationalism

Nero [Roman Emperor] 1–4, 27–29, 36, 37–42, 45, 79, 166, 192
Neostoicism, *see* Stoicism
Neilson-Terry, Phyllis 197
Norfolk 130, 172, 182, 189, 192
novels 55 n. 15, 98
   See also historical novels

Octavia, Claudia [wife of Nero] 40
O'Brien, Karen 55
Omens 2, 76, 88, 179
Osmond, Patricia 33
Owen, Mrs. Octavius Freire 131–2

Paganism
   See Druidism
Pageants
   See historical pageants
Paetus, Thrasea [Roman senator] 29–30
panoramic histories 67, 73–7, 84
   sentimentality 74–7
Parliament 88–90
   Anglo-Saxon 88
   Houses of 141, 147, 158, 174–5
Parliament Hill Fields,
   See Hampstead Heath
   See under Boudica
patriotism 16 n. 58, 104–6, 109, 114, 116, 120–4, 132, 137, 144, 147, 163, 184, 199
   Boudica as symbol of 116, 120–1, 132
   See also femininity
past and present 5, 7–8, 15, 23, 34, 49, 82–3, 85, 90, 94–6, 99, 102–3, 112, 119, 137–8, 144, 148, 163–5, 207
Paulinus, Suetonius
   See Suetonius Paulinus
Peto, Sir Morton 174
Pemberton, Henry 105–7
People's Palace (Mile End) 146
Pezron, Paul 93
Philips, Ambrose 86
Phillips, Mark Salber 55, 83
Plumb, J.H. 6
Pocock, J.G.A. 6, 53
poetry 33–4, 48, 67, 90, 93, 101, 134–43, 150, 178, 206
politics 22, 24–30, 35, 45–6, 53, 55, 61, 80–103, 112–13, 118, 126, 207
Polybius 35 n. 41, 37 n. 50
popular history,
   See under history; historical culture
Porter, Endymion 31, 47
Powell, George 57, 67–70
Prasutagus [Boudica's husband] 1, 41, 130, 136, 141, 193, 197
   called Arviragus 63 n. 44, 130
present, *See* past and present
Prichard, T.J.L. 177

Index

Prince Albert, *see* Albert
Princess Victoria 177
prophecy 116–17, 148, 162, 196, 198
public history
  See under history; historical culture
Pughe, William Owen 176–7
Purcell, Henry 70

Queenship 20, 128 n. 42, 137, 138, 145
Queen Caroline 128 n. 42
Queen Elizabeth 58
  Boudica and 17–19 n. 67, 26, 31, 51
Queen Victoria 128, 149–50, 159, 170, 192
  Boudica and 141, 147–8, 151, 159–60, 162–3, 165, 170, 173, 177–8, 182–3, 201

Ranger, Terence 6
Rani of Jhansi (Lakshmi Bai) 134
rape 2, 19, 69–72, 76, 78–9, 105, 122, 131, 188, 198
Rapin do Thoyras, Paul de 84, 88–92, 98, 174
Rational Amusement, The [no author] 113–14
Read, Charles Hercules 148, 155–7 n. 52, 160, 165
reception 11 n. 40
representations 7, 8, 12 n. 42
Rheannus, Beatus 27
Rhodes, Thomas 120–4, 126, 127, 135
Rhoscomyl, Owen 179–81
Ricks, Christopher 141
Robertson, William 81
Rome and Romans 1, 3, 18, 45, 50, 51, 65, 75–7, 86, 89, 90, 93, 105, 113, 130, 136–8, 143, 156, 165–7, 182, 193–4, 198
  anti-Catholicism 20 n. 72
  British empire and 116, 160 n. 65
    See also Cowper, William; Fletcher, John; Hannah, Ian C.; Trevelyan, Marie
  history of Rome 26–9, 38–41
  Romans named in fiction,
  Burrus (film) 198
    Caska ((Hopkins) 71–2
    Cato (Hannah) 165–6
    Comus (the Pict) (Powell) 69
    Decius (Hopkins) 71–2
    Faustinus (Bury St Edmunds Paget 1907) 193
    Julius (Lindsay) 136–7
    Junius (Fletcher) 20
    Marcus (film) 198
    Paulinus (Hopkins) 71–2
  Rome in novels 161, 165–6, 172, 174, 182, 184–5
  See also ancient Britain
Roman Britain, *see* ancient Britain
Rowlands, Henry 87
Rüsen, Jörn 14

St Albans 2, 172, 191 n. 67, 199, 201
  pageants (1907, 1953) 190–1, 193,
  See also Verulamium
Sallust 58, 79
Salmon, Thomas 84, 90–3, 102, 112
Sammes, Aylett 74–5
Savile, Henry 30
science 10, 11
Scotland 26, 63 n. 46, 73 n. 64, 96, 129–30
Scott, Sir Walter 117
Sculpture 149–50
  of Boudica
    Westminster, London *147*
    Brecknock Museum 175
    Cardiff City Hall *187*
    People's Palace, Mile End 146
    Colchester 172
Sejanus [Emperor Tiberius' favourite] 33
Seller, John 75–7
Selous, H.C. 174
Seneca, Lucius Annaeus 38
  factor in Boudican rebellion 3, 42–3
  Stoicism 29, 40, 43
Shakespeare, William 18 n. 66, 55 n. 17, 58, 194
Sidney, Philip 30, 33–4
Smith, Anthony D. 173, 181 n. 37
Smollett, Tobias 84, 96–101
  Complete History, sales 96–7
Society of Antiquaries (Elizabethan) 33, 54
Society of Antiquaries (1707) 54
South African Wars 147, 162, 180
Speed, John 77
Stamford (Lincolnshire) 172–3
Stoicism 28–30, 34
  Boudica and 42–6, 48
  Christianity and 36
  See also under Bolton, Edmund; Seneca
Stonehenge 37, 45, 49
  Boudica buried under 37, 45–6, 49, 66
Stothard, Thomas 141
  illustration of Boudica *142*
Strong, Roy 117
Squires, Samuel [Bishop of St David's] 95
Suetonius Paulinus 2, 4, 41–4, 71, 76–7, 87, 90, 127, 182, 184, 191, 194, 197–8
  unflattering description in *Nero Caesar* 47
Suffolk 172, 174, 189, 192
suicide 29, 72, 105–6, 134, 161, 185
  Boudica's 2, 4, 46, 65–6, 70, 78, 89, 105, 124, 131–2, 139
Swetnam, Joseph 58

Tacitism 27–8
Tacitus, Cornelius 1–3, 25–7, 31, 40, 48
  Agricola 2, 31, 47, 177, 183
  Annals 2, 26–8, 29, 32, 41, 43, 59 n. 30, 195

Histories 26, 27, 28, 29, 30
   Stoicism and 29–30
   Justus Lipsius and 29
Thatcher, Margaret 170
Theatre Royal Drury Lane 68, 70, 104
Thornycroft, Hamo 149
Thornycroft, John Isaac 153, 157–9
Thornycroft, Thomas 147–53
   'Boadicea group' *147*, 14–19, 153, 158–9, 183 n. 44
Tennyson, Alfred, first Baron 134, 140
Thatcher, Margaret 170
Thomas, D.A., Lord Rhondda 188
Thomas, John 174, 175 n. 16
Thomas, John Evan 174
Thomas, John Havard 186–9
   statue of Boudica *187*
Tiberius [Roman Emperor] 1, 27, 32–3, 41
Tigranes [ancient Armenian king] 41
Tindal, Nicholas 88–9
Toland, John 87
Trevelyan, Marie 147, 148, 160–6
Triads (Welsh) 176–7
Trinobantes 2, 43, 71 n. 61
Tuck, Richard 45

universities 53–4
Unwin, Christina 134, 140 n. 70

Vergil, Polydore 3
Verulamium 2, 44, 172, 177, 190–1, 202
   See also St Albans
Villa Faustini 192–3, 195
Villiers, George, first duke of Buckingham 25, 32
von Ranke, Leopold 119

Wales 3, 26, 63, 170, 171 n. 6, 173, 175, 189
   ancient history 176, 179, 180, 182, 186
      See also Ancient Britain
   antiquarianism, *see under* Morien
   archaeology in 183–4 n. 46, 185 n. 50
   'Buddug' 163, 176–78 n. 24, 177, 182, 185–6, *187*, 188, 189, 201
   and Victoria 173, 177–8, 182–3, 201
   See also Aregwedd Voeddig
   Bryn Sion 184
   Druidism in 171, 176, 181–4
      Christianity and 164, 181–2
      gorsedd 181
   Maen Achwynfan 185
   National Pageant (1909) 179–80
   'National Valhalla' 186–7
   Pageant of Gwent (1913) 180
   panoramic histories of 63 n. 44, 176
   relations with England 178–9, 181–2, 186
   See also Cardiff City Hall; *eisteddfod*; England; national identity; national narrative
Walpole, Robert 82, 95, 96, 103
Warner, Marina 146
Wheare, Degory 54
White, Hayden 10, 206–7
William III 98, 99
Williams, Edward, *see* Morganwg, Iolo
Williams ab Ithel, John 177
women's history 12, 59, 65, 125 n. 28
   and biography 126–34, 64
   tradition of 51, 59–60, 62, 120, 127, 144
Woolf, Daniel 12–13, 32, 41 n. 59, 53
Woolner, Thomas 141 n. 73, 174

Xiphilinus, John 3

The manufacturer's authorised representative in the EU for product safety is Oxford University Press España S.A. of el Parque Empresarial San Fernando de Henares, Avenida de Castilla, 2 – 28830 Madrid (www.oup.es/en or product.safety@oup.com). OUP España S.A. also acts as importer into Spain of products made by the manufacturer.

www.ingramcontent.com/pod-product-compliance
Lightning Source LLC
LaVergne TN
LVHW021942060526
838200LV00042B/1894